Cambridge Imperial and Post-Colonial Studies Series

General Editors: **Megan Vaughan**, Kings' College, Cambridge and **Richard Drayton**, King's College, London

This informative series covers the broad span of modern imperial history while also exploring the recent developments in former colonial states where residues of empire can still be found. The books provide in-depth examinations of empires as competing and complementary power structures encouraging the reader to reconsider their understanding of international and world history during recent centuries.

Titles include:

Brian Ireland
THE US MILITARY IN HAWAI'I
Colonialism, Memory and Resistance

Robin Jeffrey
POLITICS, WOMEN AND WELL-BEING
How Kerala became a 'Model'

Gerold Krozewski
MONEY AND THE END OF EMPIRE
British International Economic Policy and the Colonies, 1947–58

Sloan Mahone and Megan Vaughan (editors)
PSYCHIATRY AND EMPIRE

Javed Majeed
AUTOBIOGRAPHY, TRAVEL AND POST-NATIONAL IDENTITY

Francine McKenzie
REDEFINING THE BONDS OF COMMONWEALTH 1939–1948
The Politics of Preference

Gabriel Paquette
ENLIGHTENMENT, GOVERNANCE AND REFORM IN SPAIN AND ITS EMPIRE 1759–1808

Jennifer Regan-Lefebvre
IRISH AND INDIAN
The Cosmopolitan Politics of Alfred Webb

Ricardo Roque
HEADHUNTING AND COLONIALISM
Anthropology and the Circulation of Human Skulls in the Portuguese Empire, 1870–1930

Michael Silvestri
IRELAND AND INDIA
Nationalism, Empire and Memory

John Singleton and Paul Robertson
ECONOMIC RELATIONS BETWEEN BRITAIN AND AUSTRALASIA 1945–1970

Aparna Vaidik
IMPERIAL ANDAMANS
Colonial Encounter and Island History

Kim A. Wagner
THUGGEE
Banditry and the British in Early Nineteenth-Century India

Jon E. Wilson
THE DOMINATION OF STRANGERS
Modern Governance in Eastern India, 1780–1835

Cambridge Imperial and Post-Colonial Studies Series
Series Standing Order ISBN 978–0–333–91908–8 (Hardback) 978–0–333–91909–5 (Paperback)
(outside North America only)

You can receive future titles in this series as they are published by placing a standing order. Please contact your bookseller or, in case of difficulty, write to us at the address below with your name and address, the title of the series and one of the ISBNs quoted above.

Customer Services Department, Macmillan Distribution Ltd, Houndmills, Basingstoke, Hampshire RG21 6XS, England

Tributary Empires in Global History

Edited by

Peter Fibiger Bang
Associate Professor, The Saxo Institute,
University of Copenhagen, Denmark

and

C. A. Bayly
Vere Harmsworth Professor of Imperial and Naval History,
University of Cambridge, UK

First published 2011 by
PALGRAVE MACMILLAN

Palgrave Macmillan in the UK is an imprint of Macmillan Publishers Limited,
registered in England, company number 785998, of Houndmills, Basingstoke,
Hampshire RG21 6XS.

Palgrave Macmillan in the US is a division of St Martin's Press LLC,
175 Fifth Avenue, New York, NY 10010.

Palgrave Macmillan is the global academic imprint of the above companies
and has companies and representatives throughout the world.

Palgrave® and Macmillan® are registered trademarks in the United States,
the United Kingdom, Europe and other countries

ISBN: 978–0–230–29472–1 hardback
ISBN: 978–0–230–30841–1 paperback

This book is printed on paper suitable for recycling and made from fully
managed and sustained forest sources. Logging, pulping and manufacturing
processes are expected to conform to the environmental regulations of the
country of origin.

A catalogue record for this book is available from the British Library.

A catalog record for this book is available from the Library of Congress.

10 9 8 7 6 5 4 3 2 1
20 19 18 17 16 15 14 13 12 11

Printed and bound in Great Britain by
CPI Antony Rowe, Chippenham and Eastbourne

L'unité de lieu n'est que désordre
Seule l'unité de problemè fait centre

Marc Bloch

Contents

Part III   Comparative Histories

Preface

Tributary Empires in Global History is one of the main outcomes of a research project which we launched in 2005 under the auspices of the COST action scheme to promote comparisons of precolonial land empires, particularly the Roman, the Ottoman and the Mughal. (The web page at http://tec.saxo.ku.dk contains programmes and summaries of these meetings, as well as other relevant information.) We are deeply grateful to the European research community for making it possible to build an extensive and generously funded programme and network which has brought together a huge range of scholars from Europe and beyond and whose expertise has ranged from ancient Assyria, through Qing China to the sociology of modern political systems. Many more people were involved in the project and participated in our reflections than could possibly be represented in this book. We thank them all for their enthusiasm, work effort and inspiring contributions as the project developed while we hope that this book will reflect some of the sheer intellectual excitement of comparative research that we often felt as we got to familiarise ourselves with topics and fields previously little known to us. It reflects well, we think, on the COST-setup that they were willing not only to take a chance on us and try something entirely new to them, but also to allow us sufficient time and space for members of separate disciplines with little tradition for dialogue to get accustomed to discussing together and learning from each other. Copenhagen, Istanbul, Athens, Warsaw, St Andrews, Rethymno, Vienna, Utrecht, Rome chart a busy schedule of discussion and debate. And great thanks are due to all the institutions which accommodated our meetings and to all our organising hosts on these occasions: Björn Forsén, Giovanni Salmeri, Dariusz Kolodziejczyk, Adam Ziolkowski, Greg Woolf, Antonios Anastasopoulos, Ebba Koch, Jeroen Duindam and Claire Sottinel. In this connection, however, we would like especially to thank professor Metin Kunt who was part of the executive committee with us, and from COST Drs David Grønbæk, Fracesca Boscolo and Julia Stamm as well as Jana Gašparíková and Balázs Kiss. They have all, in turn, provided invaluable help, advice and encouragement. We are equally grateful to the editors of this series, Richard Drayton and Megan Vaughan, together with Michael Strang of Palgrave for having accepted the book. Finally thanks are due to Ruth Ireland for assistance and to Jesper Johansen Meisner, who compiled the Bibliography and Index.

At the end of this project we are delighted to note that it has been part of a growing interest in comparative studies among historians of premodern empires. Two projects, in particular, have been running parallel and engaged constructively with ours, the Stanford Ancient Chinese and Mediterranean Empires Comparative History Project, under Walter Scheidel, and The Network of Ancient and Modern Imperialisms, directed by Phiroze Vasunia. We are grateful to both and share with them a conviction that comparative history will be increasingly important to our various individual fields, not only for inspiration and opening up new perspectives, but also to prevent isolation and facilitate dialogue with the rest of the historical profession and in particular the discipline of world history. To publish our results in this series will, we hope, mark one step further in this direction.

Peter Fibiger Bang and C. A. Bayly
Copenhagen and Cambridge

Contributors

Peter Fibiger Bang is Associate Professor at the Saxo Institute, University of Copenhagen. He is a Roman comparative historian, interested in political economy, the sociology of power, state-formation and world history. He was Chair of the Network Tributary Empires Compared 2005–09 (http://tec.saxo. ku.dk). He has published *The Roman Bazaar: A Comparative Study of Trade and Markets in a Tributary Empire* (2008) and five other edited volumes. With Walter Scheidel he is editing *The Oxford Handbook of the Ancient State* (forthcoming).

Karen Barkey is Professor of Sociology and History at Columbia University. Her research has focused on historical comparisons of the Ottoman Empire to illuminate issues of state-centralisation and decentralisation, social movements as well as imperial decline. Among her books are *Bandits and Bureaucrats: The Ottoman Route to State Centralization* (1994) and *Empire of Difference: The Ottomans in Comparative Perspective* (2008). The latter was awarded The Barrington Moore Award in Sociology and the David J. Greenstone Award in Political Science.

Rudi Batzell is currently pursuing an MPhil in Modern European History and Economic and Social History at the University of Cambridge on a Kellett Fellowship from Columbia University. His thesis on 'Class Formation and Politics in 1870s' California' received the Albert Marion Elsberg Prize in Modern History at Columbia University.

C. A. Bayly is Vere Harmsworth Professor of Imperial and Naval History at the University of Cambridge and a Fellow of St Catharine's College, Cambridge. His many books on late Mughal and colonial Indian as well as global history include *Rulers, Townsmen and Bazaars* (1983), *The Birth of the Modern World* (2004) and with Tim Harper, *Forgotten Wars* (2007).

Stephen P. Blake, Center for Early Modern History, University of Minnesota has written extensively on the Mughal Empire, often in a comparative and sociological perspective. His main works include *Shajahanabad: The Sovereign City in Mughal India 1639–1739* (1991) and *Half the World: The Social Architecture of Safavid Isfahan, 1590–1722* (1999).

Fabrizio De Donno is Lecturer in Italian Studies at Royal Holloway, University of London. His work focuses on Orientalism, Modernism and Nationalism in Italy. With Neelam Srivastava, he has edited *Colonial and Postcolonial Italy*, special issue of *Interventions: International Journal of Postcolonial Studies* (2006).

David Ludden is Professor of Political Economy and Globalization in the Department of History at New York University. His research has concentrated on South India and Bengal and focused on issues of agricultural and social development in the very long term. Among his books are *India and South Asia: A Short History* (2002) and *An Agrarian History of South Asia* (1999).

W. G. Runciman has been a Fellow of Trinity College, Cambridge since 1971. He holds honorary degrees from the Universities of Edinburgh, Oxford, London and York. His books include *A Treatise on Social Theory*, 3 vols (1983–97) and *The Theory of Cultural and Social Selection* (2009).

Giovanni Salmeri is Professor of Roman History at the University of Pisa. His work has focused particularly on the history of modern historiography, ancient Sicily and Greco-Roman Asia Minor where he is currently conducting a field survey in Cilicia. Among his most recent publications is a book on comparative history edited with Bjorn Forsén, *The Province Strikes Back: Imperial Dynamics in the Eastern Mediterranean* (2008).

Walter Scheidel is Professor of Classics and, by courtesy, history at Stanford University. His interests range from ancient social and economic history to historical demography and global history. His many books include *Death on the Nile* (2002), *Rome and China* (ed.) (2009) and *The Cambridge Economic History of the Graeco-Roman World* (2007) with Richard Saller and Ian Morris as co-editors.

Baki Tezcan is Assistant Professor of History and Religious Studies at the University of California, Davis. He is the co-editor of *Identity and Identity Formation in the Ottoman World: A Volume of Essays in Honor of Norman Itzkowitz* (2007), and the author of *The Second Ottoman Empire: Political and Social Transformation in the Early Modern World* (2010). His research interests focus mainly on Ottoman political history in the sixteenth to eighteenth centuries and Ottoman and modern Turkish historiography.

Michał Tymowski is Professor of History at the University of Warsaw. He has worked extensively on precolonial African societies, political anthropology and comparative history. His most important publications include a *History of Mali* (1979), *The History of Timbuctu* (1979), *L' Armée et la formation des Etats en Afrique Occidentale au XIXe siècle – essai de comparaison* (1987), *The Origins and Structures of Political Institutions in Pre-colonial Black Africa* (2009).

Chris Wickham is Chichele Professor of Medieval History at All Souls College, Oxford, was editor of *Past and Present* and has written extensively on Late Antiquity and the early Middle Ages. Among his books are *Framing the Early Middle Ages: Europe and the Mediterranean, 400–800* (2005) and *The Inheritance of Rome: A History of Europe from 400 to 1000* (2009).

André Wink is Professor of History at the University of Wisconsin-Madison. He has worked extensively on the precolonial history of India. His books include *Land and Sovereignty in India: Agrarian Society and Politics under the Eighteenth-Century Maratha Svarajya* (1986); *Al-Hind: The Making of the Indo-Islamic World*, 3 Volumes (1990–2004) and *Akbar* (2009).

Figure 1 The patriarchs of the Eastern Catholic Churches performing funeral rites for Pope John Paul II

Source: Christopher Morris/VII Photo nr 00034066

1

Tributary Empires – Towards a Global and Comparative History

Peter Fibiger Bang and C. A. Bayly

> Brethren, we beg God, our Father, who has gathered us today to celebrate the Easter mystery of his only-begotten son in the funeral ceremony of the Shepherd of the Universal Church, that he will admit him into His peace and bestow on the Church and the world all things good.[1]

Ecumenic empire

It was Friday and the month was April, Anno Domini 2005, when these words sounded from the platform in front of St Peter's. Myriads of faithful mourners had massed into Rome and now crowded the Square and the broad avenues leading up to the Vatican to participate in the funeral of Pope John Paul II. Unprecedented numbers were listening in on radio or watching television broadcasts around the globe. Spoken in sombre, dignified, yet slightly artificial Italian by Cardinal Ratzinger, soon-to-be Pope Benedict and leading the service, this prayer initiated a carefully orchestrated series of commendations of the deceased bishop of Rome to his Heavenly Father. Alternating with rhythmically repeated chants of the Latin phrase *te rogamus, audi nos* ('we beg you, hear us'), were select representatives of the congregation praising the virtues and good offices of the former pope, each in his or her own tongue. French, Swahili, Philippino, Polish, German and Portuguese accumulated into a virtual cacophony of voices. Earlier during the mass, sections had already been heard in English and Spanish in addition to the leading languages of Latin and Italian. No one was to doubt that the Catholic Church was truly universal.[2]

Soon the performance of the ecumenical motif would reach its ritual climax as the ceremony moved towards the conclusion. Onto the stage now stepped the patriarchs, archbishops and metropolitans of the Eastern Catholic Churches.[3] Appearing against the backdrop of uniform red and gold-embroidered vestments, warn by the scores of Latin church dignitaries on parade, their variety

1

of dress and headgear was thrown into sharp and colourful relief. The late patriarch of the Coptic Catholic Church, Stephanos II Ghattas opened the pro- ceedings by purifying the coffin with incense. There was an exotic and gaudy spectacle of sundry oriental Christian traditions on display, Coptic, Syro- Malabar, Armenian and many more. Common to these churches are that they each make use of one of the many separate liturgical traditions which have developed within the several branches of eastern Christianity. As they intoned their prayers of commendation for the departed pope, it was the Byzantine rites which were followed. The patriarch of the Melkite Greek Catholic Church, Gregory III Laham, seated in Damascus, finally recited a longer prayer for the pope in Greek and Arabic.[4] The whole scenery is neatly captured with words used by the bishop Eusebius in the fourth century to illustrate the mighty reach of the court of his hero, Constantine the Great: 'For men of Blemyan race, and Indian and Ethiopian...could be seen...Each of these in their turn...brought their particular treasures...showing that they were offering service and alliance with these things ...'[5] Constantine had forever inscribed himself in the history of the Catholic Church. After he had managed to reunite the Roman world under his sole rule in AD 324, he proceeded to throw all his weight behind an attempt to ensure an institutional unity for the Church fit to mirror that of his universal realm. With the declaration of the first Nicene Creed, agreed to by an assembly of church leaders under the supervision of the emperor, the faith was put on a common formula intended for all Christian congregations to use: one empire, one church, boundless and all-encompassing.

Still sounding in the opening decade of the third millennium, the echo of Roman imperial symbolism and ritual which in late antiquity had been merged into the church tradition of Christ, the universal lord and bringer of peace, was unmistakable.[6] Enacted here on St Peter's Square was the burial of a Roman emperor, figuratively speaking, a world leader. At the ceremony, the Vatican had managed to attract or gather a staggering, and it was claimed unsurpassed, number of heads of state and other prominent political leaders to add lustre to the event and reflect the power of the Church. Here was even to be seen Protestant Scandinavian monarchs (in part still heads of renegade Lutheran churches), the Jewish President of Israel and the then president of the Islamic Republic of Iran, Mohammad Khatami.[7] Rome was, again, the centre of the world, *caput mundi*.

The funeral was conducted as a formidable demonstration of the univer- sal or ecumenical aspirations and reach of the Roman Catholic Church. Re-establishing Christian unity by bringing back secessionist congregations to the Catholic fold was an important ambition of John Paul's pontificate. He addressed the issue of ecumenism in a lengthy encyclical letter of 1995, 'ut unum sint/that they shall be one'.[8] Common prayer and dialogue were to fos- ter a mutual understanding between Christians which could pave the way for reunification; this was the basic claim and hope of the letter. By emphasising the need for dialogue, the Pope sought to build on the principles laid down during the Second Vatican Council in 1964.[9] In the 'Lumen Gentium' the Council had drawn up a new constitution for the Church. One important issue was precisely the relationship to the Eastern Catholic Churches, which we have just noted played a prominent role in the funeral rites of John Paul II. The constitution opted for tolerance of diversity:

> By divine Providence it has come about that various churches, established in various places by the apostles and their successors, have in the course of time coalesced into several groups, organically united, which, preserving the unity of faith and the unique divine constitution of the universal Church, enjoy their own discipline, their own liturgical usage, and their own theological and spiritual heritage…**This variety of local churches with one common aspiration is splendid evidence of the catholicity of the undivided Church.**[10]

Diversity was not to be suppressed; respect for long-established local traditions was itself to be taken as confirmation of the universality, the catholicity of the Church. Some hard-line minority voices saw such ecumenical openings as a dangerous concession, which they feared might corrupt the purity of Latin Christianity.[11]

In essence, this conflict was yet another expression of the age-old imperial dilemma of whether to 'spare the humble' or 'destroy the proud', 'parcere subjectis' or 'debellare superbos' in the immortal words of Vergil, the Roman poet of the Augustan monarchy later hailed under Constantine as a prophet of Christ.[12] But, as Seneca once exhorted the young Nero, clemency is among the most important virtues in a world-ruler.[13] It was quite in keeping with this advice that the Pope chose to emphasise moderation and leniency in the encyclical letter. He described the function of his office as that of a *servant* of unity; it was a ministry, he insisted. Yet, the exercise of such a public service, a *munus*, would be meaningless without power and authority, the reasoning went on. An acephalous Christian commonwealth, it would seem, was not possible. Unity, a thoroughly Roman and imperial idea, necessitated, even demanded the establishment of a hierarchy with one person at the top: the successor of Peter, the modern Pontifex Maximus.[14] At the funeral the ecumenical policy of John Paul had scored the considerable triumph that the Ecumenical Patriarch of Constantinople, the historic rival of the Roman pontiffs, together with a large number of other Orthodox church leaders had decided to attend the service.[15] Under his successor, Pope Benedict XVI, the movement towards reconciliation took another huge stride forward when in 2007 the Vatican succeeded in making the Eastern Orthodox churches recognise the historic primacy of the pope among Christian church leaders; he was the *protos* of the other *protoi*.[16] John Paul II had, in his encyclical letter, striven to make this claim more palatable by dressing it in diminutive terms. The Pope was best thought of as the *servus servorum/the servant of servants*.[17] Polite and politic, yet the underlying figure for this expression is nevertheless the old basic imperial notion of the king of kings, *rex regum* as it would be in Latin, one power above the others.[18]

However, how such supremacy is going to be articulated is always up for negotiation. Here, the notion of an almighty emperor is often more misleading than the more humble wording of John Paul II. The orthodox theologians may now in some sense be said to have conceded the pre-eminence of the Bishop of Rome, at least in theory. But the same declaration left open the question of what, if any thing, this would mean in practical terms. Later, and undoubtedly difficult, discussions still had to clarify what would be, as the document states, 'the specific function of the bishop of the "first see"' within a reunified church.[19] Imperial power, even if it is only of the mind, may claim supremacy, but in practice always has to compromise or tolerate deviance. This is a perennial problem of empire and of the premodern ones that form the topic of this book, more than most. Our volume seeks to explore from a number of complementary perspectives the tension in our understanding of the extensive empires of the agrarian past between widespread notions of unrivalled imperial might and frequent weakness in government. In historiography, we encounter it in the coexistence of inflated perceptions of overmighty despotic monarchs with widespread litanies about corrupt, inefficient and feeble administration. In the sociology of power, the problem has for some time been current as one of conceptualising alternatives to the homogeneous and compact nation state. Instead of a 'unitary' theory of statehood, sociologists have worked – to quote Michael Mann – on understanding states and societies as open-ended, 'constituted of multiple overlapping and intersecting sociospatial networks of power'.[20] Few forms of political organisation fit this template better than the extensive territorial empires of history comprising a great variety of cultural and ethnic groups. Frequently recurring themes concern centrifugal forces undermining centralised authority, the segmentation of power and the risk of fragmentation of the body politic. Finally, to the comparative historian, the problem presents itself, as Bang argues in his contribution, as one of reconciling the creation of strong state capacities with the continuation of local and regional traditions and forms of autonomy, both facilitating the mechanisms and limiting the reach of imperial rule. Empires, in our sense of the word, are composite and layered, representing a hierarchical ordering of diversity such as it was staged during the papal funeral.

Historiography, sociological theory and cultural or historical comparison form the themes of the three parts into which this book has been divided. All three dimensions are implicated in our opening example – as the stories mobilised by the Vatican to make the burial ritual resonate with the audience, as a (theological) theory of power (there must be one head) and as a comparative analysis of the character, institutions and politics of imperial authority. The residue of Roman imperialism discernable in the religious policies and pageantry of the pontiffs serves to indicate that the main concern is with large, agrarian, precolonial empires, often harbouring universal aspirations. This collection of essays is an attempt, at the most fundamental level, to re-examine, explore and develop current historical tropes and analytical models used to explain and describe the experience of vast premodern or, as we explain below, tributary empires; it is a venture in comparative world history.

Tributary empires – past, present and globally

April 2005 not only marked the end of the Pontificate of John Paul II, it was also during this month that we launched the project *Tributary Empires Compared* to stimulate dialogue and comparative analysis among students of extensive agrarian empires.[21] This book represents one of the main outcomes. The volume and more widely the project, however, represent something more than a set of reflections on world history by some of its leading scholars, valuable as that would have been. For we have also been aware throughout of the salience of the idea of *empire* in contemporary political discourse, and indeed, polemic. Our opening example was chosen precisely to illustrate that present questions of empire go well beyond the vicissitudes of current debates about American 'hyper-puissance' or the legacy of colonialism.[22] Indeed, it invites us to contemplate the question of historical continuities in relation to precolonial or premodern forms of imperialism. Through the borders it claims, the nation state of China acts as heir to the multi-ethnic agrarian empire ruled by the Qing-dynasty. Modern Russia, too, can be seen in such a light, as argued by Dominic Lieven.[23] In this book, the chapters by Garry Runciman, Walter Scheidel and David Ludden address the conditions and historical dynamics shaping the long-term reproduction and success of imperial power. Working from Indian cases, Ludden argues for the continuing relevance of deep continuities reaching back to the Mughals in reproducing power relations up to the present day.

In the post-war period, history and historical sociology has tended to fragment into subfields, such as political, economic and social history, gender history and the history of science. However, the geographical units within which these subfields have been studied have remained constant, not just since 1945 but over many generations, though their relative importance has fluctuated. National history has, of course, remained dominant at all levels from the academic histories written in European universities through to the public history represented on television or in popular magazines directed at school pupils. In the 1970s some authorities announced the decline of the nation state and its history, and it is certainly the case that the darker side of national consciousness and the national myth has been emphasised, and not just in the former fascist powers. Yet most school age students across the world are still trained up in national history and in some smaller nations, the teaching of national history has been seen as a redoubt against globalisation and the denaturing of the nation through the use of the English language.

A second unit of historical analysis to which historians and public policy makers now frequently gesture is transnational or global history, a response to the view that the world is now interconnected by flows of capital, by the diaspora of workers and refugees, and by common problems such as disease and global warming. Much of what is taught (and some of what is written) remains Eurocentric or American-centred histories of modern citizenship with a few concessions to the existence of China and India, or the problems of Africa.

With the focus directed to the 'multi-ethnic' land-empires, particularly of the classical up to the early modern or late Medieval era, our project and volume fall in an intermediate category. Our main specimens have been Rome, the Ottomans and the Mughal Empire. But the group is obviously wider. This volume also includes more extensive discussions of Han China, the Arab Caliphate, African tribal empires and the realms of the Austrian Habsburgs and Russian Romanovs. There is little tradition for dialogue between historians of these separate fields, yet the advantages of cross-disciplinary exchange are tangible. To classical historians confrontation with the more densely textured historical record of later agrarian empires may provide them with a sharper sense of the detailed working of government and power on the ground. Conversely, they bring to the dialogue an unusually mature and detailed historiography. Much of our conceptual baggage has been coined within a tradition heavily informed by the Greco-Roman experience. Encounters between these different fields serve, so to speak, to denaturalise the individual historiographical traditions and make their practitioners more aware of the implicit assumptions shaping their enquiries. Widening horizons, new perspectives and sharpened analyses are the benefits which we all stand to reap from such efforts to transcend our own fields.

Common to these empires is that they may be described as tributary, rather than commercial and colonial. Roughly speaking, they were all based on the conquest of wide agrarian domains and the taxation of peasant surplus production. Arguably this could be claimed for most monarchical states before the nineteenth century, the age of nationalism, as recently observed by John Haldon and Jack Goldstone.[24] But we have emphasised those that could credibly be called world-empires; in other words, vast empires that dominated their wider worlds and were able to absorb most of their competitors and reduce them either to taxpaying provinces or tributary client kingdoms. Their rulers saw themselves as universal emperors, claiming supremacy over all other monarchs. With respect to our key examples, these similarities are even reinforced by shared genealogies. In addition to the traditions of the Central Asian steppe, the Islamicate and Persianate cultures of the Ottomans and Mughals had strong roots in Middle-Eastern and Mediterranean antiquity (see Chapter 10 in this book).[25]

It may be justified to linger a while longer on the intellectual and political justification for our chosen emphasis. In historiographical terms, historians have found it difficult to detach the category of empire from the history of the nation. The notion of empire has been seen as a benign, or malign extension of national culture. During the nineteenth and early twentieth-century students of early empires, such as James Bryce, often used their studies of classical antiquity directly or indirectly to ponder the significance of race and race mixing for the contemporary 'seaborne' empires of the Western European nations: Britain, France, Holland, Italy and to a lesser extent the United States (see Chapters 2 and 3). From the mid-twentieth century, with decolonisation in Africa and Asia, the study of empire often served as an extension of the Whig teleology of history by which free, democratic peoples gave the gift of freedom to other, less developed races. Greek notions of the polis and Roman ideas of the citizen and the republic were indirectly enlisted in these debates on the 'dissemination of freedom'.

More recently yet, the spectacle of democratic intervention in supposedly failed states, whether in the Balkans, central Africa, Iraq or Afghanistan, has led to a further debate about the nature of empire. Is America an empire? And if so, is it a good enough empire: the position adopted, for instance, by Niall Ferguson. Or is all empire bad, founded upon 'a scandal' of oppression, whether the old British Empire or the modern American one: this is the position, for instance, of Nicholas Dirks.[26] A good deal of the debate on these issues has inevitably concentrated on those modern empires that formed the territorial holdings of nation states and were exploited by a form of dependent capitalism. Yet the debate has necessarily broadened to include some consideration of earlier empires and their own forms of control and exploitation.

In part, this is because of simple nomenclature: these modern empires attempted to derive their legitimacy from the earlier polities whose role in world history was already acknowledged and often modelled their ceremonial and their pretensions to be embarked upon a civilising mission on their histories. Yet in part, the sustained and growing interest in the empires of antiquity and the early modern world has arisen from the tendency of historians to see empire as a political category working through time (e.g. Chapter 8). It is unclear, for instance, at what point the Ottoman Empire became a 'modern' Empire. Earlier generations of historians would have located a partial transformation to modernity in the Tanzimat era after 1830, or possibly during the modernisation of Abdul Hamid II's reign and the Young Turks. But more recently, Cemal Kafadar has written of an Ottoman renaissance in the sixteenth century and some Ottoman historians see versions of Ottoman modernity in government, the acquisition of knowledge and the use of urban space actually predating similar developments in the seaborne empires of Western European nations.[27] Much the same analysis has been applied to China, where the empire of the late Qing, especially on its internal frontier has been seen as dynamic, even during the period of supposed decline and European neocolonialism in the nineteenth century. Rome, too, has its historians who have tried to identify modern traits in the development of commerce, administration and law.[28] Yet, there are also limits to the applicability of the label 'modern' and always the risk of falling into the trap of 'wee too'-ism, as it was recently termed by Lynn Struve, where everything in the past is modelled on Western modernity to serve the claims of identity politics, seeking restitution and dignity to marginalised groups and cultures, however deserving of sympathy such aspirations may be.[29] Often these debates reveal that the historical development generated within these imperial polities took a rather different turn from those connected with the early modernity of Western Europe. In the field of state-formation, the introduction of gunpowder and artillery did in significant ways give rise to very different processes in the Qing (and other Asian) Empires, as shown most recently by Nicola di Cosmo.[30] In this book Barkey and Batzell, in Chapter 14, explore the various attempts to build state capacity during the seventeenth century of the Ottoman, Russian and Austrian Habsburg empires. Discussions of this sort are a salutary reminder that we still have some way to go before we have finally managed to shed ourselves of the nineteenth-century baggage which tended to present the great agrarian empires as avatars of stagnation. The point, however, is that these extensive territorial polities have much in common in terms of state-formation and show quite strong developmental patterns of their own. Even the British Empire, by one standard a thoroughly modern, exploitative capitalist empire, continued to employ modes of coercion, recruitment and reward which were typical of its Mughal predecessor well into the nineteenth century. Indeed, as must be fairly obvious, British India has much more in common with the Ottoman Empire than it did with the British dominions in Canada or Australia.

It is not surprising then that historians of the left, the centre and the right have continued to analyse the category of empire as a continuum and that present political battles have both enlightened and politicised the historiography of earlier empires. Quite recently, indeed, *The New York Times* reported that the Comptroller General of the United States was exercised that the United States was going the way of the Romans, mired in 'imperial overstretch' and too dependent on a mercenary army of would-be citizens. A few months later Niall Ferguson who had already aroused Republican ire by claiming that the American empire was doing a bad job in Iraq compared with its British predecessor, went one stage further in what must be an ironic historiography. He compared the coming decline of the American polity to the last days of the Ottoman Empire. In order to survive and prosecute its imperial designs, America was beginning to sell off its internal and external financial debts 'to the autocracies of the Middle East and east Asia'. He argued that this paralleled the sale of the Ottoman and Egyptian debt to European nations after 1850 as the Empire made a desperate great leap forward in military and civil technology. The lesson is clear: if foreigners buy up your debt, 'capitulations' and the loss of national sovereignty will soon come afterwards.[31]

The attraction of the study of ancient empires also lies in something else again. That is the continuing lodgement and salience of their traces in our 'life worlds', in Heidegger's sense. This is not simply a question of immediate contact; it also reflects the way that our sense of the future results in a contemplation and reflection on past life worlds, as Oakeshott argued.[32] The early empires are all around us not simply in traces of the past: the ruins of Rome, the fortresses of old Delhi or the mosques of Istanbul, but in gesture, ceremonial and public dignity. The funeral of the late Pope in St Peter's Square and the Basilica was a present reminder of the myth and charisma of the Pontifex Maximus. The cardinals and bishops conjoined from across the world represented modern versions of the ancient Roman provinces, now finally extended to form a world empire. The recent exhibition of the 'terracotta warriors', 'The First Emperor' in the British Museum was a reflection on the ancient unity of China and its coming world power. Set amongst the varied antiquities of ancient and medieval Western Europe, it subliminally raised the question posed by Walter Scheidel in Chapter 11 of this book: was their an early 'great political divergence' between unified China and divided Western Europe? And might that first 'great divergence' have influenced the second and much shorter divergence between Chinese and European technology and military power in the eighteenth and nineteenth centuries?

It is not simply the charisma of objects that continues to direct attention to the study of the early empires. It is the nature of the populations that live amongst us. The decline of European empires and the openness of the United States to immigration from across the world have raised questions about how we relate to the 'others' among us. One of the striking features of early empires was the extent to which the central authority was prepared to off-lay matters of jurisdiction, especially on matters of custom, marriage, inheritance and property to the leaders of self-constituted 'communities.' In an important article, Alan Ryan argued that this did not arise from any sense of 'tolerance of difference', as in the enlightened liberal creed that arose after the European wars of religion and experience of absolutism.[33] Instead, it was the result of a fundamental spiritual relativism which accepted that each group should pursue its community custom and spirituality in so far as it did not prejudice the ideological supremacy of the empire. Modern calls, notable among Muslims, for 'jurisdiction within our own community' and the imposition of *sharia* themselves represent a much more fundamentalist understanding of state power than this suggests, of course. Nevertheless, the problems of the modern state dealing with large populations of immigrants with different customs, sensibilities and languages have reawakened an interest in how early empires managed cultural difference and managed to avoid both separatism and racism. For instance, it is interesting that Bernard Lewis, though now widely attacked for his unflattering view of the Islamic world in *What went wrong*[34] remains highly regarded for his description of intercommunity harmony in the Ottoman empire.[35] Equally, Ashis Nandy's utopian notion of India's communal harmony before British rule is highly regarded by contemporary Indian intellectuals.[36]

The debate about empire inevitably impinges on our understanding of earlier empires and the way their historiography has developed. Nevertheless, attempts to understand the characteristics of these empires and to analyse their development raises a series of methodological problems. Most importantly, these concern the problems raised by diachronic analysis, as opposed to synchronic analysis.

In the English language historiography of empire one finds two broad comparative approaches that emerged during the European Enlightenment and have persisted into today's postcolonial scholarship. One is a synchronic method of argument that compares, contrasts and studies the linkages between empires over particular and relatively short spans of time. C. J. Wickham's studies of the Christian and Muslim empires of late antiquity in the context of particular conjunctures of trade, warfare, consumption and, in this book, taxation are cases in point.[37] Another example would be Marshall Hodgson's work on Islamic gunpowder empires of the early modern period, which were linked in his analysis by similar technological and ideological adaptations.[38] In this book, the chapters by André Wink, Stephen Blake, Karen Barkey and Rudi Batzell most clearly represent this style of analysis.

The other approach could be called the diachronic typological mode, in which empires are abstracted from their historical circumstances and compared over the whole span of human history from antiquity to the industrial revolution in terms of their basic institutions: tributary demands, central court structure, ideology of rule and so on. Several of the Victorian works Bayly discusses in his chapter explicitly compared the Roman, Mughal and British Indian empires, for instance. Our own project has been structured in terms of diachronic typology; and some of the participants in our discussions, notably Peter Bang and Dominic Lieven, have devoted part of their work to this sort of approach which has just recently spawned a new major contribution by

Burbank and Cooper.[39] Both modes of writing about empire have advantages and disadvantages. They are best understood as complementary rather than mutually exclusive alternatives. The synchronic approach often appears to constrain its practitioners within a single explanatory mode, because historians of contiguous empires tend to think in the same way. Conversely, the diachronic mode sometimes appears to essentialise the concept of empire and abstract it from the particular historical contexts that render it meaningful. The later Ottoman Empire may, after all, have had more in common with the Tsarist or Austro-Hungarian empires of the nineteenth century than it had with its own early modern, let alone late medieval antecedents.

Synchronic, diachronic or some combination thereof, it bears emphasis that at a more fundamental level, our entire project has aimed to overcome old cultural essentialist boundaries by pioneering comparisons between the entities on each side of the great mental divide between the Orient and the West. When the great nineteenth-century historian of comparative law, Henry Sumner Maine, set about to compare Roman and Hindu legal systems, the result was a dichotomy of unchanging Hindu customs, stuck in traditionalism, and rational, dynamic Roman legalism.[40] By contrast, our agenda has been based on the identification of some basic similarities and comparable institutions cutting across such civilisational boundaries. This ambition we share with a 'sister' project at Stanford comparing Han China and the Roman Empire which Walter Scheidel presents in his contribution to this volume. Such comparative initiatives are and, we hope, will be increasingly important to reinvigorate and inspire the study of premodern empires. It is in this spirit that we offer this collection on *Tributary Empires in Global History* to the reader.

Comparative histories

One register in which the diachronic typological form of comparison brings great benefits is the area of historiography itself, which is the subject of the first section of the book. For since the Renaissance, and even more so since the European Enlightenment, historians themselves have placed empires as a category, from the Assyrians to the Tsars, into their own contemporary frames of time as they have imagined and discussed their structure, virtues and vices. The chapter by Bayly examines the nineteenth-century historiographies of Empire, particularly of the Mughal, in Britain, especially what may be classed as 'liberal histories' and their Indian critics and imitators. He argues that these need to be understood not only in their own right as important keys to Victorian mentalities and ideologies, but also because they have shaped, often negatively, our contemporary historiographies of empire. These, like so much else in the twentieth-century world, were conscious or unconscious reformulations of Victorian themes. Fabrizio de Dono follows with a comparison of how the Roman Empire was treated as a model and invested with different meanings in Britain and Italy in the early decades of the twentieth century. At the heart of the essay is a discussion of the Italian reception of the comparisons published in England by Lord Bryce of the Roman and British Empires. Finally Baki Tezcan presents a study of how the myth of the decadent Ottoman Empire dragging its moribund corpus through the seventeenth and eighteenth centuries was a construction created to serve the needs of modernising Ottoman and Turkish reformers in the nineteenth and twentieth centuries. Ironically, it was only with a past denounced as inefficient and despotic, that it became possible to justify a push for radical reforms which would break through the social barriers that had previously served to contain state power.

In the second section, we now take the comparisons a step further to explore various influential theories and models of imperial power. These, however, have generally been heavily influenced by the issues brought up within the predominant historiographical traditions, old as well as modern. A theme common to the essays in the previous section was precisely the expectation of the intrinsic corruption and imminent decline of agrarian empire. Garry Runciman now addresses this issue with the analytical tools of neo-Darwinian and historical sociology. These allow him to put into sharper relief the comparative advantages which enabled some empires to prevail and survive for long stretches of time. Conversely, Runciman also discusses the risk of fragmentation which seems to be a perennial problem of agrarian rule. Michał Tymowski develops that aspect further in his contribution. Premodern empires normally had miniscule provincial administrations; and power was often segmented and loosely organised. This problem has occasioned a substantial anthropological literature dealing with tribal societies. Tymowski provides an analysis and introduction to this body of work in his discussion of African tribal empires while also calling attention to the need to distinguish between these and the more durable agrarian polities with more elaborate hierarchies and socio-religious institutions at the heart of this book. The classic expression of the fleeting success of imperial conquerors, however, is connected with the fourteenth century Arab historian Ibn Khaldun's view of the transient nature of nomadic power over agrarian populations. André Wink revisits this issue in a discussion of the Mughal dynasty. How did these Central Asian Timurid conquerors manage to turn themselves into successful post-nomadic agrarian lords, is the question which informs his essay.

Long-term continuity and stability of empire as a form of domination is at the core of David Ludden's chapter. But, he points out on the basis of two Indian cases from the turn of the eighteenth century, the reproduction of hegemony is as much a process happening on the margins of empires, through the interconnected processes of fission and fusion (two concepts originating in the anthropological literature also treated by Tymowski), as at the centre. Just as Ibn Khaldun was used to complement modern anthropological theory, the concluding chapter of this section now supplements Ludden's post-colonial view of empire from the margins by introducing a Ciceronean theory of provincial rule. Giovanni Salmeri takes his point of departure from the creation of the first Roman province, Sicily, following in the wake of the victory of the First Punic War against Carthage. Later ages have remembered as a pivotal moment in the history of provincial Sicily, Cicero's victorious indictment of the oppressive governor Gaius Verres in the courts of Rome. The copious speeches published by Cicero to document his triumph later afforded Sicilian provincials during the eighteenth century with a mode of language through which to engage their distant Habsburg and later Pietmontese rulers in a dialogue over rights and privileges – an instructive illustration of how metropolitan views of empire may be appropriated by resourceful provincials to better their position within the body politic. With the rise of nationalism during the nineteenth century, this model of successful provincial service lost much of its allure. The conditions and perceptions of imperial rule significantly changed as was also demonstrated by the papers in the first section.[41]

From the identification of shared historiographical trends and tropes over the interrogation of general theoretical models, the third and final section now moves to direct historical and cultural comparisons. Picking up on the themes of agrarian or tributary empires as both overmighty and weak, Bang develops a framework for comparisons of Roman and Mughal imperial history structured around the notion of the Universal ruler. A form of statecraft often maligned and demonised, the essay attempts to move the discussion beyond or behind the expectations shaped by modernising Hobbesian theories of the sovereign state. Where the latter focus on centralisation and intensification of state-formation, this contribution rather emphasises the extensive character of tributary empires, the composite and heterogeneous organisation of authority, and the limits on the exercise of governmental power, echoing Tezcan's critique of the traditional interpretation of Ottoman history. Scheidel complements or extends this common framework for analysing world-empires by examining the long-term convergence of Roman and Han Chinese state- or empire-formation during antiquity. At the heart of all tributary empires is the appropriation of peasant surplus production. By comparing late Roman administration with that of the Umayyad and 'Abbāsid Caliphate, Wickham's contribution explores the different consequences resulting from variations in the organisation of rule and tax collection. In all these empires, the grand imperial households were at the centre of government. Elaborate rituals of pomp and circumstance, *ornamentalism* as David Cannadine has dubbed it, helped shape and structure the articulation of power.[42] Stephen Blake's chapter addresses this patrimonial aspect of the rule of emperors through a comparison of court rituals and ceremonies at the Mughal and Ottoman courts. Finally, the last chapter, by Barkey and Batzell, turns to the question of war-making capacity. They compare the different methods and responses offered by the Ottoman, Russian Romanoff and Habsburg Austrian empires to meet the challenges of the military revolution during the seventeenth century.

The gains to be had from neighbouring fields are by now widely recognised among specialist practitioners within the scholarly community. Frequent thematic volumes which band together a series of (isolated) specialist studies under the same heading enable us to learn and draw inspiration from a host of related disciplines; they help us to shed our habitual modes of thinking to look at our topics anew. The emphasis in such collections, however, generally remains on individual cases. Comparison is mostly left to the reader, the work only half done.[43] But in this book, we have attempted to redress this tendency and push the agenda a little further by making the comparisons more direct and explicit.[44] For it is precisely this analytical exercise which helps historians avoid being confined within conventional patterns of thought and pre-established models. In the chapters that follow, we hope to have demonstrated the potential of sustained comparison to stimulate reflection on how questions are framed, the material organised and explanations offered. Often the preserve of disciplines, bound by tradition and to some extent isolated by complex and difficult philologies, the study of tributary empires depend for its renewal and continued relevance on efforts to break down our accustomed disciplinary barriers and confront these different empires and their histories as well as historians with each other. Historical contextualisation is crucial; we need to move towards a global and comparative history.

Notes

1. *Messa Esequiale e Tumulazione della Salma del Romano Pontefice Giovanni Paulo II. Piazza San Pietro, Venerdi 8 Aprile 2005* (The Vatican), p. 35 (our translation): 'Fratres, Deum omnium Patrem deprecemur, qui hodie nos congregavit ad Unigeniti Filii sui paschale mysterium in universæ Ecclesiæ Pastoris exsequiis celebrandum, ut eum assumat in pacem suam et Ecclesiæ ac mondo bona cuncta largiatur'. A detailed 'guide' to the funeral is available in the excellent article on Wikipedia, providing extensive links to official documents.
2. *Messa Esequiale*, pp. 35–37.
3. In terms of liturgy and theology these churches belong within the broad family of Eastern Christianity, orthodox and others. But they have broken out and returned to, or remained in, full communion with the Latin Catholic Church. Their affairs are regulated by a decree issued during the Second Vatican Council: Available online at http://www.vatican.va/archive/hist_councils/ii_vatican_council/documents/vat-ii_decree_19641121_orientalium-ecclesiarum_en.html.
4. *Messa Esequiale*, pp. 66–70. Note that the official printed programme omits the part spoken in Arabic, and only mentions the Greek version. It is necessary to consult the televised recording of the funeral to hear this, as well as to see which clerics did what. An easily accessible link to the video recording of the funeral is available

online at http://www.washingtonpost.com/wp-srv/mmedia/world/040805–1v.htm. Recordings are also available from the Vatican home page, but we experienced technical difficulties with these.

5. Eusebius, *Vitae Constantini* IV, 7, 1–2, translation by A. Cameron and S. G. Hall in Eusebius, *Life of Constantine* (Oxford, 1999), p. 156. Fowden (1993) for a vivid analysis of how the link was forged under Constantine and his successors between the Universal Roman Empire of Late Antiquity and the universalism of the Catholic Christian Church.

6. Schneider (2006: 247–52) for an analysis of how imperial imagery entered late antique Christian iconography.

7. Cf.http://www.vatican.va/gpII/documents/delegazioni-uff-esequie-jp-ii_20050408_en.html.

8. *Ut unum sint* of 25 May 1995; Available from the Vatican home page both in Latin, and authenticated English translation, http://www.vatican.va/holy_father/john_paul_ii/encyclicals/documents/hf_jp-ii_enc_25051995_ut-unum-sint_lt.html.

9. The literature is overwhelming. Wilde 2007 is an interesting analysis of the political struggles and the mobilisation of factions during the council, if perhaps too dependent on Protestant and progressive claims to what the council should mean; balanced and magisterial is Pesch (1994).

10. *Lumen Gentium* III, 23, 72–73 (emphasis added): Divina autem Providentia factum est ut variae variis in locis ab Apostolis eorumque successoribus institutae Ecclesiae decursu temporum in plures coaluerint coetus, organice coniunctos, qui, salva fidei unitate et unica divina constitutione universalis Ecclesiae, gaudent propria disciplina, proprio liturgico usu, theologico spiritualique patrimonio. Inter quas aliquae, notatim antiquae Patriarchales Ecclesiae, veluti matrices fidei, alias pepererunt quasi filias, quibuscum arctiore vinculo caritatis in vita sacramentali atque in mutua iurium et officiorum reverentia ad nostra usque tempora connectuntur (73). Quae Ecclesiarum localium in unum conspirans varietas indivisae Ecclesiae catholicitatem luculentius demonstrat. Simili ratione Coetus Episcopales hodie multiplicem atque fecundam opem conferre possunt, ut collegialis affectus ad concretam applicationem perducatur. Available online at http://www.vatican.va/archive/hist_councils/ii_vatican_council/documents/vat-ii_const_19641121_lumen-gentium_lt.html.

11. The main document on ecumenism, the decree *Unitatis Redintegratio*, issued during II Vatican, is often seen as a fairly radical self-relativation by the Church because it admits faults committed also on its side in producing divisions within Christianity (chapter 3) and because it concedes that elements of true Christianity may be found outside Catholicism (chapter 4), particularly within the broad family of Eastern orthodoxy whose traditions the Church fully embraced (chapters 16–17), cf. Pesch (1994, chapter 6). But this needs to be put in perspective. The attitude expressed towards the various Protestant professions, apart from the Anglican Church, was considerably more lukewarm (chapter 19). In general, the decree attempts to balance between the wish to invite dialogue and an insistence on the primacy and fullness of the Catholic Church and of the Pope. 'False irenism' should be avoided (chapter 11): the basic Catholic truths were not negotiable. On several occasions, this has been re-emphasised. Apart from John Paul's encyclical letter, whose title echoes chapter 8 of *Unitatis Redintegratio*, it is worth quoting the *Dominus Iesus*, emphatically lashing out against 'relativistic theories which seek to justify religious pluralism, not only *de facto*, but also *de iure (or in principle)*' (chapter 4), drafted in 2000 by the present pope for his predecessor, when he as Cardinal Ratzinger was head of the

Congregation of the Doctrine of the Faith: The Universal Church of Christ was and is for all times the Catholic Church.

12. Vergil, *Aeneid* VI, v. 853; Another poem of Vergil, the fourth ecloga, was read by Constantine (and his Christian advisers) as a prophesy of the birth of Christ, in a speech preserved among the writings of Eusebius but ascribed to Constantine: *Oratio Constantini Imperatoris ad sanctorum coetum*, in J. P. Migne, *Patrologiae Graecae Tomus* 20, 1234–1315 (esp. chapters 18–21).

13. Seneca, *De Clementia* (best consulted in the edition of the text, translation and commentary recently published by Susanna Braund, Oxford 2009).

14. *Ut unum sint*, chapters 88–97. Sørensen (1976: 159–60) for the connection between Seneca's stoicism and Christian ideology of rulership, in which Matthew 20: 26–27 occupies a central position, emphasising humility and service.

15. The webpage at http://www.vatican.va/gpII/documents/delegazioni-rel-esequie-jp-ii_20050408_en.html lists church delegations present at the funeral. The great numbers were a considerable source of pride, cf. http://www.catholicculture.org/news/features/index.cfm?recnum=36398.

16. This happened in the so-called Ravenna document, a declaration issued by the Joint International Commission for the Theological Dialogue between the Roman Catholic Church and the Orthodox Church. Cf. http://www.vatican.va/roman_curia/pontifical_councils/chrstuni/ch_orthodox_docs/rc_pc_chrstuni_doc_20071013_documento-ravenna_en.html, particularly chapters 40–42 and 10. Even without the representative of the Russian Orthodox Church, who walked out in protest against the presence of the Estonian Apostolic Church, the document nevertheless represents a fairly significant step forward from the very guarded joint proclamation issued as the II Vatican council drew towards its close in 1965 by the Pope and the Constantinopolitan Orthodox Patriarch expressing regret over the events which led to the Great Schism of 1054, but also stating that much work still had to be done to overcome remaining differences: Available online at http://www.vatican.va/holy_father/paul_vi/speeches/1965/documents/hf_p-vi_spe_19651207_common-declaration_en.html.

17. *Ut unum sint*, chapters 88 and 103.

18. Cf. Schäfer (1974). Particularly with Pope Gregory the Great (r. 590–604), who vigorously asserted the primacy of Rome within Christianity, the title became a more or less established part of papal usage. While conceding final jurisdiction of Gregory in a conflict concerning some prelates under his sea, the patriarch of Constantinople had nevertheless stressed his own ecumenical, that is universal, standing. This worked like a red rag to a bull and got Gregory all up in arms. In lengthy letters to the Emperor and Patriarch in Constantinople respectively, the recipients were lectured on the primacy of the see of Rome and of the importance of humility advocated by the successor of Peter, the *servus cunctorum sacerdotum*, in executing his pastoral duties rather than the ungodly pride and hubris of the Constantinopolitan patriarch which upset the peace and unity of the Church. If anyone had the right to call themselves universal or ecumenical, it was the Roman pontiffs; and even though it had been granted to them by the council of Chalcedon, they had always humbly refrained from using such a scandalous and arrogant title. Gregory the Great, *Epistles*, Book V, nos. 18–20 (in the numbering of J. P. Migne, *Patrologia Latina*, Vol. 77 (Paris 1896), pp. 738–48). For discussion, though occasionally seduced by the humility claimed for himself by Gregory in the letters, see Markus (1997, chapters 2 and 6), Modesto (1989: 140–79), Richards (1980: 63–66 and chapter 13).

19. Chapters 43 and 45 of the Ravenna document. Compare the cautious observations made by the leader of the Catholic delegation, Cardinal Walter Kasper in an interview to *Vatican Radio*, 14 November 2007. Available online at http://www.oecumene. radiovaticana.org/en1/Articolo.asp?c=167345.
20. Mann (1986: 1). Hintze (1997) for an attempt to apply Mann's theoretical apparatus in an interpretation of an agrarian empire.
21. The webpage at http://tec.saxo.ku.dk contains programmes and summaries of these meetings, as well as other relevant information.
22. Cf. Cooper (2005), chapter 6.
23. Lieven (2001), Brook (2009). Further Subrahmanyam (2006) arguing for the importance of the Mughal Empire for modern Indian state-formation.
24. Haldon & Goldstone (2009: pp. 3–29).
25. But even without such genealogical links, the similarities in the style of rule are often as remarkable as the differences. See, for instance, the careful comparison of Roman and Han Chinese traditions of ruler largesse by Lewis (2009).
26. Dirks (2006), Ferguson (2004).
27. Kafadar (1994), Aksan & Goffman (2007).
28. Schiavone (2000) is an excellent and balanced discussion of the question of the modernity of the Roman Empire and its limits.
29. Struve (2004: 31).
30. Di Cosmo (2004), a contribution to a book on the *Qing Formation in World Historical Time* edited by Struve (2004). See further the contributions of Milward and Perdue to the same volume stressing the Qing as a 'normal' agrarian empire.
31. Niall Feguson, 'An Ottoman Warning for Indebted America', *Financial Times*, 1 January 2008. Available online at http://www.ft.com/cms/s/0/6667a18a-b888–11dc-893b-0000779fd2ac.html.
32. Oakeshott (1983).
33. Ryan (2007: 1–16).
34. Lewis (2002).
35. Lewis & Braude (1982).
36. Nandy (1983).
37. Wickham (2005).
38. Hodgson (1974), Vol. 3. See also Islamoglu & Perdue (2009) for a recent attempt to explore the synchronic histories of the paths followed by China, the Ottomans and India into modernity.
39. Lieven (2001), Bang (2008), Burbank & Cooper (2010).
40. Maine (1861).
41. See Forsén & Salmeri (2008) for a comparative collection of essays exploring provincial societies in the longue durée of Mediterranean history.
42. Cannadine (2001).
43. Hurlet (2008) is a recent example of such hesitant comparison; the emphasis is placed heavily on treating each case as a 'forme originale' (p. 81) and stressing the diversity of historical experience. A number of particularly successful collections of the juxtaposing kind looking at premodern empires would be Alcock et al. (2001), Morris & Scheidel (2009) and Mutschler & Mittag (2009).
44. An ambition we share with Scheidel (2009) and Dale (2009).

Part I
Historiographies of Empire

2
Religion, Liberalism and Empires: British Historians and Their Indian Critics in the Nineteenth Century

C. A. Bayly

This chapter considers nineteenth-century history writing about premodern empires, concentrating mainly on historians working in Britain and India. I focus on liberal imperialist histories of empire and their critics. Both posited a 'historicist' narrative, whereby events in the past represented the working through of powerful essences in human history, whether the spirit of liberty, racial virtue or superior spirituality. Much recent work in the social sciences has featured an all-out attack on teleologies of progress of this sort, which had been dominant during the Victorian era. From Michel Foucault to Hayden White, from the *Invention of Tradition* to *Subaltern Studies* the notion of history as an unfolding tale of civilisational and racial essences through time has been trounced in a hundred thousand pages of closely argued print. Yet from the perspective of public education and public discourse, this massive effort has been largely unsuccessful. It is symptomatic that several of the British liberal imperialist historians referred to in this paper, such as James Bryce and H. G. Keene, are quoted approvingly on Hindutva (politicised Hindu), Armenian or Greek websites for their denunciation of the Islamic empires.

Equally, the 'romance of the nation' through time remains dominant in public and popular history in Britain, India and beyond. Even today's liberals themselves resort to historicist arguments to refute the new right. Residual socialist societies, such as China and Vietnam, cling to materialist versions of ideologies that similarly stress the evolutionary progress of nations. Even within the specialist academy the tide has turned, with the rise of sociobiology, historical evolutionism and geographical determinism. Tradition, far from being accepted as 'invented' is being re-essentialised before our very eyes. Rather, therefore, than revisiting a style of history writing, long dead, quaint and fully justifying the 'infinite condescension of posterity', this paper will be examining the creation of a powerful, flexible, and now resurgent mode of thought, which originally took shape in the nineteenth century, but continues to envelop us.

In the first part of the chapter, I examine the emergence of nineteenth-century historical writing through the categories of liberalism and empire. I will then go on to discuss the intellectual and political culture of some British and Indian historians of the Victorian era who considered the Mughal, Ottoman and British empires, very often in the context of the Roman Empire. The chapter ends with a brief epilogue on the continuing relevance of nineteenth-century historiography, often in negative ways, for contemporary historians of the 'tributary' empires.

From stadial theory to liberalism c. 1750–1850

It was in the late-eighteenth century British and European Enlightenment that many of the key themes of the later liberal era historiography began to appear as literary tropes. For Edward Gibbon, as for his French coevals, Condorcet and Montesquieu, the Roman Empire succumbed to 'luxury and superstition'. As in the diatribes of Edmund Burke against the English East India Company, Eastern license and despotism had corrupted the domestic republic of virtue. In these Enlightenment works, the Islamic empires held an ambivalent position, whereas to Edmund Burke and many of his contemporary observers of India, 'Mahomedan tyranny' had corrupted an ancient Hindu constitution, in Gibbon's narrative, Islam's first appearance on the borders of Europe signalled the advent of a rational religion of human brotherhood in opposition to the corrupt caesaro-papism of the Eastern and Western Roman empires.[1] In the eyes of Warren Hastings (Governor of Bengal, 1770s) and his leading officials, the Mughal Empire of Akbar had, in works such as Abul Fazl's 'Ain-i Akbari', established a Mughal 'constitution' that protected the peasant against the exploitation of the *zamindars* (landowners).[2] This ambivalence about Muslim empire also characterised the thought of the first generation of Indian liberals in the 1820s and 1830s, such as Raja Ram Mohan Roy. For Ram Mohan, India was already being defined as a 'Hindu' space and Muslim invasions were indicted for fatally weakening an ancient Hindu constitution. Yet at its best and especially under Emperor Akbar, the Mughal regime had guaranteed religious 'rights' while creating a system of 'virtual representation' in which respectable citizens could bring their plaints and observations to higher authority.[3] Implicitly, therefore, the British rulers should carefully follow these precedents.

A second mode of Enlightenment thought abstracted these themes of virtue and good governance into a more mechanistic account of the rise of 'polite and commercial societies' through the stages of nomadism, patriarchal localism and benign imperial despotism. This was the meta-narrative of Adam Ferguson,[4] Adam Smith and their continental European contemporaries. In this account, the Roman Empire was the highest stage of the old European civilisation, while ancient India and, possibly, the Mughal and Ottoman Empires had progressed almost as far. Yet in these ancient and Eastern polities, as contrasted with modern Western Europe, two critical features were missing to consummate the transition to the modern. First, a benign division of labour based on 'moral independency' was absent. Slavery and serfdom, the *ghulam* and the *fellahin*, or a dependent merchant class, could never provide the requisite moral and economic dynamism. Secondly, a rational monotheistic religion was essential. Rome and ancient India had remained 'polytheistic,' while (though Enlightenment thinkers were ambivalent about this) Islam was essentially 'enthusiastic', lacking the supposedly rational benevolence that derived from Christ's revelation. The Roman and Islamic empires were therefore predestined to decline without giving rise to benign and commercial societies.

A homologous idea of decline was also embedded within the discourse of political thought in the Muslim and Indian worlds. Ibn Khaldun's cycle of rise and degeneration in Muslim societies had been elaborated and aestheticised within the Ottoman and post-Mughal realms. When rulers fell into luxury and men turned away from the righteous norms of the medieval ethical *akhlaq* texts, godly dominion decayed. In India, the theme of decline found widely in eighteenth- and nineteenth-century Persian and Urdu literature had a further local explanatory device.[5] Muslims in India were inclined to 'wicked innovation' (*bidah*); they took up idolatrous Hindu forms of worship. Their Empire was also corrupted from within by the venomous sale of office and the rise of Hindu *bakkals* ('grocers').

Precursors of liberal historicism

Both the 'Scottish' and the 'Islamic' versions of this trope of decline were adapted and absorbed into mid-nineteenth century British and Indian historical evaluations of the historic 'tributary empires'. But in the meantime a number of important intellectual and evidential changes had served to sharpen and reorganise these themes. First, a more professional historical style had emerged. B. G. Niebuhr and other German historians introduced the concept of imperial culture into historiography. The analysis of historical texts and archaeological findings had not only given greater precision to the dating of imperial formations, but discoveries such as those made by Napoleon Bonaparte's savants in Egypt or Henry Layard at Nineveh had greatly extended the number of known empires, making possible both extended typologies and historical sequencing.

Secondly, 'race' began to take centre stage in the analysis of the capacity for growth of human potential. Institutions such as the colonial armies and early colonial censuses had begun to classify human groups. Phrenology and race science emerged parallel with the linguistic analysis of Indo-Aryanism.[6] Thirdly, religion had 'returned' following the freethinking age of Gibbon and Voltaire. But now the capacity of different 'races' and polities to generate rational religions of mankind within putative nation states, or imperial formations became the touchstone of human progress. Religion had thereby become central to the history of progress rather than being an epiphenomenon to it, as had been the case for Ferguson or Gibbon. This was a theme common to Evangelical Protestant Christians, newly reformed Roman Catholics, Unitarians, Positivists, Mazzinians, modernising Muslims along with Hindu 'reformers' such as Brahmo Samajists and Sanatan Dharmis.

Yet the idea of secular and religious progress also re-inscribed difference more sharply than had been the case with the Enlightenment thinkers. The argument would now go: 'it is our "founding leader" or our "hero" race, rather than yours, who bears the burden of civilisation'. All these religions and sectarian tendencies scanned history to show that their own race, nation or imperial formation had once been the repository of a proper religion that marked the progress of God's reason within the human spirit. Often the thinkers of the 1840s and 1850s found that such a message had faded or been suppressed by outside conquerors or corrupt priesthoods. But the spirit, along with the polity, would reawaken. National, racial and human regeneration awaited, therefore, not only a renaissance, but also a reformation.

Using the example of Hegel, Ranajit Guha argued recently, for the Indian case, that the world-history of the state decisively drowned out the cultural drama of ordinary people and their deities (*itihasa*) at a critical moment about 1820, a position broadly echoed by Dipesh Chakrabarty.[7] It is indisputable that states and empires became the lodestones of histories in the nineteenth and twentieth centuries as argued in Guha's essay. Yet I want to enter some qualifications to this position. First, great histories of political events and of the process of deity through history existed in the Indo-Islamic tradition and this was assimilated into colonial histories, most notably in the case of the Indian official and historian of early India, H. M. Elliot.[8] There was no sudden transition from history as popular folk representation to 'statist' history. Secondly, colonial historiography in India, following Anglo-Scottish precedents, emphasised the progress of civil and commercial society and was less concerned with the state than its German equivalent. For Guha, Adam Smith, not Hegel would have made a more appropriate incubus on historical writing.[9] Thirdly, the emergence of statist narratives in the nineteenth century was itself accompanied by increasingly deep analyses of popular culture by historians. What happened was that folklore was hived off from the history of the state; popular history did not disappear.[10]

It seems to me that the key feature of the new history was its thoroughgoing historicism even more than its obeisance to the state. The word historicism, of course, is a problematic one that is used in many different ways.[11] I use it to describe historical writing that is developmental, in that history's end – the increase of human liberty and wellbeing – is believed to be inherent in its progress. This was history that was supposedly idealist, objective and coherent, rather than random or arbitrary. By contrast, much eighteenth-century historical writing had been quite static or moralistic. Even Anglo-Scottish stadial historiography was more interested in describing stages rather than understanding the moral and spiritual drivers of change.

This extreme historicism emerged in different forms and with different political implications. Not many Britons or Indians of the early nineteenth century read Hegel, but, as Guha suggests, Hegel's 'world spirit', manifested through successive religious and political formations was emblematic of the period. In the German tradition, the state, which for Hegel included entities such as the Holy Roman Empire, was a worldly emanation and incubator of transcendental spiritual progress. For later writers, particularly in the English-speaking world, empires were also significant as they aggregated different groups of human beings. In this interpretation, they were epiphenomena within which would mature a worldwide polite and commercial society, marked by free trade in goods, religion and ideas. Yet empires also failed successively, in this view, mainly as a consequence of over-centralisation and inappropriate religious zealotry. In the rebirth of nationalities at the end of empires lay the hope that new seeds of freedom and spiritual awakening would be sown. Thus Christianity spread amongst Europe's barbarians, including the Anglo-Saxons, following the fall of the Roman Empire. Similarly, British writers on India and indigenous intellectuals, such as Aurobindo Ghose, came to see the rebirth of Indian nationalities after the fall of the Mughal Empire as harbinger of new spiritual and political progress.[12]

The English-speaking world also saw early versions of the quasi-materialist form of historicism parallel to what became the dominant Marxist or Comtean theories of continental Europe. Important here was Henry Thomas Buckle (1821–1862) whose *The History of Civilization in England* was well known to Indian writers as early as 1848. Buckle's influence was at its height in the decade immediately after his death.[13] He saw history as a triumph of 'mind over matter', a phrase which he coined himself. Civilisation began in areas such as Europe where man had an easier control over the massive forces of nature. Civilisation in the East was held back by the grandeur and hostility of nature. B. B. Majumdar, writing in the 1930s, believed that Buckle's own analysis was partly based on the writing of the Bengali radical Dakshinaranjan Mukhopadyay who indicted a Brahmin moral tyranny for condemning the Bengali peasant to unending poverty and labour.[14] Yet another Bengali writer, Kali Charan Banerjee, could turn this trope on its head. Banerjee argued that the Indian farmer had learned to dominate the great Eastern deltas early in history. This allowed the emergence of the Brahminical intelligentsia whose great intellectual advances were not corrupted, as they were in the case of Western intellectuals, by commerce and moneymaking.[15] For Banerjee, Indian history, and above all the Bengali gentry, provided evidence, therefore, of the decisive triumph of mind over matter. India was not, as Buckle argued, the civilisation that had been left behind. Banerjee's paper caused a furious row between British and Indian members of the Bethune Society, a Calcutta literary body. Yet this was proof that historicism could be adapted to optimistic as well as pessimistic accounts of Oriental history.

The new historicism came in neoconservative as well as liberal guises. Hegel himself, traumatised during the 1830 revolution by rioting students, profoundly distrusted democracy. The British historians of India I shall go on to describe were at best liberal imperialists who generally emphasised the rule-making capacity of empires more vigorously than the liberating effect of popular government, even for Britain itself. Yet a dominant strain of historicism, especially for liberal Indians, was represented by Guiseppe Mazzini's style of democratic nationalism in which republican solidarity spoke to the birth of new 'messiah peoples'.[16]

Finally, what distinguished the late-eighteenth century historiography of empires from the mid-nineteenth, for both rulers and subjects, was the actual physical experience of empire. Liberal and establishment historians of the mid-nineteenth and late-nineteenth century were profoundly aware not only of the oppressions of empire, but they also feared the return of 'barbarism'. The 1789 and 1848 revolutions in Europe, the Indian Mutiny-Rebellion, the US Civil War and other calamities informed their view of the fragility of power. At the same time, the aesthetic sensibilities of the period between 1780 and 1840, centring on romanticism and 'the sublime', had given the British in India an almost tactile sense of the Mughal imperial past as they discovered, measured and sketched its great mosques and fortresses, many of which were still in use.[17] This awareness of the physicality of empire paralleled the consequences of the 'grand tour' of Italy for contemporary understandings of the Roman Empire, and the beginnings of romantic tourism in the Ottoman Empire, signalled, for instance, by the paintings of David Roberts. Here again, the Indian intelligentsia were creating a homologous sensibility. In the 1850s, the Mughal noblemen and junior civil servant, Sayyid Ahmed Khan, compiled the *Athar-al Sanadid*, a disquisition on the royal monuments and Sufi shrines of Delhi, written in a language of enquiry and regret.[18] Even in Bengal, where many Hindu writers followed colonial authorities in deploring the destruction wrought by the Muslim conquests, some gave a much more positive view of the Mughal Empire, its inclusion of Hindu subjects and its great public works.[19]

Comparative imperial historiographies in India and beyond

This more informed view of empire was the context in which a new generation of comparative historians of empire arose in the mid-nineteenth century.
Their influence remains with us today, less because of what they wrote than
as a consequence of the critiques that their contemporaries and later generations directed against them. H. G. Keene (1825–1915) stands out as the classic liberal historian of Indian empires. He wrote the *Fall of the Moghul Empire*,
a biography of the eighteenth-century leader, Madhava Rao Shinde,[20] and a
more general *History of India from the Earliest Times to the Twentieth Century*
(1876). This last went into many editions and was the standard textbook
until the history of Vincent Smith, the Anglo-Irish anti-nationalist, began to
replace it in the 1910s.[21] In historiographical terms, Keene represents a middle
stage between Mountstuart Elphinstone's 'enlightenment' *History of India* and
the professional historical works of Jadunath Sarkar and W. H. Moreland in the
twentieth century.

Keene was a former ICS officer who criticised the land-revenue policy and
over-centralisation of British-Indian Government. He was uneasy about military expenditure and frontier wars. He represented the kind of Whig radical
hostility to 'big' government that Gareth Stedman Jones and Miles Taylor[22]
both regard as typical of British radical liberalism. He had much in Common
with A. O. Hume, William Wedderburn and William Digby, all of who were
dissident Indian officials, turned founder members of the Indian National
Congress. At the same time, Keene's history was permeated with a kind of
vulgar social Darwinism.

The liberal idea that empires foundered on over-taxation and rigid centralisation was already common among both British and Indians. Two years before
the publication of *Keene's Fall of the Moghul Empire*, the *Bengalee*, the most radical
of the early nationalist newspapers, compared Britain's dominion by the sword
in India and the crushing taxation imposed on its people to E. A. Freeman's
picture of the fall of the Roman Empire.[23] Like Keene, Freeman was a liberal
historian devoted to the idea that history recorded a succession of national
liberations from despotic tyrannies. English history saw the slow deliverance
of Anglo-Saxon freedom from the oppressive Norman Yoke. Eastern tyrannies,
such as Saracen and Ottoman rule, were even more oppressive. The Ottoman
Turk was a 'monster in human form' and '[t]he pretended reforms of the Turk
[the Tanzimat] were in their own nature good for nothing' (See Tezcan's contribution below for the Ottoman-Turkish take on this issue).[24] Ironically, an Irish
pamphleteer took up Freeman's theme, claiming that English government in
Ireland was as tyrannical as the Turks' rule in Eastern Europe.

Keene's application of these liberal themes to India's Islamic empires was
significant because it was widely diffused in Britain and India at a time

when history was being institutionalised in schools and colleges. Although superficial by contemporary German standards, it modernised the themes of 'Muhammadan tyranny' foreshadowed by the historians of the later eighteenth century. It also spoke directly to the emerging Indian liberal intelligentsia and helped inform memories and sensibilities derived from family and local sources. Keene's *Fall* presented a fashionable scientific and evolutionary face of the history of race and empire. The Mughal rulers, he argued, had succeeded at first because, by taking Hindu women, they widened their genetic pool, avoiding the 'hereditary imbecility' that afflicted so many ruling dynasties. Here Keene diverged from the earlier orientalists' themes of the decadence and luxury of the harem by insisting on the scientific advantages of out-marriage by the Mughal rulers. Similarly, brutal as they were, the massacres of brothers and uncles by the successful heir that took place after Mughal successions also acted to promote the 'survival of the fittest', in Keene's neo-Darwinian view.

As with many later liberal theorists, Keene's argument tacked uneasily between institutional and racial arguments. Thus, the Mughal Empire had fallen not only because of Aurangzeb's tyranny, but also because 'immigration [from the Muslim lands] had ceased and degeneration set in.'[25] In turn, the supposed anarchy of the eighteenth century had broken out because Mughal despotism had 'emasculated' the Hindu mind. The British would need to avoid a similar result, for secular education had destroyed India's 'own spiritual traditions', leading to an inner anarchy.

There were other ways in which fashionable ideas influenced his text. Keene believed that the early Hindu Aryan invaders of India brought with them the seeds of a system of democracy that flourished on Indian soil in the form of village councils (*panchayats*) and other representative institutions. When later Muslim conquerors attempted to establish empires in the subcontinent, they were most successful when they embraced and incorporated such institutions of self-government. This the great Emperor Akbar did most successfully, while his antithesis the Emperor Aurangzeb, centralised rule and refused to tolerate difference amongst his officials or his people. Aurangzeb 'over-governed' while his 'jealous centralisation' combined with 'persecuting spirit' overwhelmed the empire. In his racial theories, Keene, therefore, anticipated the more romantic interpretation of a somewhat younger liberal imperialist historian, E. B. Havell. Havell, writing at the turn of the twentieth century, also insisted on the link between Aryanism and democracy. A former director of artisan industries, Havell argued that under Akbar the Mughal rulers had, to all intents and purposes, become 'Aryans' themselves.[26] Both Havell and Keene displayed the characteristic confusion in liberal thought between racial and institutional determinism. This confusion was apparent in the eighteenth-century stadial theorists, but had now been sharpened by the development of evolutionary ideas and the concept of progress.

Religion naturally played a prominent part in Keene's scheme. His approach seems to have been not unlike that espoused by the so-called 'fulfilment theologians' of the more radical contemporary missionary societies. In this argument, Hinduism represented a repository of some basic aspects of human religiosity that would unfold through stages of evolution. Ultimately, a rational form of Christianity would supervene, even in India, and there were already signs that Puranic Hinduism was in decline, a view echoed by many Indian writers. But the evolution of faith was severely tested by periodic retreats towards religious bigotry and exclusionism, of which the Islamic reaction of Aurangzeb was one of the worst examples in Indian history. As a result, the sturdy and destructive noxious plant of religious bigotry, 'Ficus Religiosa', as he called it, had taken root on the foundations of Indo-Mughal rule and destroyed them, thus paving the way for the British conquest of the subcontinent.

Classical and Ottoman parallels in high liberal writing

There were a number of deep themes in Keene's work that paralleled English-language liberal histories of other pre-industrial empires. For 'Hindu' and 'Muslim conqueror' in Keene's work, one could easily read 'Greek' and 'Roman'. In the popular histories of the 1870s and 1880s, the Greeks, Aryan incomers like the supposed early Hindu Aryans, spread the seeds of democracy within Europe in Antiquity. Greece not Rome was the first liberal icon. John Stuart Mill saw the Greek city-state, particularly Athens, as a true model for modern representative government in Europe.[27] Mill preferred small-scale, face-to-face societies and direct representation through public debate, as in ancient Athens, or indeed the idealised view of the Indian *panchayat*. According to these liberals, the only way that modern representative democracy could be saved from anonymity and the crushing weight of millions of individual claims of self-interest would be to encourage the sense of intimate civic virtue that exemplified the Athens of Pericles. Empire was generally inimical to such virtue. Even Athens's 'blue water' empire of commerce and culture had its exploitative, tributary aspect. In the time of Alcibiades, it had lurched toward tyranny and had been destroyed on the walls of Syracuse.

Such ideas had contemporary relevance at a time when advanced liberals were deeply uneasy about the direction of Britain's world empire. Mill himself was inclined to approve British dominion over lesser civilisations 'caught' in an earlier stage in the evolution of civil society, such as India or China. At other times, however, Mill along with the radical liberals, was fearful that the resulting despotism would lead to the corruption of domestic government and civil society. These fears were vigorously expressed, particularly in the aftermath of the Indian rebellion of 1857. The nearest equivalents to Athens's empire of settlement of trade were the British 'white colonies', Australia, Canada, New

Zealand, Natal and Cape Colony. Liberal governments in the 1850s and 1860s struggled to withdraw imperial troops even from these territories.

The Roman example was more salutary yet. All educated Britons of this period were brought up on the speeches of Cicero. They were taught to deplore the usurpation of the Roman Republic by powerful military commanders: Sulla, Pompey and Caesar. The Romans provided the foundations of European state power, but ultimately snuffed out the seed of Hellenic liberty, which had to be planted again following the barbarian invasions of the Empire and the rise of Christianity. A similar theme animated English histories. Here the rude self-government of the Anglo-Saxons and Norsemen (specifically compared with the Hindu Aryans by Keene, among others) was supplanted by the tyranny of the Norman Empire. But luckily for humanity, the 'Norman yoke' was lifted and Saxon freedom fructified the barren wastes of Norman efficiency.

Yet not all liberal historians and theorists were as ambivalent as Mill and his followers about Empire. Towards the end of the century the early Roman Empire of Augustus secured increasing approval. Lord Bryce, a liberal politician as well as a historian, applauded the spread of Roman civilisation throughout Europe and compared it directly with the British Empire in India.[28] However, Rome, like the Mughals, had declined because corrupt landlordism and unchecked imperial autocracy had undermined its military virtues. British India was built upon more solid foundations of the rule of law and the Christian virtues of its rulers.

Contemporary historians and public moralists had begun to interpret the Ottoman Empire in similar terms. According to some writers, Arab freedom and license had been disciplined and organised by Turkish realism and hardiness. The Turks here stood as a kind of eastern Norman and the Arab as a freedom-loving Saxon. Sulaiman the Magnificent, far from being an intolerant Muslim, was an Ottoman Augustus or Akbar. Despite the relative decline of the Ottomans in the face of Russia and Austria, the 'Turks' still had the capacity to adjust and modernise. The Tanzimat reforms after 1840 had shown this, despite Freeman's contempt for them. A reformed Ottoman Empire might even begin again to scale the stages of civilisation. It is intriguing that British officials in India occasionally looked over their shoulders at how a surviving multi-ethnic, but still Islamic, empire was governed. In 1873 in an article in the *Times of India*, an expatriate journal, suggested that 'Turkish officers of high rank' should be introduced into the Muslim parts of British India to command the respect of Indian Muslims, while at the same time having 'intercourse with Europeans'.[29] This was a time when the British were worried about the so-called 'Wahhabi' threat of radical Muslims to the Indian Empire and modernising Ottoman Muslims, themselves hostile to Wahhabism, could be seen as some kind of antidote. Bizarre as it was, this suggestion reflected the partly favourable view that British commentators had of the Ottoman Empire up to the 1870s. Many non-Muslim Indians thought otherwise. The Bombay *Native Opinion* stated that the idea added insult to the injury of colonialism.

Thereafter, however, Turkophobia took over as a dominant theme developed in the writings of Freeman, Bryce and others. Sultan Abdul Hamid II came to seem more and more like an Ottoman Aurangzeb, Caligula or Nero, intolerant, brutish and over-centralising. Religious persecution of Christians during the 'Bulgarian atrocities', it was assumed, had begun to erode the basis of Ottoman power, as Aurangzeb's assault on the Hindus had eroded the Mughal Empire.[30] As racial theorising became more common and standardised, the Turks were increasingly depicted as brutish and ignorant invaders from the Steppes, while paradoxically, desert Arabs were now seen as natural gentlemen and hardy democrats. This perception expressed itself with various degrees of sophistication in the work of later British arabophiles, such as Charles Doughty, Gertrude Bell and T. E. Lawrence.

Indian liberal histories and political debate: the Mughals, Romans and Britons

What I have been stressing is, first, the formative influence of liberal historicising on the nineteenth-century understanding of the earlier tributary empires. Secondly, however, that history emerged permeated with contemporary political debates. Current issues about political decentralisation and racial politics in the 1870s and 1880s formed the second major influence on history writing about India and other empires. This can be seen very clearly in the case of liberal Indian reactions to Keene's *Fall of the Moghul Empire* and the work of other similar British historians of India. The *Tribune* of Lahore was the leading upper-Indian liberal nationalist newspaper in the 1880s and 1890s. It was associated with Surendranath Banerjea, one of the key leaders of the Indian Association and the Indian National Congress. Banerjea was a devotee of the Italian democratic nationalist Guiseppe Mazzini. *The Tribune*, with its Bengali staff and Sikh proprietor, a newspaper set in the second city of the former Mughal Empire, was extremely ambivalent about Muslim rule in India. In 1883 the paper published an article 'Liberal Principles in India', discussing Keene's *Fall of the Moghul Empire* and indicating the extent to which contemporary political debates were forming the emerging historiography of Mughal India.

Keene, the *Tribune's* commentator argued, was an excellent historian and surprisingly non-partisan for an Englishman. He was to be praised for recognising that the ancient Aryans who conquered India 'possessed the germ of liberal principles and preserved them through long succeeding ages'.[31] He was right that when the Muslims acquired India they had the option either of 'ruling selfishly' or adjusting their principles to the local inhabitants so that they 'could benefit from what benefited India'. Akbar made the adjustment with great success. But the Mughals had also tried the first, 'selfish' method, to their ultimate ruin. Akbar, the newspaper wrote 'anticipated all the great liberal measures that the British have revived'. Akbar reformed the law, retained the village system of government and brought Hindus into state service. He repressed the usurpations of his co-religionists and introduced a system of local self-government. Aurangzeb had done the opposite. His rule was tyrannical. He had excluded Hindus from office and had levied special taxation on them. Continuous warfare had brought about over-centralised administration.

The *Tribune*'s editor was adapting the classical British liberal assault on colonial warfare, taxation and over-centralisation. Yet he was also framing his view of Mughal policy in the light of the violent Indian debates of the 1880s. The conservative Viceroy, Lord Lytton (a 'British Aurangzeb'), had engaged in warfare in Afghanistan and muzzled the Indian press. His successor, Lord Ripon (a 'British Akbar'), had introduced local self-government and had sought to give Indian judges limited jurisdiction over British residents of India in the famous Ilbert Bill of 1883. The proposed measure had given rise to a massive and racist agitation by local British residents, supported by newspapers such as *The Times* in London. This outpouring of vitriol paralleled, the *Tribune* implied, the religious intolerance of Aurangzeb. The paper went on to admonish Keene for equivocating on the matter and publicly stating that some aspects of the Ilbert Bill were 'premature'. Ripon's liberal principles, a continuation of Akbar's, should be pushed through to their conclusion. Indians should not only be recruited into the civil service on equal terms, they were ready for representative government.

Indian liberals indeed generally made an exception for Akbar and other Mughal rulers who were supposedly animated by a 'liberal spirit'. As the *Tribune* put it in an editorial: 'The history of Mahomedan rule is not very pleasant, it is true; but what foreign rule ever gave pleasure?' And if there were tyrants among the Mahomedan rulers of India were there not great and just rulers, too? The emperors Babur, Humayun, Akbar and Shah Jahan had allowed Hindus into high office and had not treated them as 'natives' as in (the supposedly more) enlightened British rule.[32] Yet the general run of Mughal rule was depicted as a foreign despotism, involving the loss of control by indigenous people over a cultural area already becoming a nation in many new works emerging from Bombay and Calcutta. The vision was strongly historicist. India (like Italy) had an ancient culture that was disturbed by internecine warfare and internal corruption and then debased by long periods of foreign rule. For all the faults of the caste system this allowed India to repel, or in some cases absorb, the Muslim influence (as it would under British rule which was accompanied by the evils of drink and promiscuous modernity). Otherwise, as a writer in another part of the subcontinent put it, India might have been 'denationalised' by Islam, for people, like monkeys ('which Darwin says are our common ancestors'), are blind imitators.[33]

What made escape possible, according to most Indian liberals, was not so much hierarchy, but the existence in the subcontinent of an innate spirit of freedom and an evolving 'religion of humanity'. Both India's ancient representative bodies and her religion had at times been overwhelmed by tyranny and superstition. But they would eventually triumph as India, as in the rest of mankind, moved through a natural historical evolution. On the religious side, medieval teachers and spiritual mentors, such as the logician, Shankaracharya, and the Bengali divine, Chaitanya, had constantly revived the wisdom of the rational sages of antiquity. Later, the spirit of reason entered a modernist phase in the work of the Brahmo Samajists and other nineteenth-century reformers.[34] On the political side, long ages of 'Mahommedan despotism' had given way, in the eighteenth century, to the rebirth of long-suppressed Indian nationalities such as the Marathas and the Sikhs. The rulers of these kingdoms were themselves animated by the teachings of gurus such as Guru Ramdas and Guru Nanak.

In this reading, Indic religions of humanity were superior to all types of Islam, a religion that was rigid and left no room for spiritual change and development. Of course, it was true that some signs of movement had been detected in the Islamic world. The Chishti Sufi teachers in India, associated with Akbar, had shown signs of an encompassing and rational faith. Akbar's own court faith, the *Din-al Illahi* (divine faith), was seen as a positive development, even though as a hybrid form, it was unlikely to enthuse the people. Western Indian liberals also saw in the Bahai-Babi movement in contemporary Qajar Persia a sign of the imminent emergence of a new age of Islamic rationalism and spirituality to replace arid textualism.[35] Yet most depictions of the Islamic faith in liberal Hindu and Parsi newspapers stressed not Islam's rationalism, but the opposite. Much was made of the decadence and riotousness of Muslim religious festivals, of the depravity of the Muslim masses and the fanaticism of the heartlands of Muslim India such as the North West Frontier or rural East Bengal.

Race and religion. Romans and Holy Romans; from Bryce to Toynbee

Dominant races created empires, but how far should they merge with subject peoples? Here the lessons of Rome and the Mughals for modern empires took on a different hue. As the debate about race and sex within the British Empire became permeated with social Darwinist thought after 1890, racial mixing became an issue for both British and Indian historians. Javed Majeed has noticed that there was silence and ambivalence in British writings about racial relations in the Roman Empire.[36] Many imperial administrators might have had the Roman example before them. Macaulay's ideal of 'brown Englishmen', speaking the conqueror's language echoed contemporary representations of Roman culture and the role of Latin. Yet the British could surely not marry their Indian subjects or allow them to become British citizens and governors, as provincial Gauls, Spaniards and even Africans became citizens and in some cases Roman emperors. For the British, the Roman Empire was a model, but also a warning. Bryce spelt out the reasons. For one thing, there was a much greater 'distance' between 'modern Europeans' and 'less advanced races' than between the Romans and their conquered subjects. Race did not provide a clear line of separation for the Romans. It did in India, and even more so in Africa. True, 'generations of mental culture' had produced visages full of 'intelligence and refinement' among the 'more civilised races of India.' But colour difference still 'creates a feeling of separation, even of slight repulsion'.[37]

We can glimpse a similar uneasiness about racial mixing among many Indian liberal commentators of the nineteenth century. They argued for equality in the public services with the British and for dominion status within the Empire. They most certainly did not argue, however, for racial assimilation, even though they pointed to the example of Akbar's marriages with Hindu women. It was the political example of the Emperor, not what they saw as his attempt to create a mixed Hindu-Muslim ruling group that they applauded. Religion was the integument of race. The Mughal harem, filled with Hindu women, was as suspect as Anglo-Indian marriages of the eighteenth and nineteenth centuries. The *Native Opinion* of Bombay disparaged some contemporary marriages between Hindu and Parsi men and English women. Most Indian newspapers and comments were dismissive of Eurasians, usually depicting them as loafers and drunkards. Earlier Indian ideas about the moral distraction caused by the mixing of *dharma*s (religions) were adduced, alongside modern, eugenic notions of the alarming effects of racial mixing on mental and physical powers.

Again, if religious zealotry played a part in the fall of empires, how far could true religion help to sustain them. Here Lord Bryce was a particularly interesting commentator. This liberal statesman wrote on the *Holy Roman Empire* (1864), the *American Constitution* (1884) and published a comparison between the Roman and British Empires in 1914. During World War I, as a diplomat, he collected material to substantiate charges that the Ottoman Empire had carried out genocide against the Armenians. Put together, Bryce's narrative and his contemporary political posture amounted to an archetypical liberal world history. According to him, the Romans initially expanded a rational system of law and government to create a benign world system, as the British were to do later. The Romans 'reduced the Greek theory of the Commonwealth of mankind to practice'.[38] Ultimately, however, the Roman Empire foundered for two reasons. First, its power was 'vulgarised' by amalgamation with provincial elites, especially in the East. Consequently, Rome lost its identity as a redoubt of republican virtue. This was a weak version of the problem of racial mixing.

Secondly, however, 'it is on religion that the innermost and deepest life of a nation rests'. Roman religion was primitive and corrupt. (See Chapter 3 for the Italian debate sparked by Bryce's writings.) Hence the Holy Roman Empire, parallel to the Christian Eastern Roman Empire, was ultimately more flexible and hence more stable. It was capable of 'establishing peace in the world'. It was ultimately 'an empire of opinion',[39] a term used 50 years earlier for the British Empire in India. The Holy Roman Empire had allowed the wonderful flowering of medieval European religious art and letters. One could add that Bryce's evaluation of ancient Rome and its Christian *avatar* was contemporary with the time when the English Church, under the influence of Cardinal Manning, was drifting towards Rome and the last vestiges of civil disabilities were being removed from Roman Catholics. Of course, in Britain, the study of the Roman Empire was not as profoundly enmeshed in contemporary political debates as it was in Italy or France, where colonial expansion in North Africa was justified in terms of its Roman forbear and the existence of ancient bishoprics there. Yet even in Britain, the mid-century 'culture wars' exercised a subtle influence on the writing of history.

Bryce's analysis proceeded to modern times. In time, he argued, the Anglo-Saxon race had founded two great political systems that raised the commonwealth of mankind to a new level. One was the American Republic, a decentralised polity of English law and, critically, Protestantism, quite different from the democracy misunderstood by Alexis de Tocqueville. The other was the British Indian Empire, a multi-ethnic agglomeration of agrarian interests ruled by virtue of law and administrative prestige. Unlike the Romans, or indeed the Mughals, the British had not compromised their status as a Christian ruling caste. Paradoxically, it was by *not* extending full citizenship to their Indian subjects or putting into action a programme of conversion that they had maintained the cohesion of empire.

Bryce did not deal directly with the Mughal or Ottoman empires in his works until he became a fierce propagandist against the Ottomans during World War I, alongside the young Arnold Toynbee. But his asides in *The Holy Roman Empire* leave little doubt that, like so many Gladstonian liberals, he had little time for Muslim despotism. The Mughals and Ottomans, like the Umayyad Khilafat or the Saracens before them did not rule empires, but 'mere aggregates of territories, not really unified by any administrative system'.[40] Though the Ottomans claimed to be heirs to the Caesars, it was only the Holy Roman emperors who truly filled this role. Islam itself promoted tyranny. One particular illustration of such tyranny was the debased system of farming out revenue to venal adventurers and merchant families that pervaded the Muslim polities. The Romans had their *publicani*, but the system was regulated even under the vicious Nero and it was abolished under Hadrian. The British in India had replaced Mughal revenue farming with the orderly administration of the collector. Yet in the

Ottoman Empire, revenue farming had continued and had become even more oppressive to the people than the tyranny of state officials.[41]

Most liberal historians, indeed, seemed incapable of treating Muslims equitably. True, Islam achieved grudging respect as a conquest religion, but it was never understood as an alternative version of a 'commonwealth of mankind.' According to Bryce, Islam was also easily debased in an environment such as India where it was marked by the 'tasteless and extravagant ceremonies' of Muharram. In Bryce's meta-narrative, religion and race again emerged as the main influences on historical change.

Living empires in India: experience and history

So far this chapter has considered two influences on nineteenth century and, by extension, post-colonial histories of empire: these are liberal historicism and contemporary political debates, especially those concerned with race, religion and 'local government'. A third influence, already foreshadowed by the romantic orientalists of the first half of the century, revolves around 'sites of memory' and the living traces of empire. In the case of the Roman Empire, the tilt of British Christianity towards the Papacy meant that, after 1860, many more people had physical experience of the holy city and of the Roman past. The excavations in the Church of San Clemente in Rome, undertaken by Irish Catholic fathers, for instance, seemed to dramatise the very stages of civilisation of which Buckle, Freeman, Bryce and others wrote.[42] The fathers found traces of an ancient temple of the monotheistic god of Mithras in the ruins of the pagan Roman houses of Nero's day. The level above this revealed traces of early Christian worship which broadened upwards again to a Romanesque church and finally into the glory of renaissance Christian architecture. The workings of God over time within the integument of imperial power seemed almost physically proven by such excavations. Even in the British Isles themselves, the flowering of Roman archaeology after the 1850s revealed the British as former colonial subjects, surrounded by the roads, bath houses and garrisons of their former masters. Likewise, the increase of tourism, exploration and Christian pilgrimage in the Middle East resulted in a physical awareness of its ancient empires. It was an awareness, however, that increasingly cast the Ottoman Empire and its officials in a poor light.

It was in India that the living experience of empires was most profoundly influential in their historical reconstruction. Many nineteenth-century Hindu, Parsi and Sikh liberals believed that they were inhabiting a dangerous, or even polluted terrain situated between the artefacts of two empires, the archaic Mughal Empire and the corrupt modernism of the British. Both were part of their lived experience, for they were acutely aware of the inheritance of Mughal India. Around them, the nineteenth century liberal Hindus saw the detritus of the old empire: thieving Pathan knaves, mercenary Kabuli moneylenders,

Kashmiris who sang 'obscene' songs all night in the bazaars. These Muslims, however barbarous, still saw themselves as descendants of conquerors, superior to the Hindus. Yet in fact, the *Tribune* noted, the Muslims were usually converted Hindus of the lowest sort who had played no part in the construction of Muslim empires. Besides, the commentator concluded, India had already been reconquered by the Hindus before the advent of British rule.[43]

The organisation of Indian cities seemed to dramatise the degeneracy of the old order. For instance, the new modern centre of Allahabad, with its High Court and civil lines, was surrounded by communities of former Muslim soldiers and court servants planted by the Mughal emperors, such as the Pathan settlement of Dariabad.[44] These were always depicted as centres of riot and crime. In the ancient Uttar Pradesh city of Jaunpur, a demonstration of primitive religious enthusiasm in 1883 saw guileless Hindus congregating around a Muslim preacher and his bodyguard of semi-wild Muslim hill men (*paharias*). Living traces of the past did not always summon up fear and concern, of course. In Allahabad again, there was a well-known legend that the Emperor Akbar had constructed his great fortress opposite the famous Hindu bathing place, the Sangam, because he was the *avatar* (or reborn form) of an ancient and powerful Hindu yogi. Yet the multi-ethnic nature of the Mughal Empire and the hybrid religious forms that had flourished under Muslim rule were seen by many commentators of the nineteenth century as impediments to progress. Today's post-colonial commentators tend, by contrast, to hail such examples of toleration and inclusiveness.

For many nineteenth-century Indians, again, a further danger was the manner in which British officials were exploiting these very traces of 'backwardness'. Colonial officials and scholar officials, such as the Punjab educationist, G. W Leitner, seemed to be attempting to revive a Punjabi Mughal culture as a counterweight to the English-educated Indians.[45] Everyday practice seemed to confirm the depravity of the old Empire and the hypocrisy of its British successor. British officials insisted on Indians, salaaming, bowing and taking off their shoes on their approach. According to the public moralists these manners were not suited to the modern age: they were 'the remnant of the court etiquette of a degenerate Muslim age'.[46] This degeneracy had penetrated far into the domestic life of India. The Bombay reforming press noted that even in supposedly advanced Bengal, the vast majority of women were still secluded. This again was a consequence of the 'Muhammadan thrall'. Liberal ideas once again historicised popular assumptions and attitudes. Pathans had always been seen as vigorous and dangerous. Now they were increasingly seen as representatives of a past age, to be kept from polite Indian society.

Yet there was an ambiguity here. The louder the liberal press and pamphleteers denounced the archaic features of Indo-Islamic society, the more they were faced with the relative dynamism of many south-Asian Muslim communities. Despite the arguments of Muslims themselves, notably Sayyid Ahmed

Khan, that Indian Muslims were backward, they seemed to be flourishing in many areas. They dominated the post-1857 British Indian Army and held on in the subordinate civil service. They were well-represented amongst rising entrepreneurial classes: the Kabuli moneylenders in the plains, the Punjabi Mussulman trader in Burma or the Bohras and Memons who did well in the Arabian sea trades. The more the death of the Mughal Empire or its retreat to a 'husk culture' was celebrated, the more the consequent diasporas of Indian Muslims seemed to thrive, and to some, threaten.

These expressions of disdain for the old order might be seen simply as results of what contemporary historians of south Asia call 'communalism'. In fact, such attitudes were pervasive even among those Hindus and Muslims who called for amity between the 'communities' and a common front against the British. I would argue that they were consequence of the historicising and racial essentialising of the liberal historical movement. Liberalism archaicised the Mughal; hence it archaicised Muslims and their belief systems. Historical writing of this sort was one precondition for 'communalism', rather than a consequence of it. It was the power of ideas as much as squabbles over office-holding which drove communalism into public discourse.

Let us take the case of Raja Siva Prasad, the author of the Hindu work *Itihas Timirnasak*, a history of India in the Muslim period, largely critical of Muslim rule, which it held had perverted and destroyed free and ancient Hindu institutions of Bharat Desh. ('The land of (Hindu) India') Siva Prasad had once been critical of British rule but had repented, become Deputy Inspector of Schools in the Benares region, and emerged as a major 'loyalist' in the post-Mutiny period. His work picked up some themes from British works, such as those of Elphinstone and Elliott, but it was written well before the standard British liberal histories of Keene: 'the cruelty, coercive force and decadence of the Muslims drowned us',[47] he wrote, implicating practices such as Muslim *purdah* for exacerbating modern and malign aspects of the Hindu caste system. He denounced child marriages, multiple marriages, *sati* (widow burning) and the degraded position of untouchables. All these were the consequence of Muslim rule that had blocked avenues of progress for the Hindus. Lacking the patriot-isms of Europe, Hindus were simply slaves of whatever ruler came to power. Only education and British government would remedy this.

In her recent analysis of Siva Prasad's work Manu Goswami notes how he drew on the theme of Mughal decadence and failure in the work of imperialist British historians, particularly H. M Elliot.[48] While this is certainly the case, it is important to remember, too, that Siva Prasad was not simply subservient to a dominant colonial discourse which 'othered' Muslims. These ideas had meaning for some of their readers precisely because they re-energised literary tropes such as the Sikh and Hindu responses to Muslim *jihad* ideologies. They drew meaning from old family histories, particularly among commercial communities, like those of Siva Prasad, which indicted Muslim rulers for abducting women for their harems, even while they praised these rulers' benevolence. Above all, such histories of decadence and future improvement were read in the context of the living experience of Indian liberals mentioned above, as they negotiated the dangerous detritus of two empires.

Liberalism and Muslim reform

Again, these historiographical moves should not be seen simply as reflections of Hindu-Muslim communal ideologies. Many Muslims were also scathing about the decadence of later Mughal rule and explicitly or implicitly criticised multiple marriage. Sir Sayyid Ahmed Khan had much in common with Siva Prasad, both as a historian and as a politician. The two came together in opposition to the Indian National Congress during 1888. Sayyid Ahmed's writings suggest that he can be seen as a version of a Muslim liberal.[49] He believed in progress, education and the cultivation of eugenic fitness. Like both Hindu and British liberals, he saw rational religion as the essential driver of human progress, though in a fundamentally different tradition from them, and untouched at the deepest level by international liberalism.[50] God, according to his reworked version of the eighteenth-century teacher, Shah Wali-Allah's, doctrine had planted the seed of knowledge (*ilm*) in the human mind. This was progressively revealed by the work of the Prophets and the teachers in the form of successive *sharia*s (legislations) that were appropriate to different periods of historical time. The Prophet's revelation was indeed final, but the record of it made by human beings was imperfect and must therefore be reinterpreted in the light of the advancing state of knowledge. The Umayyad Khilafat and even the Mughal Empire of Akbar had been appropriate contexts for the interpretation of sacred, literary, astronomical and other scientific lore. Yet later decadence had set in because of man's ignorance and greed. Aurangzeb and his court were trapped in stale traditionalism. The British Empire now provided a context in which education and learning could advance. The Muhammadan Anglo-Oriental College in Aligarh that Sir Sayyid founded would nurture *ilm* in a way that would preserve the Prophet's revelation and interpret Muslim science in terms of Western developments. In time, even the British Empire would pass and India's Muslims would come into their own.

Other writers of Islamic history and institutions, notably Altaf Hussain Hali and Sayyid Amir Ali held similar views. Their works and ideas also paralleled what Albert Hourani called the 'liberal age' of Arabic thought in Egypt and the Levant. But their view of the Mughal Empire was more positive than Sir Sayyid's had become by the 1870s and in this they echoed the attitude of thinkers such as Jamal-uddin Al Afghani and Mahomed Abduh to the Ottoman Empire: while internal vice may have undermined Ottoman rule, the external attack of unbelievers and imperialists was more damaging.

Alongside these intellectual constructs, there also existed a vein of political nostalgia that stood as the opposite to the hostility to the detritus of the Mughal Empire that we have seen among the more strident liberal Hindu and Parsi writers and journalists. Writers such as Abdul Halim Sharar[51] and many Urdu poets mourned for the passing of the great civilisations of the cities of Delhi, Lahore, Lucknow and Hyderabad. This sentiment was by no means confined to Muslims. As Mushirul Hasan has most recently pointed out, many non-Muslim poets and writers looked back to the hybrid cultures of the old Muslim-ruled states of south Asia as representative of a period of communal harmony.[52] The idea of Hindu-Muslim mixing and melding in the subcontinent was a pervasive one and it became more attractive as communal rioting became more regular in the 1880s and 1890s.

Professionalisation and historical evidence

One final strand of thought and analysis of the Mughal Empire must be mentioned. These were the local official and unofficial investigations of India's past carried out by settlement officers, the writers of official district gazetteers and the increasing numbers of local antiquarian societies. The works produced by these authorities were often tinged with the rhetoric of despotism and progress. Yet they generally presented a more dispassionate account of the workings of the Mughal Empire and its successors at a local level. Rather than conflict and dispossession, they necessarily stressed coexistence and compromise: they charted the service of Hindu chieftains within the Mughal army, the establishment of religious grants (*waqfs*) around which settlements and advanced agriculture developed. They detailed the forms of representation by which local magnates and merchants represented their problems and requirements to local Muslim officials. This accretion of scientific knowledge and textual remains on Mughal governance later played an important part in the early twentieth-century histories of W. H. Moreland and Jadunath Sarkar. In the nineteenth century, however, the meta-narrative of progress seemed quite divorced from this localised evidential base, at least in English-language historical writing. Even revenue officers such as Elliott or Keene, who had worked with these local materials, rarely let them influence their teleological constructions of the past. Hayden White's understanding of historical writing as a series of narrative emplotments, rather than an engagement with evidence, seems particularly apposite here.[53] Thus, throughout much of the later nineteenth century, the ideological initiative lay with liberal historicist writers for whom the agrarian empires were now, in the main, symbols of despotism and unreason. This was not necessarily because they were 'communalists' themselves. Many, indeed, believed that like-minded Muslims ought urgently be brought more fully into the national family. Their disdain for the Ottomans and Mughals was instead an outgrowth of their overriding belief in human progress.

Re-evaluations and the continuing grip of historicism: 1890s–1940s

The liberal historicist strand of historical writing continued to be influential well into the twentieth century, though increasingly transformed by nationalist and idealist conceptions of human society. A number of intellectual and political trends supported this. In the first place, the influence of Oswald Spengler's 'gigantist' history was felt in British historical writing, especially in the work of Arnold Toynbee whose *Study of History* (London, 1934–61) laid out a sequence of civilisational cycles that included the rise and decline of Rome, the Mughals and the Ottomans. Civilisations declined, according to Toynbee, because the elite's creative powers waned, leading to the withdrawal of allegiance by the people. In his scheme, religious revelation periodically initiated a new cycle of creativity, often in the period of transition between empires. Inevitably, the Ottomans and even the Mughals were too far on the downward cycle to have retained much dynamism. Toynbee's treatment of the Ottomans was, moreover, still influenced by a Gladstonian Turkophobic rhetoric, now envenomed by the Armenian atrocities. The Ottoman Empire had long since fallen prey to the dead hand of Islam and the brutalisation of the 'Turkish' character by despotism. Attesting to this continuity in the theme of civilisation and barbarism, Bryce himself wrote an introduction to Toynbee's 1916 diatribe against the Ottoman Empire.

Secondly, the theme of the corruption of Islamic empires was given new force by the propaganda that developed around British rule in Egypt after 1882. Lord Cromer's belief that an upstanding Indian-style bureaucracy would inject moral standards into the corrupt Coptic and Circassian bureaucracy (*amlah*) deposited by the Ottomans in Egypt clearly echoed earlier projects to cleanse the Indo-Islamic bureaucracy of the subcontinent. Works such as Milner's *England in Egypt* and the standard histories of India and Egypt followed this line. The rise of Indian and Egyptian nationalism after the 1880s also drove liberal historical writing towards the authoritarianism of the 'new imperialism'. Vincent Smith's *History of India*, which remained a key textbook in India until the 1960s, adopted many of the themes of progress and decline that were found in Bryce or Keene. But its essential assumption was that Indians could never form a nation. Only Britain could hold together the fissiparous entities that had emerged from the failed assimilation of Hindu to Muslim India during the Mughal period. Reflections on Egyptian and Indian history by native intellectuals began to challenge these stereotypes. The Egyptian writer, Duse Mohamed, for instance, anticipated Edward Said, by denouncing Western writers for portraying Indian rajas and Egyptian pashas as one simple essence of backwardness.[54]

A third important influence on historical writing about the Mughals and the Ottomans was the further development of racial thinking, which occurred, ironically, in the context of the re-evaluation of Islam itself. The British view of Islam, harsh and dismissive in the middle of the century, improved as 'fulfilment theology' and a new interest in human spirituality became evident after 1890. T. W. Arnold's, *The Preaching of Islam*,[55] favourably contrasted the expansion of the Muslim world through preaching and equality with the brutality of Christianity. It was almost as if the age of Gibbon had returned. This trend coincided with a new romantic conception of the glorious freedom of the Arabian spirit, manifested in the writing of Charles Doughty, Gertrude Bell and later T. E. Lawrence. Yet if the Arab was praised, the Turk, simultaneously brutalised by despotism and corrupted by luxury became an even clearer target of xenophobic orientalism.

Some Indian histories of India displayed similar tendencies. Aurobindo Ghose, a leading anti-colonial nationalist theorist of the 1900s, helped transform the liberal universalism of Ram Mohan Roy or Surendranath Banerjea by emphasising the enduring spiritual unity of India and its people. India's difference and superiority was unambiguously asserted. Yet in this unfolding of soul and land over time, the Muslim found an even more diminished role. For Aurobindo, as noted above, it was the free community of Indian peoples released by the collapse of the Mughal Empire who were the key to the subcontinent's future.[56] In this monist historical faith, the Mughals were not damned by their centralisation or their bigotry, but by the very fact that they were not of Aryavarta, the land of the Aryans. In the emerging Hindu supremacist interpretation of Vinayak Damodar Savarkar, the greatest event in Indian history was the displacement in the eighteenth century of the Mughal Empire by a modern version of *Hindupad Padhshahi*, the 'Hindu Empire of India', which he associated with the Maratha confederacy of that era.[57]

In the years between 1880 and 1940, then, historicist meta-narratives of progress and decline reached their apogee. But there were already other developments in train. A deeper technical understanding of the working of the old empires was complemented by a materialist turn in historiography, reflecting the early influence of Marxism and economic history on these disciplines. W. H. Moreland was one of the first India historians to understand the workings of the post-Mughal revenue and administrative systems of India. In works such as *Akbar to Aurangzeb* he began to bring together local histories with the meta-narrative of civilisation's progress.[58] Giving full credit to the road and canal building activities of the Mughal rulers, he was nevertheless able to argue that the British had massively extended the premodern scale of the Mughal economy through the railway, the modern canal system and the steamship. British progress began to be defined as economic and not moral progress.

A similar re-evaluation was occurring in writing about the former provinces of the Ottoman Empire. In Egypt, the hydraulic marvels of pharaonic and Hellenistic-Roman Egypt, gave way, it was increasingly asserted, to the sleep of

Islam. Only the work of British engineers on Egyptian waterworks could bring back the lush plenty of Egypt. The hydraulic engineer, Sir Charles Wilcocks, made a similar analogy between ancient Mesopotamia and a British ruled Basra province.[59] What had been achieved in the Indian Punjab would be achieved in the new Iraq. Indeed, for a brief period between 1914 and 1926, the British began to accumulate information on Ottoman rule in Mesopotamia similar to what they had acquired by 150 years of rule in post-Mughal India. In general, this was deployed to the discredit of Ottoman administration in three provinces that had only been lightly touched by the Tanzimat reforms. Administrators such as those of A. T. Wilson, Sir J. Haldane and Sir Arthur Dodds, described Ottoman administration as a skin-deep affair. The sultan's officers had merely played off the great clans, such as the Muntafiq and the Howeitat, against each other; administration had been venal, justice brutal. Yet not all officers saw it in this light. Stephen Longrigg noted that Ottoman rule had taxed the country lightly and that strenuous efforts had been made in the late eighteenth and early nineteenth century to create a class of prosperous peasant landowners.[60] The British, with their widespread predisposition to conservative rural magnates, had halted and reversed that progressive tendency.

Despite the beginnings of the 'materialist turn' in empire historiography and the accumulation of material on local governance and the condition of the peasantry, the old themes of race and religion died very hard.[61] This was because they spoke directly to the nationalist and religious concerns of the day. In the case of the Ottomans, Sir Hamilton Gibb, the leading English-language historian of the Ottoman Empire, saw Islam as a great church, with state power a mere penumbra to it.[62] His co-worker Henry Bowen believed that the Empire had begun to flounder in the eighteenth century when vigorous and intelligent European and Circassian elites were replaced with Turks and other unregenerate Asiatics. Quite apart from the racialist bias, this was not in fact the case.[63]

This dichotomy between the new materialism and the continuing hold of racialised progressivism was also apparent in the historiography of the other two empires, the Mughal and the Roman. In the case of the Mughals, the technical, if imperialist, approach of Moreland was paralleled by that of the leading Indian historian of the period, Sir Jadunath Sarkar.[64] His detailed analysis of Muslim geographical texts and revenue data did not prevent him from arguing that the fall of the empire was mainly due to the fanaticism of Aurangzeb and the rise of the 'hardy' Maratha soldiers on the western Indian plains. Similarly in the case of Rome, the technical prosopography of Ronald Syme, A. H. M. Jones' analysis of the effects of cholera on the Empire and J. B Bury's detailed work on administrative history attested to the influence of historical materialism and realist history. Yet the wider stage was still filled with grand structures of civilisational rise and decline in the style of H. V. Breasted, the American historian, Arnold Toynbee and influential German racialist conservatives.

Conclusion: the liberal era and modern historiography

It is evident that much that has been written since the 1950s on the great agrarian empires has to one degree or another attempted to escape from the assumptions of the earlier period. Yet I would argue that post-war and post-colonial histories are still heavily influenced by the themes of the liberal imperialist era. In the Mughal case, while within the academy, racial and religious constructions of its history have been increasingly squeezed into the territory of the Hindu right, many of the historicist and evolutionary assumptions of the older historiography are alive and well at a popular level. Romila Thapar, India's leading historian, has consistently argued against right-wing textbooks that portray Muslims in India as brutal 'others', invaders of the subcontinent rather than one strain in its culture. Aurangzeb remains a major player in this drama. It is revealing that several of the fullest entries on the worldwide web under the name 'James Bryce' contain articles by Hindu right wingers, praising that liberal imperialist author for his view that 'race mixing' – in this case between Hindus and Muslims – had led to, and would lead to political collapse. Other references to 'Bryce' in English and French allude with hatred or approbation to his diatribes against the 'genocidal' Ottoman 'Turks' of 1915. In the case of the Ottomans one might see a resurrection of some of the themes of 'the dead hand of Islam' in some recent work of Bernard Lewis, who remains nevertheless one of the great historians of the Empire and of modern Turkey. What might be called 'auto-orientalism' also remains a powerful force. A recent exhibition in London, coinciding with Turkey's move towards the European Union, mounted a picture of the racial and cultural drama of 'the Turks' over a millennium. The Ottoman Empire was represented as a reflection of specifically Turkish cultural dynamism and adaptability.

Meanwhile on the academic front, revaluations have largely centred on refuting the powerful historicist assumptions of the liberal era. In the work of materialist and Marxist writers such as Irfan Habib, Sevcet Pamuk or de Ste. Croix, the dynamic of class struggle has replaced the earlier emphasis on race and religion. The teleological narrative has changed its form, but not always its thrust. In the Indian historiography, for instance, the Emperor Akbar has been transformed into a prophet of Jawaharlal Nehru's Indian 'secularism' of the 1950s. Of course, not all history is still written in the shadow of the Victorians. The post-1980 generation of specialists has called into question even this materialist teleology by questioning the whole issue of 'tradition and modernity'. The sharp distinction between incoming conqueror and local society that often formed the thrust of nineteenth-century histories has similarly been abandoned. Instead, historians have painted a picture of the assimilation of local elites into imperial cultures, blunting the old picture of the 'revenge of the provinces'. This has been the theme of writers as varied as

Greg Woolf, Metin Kunt, Hasan Kayali and Kumkum Chatterjee on the three empires. Foucauldian paradigms have been applied to the discourses of empire. Equally, the work of Edward Said prompted a whole revaluation of the theme of despotism as it was applied to all three empires. Revenue farming, the height of tyranny to the Victorians, has sometimes been seen as a successful and appropriate form of state-building in recent writings on the three empires. Yet even where the Victorian stereotypes have been overturned, it was the issues selected by the nineteenth-century writers that particularly attracted the revisionist attentions of their successors. To this extent, their influence remains inescapable and even our own project in this volume distantly reflects their desire to compare empires diachronically as a yardstick for human progress or degeneration.

This essay has discussed a period when the Roman, Ottoman and Mughal empires existed in the same frame of time, namely in the *imaginaire* of nineteenth-century and early twentieth-century liberal historians and their domestic and indigenous critics. During this period, historiography was influenced by three fundamental forces. These were, first, the historicist structure of liberal and post-liberal thought itself; secondly, the political conflicts and controversies of the era, such as the debate over Indian reform or the 'Bulgarian atrocities'. Thirdly, the ruminations of intellectuals were powerfully affected by the living evidence of empire all around them, be it the heritage of post-Mughal Muslim diasporas in India or echoes of the Tanzimat reforms heard by British scholar administrators in Egypt and later Mesopotamia. It was (and remains) this powerful combination of intellectual practice and everyday experience that gave the historicist, racial and religious understandings of the old empires their staying power. Even today, popular opinion remains largely in its thrall, while academic work still struggles to escape from and refute its meta-narratives.

Notes

1. For the background, see Pocock (2002, vol. 1: *The Enlightenment of Edward Gibbon, 1737–64*).
2. Cf. introduction of Francis Gladwin (1800)'s translation of *Ayeen Akbery or the Institutes of the Emperor Akber.*
3. Roy (1999) (*India Gazette*, 17 December 1829).
4. Ferguson (1789).
5. Russell & Islam (1969).
6. Kapila (2007).
7. Guha (2002); Chakrabarty (2000).
8. Elliot & Dowson (1851–55).
9. Rothschild (2001).
10. Peter Burke analyses this process in (2005:3–6).
11. Iggers (1995).

12. Aurobindo (1958: 396).
13. Buckle (1916); *Encyclopaedia Britannica*, 13th edn, 1926, 3–4, p. 732.
14. Majumdar, 1934, vol. I, *Bengal*: 116–18; *Bengal Harukaru*, 2, 3 March 1843.
15. Report on the Bethune society meeting, *Native Opinion*, 26 December 1875.
16. Bayly (2008).
17. Cf. the paintings of Thomas William Hodges, Thomas and William Daniell. De Almeida & Gilpin (2005); Tillotson (2000) for general discussions of British artists and their vision of India. David Roberts's representations of the mosques and palaces of the Middle East, though searching for Christian signs, may have achieved something similar for the Ottoman and pre-Ottoman world.
18. Troll (1972).
19. For example 'The Moghul and British Empires Compared', a set of ten articles, *Hindoo Patriot*, May–June, 1854.
20. Keene (1891).
21. Smith (1906).
22. Jones (1983); Taylor (1995).
23. *Bengalee* cited in *Native Opinion* (Bombay), 25 January 1874.
24. Freeman (1877).
25. Keene (1887: 278).
26. Havell (1918) (this text was based on numerous articles he had written from the 1880s onwards).
27. Biagini (1996).
28. Bryce (1914). See also De Donno's analysis in Chapter 3 of this book.
29. *Native Opinion* (Bombay), 23 September 1873 'Lack of Sympathy between the rulers and ruled.' *Times of India*, 8 September 1873.
30. Jake Grout-Smith, 'British perceptions of Turks and Arabs, c. 1879–1914' unpublished Cambridge dissertation, MPhil in Historical Studies, 2004.
31. 'Liberal Principles in India,' *Tribune*, 30 June 1883.
32. *Tribune* (Lahore) 12 November 1881.
33. *Native Opinion*, 15 June 1873, 'Nationality'.
34. This evolutionary religious and secular history is succinctly expressed in Banerjea's oration of 1876 on Mazzini, see his *Collected Works* (1922: 48–56).
35. Cf. the long series of articles on the Bahis/Bahais in *Native Opinion*, March–April 1973.
36. Majeed (1999: 88–110).
37. Bryce (1914: 59).
38. Bryce (1904: 413–14).
39. Ibid., p. 418.
40. Bryce (1914: 7).
41. Ibid., pp. 31–32.
42. See *La Chiesa di San Clemente* (Rome, 2002), history of the church and excavations available on site.
43. *Tribune*, 24 January 1883.
44. Bayly (1975).
45. *Tribune*, 29 October 1881.
46. Ibid., 26 March 1881.
47. *Itihasa Timirnasaka* (1873), p. 87 cited by Goswami (2004: 183).
48. Ibid., p. 184.
49. Troll (1978).

50. Cf. Devji (2007); Devji effectively argues that Muslims had their own form of evolutionary historicism, but its essence was wholly different from the Western or Hybrid Indo-Anglian one.
51. Sharar (1975).
52. Hasan (2005).
53. White (1975).
54. Mohamed (1911: 4).
55. Arnold (1893).
56. See Note 8 above.
57. Sarvarkar (1972), esp. p. 59.
58. See also Moreland (1929).
59. Wilcocks (1925).
60. Longrigg (1925).
61. Bayly (2002).
62. Gibb & Bowen (1950–57).
63. Review of Gibb and Bowen, *Islamic Society* by Itzkowitz 1962.
64. Sarkar (1935).

3

Orientalism and Classicism: The British-Roman Empire of Lord Bryce and His Italian Critics[1]

Fabrizio De Donno

In this chapter, I aim to explore the impact of James Bryce's *The Roman Empire and the British Empire in India* (1901) on the early-twentieth-century Italian historiography of Rome. I will particularly focus on the reception in Italy of Bryce's comparative discussion of the notions of assimilation, denationalisation of subjects and decline in the Roman Empire and in the British Empire in India. I will in this way attempt to show how the genre and themes of Bryce's work inspired a similar comparative approach in Italy and gave rise to responses among the prominent Italian historians of Rome of the early twentieth century, and in particular in Ettore Pais. My contention here is that the Italian commentators elaborated a contrasting rhetoric and use of the trope of Rome which, on the one hand, responded to the British domestication of Rome and, on the other, reflected Europe's and Italy's cultural, political, and social concerns of the time.

James Bryce and the comparative historiography on the British and Roman Empires

In his *The Roman Empire and the British Empire in India*, James Bryce wrote that 'there is nothing in history more remarkable than the way two small nations created and learnt how to administer two vast dominions; the Romans their world-empire [...] and the English their Indian empire'.[2] Bryce's comparative analysis of the British and the Roman Empires constitutes an example of an established genre of historical writing which developed in Britain between the late nineteenth and early twentieth centuries. Professor F. Haverfield – a historian of Roman Britain and a contemporary of Bryce – spelt out the reasons and ideas behind the British interest in imperial Rome in his inaugural address to the Society for the Promotion of Roman Studies in 1911. He started by recognising the debt to Theodor Mommsen for making Roman history a 'newborn' and a 'more technical' subject, while also stressing that it had been

Mommsen's merit if the general European interest in the history of Rome had shifted its focus from the republic to the empire.[3] Haverfield then went on to discuss in detail what had made Roman history, particularly with regard to Britain, 'the most instructive of all histories'.[4] Although the republican constitution of Rome offered 'the one true analogy to the seeming waywardness of [the] English constitution', what was more important was how the Roman 'imperial system [...] light[ed] up [the British] Empire, for example in India, at every turn'.[5] What especially concerned the British Empire was 'the methods by which Rome incorporated and denationalised and assimilated more than half its wide dominions, and the success of Rome [...] in spreading its Graeco-Roman culture over more than a third of Europe and a part of Africa'.[6] Other valuable comparisons involved the 'Roman frontier system' partly because it pointed to problems of decline, but also because it was what 'has given us all modern western Europe'.[7] This last aspect was also relevant to the 'three and a half centuries during which Rome [had] ruled Britain'.[8]

The use of Roman history in Victorian culture and thought, with particular reference to the shifting concern from republicanism to imperialism, dated back to the late nineteenth century. In his *The Expansion of England* (1883), for instance, John R. Seeley claimed that, while the Roman republic was praised for its 'freedom', the Roman Empire was held in favour for its 'civilisation'.[9] If Roman republicanism had been traditionally associated with liberty in opposition to the Roman despotic imperial rule, this new wave of writings extolled imperial Rome for bringing about 'the modern brotherhood or loose federation of civilised nations'.[10] Similarly, in his article entitled 'The Imperial Ideal' (1905), the historian W. F. Monypenny clearly outlined the character and nature of the transition from ideas of 'Nation' and 'Nationality' to those of 'Empire' and 'Imperialism'. He argued that 'power and dominion rather than freedom and independence are the ideas that appeal to the imagination of the masses; men's thoughts are turned outward rather than inward; the national ideal has given place to the Imperial'.[11]

This fin-de-siècle European interest in the history of imperial Rome, as Raymond F. Betts has argued, 'provided pleasing undertones to the litany of the new imperialism'.[12] According to Richard Hingley, in fact, the Roman Empire became an intrinsic trope of British imperial discourse and articulated three themes in particular: imperialism, Englishness and Romanisation.[13] The Roman conquest of Britain was seen as the key moment in which the transmission of civilisation, imperial character, and Christianity took place between Rome and Britain.[14] The idea of 'Romanisation' was associated with 'civilisation' and 'progress', and 'the civilising mission linking Rome and Britain appear[ed] united in the form of a linear continuity of progress through time'.[15] In this sense, the idea of Romanisation was influenced by evolutionary and diffusionist theories,[16] as well as, as will be seen in this essay, by the interaction between orientalism and classicism. Rome was thus used in order to define categories of otherness and racial mixing within the context of the British Empire: from the native Britons (the Welsh, Irish and Scots, or 'Celtic subaltern'), who had had less or no contact at all with the Romans, to the 'less racially compatible' non-Christian colonial Asians and Africans (but in particular the Indians) whom the English compared to Rome's African subjects.[17] Notions of otherness, racial mixing, and Englishness, were however subject to nuances, and in general terms the English imperial spirit was considered to be more the result of a 'mixed genetic inheritance, including ancient Britons, classical Romans, Anglo-Saxons and Danes'.[18]

One important effect of the use of the notion of Romanisation in conjunction with evolutionary thought was, of course, that it defined Englishness against Romanness. What emerged from the juxtaposition between England and Rome, essentially, was the distinction between the modern liberal character of the English and the ancient despotic character of the Romans. By discussing Roman imperial despotism, in other words, Bryce and his contemporaries had the opportunity to address and celebrate British liberal imperialism. As Raymond Betts has argued, the British Empire was defended not by means of military analogies with Rome, but on the basis of racial and customary contrasts. In the British Empire, for instance, as opposed to the Roman, the liberal character of imperial rule was primarily determined by the fact that force was admitted only 'as necessary rather than as desirable'.[19] If Rome as an ancient power had been 'tyrannical and exploitative', therefore, modern British rule was seen as 'humanitarian and commercial'.[20]

The political discourse of liberal imperialism that emerges from the comparative work of Bryce and his contemporaries deals with notions of ethnic fusion, citizenship, militarism and societal refinement, and addresses them within the rhetorical contexts of republican virtue and imperial corruption. The idea of civil society which these British historians come to embrace finds its roots in eighteenth-century political thought and in particular in Adam Ferguson's *An Essay on the History of Civil Society* (1767). John Pocock has shown how Machiavelli's republican writings and use of the trope of Rome inspired James Harrington's *Commonwealth of Oceana* (1656) and influenced eighteenth-century political philosophers such as Adam Ferguson.[21] In his *An Essay*, Ferguson saw history develop from barbarism to civilisation in parallel with the transition from military conquest to commerce. If the patriotic citizen of the republic fought out of virtue and solidarity, as society became more refined the relationship between citizens was characterised by specialisation and commerce. This is the moment when armies became professional and defence was left to those paid for the purpose. As Pocock puts it, the history of the republic 'tended to become one of the self-corruption of virtue by virtue'.[22] The progress of civilisation turned out to be more the cultivation of secondary values inextricably linked with the division of labour and the specialisation of personalities. In the eighteenth century, Britain saw itself as a civil society whose virtue was under the threat of corruption by virtue itself. For Ferguson, the solution to this problem was for members of society to retain their political persona by not ceasing to be a citizen. As a Scot and a key figure of the Scottish Enlightenment, Ferguson wished to ensure that citizenship would be accessible to all British people.

With the transition from republicanism to imperialism in nineteenth-century British liberal thought, however, new and orientalist inspired notions of race and religion came to have an impact on ideas of civil society and citizenship, with particular reference to the context of British India and ancient Rome. As C. A. Bayly has shown in his chapter in this volume, Bryce's comparative work is an example of a 'liberal history' of empire where race and religion are both the main agents of historical change, and what distinguished Bryce's genre from the histories of the late eighteenth century: not only that of Ferguson but also those of Edward Gibbon and Montesquieu.[23] Bayly locates Bryce's comparative work on the Roman and British Empires in the wider context of Bryce's work, and shows how, together with his two previous books on the *Holy Roman Empire* (1864) and on the *American Constitution* (1884), Bryce's overall historical output 'amounted to an archetypical liberal world history'.[24] In this history, it is rather the Holy Roman Empire, based on the rational and monotheistic religion of Christianity, that offered more stability. For Bryce, however, the two great political systems of the modern age had been founded by the Anglo-Saxon race: the first was the American Republic, 'a decentralised polity of English law and Protestantism'; the second was the British Empire in India, 'a multi-ethnic agglomeration of agrarian interests', which was ruled 'by virtue of law and administrative prestige' and where the British maintained the cohesion of the empire by not compromising 'their status as a Christian ruling caste' and 'by not extending full citizenship to their Indian subjects'.[25] A political persona was thus denied to Indians on racial and religious grounds because it was feared that assimilation might affect English virtue and civil society and lead to the collapse of the empire.

If, as Hingley has argued, British commentators developed an interest in imperial Rome after Mommsen had depicted Roman Italy as 'a suitable role model for the new states and would-be empires of Germany and Italy',[26] in turn, the comparative use of imperial Rome developed by the British liberal historians soon began to prove influential on continental historians of Rome. The widespread interest in Roman history was also due to the fact that, as Catherine Edwards has pointed out, 'different nations [...] competed sometimes to identify with Rome'. Such identification went to the extent that professional historians often created overlappings between 'the mechanism of Roman imperial administration' and the 'concerns of statesmen in Germany,

Britain, and elsewhere, charged [...] with the administration of growing empires'.[27] If, as Betts asserts, references and allusions to imperial Rome had served as 'heuristic reinforcement'[28] in British imperial thought, in Italy the idea of Rome served many nationalistic purposes. While the idea of republican Rome had been at the heart of the *Risorgimento* movement of independence and the process of national unification, imperial Rome became a central theme in nationalist and colonial ideology from the late nineteenth century, as well as a rhetorical trope with specific anti-British and anti-liberal connotations in fascist political discourse.[29] Bryce's comparative work in general, and his essay on imperial Rome and British India in particular, had a considerable impact on the Italian historiography of Rome. Although Bryce was not the only British author to have an impact in Italy, he was undoubtedly the best known and most influential among figures such as Ettore Pais, Guglielmo Ferrero, and Gaetano De Sanctis.[30]

Orientalism and classicism: the comparative perspective in England and Italy

Bryce's comparative perspective is an example of the interplay between orientalism and classicism. As Javed Majeed has demonstrated, such perspective was part of a general trend of British comparative attitudes to India which originated with British orientalism in the eighteenth century, when Sir William Jones compared Sanskrit with Greek and Latin and 'laid the foundation of the study of Indo-European languages as a family'.[31] The comparisons between Sanskrit and Latin as ancient Indo-European languages suggested that Indian and Roman civilisations were linked by a genealogical relationship whose evolution culminated in modern European civilisation. In the British scholarship on British India and imperial Rome, Indo-European or 'Aryan' genealogies informed comparisons and contrasts between 'historical eras' as well as 'between cultures in the same era'.[32] In these comparative perspectives, the Aryan family of languages also provided the racial maps that underpinned the comparative observations in law and history.[33] Thus, to compare British India with ancient Rome pointed to some aspects of the contemporary antiquity of India, while the modernity of imperial Britain was defined against the antiquity of both contemporary India and ancient Rome. The link between Rome and Britain also connoted the progressive nature of European history and civilisation as opposed to the static nature of India. Another example of this kind of comparison was Henry Sumner Maine's *Ancient Law* (1861), in which contemporary Hindu law was compared to ancient Roman law.[34]

This interplay of orientalism and classicism is central to Bryce's construction of the idea of ethnic fusion and assimilation in the British and Roman Empires. The idea of racial difference between the conquering and conquered races, which is underpinned by such interplay, represents the key contrast between the two imperial systems:

> the relation of the conquering country to the conquered country, and of the conquering race to the conquered races, are totally different in the two cases compared. In the case of Rome there was a similarity of conditions which pointed to and ultimately effected a fusion of the peoples. In the case of England there is a dissimilarity which makes the fusion of the people with the peoples of India impossible.[35]

What 'contributed more to the fusion of the races and nationalities that composed the Roman empire' is exactly 'the absence of any physical and conspicuous distinctions between those races'.[36] On the other hand, in British India race and religion constituted obstacles to fusion. In racial terms, the colour of the Indian skin 'creates a feeling of separation, perhaps even of slight repulsion' and this particularly formed 'an insurmountable barrier to intermarriage' and 'intimate social relations'.[37] Religion, like race, is an impediment to fusion as the lives of Hindus and Muslims are shaped by their religious practices.[38] Religion can create 'a sort of nationality within a nationality'.[39] In sum, 'the English are too unlike the races of India [...] to mingle with them [...] or to come to form one people. [...] The races of India [a]re all of them far behind the English'.[40] For Bryce, as will be seen, the analogy between British India and imperial Rome also legitimated the British despotic rule of India. Bryce's use of Rome's policies of ethnic fusion should, of course, be situated within the context of the discussion of imperial corruption and decline. As Majeed has pointed out, in Bryce's work imperial Rome is treated as a 'cautionary tale' with particular regard to the question of assimilation.[41] At the same time, however, Bryce's insistence on depicting the absence of racial notions in the context of ancient Roman imperialism also lays emphasis on the 'modernity' of the British 'imperial category of race'.[42] In order to effectively assess Bryce's argument, it is therefore important to stress that, if on the one hand, he considers Britain to be 'heir to an imperial Roman enterprise', on the other, he also distances Britain 'from this earlier enterprise, particularly because of the dangers of assimilation it implies'.[43] In many respects, this ambivalence in the British approach to Rome proved crucial in soliciting the response of the Italian historians. Before moving on to explore such response, however, it is important to dwell a little more on the relationship between orientalism and classicism in Europe and in Italy in particular.

The approach to Roman history according to the new Indo-European or Aryan family of languages and races involved a similar process of interaction between orientalism and classicism as that described with reference to Greek history by Martin Bernal's *Black Athena: The Afroasiatic Roots of Classical*

Civilisation (1987). Bernal in this book gives an account of the changes that took place in the European academic approach to Greek history in the aftermath of the establishment of orientalist philology between the late eighteenth and the nineteenth centuries. He distinguishes between the traditional approach, which he calls the 'Ancient' model and that was based on classical sources, and the new approach, which he calls the 'Aryan' model and that was mainly influenced by nineteenth-century comparative philology, historical linguistics and anthropology. While the first approach saw Greece as 'Levantine' and 'on the periphery of the Egyptian and Semitic cultural area', the new model saw Greece as European and, in some extreme cases, even denied the influence that Egyptians and Phoenicians had exerted on it, and claimed that the Greeks were a mixture both of Indo-European tribes arrived from the *north* and of indigenous subjects. If Bernal devotes his book to urge scholars to 'overthrow the Aryan model', he also claims that this model came in vogue when it became intolerable for nineteenth-century Europeans to think that Greece – 'which was seen not merely as the epitome of Europe but also as its pure childhood' – had been 'the result of the mixture of native Europeans and colonizing Africans and Semites'.[44] Even more importantly, Bernal maintains that the Aryan model's rejection of the Phoenicians' influence on Greece coincided with the rise of racial anti-Semitism in France and Germany in particular. Furthermore, Bernal also points out how French and German scholars associated the Phoenicians with the English as 'the proud manufacturing and merchant princes of the past and present'.[45] Interestingly, the English liked the association and admired the Phoenicians. On the continent, in the meantime, the Aryan model had begun to affect the approach to Roman history too, and from Niebuhr and Michelet to the early twentieth century, the Punic Wars came to constitute a historical reference for the racial struggle between the Aryan Romans and the Semitic Carthaginians.[46] As Robert Young has pointed out, the French orientalist Ernst Renan in particular had been responsible for putting forward the idea that history in general had taken on 'the form of a dialogue, or conflict, between the Aryans and the Semites'.[47] Indeed, in France commentators associated the French to the Aryan Romans and the British to the Semitic Carthaginians in order to discuss Anglo-French tensions. Similarly, Italian historians of Rome, and Pais in particular, borrowed the same historical reference to discuss Anglo-Italian tensions.

The new Aryan approach to Roman history had a varied impact on the Italian historiography of Rome. While it was generally adopted by most historians, Pais remained more sceptical and continued to draw on the ancient sources rather than on the modern comparative method.[48] This notwithstanding, he often borrowed the parlance of the new method, even if such borrowing at times implied a criticism of the findings of the new approach. A clear example of this is found in one of his earlier works on Magna Graecia and Sicily, where he clearly stated that his aim in the book was to deal with the 'great historical problem' of whether the European Mediterranean was more Aryan or Semitic.[49] While Pais occasionally made references to Aryanism and, as will be seen, often addressed the British as Semitic, his engagement with orientalism and the comparative method remained more ambiguous. In a lecture on *La storia antica negli ultimi cinquant'anni con speciale riguardo all'Italia* ('Ancient History in the Last Fifty Years with Special Regard to Italy'), which he delivered at the University of Rome in 1911, Pais gave an account of the latest methodological developments in the history of classical antiquity in Europe. Although Bryce is not mentioned here, other English scholars such as Henry Sumner Maine and the new comparative methods concerning philology, ethnography and law, are acknowledged as having 'opened new fields of investigation for the understanding of the moral and social ideas of the classical world'.[50] At the same time, however, he warns that these scholars' supposedly original work may be in fact misleading as it 'projects on to the ancient world that light which comes exclusively from the modern world'. Although 'ingenuous', such reconstructions often lack a 'solid scientific basis'.[51] Pais does not completely reject them, but he situates himself and his approach between the *Risorgimento* and Mazzinian tradition of historians of Rome including Atto Vannucci, and the new tradition of scholarship of Germany and Britain.[52]

There was, of course, a nationalist slant in his position. The Aryan method often stereotyped contemporary Italy as a decadent remnant of ancient glories and set it in contrast to the more modern northern European nations. As a result, the general reception of Aryanism in Italy remained controversial.[53] Reliance on the ancient sources rather than the new method thus also equalled to denying the northern and Indo-European origins of classical Greece and Rome, and avoiding the consequent domestication of classical antiquity on Britain's and Germany's part. In the same lecture, Pais even made reference to the foundation of an 'English Society for Roman Studies' presided by Haverfield, but particularly stressed, with a messianic and Mazzinian tone, that such events should make the Italians reflect both on the impact of Latin civilisation on the modern West, and on modern Italy's duties towards its own ancient past. He thus concluded by inviting the *Istituto storico italiano* ('Italian Historical Institute') to be the 'symbol of the nation' and to lead Italy into a new phase in the study of ancient Roman history – a field of study that, after all, 'can only be meaningful to and loved by those people of Latin culture and blood'.[54] Interestingly, though, he often borrowed the findings of the comparative method and he certainly developed a comparative approach to Roman history himself. While Pais mostly relied on what Bernal has called the ancient model, the Italian also engaged indirectly with the new Aryan model. The most controversial aspect of Pais' engagement with orientalism concerns the Italic peoples and the foundations of the Roman Empire. If he agreed that the Romans fused all the Italic peoples into one people and went on to unify Italy, Europe and the Mediterranean, he never clearly embraced the idea that the Italic races were of Indo-European lineage. Paradoxically, however, while describing the process of Romanisation of the Italian peninsula, he made reference to the linguistic work of one of Italy's leading scholars of Indo-European philology, Graziadio Isaia Ascoli.[55]

In actual fact, the comparative perspective involving the interplay of orientalism and classicism in Italy focused on the idea of Italian unification through ethnic Romanisation. Already during the *Risorgimento*, Italian nationalists such as Giuseppe Mazzini associated the idea of national unification with that of a Roman 'rebirth'. In Mazzini's 'religion of humanity', the notion of a 'third' Rome as the historical and political centre of the Italian nation and as a legacy of imperial and papal Rome was imbued with notions of universalism, Romanisation and unification. Mazzini believed that the dying Europe of the Papacy, of 'Empire', of the monarchy and the aristocracy, would be awakened by the Young Italy's and Young Europe's projects he led.[56] Mazzini's building of a new humanity, however, was Eurocentric and concentrated on a European brotherhood which would bring liberty to the rest of mankind. Mazzini's notion of Roman rebirth, in fact, also referred to the possibility of Italian influence in Africa and the Mediterranean.[57] In 1859, two years before the proclamation of the Kingdom of Italy, the future prime minister of Italy and a nationalist, the Mazzinian Francesco Crispi, had spoken of Africa as 'the ghost of the past and the hope and desire of the future'.[58]

In post-unification Italy, the classicist tradition of the *Risorgimento* mingled with a growing orientalism, which developed the Indo-European concept within the context of the ethnology of Italy and Rome. Angelo De Gubernatis, a leading Italian orientalist, reconstructed the history of Aryan Italy by means of a succession of declines and rebirths of Rome. The modernity of the 'third' Aryan Rome of united Italy was defined by parallels between contemporary India and the 'first' Aryan Rome.[59] The evolution and progress of Rome was reconstructed through the Hindu myths and customs which had evolved from Hinduism to Roman paganism and then to Christianity.[60] The modernity of united Italy and the third Rome was established by showing that the same myths now belonged to popular culture and folklore.[61]

Such visions of Italy and the third Rome within Indo-European civilisation influenced the ethnological and historical writings on the origins of Rome. Among the chief orientalists who influenced ethnology and history was Francesco Pullè. His *Profilo antropologico d'Italia* ('Anthropological Profile of Italy', 1898) reconstructed the ethnic make-up of Italy in pre-Roman times and gave an account of the *northern* origins of the Italics and the Latins, and of Rome's unification and ethnic Romanisation of Italy.[62] Such accounts were particularly criticised by Italy's leading anthropologist of race, Giuseppe Sergi, who argued that the origins of the Italics were in the Horn of Africa and not in India, and that the European races were, therefore, Eurafrican and not Indo-European.[63] Fascinatingly, such a theory had an impact on Italian orientalism and on the work of Carlo Conti Rossini in particular, who wrote extensively on Italian East Africa with particular reference to how Romans, Italians and Ethiopians shared the same religion, Christianity, and the same place of ethnic origin, the Horn of Africa.[64]

While neither the Indo-European nor the Eurafrican ideas fully shaped Pais' approach, he was no doubt certain that Roman history should be rewritten as the first stage of Italian history. He traced the origins of Rome back to the Greek colonisation of Italy and the hybridisation of the Greeks with the Samnites, Latins and Etruscans, and described Rome's expansionism by recounting the Roman victories against the Gauls and the Carthaginians.[65] The origins of Italy, of course, dated back to when the Roman republic assimilated the Etruscans and went on to unify Italy.[66] The unification of 1861 was seen as the repetition of that first unification and Romanisation of Italy. In a speech delivered in 1911 on occasion of the 50th anniversary of Italian unification, Pais particularly praised the means used by ancient Rome 'to cement the unity of the Italian people and fuse all the different Italic races', while also stressing that Rome's expansion 'should be remembered in order to indicate the path that Italy should follow for the future'.[67] These Italic races to which Pais refers, however, were not the Indo-European Italics coming from the north identified by orientalist scholarship. It was not until the publication of Bryce's work in Italy, in fact, that Pais and his contemporaries dealt with the new comparative method in a more engaging manner.

James Bryce and the Italian historiography on the Roman Empire

Bryce's work was translated by the leading jurist and scholar of Roman law, Giovanni Pacchioni, in 1907 and was reviewed by the scholar and later minister and senator of Italy, Arrigo Solmi, in 1912. Pacchioni, in his introduction to the translation, particularly praises Bryce for being able to 'illustrate in ingenious ways the past with the present and the present with the past', and to 'identify analogies between events from distant centuries seemingly irrelevant to each other'.[68] Solmi, on the other hand, is more critical and dwells more on the differences between the two empires which Bryce unearths as regards the issue of fusion. For Solmi, it is Rome – and not Britain – that gave 'the historically strongest impulse towards the unification of mankind'.[69] It is Rome that truly communicated to all subjects its civilisation, language, law and, later, even religion. These policies, against which Bryce defines British imperialism, would continue to be the focus of discussion in much of the Italian historiography of Rome of the early twentieth century. While only part of this scholarship was informed by Italian nationalist and fascist ideology, there is an overall tendency in this historiography to devote a great deal of space to the criticism of modern – and in particular British – imperialism. The British Empire and its liberalism are thus attacked both by anti-imperialist commentators, and by nationalist commentators such as Pais who praise imperialism primarily in reference to Italian expansionism.

Pais, De Sanctis and Ferrero reacted to Bryce's work in ways which were as diverse as their political and religious stances, as well as their methodological approaches to the study of the history of Rome. Pais, as the next section will show in detail, was undoubtedly the fiercest critic of Bryce.[70] His work was informed by the gradual deterioration of the relationship between Italy and other western nations – and Britain in particular – following on two political events: the Versailles treaty of 1919, and the Italian invasion of Ethiopia and the proclamation of the Italian Empire in 1936. In the aftermath of each of the two events, Pais published a book on the relevance of Roman history to contemporary politics: *Imperialismo romano e politica italiana* ('Roman Imperialism and Italian Policy', 1920) and *Roma: Dall'antico al nuovo impero* ('Rome: From the Ancient to the New Empire', 1938).

Both books were influenced by Bryce's comparative method. In the first of the two books, Pais explicitly mentions Bryce while addressing the 'superiority' of the Roman Empire over the British Empire.[71] The book was not an 'attack' on British imperialism alone, but also on American and French imperialisms. Pais gives an account of how, in his view, these powers seemed to obstruct the path to Italian national regeneration and affirmation. The threats to national affirmation, however, also came from within. The text deals with the spread of international socialism in Italy and its pacifist and neutralists tendencies. Although already present before the war, these tendencies returned even stronger during the so-called *biennio rosso* ('red two years'), a period characterised by socialist uprisings as well as by condemnation of Italy's participation in World War I. These internal crises, as well as the 'humiliation' of Italy's World War I 'mutilated victory', were the factors which fascism had set out to challenge from its origins. Thus capitalism and liberalism on the one hand, and socialism on the other, are challenged by Pais' earlier book by means of reference to the greatest of all 'Italian' heritage: the Roman heritage. Roman values are here contrasted to capitalist and socialist values, and implicitly associated with nationalist and fascist ideology. Many of the features of Roman imperialism – from its agrarian nature to its assimilative policies – are used to discuss the underpinnings of fascist ideology in the first book, and the general success of fascism in the second.

Both De Sanctis and Ferrero also dealt with issues and methodologies inspired by Bryce and his genre. However, as opposed to Pais, their criticism of British and modern imperialism derived from their engagement with republican thought. De Sanctis was a Mazzinian and a Catholic who wrote a famous history of Rome from the origins to the foundation of the empire. In his *Storia dei romani* ('History of the Romans', 1907–23), while he embraced the Indo-European lineage, he depicted Rome both as a symbol of Italian unification and as embodying the *Risorgimento* ideals of liberty. De Sanctis had an anti-imperialist approach to Roman history.[72] His explicit engagement with Bryce – although essentially critical – occurs in another work, *Dopoguerra antico* ('Ancient Post-war Period', 1920). In this essay, written in the aftermath of World War I, De Sanctis used the trope of Rome to criticise the contemporary imperialist tensions which had led to the war. His republicanism became an antidote to the new imperialism as the relevance of the *Risorgimento* and its ideals of liberty had resurfaced in this post-war period. It is during this time that he set out to write the last part of his *Storia dei Romani*, that is, the foundation of the Roman Empire.[73] Although the mention of Bryce is made while discussing the negative aspects of Roman imperialism, De Sanctis praised the Roman policies of assimilation criticised by Bryce. De Sanctis considered such policies the only positive aspect of Roman imperialism since 'no other imperial people can boast an equally magnanimous treatment of their subjects' – an aspect that rendered Roman imperialism a lesser evil compared to other types of imperialism.[74] Despite this positive note on Roman imperialism, however, De Sanctis criticised Roman expansionism in the 'Orient', and, ironically, built this criticism on issues of ethnic fusion in the Roman Empire. According to De Sanctis, it was imperialism in itself that had led to corruption, exactly because, through the opening of the Roman citizenship to African and Eastern races, the Romans had 'weakened' their ethnicity and, therefore, their virtue. This was a factor which had played an important part in the 'decadence of the political life in Rome'.[75] To him, it was the Greeks who ultimately represented the ideals of liberty, and he thus wrote a history of the Greeks, *Storia dei greci* (1939), in reaction to the strengthening of the fascist dictatorship in Italy in the 1930s. For De Sanctis, as for Bryce, imperial Rome had marked the end of liberty, and if the twilight of the classical world had not been definitive, this was only due to the rebirth of the Latin world in the 'barbarous West' (namely, the Holy Roman Empire); an event which had built the foundations of the Christian era.[76]

Guglielmo Ferrero, on the other hand, was a liberal and a democrat who wrote various important works on Rome, such as *Grandezza e decadenza di Roma* ('The Greatness and Decline of Rome', 1902), known internationally and translated into many languages.[77] Piero Treves maintains that Ferrero contributed to a general reawakening of the interest in the history of the Roman Empire both in Europe and in Italy. Ferrero's approach to Roman history, Treves continues, reflected contemporary liberal concerns such as 'the problem of legitimacy and of the administration of an empire, equally ancient and modern, ruling multiracial subjects or peoples'.[78] Treves locates Ferrero's historiography among the liberal currents of historiography of empire of British historians such as Bryce and Cromer, while stressing that Ferrero's interests lay more in the ethical reconstruction of the history of the empire.[79] Indeed, Ferrero's work was in many ways yet another critical response to the transition from republicanism to imperialism in the European historiography on Rome. Already in 1898, in a work entitled *Il militarismo* ('Militarism'), he had stated his position with regard to Roman imperialism as he argued that the Roman conquests, from the Punic wars to the expansion of the empire, were only 'bloody speculations of an aristocracy of financiers and soldiers'. Such aristocracy was 'arrogant and violent beyond any imaginable bestiality', and its greatness consisted in having reduced 'the wealth of many nations into the patrimony of a few families', and 'the strength of many lively and industrious peoples' into 'the passivity of a few groups of slaves'.[80]

Ferrero's interest in the history of Rome, however, was also dictated by an interest in the progress and decadence of peoples, with special reference to the contemporary decadence of Latin peoples and the progress of North-Western Europe and the United States. Ferrero's historiography was also based on Aryan genealogies, and sought to address, also by means of ethnic comparison, how an ordered society became corrupt. For Ferrero, the history of Rome was an ideal and complete history showing how the virtue, simplicity and purity of ancient customs became corrupt by luxury, greed and ambition, and thus led to decadence.[81] Such processes of corruption and decay, according to Ferrero, were relevant to the modern world and to the new imperialism, with particular regard to empires like the British and nations such as the United States.[82] In this context, Ferrero even wrote a distinct comparative work on Ancient Rome and the United States.[83] Ferrero, like De Sanctis, thus appears dissatisfied with Bryce's emphasis on Roman imperialism and corruption rather than on republicanism and virtue. On the other hand, for historians like Pais, the task was that of exalting Roman imperialism by overturning Bryce's perspective. Such variety of approaches reflected, of course, the richness of political ideologies in the national and international contexts in which these authors operated.

The Roman heritage and political thought in Britain and Italy

Britain and Italy, in the British and Italian works respectively, are thus depicted as heir to Rome. For historians such as Bryce, Rome represented the ancient tradition of European imperial rule, which the modern imperial enterprise of Britain had 'resumed.' On the other hand, for Pais Rome represented the tradition of national unity 'repeated' by modern Italy. While Bryce was mainly interested in the history of the empire and issues of decline, Pais concentrated on the period that spanned between the final stages of the republic and the formation of the empire. The two books by Pais deal in particular with this period: the first book treats the expansion of the Roman republic in conjunction with the radicalisation of Italian nationalism, while the second deals with the foundation of the Roman Empire in parallel with that of the Fascist Empire.

Bryce constructed his idea of the tradition of European rule and unification of mankind by linking Rome's ancient attempt and England's modern attempt. He explained how Rome brought all the Mediterranean regions and the western countries as far as Caledonia under one government, thus producing 'a uniform type of civilisation which was Greek on the side of thought, of literature, and of art, Roman on the side of law and institutions.'[84] Then came Christianity, which, by giving one religion to all these regions, deepened their sense of moral and spiritual unity. It was, Bryce goes on to say, with the intellectual impulse of the Renaissance and the discoveries in Africa and America that the process was resumed more swiftly by the emerging European nations, among which England led the way.[85] He thus envisages the diffusion of European civilisation in most regions of the world within a measurable time. This process of unification of mankind is characterised by two efforts of 'Nature': in the earlier effort the 'principal agent' was Rome; in the later Britain.[86]

Bryce's engagement with liberal ideology by means of the trope of Rome is articulated with regard to how commerce is opposed to militarism, and racial and religious separation to assimilation and fusion. Bryce bases his argument on the Roman notion of *Imperium*, but modifies it on the grounds of the alleged difference among the three territorial groups within the British Empire: the self-governing colonies, the Crown colonies, and the Indian territories which are 'ruled by or dependent on the sovereign of Britain'.[87] In the self-governing territories, which for Bryce most typify British imperialism in contrast to the Roman type, Britain rules according to the notion of *Imperium et Libertas*.[88] These Dominions are administered by a reproduction of the liberal and democratic government which rules England itself, and therefore are not subject territories. Similarly, the Crown colonies have little to do with Rome as they are scattered around and too diverse to be treated as a body. It is in India that Britain rules as a Roman *Imperium*. Such a rule is more fitted to Indian society where, in Bryce's view, despotism was already there when the British arrived. British modernity is thus defined against the despotism of contemporary India and ancient Rome. Despotism, moreover, is also associated to the idea of militarism. Thus, as Rome in its empire, Britain is said to have imprinted a military character on its rule in India.[89] The commercial nature of the British enterprise is understated in this case: even if the British went to India as traders, they had to resort to arms in order to keep order and peace because 'society is not in India, as it is in England, an ordinary civil society occupied with the works and arts of peace, with an extremely small military element.'[90]

The legacy of Ferguson's idea of civil society is undoubtedly felt in Bryce's rhetoric of liberal imperialism. Bryce's allusions to civil society in England refers to the reasons why citizenship was to be maintained in the self-governing democratically ruled parts of the empire and not in India, where society, like in ancient Rome, was primitive. Although the India Act of 1833 declared that an Indian 'might be named Governor-General of India', in actual fact the higher government posts were reserved for 'men of European stock'. [91] For Bryce, the difference between the Romans and the races they conquered was minimal, while the British in India, by virtue of Indo-European genealogies, felt they dealt with an 'ancient' race distant from the modern Europeans. While these British anxieties about racial assimilation in India, as Majeed points out, sprung from fear of a 'creolisation' of imperial culture, they were also related 'to the growth of Indian nationalism and its challenge to British rule, and the need to preserve the Indian Civil Service as a monopoly of European officers'.[92] The threat of British decline in India is thus dealt with by means of a narrative of Roman decline with reference to the loss of character and virtue of the Roman political persona. If assimilation, on the one hand, contributed to the unity and the strength of the empire and to the creation of an 'imperial nationality'[93], on the other, it was responsible for the erasure of Roman character, virtue and history:

> It was the influence upon the City of the conditions which attached to her rule in the provinces that did most to destroy not only the old constitution but the old simple and upright character of the Roman people. The provinces avenged themselves upon their conquerors. In the end, Rome ceases to have any history of her own.[94]

What should also be borne in mind, as Bayly has argued, is that the idea of race and that of virtue went hand in hand at this time. If the Roman Empire foundered, this was a consequence of the 'vulgarisation' of its power 'by amalgamation with provincial elites, especially in the East', and of the loss of Rome's identity 'as a redoubt of republican virtue'.[95] Bryce's warning in respect to Rome is also used in terms of reassurance: thanks to the anti-assimilative policies, British rule in India is depicted as showing no sign of weakness. If there is a threat to British power, for Bryce this lies in the provocation of discontent among the Indian subjects as a result of 'laying on them too heavy a burden of taxation'.[96] The distance that the British have created between themselves and the Indians will no doubt allow England to preserve its virtue and erase any fear of a possible collapse of its empire. Bryce's conclusion is eloquent: 'England was great and powerful before she owned a yard of land in Asia, and might be great and powerful again with no more foothold in the East'.[97]

Bryce's discourse of liberal imperialism is subverted in Pais' work by means both of praise for the agrarian and military nature of Roman colonialism, and of contempt for the commercial nature of imperial Britain. More importantly, Pais condemns Bryce's conceptions of race and religion and praises the notion of imperial nationality, which for him is central to the definition of Italian national identity. In *Imperialismo romano e politica italiana*, while implicitly referring to the advent of the fascist movement led by Benito Mussolini, Pais addresses the new political, military and agrarian reforms in Roman style enunciated by 'eminent men'.[98] What Pais advocates in this text is the need for Italy of a demographic colonialism which would serve both nationalist expansionism and the need of Italian emigration. The considerable flows of Italian emigrants leaving for the New World or other countries are, in fact, central to the work of reform of fascism which Pais discusses. Land reclamation in Italy was one solution to the problem. Even more important was to 'guide' and 'direct' the migrant flows. Pais, with the fascists, believed that emigration should be directed to the Italian colonies, so that the Italian emigrants and their children would not be lost to foreign countries.[99] The model of Roman demographic and agrarian colonialism in this sense was useful to associate emigration with 'imperialistic pride',[100] as imperialism came to be seen by Italian nationalists as the main instrument for the nation's defence and regeneration. The full 'rebirth' of Italy, according to Pais, depended on the re-establishment of the balance of power in the Mediterranean; a balance primarily undermined by British imperialism.[101]

What underlies Pais' discussion is the populist idea that Italy is a 'proletarian nation.' Such an idea both provided legitimacy for the national affirmation on the international stage, and proposed more cohesion within classes in a deeply divided country facing the serious challenge of a socialist revolution. Italian nationalism had been built on the notion that Italy was a 'proletarian nation'. Enrico Corradini, the leading Italian nationalist, developed this idea in the 1910s. For Corradini, imperialism was the natural step forward from nationalism[102] – a shift which reflected once again the transition from republicanism to imperialism both in European political thought and the historiography of Rome at this time. He applied to nations the socialist notion of solidarity among subordinated classes, and claimed that, in the same way as subordinated classes are proletarian classes, so subordinated nations are proletarian nations. Thus, international socialism is transformed into national socialism, and Italy, as well as all the other subordinated nations, become proletarian nations. According to Corradini, the imperialism of the Great Powers is also possible thanks to the pacifism of the proletarian nations and their lack of expansionist ideals. Emigration is particularly blamed in reference to this lack as the migrants from proletarian nations are said to provide energy for more powerful and wealthier countries. By settling in foreign countries and not in the Italian demographic colonies, Italian migrants become 'wasted' while giving form to a sort of 'anti-imperialism of servitude'.[103] Thus it is crucial that emigration from Italy be directed towards its overseas possessions. In this way, nationalism is described by Corradini as the doctrine to employ in order to instil into Italians a national and imperial consciousness. Mazzini's 'religion of humanity' and ideas of insurrection constitute, together with socialism, the intellectual bases of Corradini's proletarian nationalism. Proletarian nations, according to Corradini, must react against the materialist imperialism of plutocratic nations, and develop spiritual forms of imperialism in which the doctrines of national consciousness and internationalism are conceived in messianic (Mazzinian) terms. Thus, the international struggle, conquest and imperialism – as opposed to emigration and pacifism – are the path to Italian national affirmation.[104] Following on from Corradini's nationalist discourse, intellectuals that served fascist pursuits between the 1920s and 1930s, including Pais, developed a rhetoric of fascist imperialism and leadership among oppressed nations aimed at challenging the 'plutocratic', or indeed liberal imperialism of leading commercial powers such as Great Britain.

Imperial Rome is, of course, the rhetorical trope used by Pais to discuss Italian nationalism and imperialism. The idea of *Imperium*, racial and religious assimilation, agrarian and demographic colonialism are the ideological underpinnings of Pais' 'fascist' history of Rome. These concepts are naturally developed with an anti-democratic, anti-liberal and, above all, anti-British slant. Pais explicitly criticises Bryce for not dealing with the way in which Rome and England have ruled respectively Egypt and India, and for thus failing to discuss 'the great wisdom with which Rome was able to cement the union between the different peoples and races within the empire'.[105] Pais here stresses the idea that what Bryce considers a weakness in the Roman Empire – that is, the Roman assimilation and denationalisation of the imperial subject – is instead its strength:

> England, that has created such a vast empire, distances itself from the indigenous people over whom it has extended its rule. [...] How superior is Rome's enterprise! Wherever Rome takes its eagles, there the colonists not only defend and cultivate the land, but they assimilate the natives and create a strong bond between them and the Eternal city. [...] The provincials will aspire, in the same way as the children of Italy, to command legions, to the highest magistrateship, and more than one provincial will even dress the vest of emperor.[106]

Pais also establishes the 'moral superiority' of Italian agrarian colonialism while, this time implicitly, referring to British oppression:

> Italian imperialism will not mean cruel wars and the despoliation of the conquered people, but the natives' participation to the laboriousness in the

fields.[...] A participation which will find its peak in the moral elevation of the thought and laws which unite all peoples. Italy's aim is not to oppress other peoples, but to defend their rights.[107]

Pais makes also reference to a new law implemented in 1917 in Italian Libya, according to which a new special Italian citizenship had come into being for the natives. He consequently compares this event with 'the wisdom with which Rome assimilated all the Mediterranean peoples'.[108]

In his comparative history, however, Pais also criticises international socialism. According to him, assimilation and fusion in 'fasces' of workers from different nations is an impossible task.[109] The presence of Bryce is felt even in this instance as Pais comments on the difficulty on the part of a British worker to fuse into one with an Indian worker due to the British conception of racial and civilisational superiority. The alternative to international socialism is, of course, national socialism, but only for those nations like Italy, which have traditionally shown inclinations towards fusion and assimilation. Here, the Roman fasces will include all Italian classes and will give way to the fascist 'third way' of corporativism.[110]

Militarism, in turn, is described as the 'defensive' means to accomplish the nationalist and fascist goals of *Imperium*. Assimilation and the authority of the State will be imposed through military means. According to Pais, the military defeats of Italy were no sign of aversion to militarism. By means of analogy with the expansionist wars of republican Rome, he goes so far as to claim that in the same way as 'the Romans became more tenacious and courageous after the first defeats' in the Samnite and Gallic wars, so the Italians became stronger after the defeat of Caporetto during World War I – a defeat which 'prepared for the great victory'.[111]

Race and Religion are also seen as unifying and assimilative forces by Pais. There is ambiguity in the way in which he describes Roman religion, though. Rather than discussing paganism, he speaks of Roman Catholicism without clearly separating it from the history of imperial Rome. He thus uses the Roman Catholic idea of universal brotherhood to outline 'the thought and action of a new social order' which proposes 'the destruction of old [racial] prejudices' so that 'a man of white race can see a brother in a black man and in a Chinese man'.[112] Interestingly, though, an anti-Semitic presence typical of the genealogies derived from the Aryan model is felt in Pais' rhetoric. On more than one occasion Pais speaks of a Semitic threat to Europe while referring first to Carthage and then to Islam. This is due to the 'fanaticism and greed' of Semitic people, against which, first Rome and then Europe, needed to defend themselves.[113] During the Punic wars, Rome had to fight the Semitic Carthaginians as they did not tolerate commercial competition from people of different race and religion. Carthage in this way becomes a rhetorical trope to discuss the imperial policies of Britain outlined by Bryce, as well as Italy's desire to challenge Britain in the Mediterranean, particularly in the aftermath of the invasion of Ethiopia. A parallel rhetoric of anti-Semitism is also developed by referring to how Europe faced another Semitic threat, this time from Islam, after the collapse of Rome.[114]

Pais' later book, *Roma*, continues to develop the themes of the previous book but with an enhanced tone of legitimacy resulting from the increased confidence of fascism after the proclamation of the empire. For Pais, fascism and the empire are the glorification and the recovery of the history of Rome.[115] Indeed, here Pais forcefully argues that the study of the history of ancient Rome, which provides the greatest examples of 'physical and moral vigour', and of 'independence and national dignity', should inspire the 'education of the new Italy'.[116] Mussolini is in this way praised for having re-established 'social order' and the balance of aspirations among various classes by 'inspiring himself to the example of ancient Rome' and 'giving full authority to the State'.[117] Moreover, fascism's work of land reclamation and renewal of social institutions in Italy is discussed by means of comparison to the industriousness of the Romans. In the international context, the invasion of Ethiopia is seen as an action of defence from the attack of nations which dominate the Mediterranean, and is thus compared to the Roman wars of expansionism. Race and religion, at the same time, are once again discussed in assimilative terms. Pais claims that under the auspices of the Duce and of an Italian Pope, the concept of the political unity of all the races of Italy is associated with the 'universalism of Christian morality and of Latin culture'; both of which have been created by the 'genius of Rome'.[118] As in the previous book, Semitism remains a worrying issue. Interestingly, as Mariella Cagnetta also points out, Semitism is associated to mercantilism while Romanness (as well as Aryanness) to spirituality.[119]

In a section of Pais' book, whose title 'Imperialismo romano e imperialismo britannico' ('Roman Imperialism and British imperialism') recalls the title of the Italian translation of Bryce's book, Pais' discussion focuses mainly on two comparisons: first, the commercial civilisation of imperial Britain as opposed to the agrarian work and the pacification carried out in the Roman Empire; and second, Rome's assimilation and denationalisations of imperial subjects as opposed to the British bar to ethnic fusion which is here attributed to British racism and contempt for coloured people. Pais holds that the federation of states which constitutes the British Empire has no solid foundations because of the empire's commercial and racist policies. As a result, according to Pais,

> The time is not far when England will be called to reconsider its policy lacking in ideal and determined by immediate mercantile profit, not always

inspired by sentiments of dignity, friendship or faith; these, in fact, were the ideals of Rome inherited by the modern Italians.[120]

In order to demonstrate the exploitative nature of British commercial civilisation, Pais creates an association between, on the one hand, Britain and Semitic Carthage as commercial empires and, on the other, between ancient Aryan Rome and Italy as agrarian empires of pacification. He then goes on to explore the implications of these associations within the context of India. Pais first refers to Carthage which,

> moved by selfish feelings like Britain, turned all its care to commercial and financial interests, [...] thus bringing harm to the colonies. As a result, Cadiz and Utica abandoned their political metropolis and joined its enemy, the Romans, as these offered them better life conditions.[121]

The implication here is that India would abandon Britain to join fascism, as Cadiz and Utica had abandoned Carthage to join Rome. Pais based his claims on the grounds of the undermining of Indian industries by the British, and the imposition of the products of English factories on the Indian market.[122]

As opposed to Britain, Pais goes on to say, Rome assimilated its subjects through pacification and gave them its laws. It forced them to cultivate the land and erect imposing buildings, and develop their skills with the arts and science.[123] Moreover, far from being an oppressive and tyrannical empire, Rome granted citizenship to all subjects and made emperors of provincials.[124] While referring to the laws proposed by Lord Macaulay in order to allow Indians into the Indian Civil Service, Pais maintains that this law was made unwillingly and simply to concede nominally a right which in reality would never be granted. The English, according to Pais, would never let an Indian take the highest governmental posts in England.[125] In Pais' rhetoric, therefore, it is imperial Britain that is tyrannical and oppressive. Contrary to what Bryce asserts about the decline of the Roman Empire, Pais argues that British assumption of racial superiority and its non-assimilative policy will eventually cause the subjects' rebellion and the consequent decline of the British Empire.[126] It is interesting to note that this fascist appropriation of Roman antiquity proved influential even outside of Italy in that it eventually led to a change in British and German attitudes to Roman history.[127]

Indeed, after the conquest of Ethiopia and the proclamation of the empire, India came to occupy a more significant place in fascist policies in the light of the heightened tensions between Italy and Britain. Fascism was to provide support to India by virtue of its being another proletarian nation and in the name of their common ancient Aryan civilisation. The orientalist Carlo Formichi, for instance, established many geographical, civilisational and political affinities between Italy and India, particularly in their being enemies to Britain.[128] He reminded both Indians and Italians that

> Italy has neither political nor territorial ambitions in India. Only one motive guides it; clear and confessable: to perform even in regard to India the duty which the Duce has assigned to the third incarnation of Rome: to promote, establish and defend justice in the world. [...] the Duce affirmed that only when the unity of Mediterranean civilisation, which was East and West, had been broken by the birth of a new and non-Mediterranean civilisation, only then the relationship between East and West became one of subordination and of material convenience, thus destroying any creative collaboration.[129]

While creating parallels between India and Italy as ancient civilisations ruled by foreigners for centuries, the orientalist laid emphasis on how India, like Italy, would achieve once again greatness through independence and rebirth.[130] Formichi, therefore, claims that it is fascism's duty to contribute to the Indian awakening by offering anti-British support.[131] Formichi thus praises the nationalist Subhas Chandra Bose and his 'doctrine of *Camyavada* (doctrine of Harmony)' which combines 'constructive examples of revolution in Europe with Hindu nationalism', thus suggesting that some 'socio-ethical ideas of Bose had been inspired by fascism and national socialism and applied to the Indian movement'.[132] It is paradoxical, however, that these anti-racist attitudes of fascism coexisted with fascist racial legislation involving blacks and Jews and implemented at home and in the empire from 1937 to 1941.[133] In the racial theories that supported this legislation, as in the above-examined books of Pais, Semitism, with particular regard to the Jews, remains associated to the alleged capitalism and racism of the British Empire.

Conclusion

In this essay I have discussed the extent to which early twentieth-century Italian historians of Rome responded to Bryce's comparative genre on the British and the Roman Empires. The dimension of Bryce's impact has been assessed within the context of the transnational discourse of imperialism typical of the age, and in the light of the fundamental role played by Roman history in it. The analysis of the reception of Bryce in Italy has offered particularly telling examples of how Rome was domesticated in various national contexts, but also of how Bryce's comparative genre appealingly and profitably mingled Roman history with world history on an unprecedented scale. If the interplay between orientalist and classical scholarships was instrumental in the formation of Bryce's comparative genre, the Italian historians' re-elaboration of Bryce's standpoints also contributed to the widening of perspectives in the use of imperial Rome in global history. Ferrero and De Sanctis, for instance, while adopting a republican stance, elaborated Bryce's concerns with Roman decline in order to describe the new imperialism on both sides of the Atlantic as a disease of contemporary history. Pais, too, gave a new international dimension to his engagement with Roman imperialism, even if his approach was particularly utopian and telling of the messianism surrounding Italian nationalism and fascism. The questions of virtue and societal refinement were interestingly used and reworked by all historians in support of their principal argumentations, and in all cases such issues acquired a new value and global dimension which was informed by the new findings of orientalist scholarship, with particular reference to the predicaments emerging from the new racial and religious lineages. Last but not least, the new global histories and the world of academia that produced them no doubt formed alliances with and served Western political thought, with specific regard to debates on democracy, liberalism and socialism, and their fascist rejections, within the context of the international relations of the new imperialism and its racial and religious tensions. In this sense, the relevance to our contemporary age of these works and the questions they raise can hardly be underestimated.

Acknowledgements

I would like to thank Chris Bayly, Peter Fibiger Bang and Javed Majeed for their comments on earlier drafts of this chapter.

Notes

1. All translations from the Italian texts are my own unless specified otherwise.
2. Bryce (1914: 1).
3. Haverfield (1911: xiv).
4. Ibid.: xviii.
5. Ibid.
6. Ibid.
7. Ibid.: xix.
8. Ibid.
9. Seeley (1909 [1883]: 274).
10. Ibid.: 275.
11. Monypenny (1905: 6).
12. Betts (1972: 151).
13. Hingley (2000: 2).
14. Ibid.: 4.
15. Ibid.: 122.
16. Ibid.
17. Ibid.: 4, 10.
18. Ibid.: 3.
19. Betts (1972: 153).

20. Ibid.: 154.
21. Jenkyns (1992: 4–5).
22. Pocock (2003[1975]: 499–501).
23. Bayly in Chapter 2 in this book.
24. Ibid.
25. Ibid.
26. Hingley (2000: 22).
27. Edwards (1999: 11, 14).
28. Betts (1972: 158).
29. Maria Wyke (1999: 189) explains that 'already in 1798 the *risorgimento* revolutionaries had attempted to found a new Roman republic replete with senators, tribunes and consuls instead of popes, priests and martyrs, and continued in their political discourse, in coins, seals, standards, public ceremonial and street festivals, to secularise the monuments and landscape of papal Rome and to replace Christian with civic symbols'. Moreover, Peter Bondanella (1987: 159) illustrates how Giuseppe Mazzini 'emerged in the years before the European uprising of 1848 as the most influential spokesman for republican nationalism, driving out French and Austrian influences, and returning the peninsula to its former glory with Rome as its necessary capital.' For a comprehensive account of the role of Rome in the Italian *Risorgimento*, see Springer (1987). On the role of Rome in Italian colonial ideology see Chabod (1996), in particular pp. 235–61. Bondanella's work also deals with the role of Rome in fascist ideology, while other treatments of fascist classicism include: Stone (1999), Luciano Canfora (1989 and 1980) and Gentile (1996).
30. The other two prominent authors of this genre of historical writing were Lord Cromer and C. P Lucas. See for example Cromer (1910) and Lucas (1914).
31. Majeed (1999: 90).
32. Ibid.: 90–91.
33. Ibid.: 100.
34. Ibid.: 91.
35. Bryce (1914: 58–59).
36. Ibid.: 61.
37. Ibid.: 59.
38. Ibid.: 62.
39. Ibid.: 62–63.
40. Ibid.: 69.
41. Majeed (1999: 108).
42. Ibid.: 106.
43. Ibid.: 108.
44. Bernal (1987: 1–2).
45. Ibid.: 341.
46. Ibid.: 342
47. Young (1995: 85).
48. See Pais (1908: 13–23). Here Pais compares the account of the peoples of ancient Italy of Strabo with that of new disciplines such as linguistics, anthropology and craniology, while expressing his scepticism on the latter approach.
49. Pais (2007 [1894]: 8–9).
50. Pais (1922: 5). Lecture delivered in October 1911 at the University of Rome by invitation of the *Società italiana per il progresso delle scienze* (Italian Society for the Progress of Sciences).
51. Ibid.: 19.

52. Ibid.: 10. Pietro Treves (1962: 725–26) points out that the republican and Mazzinian Vannucci was more a follower of Niebuhr than a contemporary of Mommsen.

53. De Donno (2006: 396–97).

54. Pais (1922: 29).

55. Pais (1938: 135).

56. Mazzini, 'Dell'iniziativa rivoluzionaria in Europa', in 1861, vol. 5: 55. Clara M. Lovett (1982: 138–39) situates the trope of the Roman republic within Mazzini's thought and action with particular reference to the establishment of the Roman Republic. She argues that 'from an ideological point of view, the Roman Republic reflected nearly two decades of debate among democratic intellectuals about the aims of the national revolution and the means to carry it out. Discussion within the national assembly revealed the emergence of broad consensus in the democratic camp concerning the need for an egalitarian, secular and socially responsive political system for Rome and eventually for the whole of Italy. Although surrounded by enemies at birth and short lived, the Roman Republic embodied more clearly these main principles of democratic ideology than any other revolutionary government of 1848–49'. Indeed, Mazzini's project was based on a republicanism which, after providing ideas of freedom for the French and American revolutions, was to bring liberty to Italy and to all the other oppressed peoples of Europe.

57. Mazzini (1877 [1857]: 38).

58. Crispi (1890: 240).

59. De Gubernatis (1886: 6–7, 21–22).

60. See De Gubernatis (1899).

61. See De Gubernatis (1867, 1888 and 1890) .

62. Pullè (1898: 19–168).

63. Sergi (1898, 1901).

64. Conti Rossini (1913, 1937: 171–203).

65. Pais (1898, vol. I, part I: xii–xiv).

66. Ibid.: xii and xiv.

67. Pais (1920: 26–27).

68. Bryce (1907: x).

69. Solmi (1908: 257).

70. Pais was a scholar of Ancient History. He graduated from Florence University and then went on to study in Berlin with Theodor Mommsen. He taught at various universities in Italy as well as in the United States and France. He wrote extensively on the origins of Rome and on the empire, and translated into Italian the histories of Rome by Mommsen, Edward Gibbon and others. In 1922 he was nominated Senator of fascist Italy.

71. Pais (1920: 113).

72. It should be noted, however, that De Sanctis was in support of Italian colonialism. This was a reflection of his Catholicism. He sided with the Catholic Church's support of fascist colonialism as he thought colonialism would be a means to unify the Church and the state. Moreover, his idea of Italian colonialism was anti-plutocratic and therefore anti-British. Thus, despite his opposition to fascism, his attitude towards colonialism came to be – albeit not by choice – in line with that of fascism. See Canfora (1989: 250–51, 266).

73. Treves (1962b: 1223).

74. De Sanctis (1962: 1275). In a note, De Sanctis invites the reading of Bryce's work but stresses that Roman imperialism was very different in essence from British imperialism. The latter in effect was far from '*offerre victis proprii consortia iuris*' (Note 2, p. 1275).

75. De Sanctis (1962: 1277–78).
76. Ibid.: 1282.
77. The English translation is entitled: *The Greatness and Decline of Rome* (London: Heinemann, 1907–9), 5 vols, trans. by Alfred Zimmen.
78. Treves (1962: 273).
79. Ibid.: 273–74.
80. Ferrero (1898: 136).
81. Ferrero (1910: 39).
82. Ibid.: 41.
83. See Ferrero (1914).
84. Bryce (1914: 3).
85. Ibid.: 3–4.
86. Ibid.: 4.
87. Ibid.: 5.
88. Bernard Holland (1901: 1–2) explains the different connotations of the terms *Imperium* and *Libertas* within the contexts of the Roman and British Empires, and implicitly refers to the modern nature of the British enterprise: 'the expression *Imperium,* as used by the Romans, meant neither geographic space nor populations, but in the earlier times a military and subsequently a political power, whether exercised by an individual or a State. It most nearly corresponds to our words "command", "rule", or "control", and we speak in the Roman sense if we talk of "exercising empire". [...] If *Imperium* is power over others, *Libertas* may be defined as power over oneself, whether the "one" in question is a person, or corporation, or a nation'.
89. Bryce (1914: 12).
90. Ibid.: 13.
91. Ibid.: 41 and 46.
92. Majeed (1999: 106).
93. Bryce (1914: 40).
94. Ibid.: 70.
95. Bayly in Chapter 2 in this book, p. 34.
96. Bryce (1914: 77).
97. Ibid.: 78.
98. Pais (1920: xlii).
99. Ibid.: xlv.
100. Ibid.: xlvi.
101. Ibid.: xxxii.
102. Corradini (1914: 14).
103. Ibid.: 40.
104. Corradini (1914: 42–46).
105. Pais (1920: 113).
106. Ibid.: 200.
107. Ibid.: XLVIII.
108. Ibid.: 124.
109. Ibid.: xxiii.
110. Alfredo Rocco (1973) was the intellectual figure behind the development of the idea of corporativism in Italian nationalism and fascism.
111. Pais (1920: xviii).
112. Ibid.: xxix.
113. Ibid.: 11, 66.

114. Ibid.: 66–67.
115. Pais (1938: 55).
116. Ibid.: 459.
117. Ibid.: 461.
118. Ibid.: 396.
119. Cagnetta (1973: 92).
120. Pais (1938: 436).
121. Ibid.: 430.
122. Ibid.: 430–31.
123. Ibid.: 426.
124. Ibid.: 428.
125. Ibid.: 429.
126. Ibid.: 428.
127. While discussing the fascist archaeological and cultural engagement with imperial Rome, Grahame Clark (1939: 198) concluded that 'by subsidizing excavations and publications, organizing exhibitions and by means of flamboyant but well-calculated gestures, Signor Mussolini has striven to awake in the Italian people a sense of their imperial destiny. In pursuit of his policy he has been able to wield influence far beyond anything available to the governing power in a democratic country'. According to Hingley, Clark's attitude towards the fascist use of imperial Rome in both thought and practice led to a decrease of popularity in Britain of the 'references to comparisons between the British and Roman imperial missions'. Hingley (2000: 189, note 53). Moreover, Catherine Edwards (1999: 15) argues that the fascist use of Rome eventually triggered a distancing of Germany from ancient Rome.
128. Formichi (1942: 10–11).
129. Ibid.: 14–15.
130. Ibid.: 31–32.
131. Ibid.: 10.
132. Ibid.: 186.
133. De Donno (2006).

4

The New Order and the Fate of the Old – The Historiographical Construction of an Ottoman Ancien Régime in the Nineteenth Century

Baki Tezcan

'The seraglio, with closed portals jealously guarded, is the shrine of autocracy; but the mosque, with its doors wide open from dawn till after sunset, inviting all to enter for repose, meditation, or prayer, is the temple of democracy.' With some modifications, such as replacing the seraglio with a presidential palace, this statement could well belong to a Muslim democrat movement of today. But it actually belongs to Adolphus Slade, a British navy officer who spent many years in the Ottoman Empire during the nineteenth century.[1] Slade argued that the Ottoman monarchy used to possess a 'constitution: defective, and in a state of chronic disorder, but still a roughly balanced system.'[2] As noted by Bernard Lewis, Slade saw the modernising reforms of Mahmud II and Reşid Pasha in the first half of the nineteenth century as a 'subversion of the ancient Turkish constitution' or a 'subversion of the liberties of his (Turkish) subjects:'

> These expressions are strikingly reminiscent of the language used by the pro-Parliament jurists during the English Civil War of the 17th century and its aftermath. The doctrine of the ancient constitution of England and the immemorial rights of Englishmen are central to the arguments which were used to justify Parliament against the King in the Civil War and, in a different way, in the ensuing struggles of the later 17th and 18th centuries...Slade applied these characteristically English doctrines to the Turkish situation, and pursuing them in great detail, found that they fitted.[3]

According to Slade, this ancient Turkish constitution was based on the law of the land that consisted of the *shari'a* and custom. It was protected by the *ulema*, local notables and the janissaries. Slade regarded the janissaries as a 'chamber of deputies', constituting the 'legal opposition in the state', 'engaged in shielding the rights of feudality, of democracy, of theocracy (according to the portion of the empire,) from the abuse of power in the hands of pashas ... It was the sultan's prerogative to send a pasha; but it was their business to see that he governed *according to law*':[4]

> Their power had frequently occasion to be brought into action; but as very little attention was given to Turkish internal policy by Europeans, on whose accounts alone we have had to rely, so their motives were generally misunderstood, their acts maligned. The deposition of the grand vizier, the firing of the city, a demonstration against the seraglio, would excite sensation at Pera, and would be ascribed solely to their licentiousness. No one asked whether undue authority had been exercised, whether a new tax had been imposed, a monopoly granted, or a corporation oppressed ... [5]

If one wished to do so, Slade's views could well be corroborated by other authors who commented on the Ottoman political system in the eighteenth century. For Count Luigi Ferdinando Marsigli (d. 1730), who spent a long time with the Ottomans, the Ottoman Empire merits the name of democracy rather than a monarchy or an aristocracy.[6] Sir James Porter, who served as British ambassador in Constantinople for 15 years in the second half of the eighteenth century, asserted that the Ottoman government was 'a species of limited monarchy'. He went to great lengths in defending his observation in response to a contemporary who claimed that because of 'their long residence' in the Ottoman Empire, Marsigli and Porter had so reconciled to the country and people as to make them 'unwilling to admit that [the Ottoman government] should be denominated a despotism'.[7] Porter regarded the Ottoman army as 'a powerful check upon the Grand Signor [i.e. the Sultan]', and the upper ranking jurists as the 'hereditary guardians of the religion and laws of the empire'.[8] The views of Marsigli, Porter and Slade on Ottoman political history, especially those related to the janissaries, the depositions they staged and the ancient constitution, did not have much of a following in Ottoman historiography with some significant exceptions, such as the works of Cemal Kafadar and Donald Quataert, and the insights of Şerif Mardin.[9] More than 170 years after Slade started writing on the Ottomans, two historians of Ottoman literature, Walter Andrews and Mehmet Kalpaklı, echo Slade's perspective:

> The movement in England from late-Tudor absolutism to an increasingly limited monarchy under the Stuarts is well defined and widely accepted. In the Ottoman Empire, there appears to be a parallel to the English case in the double enthronement (1618 and 1622) of the mentally incompetent Mustafa I sandwiched around the deposition and regicide of (Genç [the Young]) Osman II.[10]

Unlike Slade, however, Andrews and Kalpaklı are hesitant in pushing their case beyond 'appears to be'. They are very much justified because as two historians of literature they could not locate a work of political history that argues for an Ottoman movement towards limited government in the seventeenth century. According to the prevalent view in Ottoman historiography at the beginning of the twenty-first century, the regicide of Osman II, or other depositions of the seventeenth and eighteenth centuries, are nothing but military rebellions, hence signs of the decline of the Ottoman Empire, or of a transition the final destination of which is not clear. In the absence of a comparative study on the question of the politics of Ottoman depositions as of the year 2005,[11] Andrews and Kalpaklı hesitate to offer any conclusions: 'Why movements towards limitations on monarchical absolutism are seen as an advance in the one case and as a decline in the other we will leave to non-literary historians to thrash out'.[12]

Why indeed? How are we led to believe that the English Civil War and the 'Glorious' Revolution of 1688 are an advance in the history of limited government while the Ottoman depositions are simply signs of decline? Why did Slade's views on the ancient constitution have so few followers in Ottoman historiography? If there was indeed a very clear case to be made for limited government in the Ottoman Empire of the seventeenth and eighteenth centuries, how come the political legacy of this era has been both neglected and misrepresented as corruption and decay? The response to this question is complex and might well require a book-length study. This chapter will simply focus on the historiography of the New Order that came into being in the aftermath of the annihilation of the janissaries in 1826. I argue that because of the particular polity that the New Order aimed at constructing by an autocratic modernisation, it either destroyed or radically weakened the central sociopolitical institutions of the Ottoman Empire, the *ulema* and the janissaries, which had been successful adversaries of absolutism in the past. There is no question about the fact that this purge turned the Ottoman modernisation into a relatively successful enterprise as far as the building of a modern centralised state is concerned. The present study, however, focuses on the hazards of modernisation, especially those that pertain to the development of sociopolitical institutions that check the powers of the royal (or state) authority in a given polity. In that regard, the Ottoman modernisation erased the most powerful institutions of legitimate sociopolitical opposition in the empire that had created an indigenous model of limited government in the seventeenth and eighteenth centuries. This erasure was extended into the ways in which these institutions and the period of their heyday were to be remembered. The historiography of the New Order, the perfect example of which is Ahmed Cevdet's *Tarih-i Cevdet*, or the *History of Cevdet*, thus came to represent the Ottoman Empire of the seventeenth and eighteenth centuries as a corrupt version of the patrimonial empire of Süleyman the Magnificent, ever in decay since the late sixteenth century. In short, the modern roots of the decline paradigm in Ottoman history, according to which 'the Ottoman Empire, after a phase of continuous military conquest and territorial expansion from the early fifteenth century through the reign of Süleyman I (1520–1566), entered a prolonged period of steadily increasing military decay and institutional corruption',[13] are to be found in the historiography of the Ottoman New Order.

Although the designation 'New Order (*nizâm-ı cedîd*)' was introduced during the reign of Selim III (1789–1807) mostly to refer to military matters and has been used in scholarship in reference to his reign,[14] I believe it is more appropriate to date the beginning of this epoch to 1826 when Mahmud II destroyed the janissaries, the guardians of what came to be known as the *ancien régime*, or the Old Order (*nizâm-ı 'atîk*).[15] My use of the term New Order also encompasses the *Tanzimat* (reorganisation) period, usually dated 1839–76, as I believe the *Tanzimat* could not be executed the way it was had the janissaries been around. The royal edicts known as the Tanzimat (reorganisation, 1839) and Islahat (reform, 1856) bills, which were issued by the bureaucrats of Mahmud II's son and successor Abdülmecid (1839–61), and since then have been regarded as milestones of Ottoman modernisation, were the products of the same autocratic centralisation policy that had destroyed the janissaries. While both Abdülhamid II (1876–1909) and the Young Turks of the Committee of Union and Progress shifted gears on the course of Ottoman modernisation,[16] the period denoted by the New Order may well be extended all the way to the end of the Ottoman Empire, and even to early republican Turkey for the defining characteristics of the New Order, an autocratic centralisation, was well in place until, at least, 1950.[17] The political experience of modern Turkey since 1950 has somewhat undermined the New Order by *relatively* democratising and decentralising the polity. Recently, one of the last fortresses of autocratic modernisation, the presidential palace that had replaced the seraglio in 1923, fell as well when Abdullah Gül, a man from an Islamist background, moved in there as the eleventh president of the republic in 2007. In terms of Slade's metaphor with which this chapter started, the shrine of autocracy may well be transformed into a temple of democracy in the future. The key question for the future is whether it will be possible to create a secular temple that leaves its former site, the mosque, truly behind.

In the first section of this study I briefly discuss those features of the Ottoman New Order that are of relevance to the historiographical discussion of this article. I suggest that the central feature of the New Order was autocratic centralisation, and that the destruction of the janissaries has to be understood *primarily* within this context that is tied to the internal political dynamics of the empire even though it is usually discussed within the context of military reform which is presented as a matter related to the security of the realm vis-à-vis external powers. Military reform was an essential component of autocratic centralisation as the state was in need of reliable military forces to execute its centralisation policies. After pointing out that Mahmud II and his successors destroyed most of the institutions that defined the Ottoman Empire politically, I argue that the retrospective construction of a corrupt *ancien régime* in perpetual and irredeemable decay that could only be saved by destruction was the only way to legitimise the New Order. I show this by an analysis of certain significant introductory sections of Ahmed Cevdet's *History of Cevdet* that include Cevdet's understanding of state-society relations and its close relationship with the autocratic modernisation of the New Order. I also indicate how Cevdet's short summary of Ottoman history up to 1774 started the series of revisions in Ottoman historiography that ended up creating martyrs of reform who lost their lives in the hands of reactionaries since the early seventeenth century, making it extremely difficult to look at the seventeenth century in any other way than a time of decline.

The single most important feature of the New Order was centralisation and the considerable increase of royal authority in the empire to the detriment of any checks and balances. Not only were the janissaries destroyed, but the powerful local governors who enjoyed local autonomy in their provinces were crushed as well. The long-lasting internal political peace of the eighteenth century came to an end as the social consensus achieved with the recognition of the socio-economic and political privileges of the provincial notables as well as the janissary corps became a distant memory. More often than not, however, the centralisation efforts had high costs. The execution of Ali Pasha of Yannina (1822), who was the *'de-facto* ruler of an area with a population of one and a half million, including those portions of present-day Greece and Albania south of a line Durazzo-Monastir-Salonica, but excluding Attica and the Islands',[18] was, for instance, soon followed by Greek independence. The new army of Mahmud II that replaced the janissaries did not prove to be as useful as its predecessor and was routed by the army of Egypt both in 1832 and 1839, damaging the authority of the sultan in his relationship with the governor of Egypt, and also inspiring Mahmud II and Abdülmecid to ask for help from imperialist powers, such as Russia and Great Britain, which led to a series of developments that arguably made the Ottoman Empire a semi-colony of European powers.

If the janissaries were indeed destroyed to stop the military and territorial decline of the empire, it turned out to be a useless decision as the empire lost many more wars and territories in the century following their destruction than it had in the preceding one. Contrary to the hegemonic interpretation of the 'Auspicious Event (*vak'a-ı hayriye)*', which is the name given to the destruction of the janissary corps, the end of the janissaries was *not* simply a military matter. 'The main obstacle to the sultan's attempts to found Western-style military

training had emerged from the Janissaries' is a typical statement that intro-
duces the events leading to the annihilation of the corps.[19] Yet the janissaries
were actually not categorically opposed to the foundation of an army trained
in the Western-style. The idea of a new army was first put forward during the
reign of Selim III who established the 'army of the new order' in 1793. Since
Selim III was deposed as a result of a janissary rebellion in 1807, the opposition
of the janissaries to an army trained in Western-style became a well-established
historical truth in Ottoman history. However, there is a serious problem in
this reasoning. As noted by Reşad Ekrem Koçu, 14 years had passed between
the foundation of the army of the new order in 1793 and the deposition of
Selim III in 1807. Thus had the janissaries been really concerned with the foundation of a new army that could rival them, they would have staged a rebellion
in 1793 when the 'army of the new order' had only 1602 recruits including its
officers, and not waited for 14 years after which merely one division of this
new army numbered 24,000.[20] According to French newspapers, when French
military consultants had arrived in Istanbul in 1794, they were welcomed by
the janissaries with presents.[21] This piece of news does not give the impression
that the janissaries were categorically opposed to Western-style military training, either. What made them nervous was the possibility that this army could
later be used to disfranchise them. Moreover, the record of events prior to the
1807 rebellion suggests that popular protests were much more about the new
taxes that were levied in order to finance the army of the new order than about
the new army itself. A new army could not be raised without new taxes, and
Ottoman subjects were mostly not interested in taxing themselves any further.
Thus the 1807 rebellion could well lend itself to an interpretation that would
portray it as a justified act of political protest.[22]

When Mahmud II reintroduced the idea of a new army in 1826, the janissaries did not protest in the first instance. According to Kemal Beydilli, it was
rather Mahmud II who had studiously provoked the janissaries to revolt and
thus found an occasion, long-planned, to massacre them.[23] That Mahmud II
deliberately and cautiously undermined the power of the janissaries is noted
by contemporaries.[24] The detailed preparations made for the developments of
the 'Auspicious Event' suggest that the revolt, its suppression, and the eventual
annihilation of the janissaries were not spontaneous events.[25] Also the almost
30,000 people who were banished from Istanbul in the aftermath of the event
suggest that the janissaries were deemed to command public support even after
many of them were massacred during the suppression of their revolt and its
aftermath.[26] In short, neither the 1807 nor the 1826 rebellions of the janissaries were simply reactions against Western-style training.

Mahmud II's massacre of the janissaries was primarily a political action
designed to clear the polity from all sources of opposition that might be in his
way during his major restructuring of the Ottoman state. Ottoman historians

agree on the observation that the centralisation efforts of Mahmud II which led to the empowerment of royal authority in the empire would not have been possible with the presence of the janissary corps. The destruction of the janissary corps in 1826 is thus represented as the most important action undertaken by Mahmud II which made everything else that followed possible.[27] With the janissaries gone, Mahmud II had a free hand to do whatever he would like to, from closing down the coffee houses of Istanbul, which rendered any public critique of the monarch impossible, to effectively offering British merchants lower taxes in internal trade than the ones paid by the local Ottoman merchants, which secured him British military help against his unruly governor of Egypt, Mehmed Ali.[28] A military recovery, which the destruction of the janissaries was supposed to bring about, did not really take place:

> With Janissaryism the Ottoman dynasty had traversed five centuries, defiant and self-reliant: without it, in the course of thirteen years (between 1826 and 1840) it was twice on the brink of destruction, and was saved each time from falling into the abyss by the friendly arm of foreign intervention.[29]

While the friendliness of the foreign interventions that saved Mahmud II from his own governor of Egypt may well be debated, the main thrust of the observation above is well taken. The Ottoman Empire did not last for another century after the destruction of the janissaries, and its last 96 years were not suggestive of a military recovery. Yet as far as internal politics was concerned, the institution of the sultanate became stronger than ever after the abolition of the janissary corps.

With the janissaries out of his way, Mahmud II moved next against the *ulema*. İsmail Kara suggests that

> until the abolition of the Janissary Corps in 1826, the palace preferred to create alliances with the *ulema*. This was an attempt by the palace to divide and rule by setting the two largest centres of potential oppositional power, the Janissaries and the *ulema*, against one another. However, support for the palace against the Janissaries did not strengthen the power of the *ulema* but, on the contrary, weakened it. [After the annihilation of the janissaries] the *ulema* – by then the only force capable of counterbalancing the palace – was pushed further into the background.[30]

Just a few months after the annihilation of the janissaries in 1826, Mahmud II established the Ministry of Royal Foundations in order to centralise the administration of foundations that had been supervising local services related to such public and communitarian functions as education, health, water supply and religion for centuries. Gradually, during the reigns of Mahmud II and Abdülmecid (1839–61), this ministry took over the administration of all foundations, including those that had been established by private individuals in various parts of the empire and had local trustees, mostly from among the members of the *ulema*. These foundations provided the link between local notables who founded them, the local people who made use of them, and the local scholars of law and religion who made a living by administrating or working at them. By centralising the administration of foundations, Mahmud II and Abdülmecid not only dealt a heavy blow against the relative independence of the *ulema* from the state, but also destroyed a centuries-old tradition of local governance.[31] The members of the *ulema* were weakened further during the reigns of Mahmud II's successors as new legal institutions were founded which gradually came to replace the ones controlled exclusively by the *ulema*.

How could Mahmud II muster all the political power to execute his state centralisation programme which destroyed every possible source of organised opposition? This is an important question a satisfactory answer for which is beyond the central topic of this article. However, there are three principles which he seems to have followed that may shed some light to the question. First, as noted by Kara above, Mahmud II never moved against the janissaries and the *ulema* at the same time. He allied with the latter in order to move against the former. And after eliminating the former, he moved against the latter. Second, the sultan successfully exploited some of the existing differences within these political bodies. Thus he allied himself with the most powerful officers of the janissary corps against the rank-and-file janissaries and thus deprived the latter of experienced leadership. As for the *ulema*, Mahmud II supported palace graduates in judicial careers, appointing two such muftis during his reign when he needed the backing of the *ulema* for the legitimacy of his centralisation policies.[32] Other members of the *ulema* who aspired for high office during his reign had no choice but to realise that they had to support the sultan, especially after the destruction of janissaries, who in the past had been able to counter absolutist policies. Third, Mahmud II secured the backing of foreign powers for his reforms in return for unprecedented concessions, such as the promise of closure of the straits to any foreign power but Russia, or beneficial commercial tariffs to the British.[33] The suppression, by foreign intervention, of Mehmed Ali's army, which was the most organised civil war adversary the Ottomans ever had, must have had a quieting effect on potential rebels. Clearly, this sultan was not going to hesitate in inviting foreign troops to his empire.

A related and perhaps more important question is the socio-economic background of the political power that Mahmud II and his allies were able to muster. Once again, a proper answer is beyond the subject matter of this article. However, it is probably to be looked for within the developments that surround the acceleration of the growth of capitalism in the West, and its international repercussions, such as the rise of European imperialism and its local collaborators. Certain segments of Ottoman society, such as some of the merchant groups the members of which were primarily trading with European merchants, were better positioned to integrate themselves into the dynamics of Western capital than others, mostly because they were privileged by foreign merchants in commercial transactions – these happened to be primarily non-Muslim merchants.[34] Other than local merchants, European capital also needed specific regulations that would make its most profitable flow through the empire as effortless as possible. This need coincided with the state elites' interests in building a more centralised state administration which required the suppression of institutional opposition in the empire. In short, both the Ottoman bureaucracy and Ottoman merchants dealing with international trade frequently became willing partners of international capital despite the fact that their interests may have conflicted in other areas. Thus foreign powers lent their support to the centralising policies of Mahmud II and his successors, implicitly encouraging the destruction of the janissaries who would rather keep European capitalism within certain boundaries in the empire in order to protect local capital. The destruction of the janissary corps became one of the major 'hallmarks of further Ottoman integration into the world market'.[35] Not only did foreign powers secure a friendly administration to European capital, but they also prevented Mehmed Ali, the Ottoman governor of Egypt, from reaching Istanbul where he could have taken over the imperial administration by forcing the sultan to appoint himself or his son İbrahim to the grand vizierate. A strong Ottoman Empire under the leadership of Mehmed Ali and his family could stand on its own feet without foreign military help and become an international power to reckon with as opposed to a weak player whose survival depended on its exploitation of the European balance of power politics.

Rather than accounting for the deeds of Mahmud II and his New Order in the nineteenth century, however, this article is about the historiography that the New Order produced on what it came to call the Old Order, that is the Ottoman Empire before 1826. The centralising reforms of the New Order did not simply constitute a reorganisation of the administrative, judiciary and military functions of the state, but amounted to an autocratic coup that destroyed every possible source of organised opposition. Having destroyed the sociopolitical institutions that had defined the Ottoman Empire for centuries, the New Order had now to produce a new history that would connect it with its past in a meaningful fashion. The critical question was how one could establish this connection: how could one legitimise the destruction of the past but still claim political continuity, how could the New Order be Ottoman if it destroyed everything that defined the Ottoman political order? The task of figuring out a reasonable response was given to a junior jurist, Ahmed Cevdet.

While it may sound contradictory that a jurist was given the task of producing a new Ottoman history for the New Order which, as I argued above, destroyed the autonomy of the *ulema*, a closer look at Ahmed Cevdet suggests that there is no contradiction. Ahmed Cevdet was the perfect jurist for the job because he was one of the new jurists who were bureaucrats first and jurists second. After a traditional education in his native Lofça (Lovec in modern Bulgaria), Ahmed Cevdet came to Istanbul at the age of 16 in 1839. This was also the year when the grand vizier Mustafa Reşid Pasha announced the royal edict of Gülhane which launched the *Tanzimat*, a period of reorganisation for the Ottoman state, and thus took the first step in the consolidation of the New Order. Ahmed Cevdet had the right family connections that brought him quite close to the household of Reşid Pasha, who took him under his protection. Another powerful patron of Ahmed Cevdet was Arif Hikmet Bey.

Among the two patrons of Ahmed Cevdet, it is the latter who better symbolises the New Order despite the fact that Reşid Pasha was one of its chief architects and Arif Hikmet its grand mufti. What makes Arif Hikmet such an embodiment of the New Order is in his title, *bey*, or *beyefendi*. The title *bey*, or *beg*, was an Old Turkish word that at some point in history was used by rulers.[36] Later on it became a title mostly assumed by mid-level civil-military adminis-trators, local notables and their sons. Characteristically, it was not used by the members of the *ulema*, who were all *efendis*, unless a particular man had started his career in the imperial administration and became a jurist later – quite a few such men were manumitted slaves. Men who had such mixed backgrounds and used the title *bey* usually did not make it into the higher levels of the judicial hierarchy.[37] Yet Arif Hikmet became grand mufti in 1846, the highest position a jurist could achieve in the Ottoman Empire but was still known as a *bey*, or a *bey-efendi*. While the fact that his grandfather and great-grandfather had both been viziers would qualify him to use the title *bey*,[38] such a usage was extremely rare for a mufti who was the chief of all *efendis*.[39] In the early nine-teenth century, the judiciary had come closer under the control of the state than it ever had, making even muftis aspire to the prestige of the civil-military administration. The deflation of the *efendi* title continued more radically dur-ing the republican era in Turkey. Today it is mostly used in Turkish cities when an apartment dweller is calling her doorman. It seems, then, although Ahmed Cevdet was a junior jurist, given his patrons, one would expect that he had very different ideas for the political role of the jurists. This expectation is well born out by his work.

I suggest that Ahmed Cevdet legitimises the New Order by appropriating certain well-known notions of decline from the Ottoman political tracts of the seventeenth century. Thus he presents himself as an intellectual from within the Ottoman tradition. Yet he actually alters these notions so radically and deploys them in such different contexts that he ends up arguing something that his seventeenth century predecessors would never have imagined. If one were to compare Ahmed Cevdet and Katib Çelebi, two authors who were inspired by Ibn Khaldun, a fourteenth-century historian from North Africa, one is first struck with a resemblance. They both adopt Ibn Khaldun's statement that the life span of a state 'corresponds to the life (span) of an individual; it grows up and passes into an age of stagnation and thence into retrogression'.[40] Yet there are two major differences between Katib Çelebi and Ahmed Cevdet that end up producing very different meanings. For Katib Çelebi, who wrote in the mid-seventeenth century, the state signifies primarily the society: 'the state, which means kingdom and sultanate, consists of a human society [based] on a certain kind of custom'.[41] It is the society that constitutes the state and the custom that governs them both. Yet for Ahmed Cevdet, the relationship seems to be the other way around: 'the Ottoman society, which the [state] constituted ...'[42] Ahmed Cevdet's preoccupation with the state rather than the society is also noted by others.[43] Thus throughout his discussion, what Ahmed Cevdet is interested in doing is saving the state, if necessary, as I will suggest below, by sacrificing certain social formations.

Second, Katib Çelebi's understanding of the realm of operations that one could perform in order to postpone the ultimate end of each human society is much more limited than that of Ahmed Cevdet. For Katib Çelebi certain socio-political changes are irreversible. For instance, the number of men enlisted in the central army corps has been increasing on a steady fashion since the reign of Süleyman. Katib Çelebi argues that it is simply impossible to bring the numbers back to the level that they were during Süleyman's reign. All one should expect and plan for has to be a gradual slowdown in the increase of numbers that may eventually lead to a decrease. More importantly, however, Katib Çelebi emphasises the importance of acting with the consent of the concerned parties. According to him, it is only with the consent of the soldiers that one can find a long-term solution that would be suitable for the interests of 'both parties'. Thus Katib Çelebi recognises the members of the corps as a party in their own right and suggests to the imperial administration that it seeks their consent in any attempt at reform. He even implies that the supremacy of the soldiers in the body politic may well be tolerated in certain conditions.[44]

Ahmed Cevdet, however, could not care less about the consent of anyone. He could not let the administration of the state and the soldiers constitute two parties in a conflict. In his understanding, because human beings are apt to conflict, they give up all their individual and collective rights to the government and pledge to accept its decisions over them.[45] It is important to emphasise the term "collective" in this context. The surrender of collective rights amounts to an end of privileges enjoyed by certain groups in society by virtue of which those groups could challenge royal authority. The janissaries and the *ulema* were two such groups that lost their collective rights in the process of the autocratic modernisation that the New Order executed. It is, then, not a coincidence that the royal edict announcing the destruction of the janissaries addresses the 'people':

> Hence, let all the congregation of the Muslim people, and the small and the great officials of Islam and the Ulema, and the members of other military formations and all the common folk be one body. Let them look upon each other as brethren in faith. Let there be no differences between you. Let the great ones among you look with a merciful and compassionate eye upon the little ones, and let the minor ones, moreover, in every instance be obedient and submissive to their superiors...[46]

This first Ottoman appeal to people at large is more about destroying the powerful social groups that could and did limit royal authority in the past than it is about bringing equality to all. Equality in this context of autocratic modernisation meant equality in the sense of the lowest common denominator, which made the society as a whole weaker against the state than it had been before. The state according to Ahmed Cevdet, then, was all-powerful. The society, on the other hand, consisted of equally weak people who did not have any collective rights and thus could never be a party in a negotiation with the state. They had to abide by the state's decisions, which were supposed to be for the good of all. With this understanding of a strong state reminiscent of *Leviathan*, Ahmed Cevdet develops a very different position on the ages of the state and the remedies that may lend it a longer life. Unlike Katib Çelebi, who believes that a state in its old age cannot become young again, Ahmed Cevdet argues that it is possible for a state in decay to be renewed, to be regenerated. Yet, he says, it usually takes great revolutions to realise that regeneration.[47] Not surprisingly, the specific revolution Cevdet has in mind is the annihilation of the janissaries by Mahmud II in 1826.[48]

Ahmed Cevdet thus turns both Ibn Khaldun and Katib Çelebi upside down. Ibn Khaldun had suggested that each dynasty was doomed to extinction. Katib Çelebi, who was inspired by him, amended his approach and suggested that extinction was not inevitable. If one found the right cure for its age, the life of the state could be extended. Ahmed Cevdet, on the other hand, came to claim that the state could be regenerated, could return to its youth, through a revolution.[49] In order to make his suggestion work, he discarded the human analogy that corresponded to the three ages of the state, and applied instead the model of a tree for the Ottoman state. The seed of the tree was sown by Osman I. It reached perfection during the reign of Süleyman the Magnificent. Then, to paraphrase Cevdet, the tree oscillated between springs of order and power, and autumns of rebellions and malediction, eventually reaching a stage close to annihilation. Finally Mahmud II appeared and saved the state by destroying 'the disturbing defects and the harmful insects that infested the tree of government, and cutting some dried and exorbitant branches'. Abdülmecid continued his father's job and gave the sultanate the 'bloom of youth'.[50]

The contrast between Katib Çelebi and Ahmed Cevdet could not be more stark. For the former, the state consists of society which is constituted by certain parts. If there is a need for reform, the administration has to seek the consent of the relevant parts. Cutting them off is not an option because then the society would lose its equilibrium. For the latter, however, the administration has the liberty of dispensing with any parts of the society that it deems harmful because the society has already relinquished all of its collective rights to the state and pledged to accept its decisions which are by definition for the good of all. The all-powerful state, then, can quickly refashion its society which consists of individuals who are all equal to each other in their weakness vis-à-vis the state, as the royal edict which orders the destruction of the janissary corps implies.

The central assumption behind Cevdet's work is, then, that the state may, if and when faced with a great threat to its proper functioning, destroy a social group that obstructs its proper functioning. Ahmed Cevdet's history, the *Tarih-i Cevdet*, thus becomes a work which was intended to prove that the Ottoman state did indeed face a great threat and that this threat could not be overcome with any other method than annihilating the janissaries.[51] It was the Ottoman Academy of Science that had commissioned Ahmed Cevdet with writing his history. The task assigned was very specific in the expected timeframe that the work should cover: 1774–1826. Ahmed Cevdet, however, was commissioned in 1853, some 14 years after the death of Mahmud II and the proclamation of the *Tanzimat* both of which occurred in 1839. Thus for a work commissioned in 1853, the logical date to end the coverage would be 1839, completing the history with the end of a reign as in the more traditional historiography, or with a major event, the *Tanzimat*, which, we believe, defined the nineteenth century. Yet in 1853 for the members of the Ottoman Academy of Science, most of whom belonged to the political elite of the imperial capital, the defining moment for their era was not so much the proclamation of the *Tanzimat* but rather the annihilation of the janissaries. It was after the 'Auspicious Event,' which rendered the Ottoman society defenceless against its government, that the new political elite could introduce the *Tanzimat*, which came to include heavier taxation and obligatory military service: 'The people as a whole regretted the Janissaries; they felt, as if by instinct, that their sole dike against absolute power had been overthrown, that their liberty had been destroyed …'.[52] Thus it was the annihilation of the janissaries in 1826 that made the whole autocratic modernisation programme possible, hence the commission to produce a history that would culminate in 1826.

Cevdet implies the specific task of the *Tarih-i Cevdet*, and the manner in which it is to be executed, in his introduction where he provides a summary of the events he will cover in the upcoming volumes. This chapter lays out the main thrust that was to guide Ahmed Cevdet in his representation of the period 1774–1826, which was specifically assigned to him in his commission to write a new history. In 1774 the Ottoman-Russian war that had started in 1768 came to an end when the Ottomans accepted defeat. The resulting Küçük Kaynarca Treaty was embarrassing for the Otttomans as it involved the loss of Ottoman suzerainty over the Crimean Khanate that had been established by the descendants of Genghis Khan in the first half of the fifteenth century and been under Ottoman protection since the late fifteenth century. Ahmed Cevdet states that in the aftermath of the Küçük Kaynarca Treaty of 1774, the Ottoman Empire could neither free itself of its internal troubles, nor the external ones. He is quite correct in this observation. The Crimean Khanate was annexed by Russia in 1783. The Ottomans lost yet another war against the Russians and signed the Treaty of Jassy in 1792, recognising the Russian annexation of Crimea. In 1798, Napoleon Bonaparte invaded Egypt; in 1804 a rebellion started in Serbia that eventually brought about Serbian autonomy. Selim III attempted to establish his 'New Order' in the empire that involved, among other things, a new army and new taxes. As discussed above, the rebels brought all of this to an end when they deposed Selim III in 1807. Another Ottoman-Russian war ended with a Russian victory that led to the Russian annexation of Bessarabia in 1812. While Napoleon was ousted from Egypt with British help, the Ottomans lost their control of Egypt to their governor Mehmed Ali who established himself as an autonomous ruler there. Last but not least, in 1821 a rebellion broke out in the Peloponnese that could only be controlled with the help of the Egyptian army in 1825 – this control proved to be temporary as the Ottomans had to recognise the independence of Greece in 1832 after several diplomatic and military interventions by European powers. In short, Ahmed Cevdet is right in pointing out that between 1774 and the 'Auspicious Event' of 1826, the Ottoman state experienced continual disturbances. What is problematic is Cevdet's interpretation of the 'Auspicious Event,' through which, Cevdet asserts, Mahmud II 'cleaned the gardens of the state from the filth of [the rebels'] bodies'. Then, Cevdet adds, in the spring of the caliph-ate of Abdülmecid the Ottoman state found new life thanks to the *Tanzimat*. According to Cevdet's presentation, the state was in a process of decay that could not be halted because of the rebels' opposition. Thus there was no other way out of the abyss but to destroy the rebels, that is to say the janissaries.[53]

In this narrative of inevitability, the rebellion against Selim III, which brought about his deposition in 1807, is pivotal. As noted by Christoph Neumann, this rebellion has to show for all intents and purposes that the corruption of the janissaries was irredeemable.[54] As argued above, however, the rebellion is far from proving that the janissaries were categorically against the idea of 'trained soldiers'. So Ahmed Cevdet had to intervene in order to turn this event into a death sentence for the janissaries. As Neumann demonstrates, this intervention consisted of a highly selective use of the sources available to him. Many of the socio-economic reasons that led to the rebellion,[55] which were recounted by earlier historians who wrote about the event, were omitted by Cevdet. Cevdet also did not reflect the critical approach some of his sources had adopted toward the reforms of Selim III. Thus he developed a relatively homogenous narrative of the rebellion which cast the janissary corps as an organisation that was impossible to reform. Neumann suggests that Cevdet's take on the deposition of Selim III was definitive for the way in which this event was to be recorded in Ottoman historiography after Cevdet.[56]

Cevdet's critique was not only directed against the janissaries. Another group that was targeted was the jurists. While some of the criticism that Cevdet brought was not new in the Ottoman tradition, other points he made placed him right within the New Order. As Neumann indicates, Cevdet was critical of certain privileges accorded to high-ranking jurists who secured their offspring a position in the judicial hierarchy whether or not they were qualified. He was also critical of their active role in rebellions. Yet unlike his strong verdict against the janissaries, Cevdet does not suggest the destruction of the judicial structure of the empire. Instead, he proposes to turn jurists into simple functionaries of the state responsible for the application of the law and nothing else.[57] Thus Cevdet's ideal jurists would never even think of alternative articulations of the law that could oppose governmental policies, they would rather take the policies as the guidelines according to which the law needs to be interpreted and applied. This take is very much in line with Cevdet's understanding of the relationship between the state and society. In his view the constituents of society give up all of their individual and collective rights to the state in order to live together. The jurists cannot be allowed to form an exception. Not surprisingly, the policies of the New Order were directed to the same outcome by alienating the traditional financial resources of jurists by forming a Ministry of Foundations, and also introducing new legal institutions that could be more closely controlled by the state.

In short, Cevdet's answer to the question of how to legitimise the autocratic New Order focuses on the state and the irredeemable corruption of the old institutions. Having destroyed the janissaries and weakened the jurists, the Ottoman state was stronger than ever with no organised opposition left to stand against it. It was the state that was supposed to provide the bond of continuity with the past. It was also the state that, thanks to its regeneration after the destruction of the janissaries, was going to extend the Ottoman grandeur into the future. But just as important as the state was the claim that the old institutions had become irredeemably corrupt. The moment the author gave even one iota on the latter position, the destruction of these institutions would become questionable. Thus by virtue of its task of legitimising the New Order, especially the annihilation of the janissaries, the historiography produced by Cevdet could not even come close to recognising the Ottoman seventeenth and eighteenth centuries for what they were. To the contrary, he *had to* represent this period as the patrimonial empire manqué because only as something that failed to live up to the standards of something else could the Ottoman Empire of the seventeenth and eighteenth centuries, and its institutions, be represented as irredeemably corrupt forms of their supposedly perfect versions. Rather than recognising what the institutions of the patrimonial empire had been transformed into during these two centuries, the historiography of the New Order insisted that the Ottoman institutions of the seventeenth century had to be judged against their supposedly perfect versions that preceded them. Thus was the Old Order sentenced to death.

The death sentence issued against the Old Order required that its history be revised. If the institutions of the Old Order were in decay since the reign of Süleyman as Cevdet suggests, their history had to be rewritten with a view to create a homogenous narrative since that time. In his history, Cevdet carried the absolute need for radical reform, which he argued was behind the destruction of the janissaries, a couple of centuries earlier. Then he asked a hypothetical dignitary of the Old Order why they did not abolish the janissaries and reform the military institution. The response was that very few people knew these things, and those who knew did not have the courage to express their views. This hypothetical dignitary states that the reason the reforms could be accomplished later was because the great harm done to the Ottoman state obliged everyone to confess that it was impossible for the state to endure without the 'renewal of the system'.[58] In short, Cevdet turned the 'renewal of the system' into a necessity as of the late sixteenth century when he saw the first major signs of decline.[59] There was indeed a large literature of decline that was produced in this period by writers of political treatises. Yet, as argued by Rifa'at Ali Abou-El-Haj, these men were self-interested members of the political elite who were adversely affected by the socio-economic transformation of the sixteenth century and the rise of new sociopolitical forces in its aftermath.[60] The contemporary historiographical products were far from anything that would render the 'renewal of the system' a necessity. To the contrary, early seventeenth century historiography sentenced supporters of ideas that were suggestive of system renewal very harshly. Osman II, for instance, was toying with the idea of replacing the janissaries with a mercenary army and did not hesitate to abolish certain privileges of the *ulema* before he was deposed and murdered as a result of a rebellion that brought together janissaries and many members of the *ulema* against the sultan in 1622. Although the murder of the sultan is strictly criticised in contemporary sources, the deposition is tacitly approved as most of the early-seventeenth century authors agree in their critique of Osman II's policies. Thus the rebellion of the soldiers became a legitimate act of revolt in order to uphold the Ottoman order. [61] This interpretation was at odds with the way in which Ahmed Cevdet would like to portray the period and presented a significant inconsistency that needed to be smoothened out. The necessary revisions were started by Cevdet himself in the new version of his introduction to his history.

Although Cevdet's history is best known for the period it covers, that is 1774–1826, I would suggest that it also set the tone for the way in which pre-1774 Ottoman history was to be represented. Cevdet had written a summary of Ottoman history up to 1774 in the introduction of his first volume that appeared in 1854. Thirty years later, when Cevdet published the first volume of his work's new edition, he had mainly done some structural changes in the presentation of his material. However, there were a few critical alterations introduced into the narrative of events as well. One of these had to do with the depiction of Osman II whose absolutist policies, deposition and regicide were mentioned above. Most of the seventeenth century historiography that covered the reign of Osman II blamed his court for the deposition. It was the self-interested corrupt advisers of Osman II who had led him onto a path that threatened the continuation of the Ottoman order. The contemporary historiography was so overwhelmingly on the side of the soldiers and so strongly against the court of Osman II that Cevdet must have found himself in trouble. He had to find an angle to approach this event without showing the janissaries in a positive light, which would create a major inconsistency for his narrative of the Old Order. In the first version of his history which he wrote in the early 1850s, his solution was to emphasise the critique of the courtiers one finds in the contemporary historiography without saying anything about the janissaries.[62]

When Cevdet revisited Osman II in the early 1880s, he had a better idea that would serve his overall purpose much more appropriately. If one could transform the deposition of Selim III into a pivotal event which stands as proof that the janissaries were irredeemably corrupt and had to be annihilated – as Cevdet had already done – why could one not use the same scheme for an earlier event? This would strengthen Cevdet's argument about the long-standing necessity of "system change" since the late sixteenth century. It is in this frame of mind that Cevdet reinvented Osman II as a martyr of reform in the second edition of his history:

Sultan Osman Khan II was enthroned at the age of fourteen. Despite his youth he tried extraordinarily hard to reform the conditions of the state. But unfortunately, because the affairs [of government] had been taken off the rails, the disposition of the soldiers had become vicious, and the [rebel-soldier] bullies had gotten on in the world, he was deposed and martyred in a great rebellion that happened four years later in Istanbul.[63]

As I have argued elsewhere, this representation of Osman II took hold in late Ottoman historiography and also passed on to the historiography produced in modern Turkey. Soon Osman II was proclaimed to be the chief of the 'party of renovators' who included, not surprisingly, Selim III and Mahmud II. He was even to be awarded the epithet – retrospectively, of course—'Genç', or young, which may have been a way of bringing him closer to the Young Turks, some of whom were claiming his legacy. The Young Turks, many of whose ideas were of Western origin, had seized power and were in need of a history which would provide them with an indigenous ancestry. They needed to show that their ideas were not foreign to the Ottoman tradition. It was in this context that Osman II acquired his epithet, the 'young'.[64] Thanks to Osman II's new representation, Cevdet's argument that the necessity for 'system change' had been there since the late sixteenth century could now be supported. Osman II saw this need and thus wanted to get rid of the janissaries as well as radically reform the *ulema*, yet these rotten groups stopped him by a deposition and regicide. This depiction of Osman II and his deposition helped consolidate the portrait of the Old Order as a corrupt system in decay and thus provided further legitimacy for the New Order that destroyed the janissaries and other institutions of the Old Order.

Another significant theme that came to be discussed in the later stages of the New Order was the adoption of Western civilisation. Not surprisingly, Cevdet also contributed to this theme, which was very closely related to his argument about the absolute necessity of 'system change'. Osman II and Selim III were not the only Ottoman sultans who were deposed. There could be other ones who might well have been cut out for the job of representing the heroic reformers of the Old Order. One such sultan was going to become Ahmed III (1703–30). He was deposed as a result of a rebellion in 1730. Yet the rebellion had some very well established and fairly legitimate causes so much so that Cevdet could not help being critical of Ahmed III and his grand vizier Ibrahim Pasha. In his second edition, however, Cevdet qualifies himself. It was in that era that the Ottoman state thought of following the path of a 'new civilisation', and took the first steps in that direction, including the introduction of the printing press to Muslim masses.[65]

Cevdet is not responsible for the later development of the idea that Westernisation was an absolute necessity for the Ottomans. Yet it was from his angle of a 'new civilisation' that the whole idea of a 'Tulip Age' developed in modern Turkish historiography which found an early, heroic, but failed attempt at Westernisation in the latter half of Ahmed III's reign that came to an end at the hands of the janissaries and other rebels, who were to be labelled reactionaries.[66] The age is named after tulips that had become more popular than ever in this era among the members of Ottoman court society. The period is chronologically marked by the grand vizirate of Ahmed III's son-in-law, Nevşehirli

Damad İbrahim Pasha, who held office from 1718–30, and starts with the Passarowitz Treaty of 1718 that ended the Ottoman wars with the Habsburgs and Venice, bringing peace to the Ottomans in return for territorial losses to the Habsburgs as well as some recoveries from the Venetians. During the Tulip Age the Ottomans are supposed to have turned towards the West and initiated Westernisation. It is indeed true that diplomatic relations with the West were somewhat intensified during this period. Yet it is difficult to talk about the beginnings of Westernisation. Nor is it possible to label the rebels who deposed Ahmed III as enemies of Westernisation as they were reacting to the conspicuous consumption of an early modern court society rather than anything else. The recent work of Can Erimtan persuasively questions the assumption that there was such a thing as the Tulip Age during which the Ottoman Westernisation started, and demonstrates that this age was a historiographical construct of the Young Turk and early republican eras.[67] In support of Erimtan, I would suggest that the rebels who deposed Ahmed III do not seem to have reacted against what one would perceive as Westernisation, as evidenced in the continuing functioning of the printing press in the aftermath of the 1730 rebellion. Had the issue of contention been really about Westernisation, one would expect that the crowds would destroy the press where, incidentally, earlier in the same year the first Turkish illustrated book, which included, among other things, representations of naked women, was published. Yet the press continued properly to function, producing more titles after 1730 than it did before.[68]

While Cevdet cannot be held responsible for later developments in Ottoman historiography produced in the latter years of the New Order and then in modern Turkey, he did inspire a certain approach to Ottoman history that has continued to influence his successors, which may be summarised in the following way: the New Order was a necessity that finally brought the 'system change', which had been long overdue, to realisation. The Old Order had been perfect once upon a time, but then it decayed to such a low point where it was simply irredeemable. There were many earlier attempts at reform which were executed by some select rulers who could see the need for it, but all of these attempts were frustrated by the janissaries and the *ulema*. Thus the janissaries had to be annihilated and the *ulema* had to be taken under close state control. Then a 'system change' could be realised by moving towards a 'new civilisation'. That is what Mahmud II and his son Abdülmecid were doing. Situated where he was, Cevdet could not represent it in any other way. He was chosen for providing historical legitimacy for the New Order. And he did his job perfectly. He did it so well that the theme of continuous decay since the reign of Süleyman followed by regeneration in the nineteenth century has been the definitive approach to Ottoman history. Thanks to this historical plot, the New Order came closer to the original Ottoman grandeur than the preceding two-and-a-half centuries which could simply be summarised as the decline of the

Ottoman Empire. Thus it is not surprising that most modern studies done on Ottoman history have concentrated on the period up to the sixteenth century, or the nineteenth century. Imagining positive political development in the seventeenth and eighteenth centuries, let alone something like a limited monarchy, became impossible. This period could only be referred to as a corrupt ancien régime in decay.[69]

Notes

1. Slade (1867: 17). Some of the material in the opening of this chapter (pp. 74–6) I have previously discussed, at greater length, in Tezcan (2009a).
2. Ibid.: 10.
3. Lewis (1980: 220).
4. Slade (1837, vol. 1: 303, 304, 305, 306).
5. Ibid., 303–04.
6. Marsigli (1732: 31); Timur (1989: 121).
7. This contemporary was William Robertson; see his *History of the Reign of the Emperor Charles V* (1769), vol. 1, 388–89, n. 42. Sir James Porter responded to him in the lengthy introduction he wrote to the second edition of his work: *Observations on the Religion, Law, Government, and Manners of the Turks* (1771: xiv–xxxvi).
8. Porter (1771: xxviii, xxxi).
9. Kafadar (2007), the text of which was presented at a Mellon Seminar in the Department of Near Eastern Studies at Princeton University in 1991; Quataert (1992) and Mardin (1988: 23–35).
10. Andrews & Kalpaklı (2005: 322).
11. I should acknowledge two monographs that focus on two depositions, that of Osman II in 1622 and Mustafa II in 1703, respectively Piterberg (2003) and Abou-El-Haj (1984).
12. Andrews & Kalpaklı (2005: 323).
13. Hathaway (1996: 25).
14. There are also some earlier references, see M. Tayyib Gökbilgin, 'Nizâm-ı Cedîd,' *İslâm Ansiklopedisi* [*İA* hereafter], vol. 9, 309–18, at 309.
15. For an early use of the term *ancien régime* (*nizâm-ı 'atîq*), see Ömer Fâ'ik Efendi (1979).
16. For Abdülhamid II's Islamist policies, see Karpat (2001); for the formative period of the Young Turks and their ideas, see Hanioğlu (1995 & 2001).
17. Zürcher (1993: 4–5) makes a strong case for the political continuity between the end of the Ottoman Empire and the early republican period.
18. Skiotis (1971: 220).
19. Göçek (1996: 69). Göçek is actually to be commended for her awareness of janissaries' socio-economic and political role in her work.
20. Koçu (2004: 402–03); Gökbilgin, 'Nizâm-ı Cedîd,' 312.
21. Timur (1989: 133–34, 157, n. 50, citing a contemporary French paper).
22. Koçu (2004: 402–04); Aysel Yıldız (2008: v), who produced the most detailed study of this rebellion, argues that 'the May 1807 Rebellion cannot simply be defined as a fight between the reformists and the anti-reformists, but it rather lies at the core of a struggle for the throne, the Eastern Question and a complex web of socio-economic and religious problems of the Empire'.
23. Kemal Beydilli, 'Mahmud II,' *Türkiye Diyanet Vakfı İslâm Ansiklopedisi* [*İA2* hereafter], vol. 27, 352–57, at 354.

24. MacFarlane (1829, vol. 2: 110); cited by Mardin (1962: 148).
25. For a record noting the expenditure for the bread distributed to the people involved in the 'Auspicious Event' by the imperial administration, see Mutlu (1994: 22, n. 52). The most detailed, but also quite outdated, account of the events in English is provided by Reed (1951). For a recent re-assessment of the Ottoman and modern Turkish historiography on the 'Auspicious Event,' see Üstün (2002).
26. See Mutlu (1994: 23).
27. See, for instance, Beydilli, 'Mahmud II,' 354.
28. Timur (1989: 142–44); Mübahat Kütükoğlu, 'Baltalimanı Muahedesi,' *İA2*, vol. 5, 38–40.
29. Slade (1867: 15).
30. Kara (2005: 163–64).
31. For the ministry established by Mahmud II, see Nazif Öztürk, 'Evkâf-ı Hümâyun Nezâreti,' *İA2*, vol. 11, 521–4.
32. Heyd (1961: 81–2).
33. The promise to Russia was part of the Hünkâr İskelesi Treaty; see Kemal Beydilli, 'Hünkâr İskelesi Antlaşması,' *İA2*, vol. 18, 488–90; for the trade agreement with Britain, see n. 28 above.
34. Göçek (1996: 96–97).
35. Quataert (1994: 825).
36. See M. Fuad Köprülü, 'Bey,' *İA*, vol. 2, 579–81.
37. For three examples from the sixteenth century, see the biographies of Mahmud Bey, Mehmed Bey and Ömer Bey, in Nev'îzâde 'Atâ'î, *Hadâ'iku'l-hakâ'ik fî tekmileti' ş-şakâ'ik*, 2 vols (Istanbul, 1268AH), reprinted with indices in *Şakaik-ı Nu'maniye ve Zeyilleri*, ed. Abdülkadir Özcan, 5 vols (Istanbul: Çağrı Yayınları, 1989), vol. 2, 309, 462, 320–21, respectively.
38. Mustafa L. Bilge, 'Ârif Hikmet Bey,' *İA2*, vol. 3, 365–66.
39. As far as I could determine, the only other grand mufti who was a *bey-efendi* before Arif Hikmet was İbrahim Beyefendi (d. 1798), whose grandfather was a grand vizier, see Mehmet İpşirli, 'İbrâhim Beyefendi,' *İA2*, vol. 21, 290–91. For a list of Ottoman muftis reaching to the last decade of the empire's life, see *'İlmiye Sâlnâmesi* (Istanbul: Matba'a-ı 'âmire, 1334AH, 322–641).
40. Rosenthal [Ibn Khaldûn] (1958, vol. 1: 346).
41. Katib Çelebi, 'Düstûrü'l-'amel li-ıslâhi'l-halel,' published as an appendix to 'Ayn 'Alî's *Kavânîn-i âl-i 'Osmân der hulâsa-ı mezâmin-i defter-i dîvân* (Istanbul, 1280AH), 119–40, at p. 122; for further references to society, see also pp. 123, 124, 129, 130.
42. Ahmed Cevdet, *Ta'rîh-i Cevdet*, 2nd ed., 2nd imprint, 12 vols (Istanbul: Matba'a-ı 'Osmâniye, 1309AH) [*Ta'rîh II* hereafter], vol. 1, 29.
43. Neumann (1994: 277).
44. Katib Çelebi, 'Düstûrü'l-'amel li-ıslâhi'l-halel,' 130–33.
45. Ahmed Cevdet, *Ta'rîh II*, vol. 1, 16.
46. Translation by Reed, 'The Destruction of the Janissaries in 1826,' 247; cited by Mardin (1962: 174, n. 9).
47. Ahmed Cevdet, *Ta'rîh II*, vol. 1, 18.
48. Cevdet actually wondered whether his enthusiasm for the destruction of the janissaries was indeed right; see his letter to Sadullah Pasha from 1884 in his *Tezâkir*, ed. Cavid Baysun, 4 vols (Ankara: Türk Tarih Kurumu, 1953–67), vol. 4, 219. Incidentally, this letter also shows that Cevdet was well aware of other types of revolution.
49. Neumann (1994: 225).

50. Ahmed Cevdet, *Ta'rîh-i Cevdet*, 1st ed., 12 vols (Istanbul, 1270/1854–1301/1884) [*Ta'rîh I* hereafter], vol. 1, 71.

51. Christoph Neumann (1994) recently argued that the main purpose of the *History of Cevdet* is to legitimise the *Tanzimat* (reorganisation) reforms initiated by Abdülmecid (see especially pp. 275–83). I do not necessarily disagree with this statement, but rather draw attention to a more immediate purpose, the legitimisation of the destruction of the janissary corps. The close connection between the two aims and Ahmed Cevdet's concern with justifying the destruction of the janissary corps was also noted by Meriç (1981: 119).

52. Fontanier (1829, vol. 1: 322), cited and translated by Mardin (1962: 165 n. 108).

53. Ahmed Cevdet, *Ta'rîh I*, vol. 1, 70–71.

54. Neumann (1994: 131).

55. See note 22 above; and further Ubeydullah Kuşmani & Ebubekir Efendi (2007).

56. Ibid., 130–34.

57. Ibid., 108–29.

58. Meriç (1975: 140), see also 139 for the use of 'usul' to refer to system.

59. This is the impression one gets from his remarks on the death of Sokollu and the reign of Murad III; Ahmed Cevdet, *Ta'rîh II*, vol. 1, 42.

60. See Abou-El-Haj (1995: 282–92).

61. See Piterberg (2003) and Tezcan (2002).

62. Ahmed Cevdet, *Ta'rîh I*, vol. 1, 24.

63. Ahmed Cevdet, *Ta'rîh II*, vol. 1, 48.

64. The first text that I could locate in which this epithet is used for Osman II was authored by a former Young Turk and was published in the early 1910s; see Mehmed Murad, *Ta'rîh-i Ebû'l-Fârûk: ta'rîh-i `osmânîde siyâset ve medeniyet i'tibâriyle hikmet-i asliye taharrîsine teşebbüs*, 7 vols (Istanbul), (1325–32 AH, vol. 5: 9).

65. Ahmed Cevdet, *Ta'rîh II*, vol. 1, 67–68.

66. The most influential work in this regard was Ahmed Refik [Altınay]'s *Lâle Devri, 1130–1143* (2nd ed., 1913).

67. Erimtan (2008).

68. The book in question is *Ta'rîhü'l-hindi'l-garbî el-müsemmâ bi-Hadîs-i nev* (Istanbul, 1142/1730), which, although published anonymously, was authored by Mehmed Su'ûdî in 1583.

69. Cevdet's continuing influence on Ottoman historiography, however, was not simply the result of his mastery of historical prose. It had much more to do with the continuing condition of autocratic modernisation that started with the annihilation of the janissaries into the republican period in Turkey, which forms the subject of another article by the present author (2009).

Part II
Theoretical Perspectives on Empire

5
Empire as a Topic in Comparative Sociology

W. G. Runciman

To a comparative sociologist, empires have a twofold interest. They are, in the first place, a distinctive type of social formation. They are neither big societies on the one hand nor leagues of independent societies headed by a dominant partner on the other: they involve the exercise of domination by the rulers of a central society over the populations of peripheral societies without either absorbing them to the point that they become fellow-members of the central society or disengaging from them to the point that they become confederates rather than subjects. But empires are interesting also on account of their impermanence: they are easier to acquire than to retain. The prospect of disengagement may look for a time as remote as the prospect of absorption. But no empire lasts forever, or anything like it. Why not?

I

Empires may be as loosely controlled as Austro-Hungary under Franz-Josef or as tightly controlled as Peru under Pachacuti and Topa Inca. The peripheries may be as geographically remote as the Philippines from Spain, or as close as Tibet to China. The centre may be represented in the peripheral territories by a handful of traders, missionaries and soldiers or by large commercial enterprises, implanted networks of temples, mosques or churches, and permanent military garrisons. The peripheries may be colonies or vassals or tributaries or clients of the centre. But the most useful single word for the relationship is 'protectorate' as Lord Halsbury defined it in 1890: 'a convenient state between annexation and mere alliance'.[1]

In what follows, I approach the study of the 'convenient state' from within the terms of current neo-Darwinian sociological theory.[2] This precludes any teleological narratives of empires' predestined rise and fall. It also precludes any would-be law-like generalisations into which all empires could supposedly be fitted. Each empire on record has its own path-dependent history. But they have in common that they are all outcomes of the same underlying evolutionary process of heritable variation and competitive selection as cultures and societies generally. Neo-Darwinian theory is not concerned with the life-stories of the people who are the individual carriers of the strategies which are acted out in phenotypic behaviour but with the items or complexes of information or instructions which determine the collective behaviour-pattern of the population of which the individual carriers are members. This idea is by now thoroughly familiar in biology, where selection is seen as acting on the phenotypic effects of genes which transmit instructions for making protein molecules from organism to organism. It is less familiar in sociology. But both cultural evolution, in which selected 'memes' (the convenient shorthand term for the constituents of representations, beliefs and attitudes which affect phenotypic behaviour) are transmitted from mind to mind by imitation or learning, and social evolution, in which selected rule-governed practices define institutional roles which are occupied and performed by successive individual incumbents, work in a similar path-dependent but open-ended way. The capacity of the critical memes and practices to sustain an empire in being then depends on the extent to which their local environment either enhances or diminishes their probability of continuing reproduction. Sociologists can accordingly borrow with profit from biologists a 'reverse engineering' approach.[3] They can examine in hindsight more and less long-lasting empires in such a way as to infer the features of their design which have enabled the rulers at the centre to maintain their hold over the peripheries without being driven to either absorption or disengagement.

Short-lived empires are of little value for this purpose, since they haven't had time for what might have been adaptive memes and practices to evolve. The reasons are as a rule easy to see. Sometimes, the empire is predictably incapable of outliving its founder, like those of Asoka or Charlemagne (see further Tymowski and Wink below). Sometimes, the founder has no sooner succeeded in establishing his empire, like Lugal-Zagesi, than he finds himself put on display in a neck-stock outside the city gates by Sargon of Agade.[4] No sooner does Hitler succeed in extending the German *Reich* across virtually the whole of Europe than he provokes both the Soviet Union and the United States into a war in which Germany is totally defeated. But there are empires in the archaeological, ethnographic and historical record which lasted quite long enough to call for explanation as such, from the first Mesopotamian and Egyptian empires through the Hittite, Assyrian, Iranian, Hellenistic, Roman, Byzantine, Chinese, Islamic, Aztec, Inca, African, Mongol, Venetian, Javanese, Malaccan, Ottoman, Spanish, Portuguese, Dutch, British and Austro-Hungarian empires to the heyday of late nineteenth-century colonialism and then the twentieth century with its mixture of annexations by some and abdications by others. The success of the longer-lasting has often had much to do with what, from a sociological perspective, has to be regarded as luck – the contingencies, that is, of individual ability and temperament, or of the location and accessibility of valuable mineral resources, or of the nature and timing of technological advances in the means of waging war. But whatever the combination of accident and design in any chosen case, some imperial societies have found better ways to prolong the 'convenient state' than others have.

II

Imagine yourself a contemporary observer of the Roman Empire in the year of Diocletian's abdication in 305 and then of the British Empire in the year of Victoria's diamond jubilee in 1897. You would surely have been impressed, and perhaps even dazzled, by their size and strength. But would you have foreseen in either case how little longer they would last?

In 305, the Roman Empire had recovered with remarkable effectiveness from a period of breakdown and disorder in which it had virtually fallen apart. Defeat at the hands of Persia had been avenged, the Danubian marches pacified, the intruding German war-bands held at bay and the territories which had been controlled by Postumus in the West and Zenobia in the East reintegrated. An army half a million strong controlled the frontiers, provisioned by a system of taxation in which payments in kind offset the effects of price-inflation. Both central and provincial government were staffed by a bureaucracy answerable directly to the emperor. Landowners and, increasingly, bishops held their local populations under close control. During the fourth century the state managed to penetrate society more deeply than ever before, intensify its hold on economic resources, erect a new splendid capital in the east and develop a more elaborate system of law while promoting Christianity as the new empire-wide form of religious worship.[5] Yet within a few generations, the defeat and death of Valens at Adrianpole was followed by the settlement of the Visigoths within the imperial frontier, the sack of Rome by Alaric, the abandonment of Britain, the installation of the Burgundians to the west of the Rhine, the seizure of Carthage by the Vandals, Odoacer's occupation of Ravenna and the by then irrelevant deposition of Romulus Augustulus in 476.

Similarly, the success of the British Empire was self-evident at the close of Victoria's reign (see Chapters 2 and 3 in this book). India was the jewel in her crown, but British schoolchildren were brought up to see it as a matter of course that so much else of the world as depicted in their atlases was also coloured red. The global supremacy of the Royal Navy matched that of the Roman legions. The financial hegemony of the City of London gave successive British governments an influence over other countries, and particularly the territories of the imperial periphery, out of all proportion to the size of Britain's own domestic population. District commissioners dispensed local justice at the same time that Christian missionaries reinforced political with ideological hegemony. Yet behind the façade of imperial pageantry was a continuous sequence of crises, improvisations and local wars which time and again failed to produce lasting solutions to the problems which had given rise to them. It turned out to be a very short series of steps from naval and military retrenchment to colonial self-government and imperial abdication.[6]

Nor is it as if the rulers of either Rome or Britain had ever won over the hearts and minds of the populations of their protectorates to the extent that the panegyrists of *pax Romana* and *pax Britannica* affected to believe. The cultural influence exerted by both Roman and British elites on the populations of the peripheries can be demonstrated readily enough. But the attraction of the British lifestyle to the polo-playing rulers of the Indian princely states is as misleading an indicator as the attraction of the Roman lifestyle to the belted and bejewelled chiefs of the German tribes. Spectacular ceremonials, artful rhetoric and well-deployed symbols do not, whatever the imperial propagandists may suppose, transmit to the populations of the peripheries by either imitation or learning memes which will reconcile them to their subordinate status. This was as true of the reluctant middle-class liturgists of Roman Egypt whose resentments are eloquently documented in the surviving papyri[7] as it is of the middle-class representatives from every province in British India who attended the first meeting of the Indian National Congress in Bombay in December 1885. Proconsular sentiments of benevolent paternalism, whether enunciated by Cicero in Cilicia[8] or Lord Cromer in Egypt[9], do not turn resigned acquiescence into active enthusiasm. Paternalism implies guidance towards maturity; and that in turn implies an impending entitlement to equal treatment either as a fellow-citizen, of whatever appropriate rank, of the central society or as an independent partner in what may still be an unequal relationship but is no longer one of fatherly protector to protected child.

III

To many of the rulers of even the most durable-looking empires, the difficulties which they face in holding on to them are as familiar as they become in due course to their historians: the costs are so high, the distances so long, the frontiers so exposed, the revenues so elusive, the administration so cumbrous, the resentments so intractable, the ethnic and tribal loyalties so entrenched, the trade routes so riddled with extortion, contraband and piracy, the enmity of rivals so threatening and the monopoly of superior military technology so short-lived. But given the resources at the disposal of the centre compared with the peripheries, is there no way in which its political, economic and ideological power can be deployed which will maintain an empire in being for as long as the imperial society itself?

Rulers know that coercion alone will not keep an empire in being indefinitely. The ideology of the imperial centre has to be minimally acceptable to the population of the peripheries and economic exploitation kept sufficiently within bounds for the sources of the revenue which the centre extracts from the peripheries not to be exhausted. The locally optimal design will, accordingly, be one in which the practices defining the roles to which there attaches the power of the imperial centre are mutually adaptive across all three dimensions of social design space. There must be effective collaboration between the viceroys, generals, governors and commissioners who control the means of coercion, the planters, contractors, farmers, entrepreneurs and financiers who control the means of production, and the teachers, ecclesiastics, missionaries, propagandists and local notables who control the means of persuasion. This does not mean that they need to behave in a manner that is culturally defined as 'well': corruption and favouritism may be more effective in aligning the interests of rulers and ruled than the impartial administration of policies and ordinances imposed on the peripheries from the centre.[10] But successive incumbents have to succeed one another in stable political, economic and ideological roles which evolve neither in the direction of drawing the population of the peripheries directly into the centre, like the absorption of Scotsmen into England's governing class or of *inquilini* into Rome's, nor in the direction of releasing them altogether from control, like Britain's abandonment of India or Rome's of Britain.

For all the many differences between one empire and another, there is a dilemma which confronts the rulers of them all. The roles whose incumbents are charged with exercising political, economic and ideological control over the peripheries are, by definition, intermediate. Whether their incumbents are recruited locally from native-born members of the peripheral population, like tribal chiefs in British Africa, or descended from the initial conquerors, like the Macedonians in Egypt, or despatched from the centre for a fixed term of office, like a Florentine *podestà* serving for six months in Castiglione, the power vested in their roles must not be so great that they are effectively beyond the reach of the centre nor so limited that the centre's control of the periphery becomes no more than nominal (cf. Ludden below).[11] There is an inherent risk that a colonial elite hitherto loyal to the imperial government, like those of both British and Spanish America, may come to demand a degree of privilege culminating in independence. Conversely, formal acknowledgement of subordination, like that of the German *Reichstädte* to the Holy Roman Emperor, may be little more than a diplomatic device to help them resist encroachment by predatory neighbouring states.[12] The Venetians, having conceded local autonomy to Padua and Vicenza, then found themselves confronted by rebellions which would not have occurred if those cities had been annexed in the way that, for example, the four remaining free German cities were by nineteenth-century Prussia.[13] But if the centre is perceived in the periphery as too weak for the threat of annexation to be credible, disengagement becomes a correspondingly more realistic ambition. The rulers of the central society may, if their coffers are full, their armies well manned and equipped, and their ideological hegemony unquestioned, put down periodic rebellions, depose overmighty satraps, reintegrate breakaway provinces (or, in Islamic empires, caliphates), suborn potential opponents, disperse and resettle hostile local populations and apply the maxim 'divide and rule' to good effect. But for how long?

There is no lack of ingenious institutional designs on record by which imperial rulers and their agents have sought to maintain their political, economic and ideological control over their peripheries (Wickham discusses two of these in his contribution below). They include, for example, the military-agrarian settlements planted in outlying territories by the Qing emperors of China, the Ottoman sultans' allocation of timars on conditional tenure to descendants of the pre-Ottoman nobility or the Mughals' use of hand-picked *mansabdars* drawn from Muslim soldiers outside of India together with a minority drawn from the Indian population. But practices adaptive in the short term can turn out to be maladaptive in the long, often because they themselves change the environment in ways which diminish their probability of ongoing reproduction. This is not simply because the central society is drawn into territorial expansion beyond the point where the costs of maintaining control can be covered by the revenues available, or because of the hamfistedness of its local representatives, or because its policymakers underestimate the resistance which may be provoked by demands regarded as arbitrary or extortionate. Renegotiation of practices is intrinsic to the ongoing process of heritable variation and competitive selection by which social evolution is driven, and it is bound to be more problematic when the parties to it are neither fellow-members of a single society nor independent representatives of separate ones. Thus, tax-farming can seem a promising device for extracting resources from the peripheries without burdening the central exchequer with the costs of collection only for it to aggravate both the rapacity of the collectors and the resistance of the payers. Schools and mission-stations can seem a promising device for imposing on the children of the peripheral population the ideology of the centre only for the children to use their education to repudiate it (see also the discussion of Salmeri in Chapter 9 in this book). The recruitment of adult males in the peripheries into the army of the central society can seem a promising device for reducing the risk of rebellion only for the troops so recruited to mutiny. The dilemma then confronts the rulers once again: they have to choose between an exercise of power which will lead them in the direction of annexation and an exercise of diplomacy which will lead them in the direction of disengagement.

Rulers and their advisers can apply their ingenuity no less to devising strategies of cultural imperialism than to designing political, economic and ideological practices and roles which will maintain the 'convenient state'. But not only do they have to recognise that the doctrine of benevolent paternalism and a *mission civilatrice* is more convincing to the population (including, where it applies, the electorate) of the centre than of the peripheries. They have also to recognise that the creation of an 'empire of the mind' in which the art, science, technology, dress, manners and lifestyle of the centre are adopted in the peripheries by imitation and learning may do nothing to persuade their populations of the merits of their institutional relationship of subordination to the centre. Popular enthusiasm for the game of cricket in the West Indies and the Indian subcontinent is not inconsistent with strongly anti-British beliefs and attitudes. Nor does active manipulation of the information transmitted to the peripheries ensure that the hearts and minds will be any more likely to be influenced in the way that the rulers intend: look, for instance, at how little success the rulers of the Soviet empire had in substituting Marxist–Leninist for Islamic memes in the heads of the populations of their Central Asian peripheries.[14] There is no more a winning combination of memes in cultural design space than there is of practices in social design space by which imperial rulers can prevent the ongoing process of heritable variation and competitive selection from working to their disadvantage.

IV

There is, perhaps, a further way in which a neo-Darwinian approach can help to account for the impermanence of empires. Natural, as opposed to cultural and social, selection may seem relevant only to the extent that it has given all members of the human species their innate disposition for ethnocentricity and xenophobia. But in the past few decades, advances have been made from within the neo-Darwinian paradigm in palaeoanthropology, behavioural ecology, evolutionary psychology and evolutionary game theory which between them have brought to the top of the agenda of the human sciences the fundamental question how human groups and communities are held together at all once they have grown in size beyond the point that kin selection and reciprocal altruism are by themselves enough to explain it. It would be plausible to expect, given our biological inheritance, that aggregations much larger than the hunting and foraging bands in which our ancestors lived for hundreds of thousands of years would inevitably descend into anarchy. But big societies are often able to continue in being indefinitely despite both protracted internal conflict and defeat in war. Somehow, millions of unrelated strangers who interact directly with no more than a hundred or two of each other conform sufficiently to the same acknowledged notions of

behaviour for large societies to remain stable enough for sociologists to analyse and compare them.

If natural selection had not given us our unique capacity for language, and
therewith for rapid and cumulative cultural evolution, large societies could not
hold together at all. But once that had happened, and then, many millennia
later, the further transition had been made from hunting and foraging bands to
expanding communities of sedentary agriculturalists and town-dwellers, selective pressure strongly favoured those populations whose members implemented
two complementary strategies: on the one hand, punishment of non-conformists within the group (including a willingness to punish those who refused to
punish the non-conformists)[15], and on the other conditional co-operation with
other groups outside the reach of punishment. Social, as distinct from cultural,
evolution[16] brought into being economic, ideological and political institutions
within which power was exercised through formal roles whose incumbents succeeded one another independently of purely personal or familial relationships.
To some of these roles there attached the capacity to punish nonconformists
by the delegated exercise of economic, ideological or political sanctions, and
to others (which might be occupied by the same individuals) there attached
authority to negotiate with out-groups on behalf of the in-group. This, in the
broadest and simplest terms, is the way in which competition within and
between increasingly large societies has been acted out for the past 10,000 years –
a very short period in the timescale of evolution, but long enough for cultural
and social selection to generate the extensive range of inherited variants which
make up the agenda of comparative sociology. Empires, and the different forms
they take, are a part of that agenda. But I do not think it is purely fanciful to
suggest that human beings are innately better fitted to sustain ongoing institutional relationships either within or between large autonomous societies, and
that Halsbury's 'convenient state' cannot but be difficult to sustain for reasons
which lie deep in the past evolution of the human species as such.

Notes

1. In a Foreign Office memorandum quoted by Burroughs (1999: 194).
2. Cf. my own *A Treatise on Social theory*, 3 vols (Cambridge, 1983–1997) and *The Theory
    of Cultural Selection* (Cambridge, 2009) for a comprehensive attempt to develop a
    Neo-Darwinian approach to the study of human society.
3. On which see Dennett (1995: 212–20).
4. Oates (1979: 28) says of Lugal-Zagesi 'His "empire" did not long endure and, after
    two decades of successful rule, he was defeated in battle and brought in a "neck
    stock" to the gate of Ekur at Nippur to be reviled by all who passed by'.
5. Jones (1964); Garnsey & Humfress (2001); Kelly (2004).
6. The contrast between outward certainty and fragile foundations is well brought out
    by a comparison of chapter 9 with chapters 10 and 11 of Cannadine (2001).

7. Selected examples are cited by Lewis (1983), chapter 8 ('Census, Taxes, and Liturgies; or, Rendering unto Caesar').
8. Cf. the letters *ad Familiares* (ed. Watt; Oxford: Clarendon Press, 1982), xv.iii.2 and xv.iv.14.
9. Owen (2004), in particular chapter 16 on the shortcomings of his paternalist style of rule.
10. Cf. Elliott (2006: 229): 'In practice, the spread of systematized corruption [in Spanish America] endowed the imperial structure with a flexibility that its rigid framework appeared to belie'.
11. A classic discussion is Weber (1972: 580–624).
12. Wilson (1999); Hartmann (2005).
13. The limited loyalty bought by the concession of autonomous 'home-rule' to cities of the *terra firma* was revealed by their instantaneous defection following in the wake of the disastrous Venetian defeat to the league of Cambrai at Agnadello in 1509. Classic is Lane (1973: 226, 243).
14. For an introductory survey, see Lapidus (2002), chapter 29.
15. On the evolutionary significance of 'strong reciprocity', see Gintis (2000)
16. On the transition from cultural to social evolution, see Runciman (2001).

6

Early Imperial Formations in Africa and the Segmentation of Power

Michał Tymowski

Empire is an important and commonly used term that is difficult to define. This is not an isolated case. Similar difficulties are encountered when defining other terms, such as the city. A reason for the difficulty is the historical mutability of the phenomena to be defined. Broadly speaking, there are two ways which allow us to take this historical mutability into consideration.

The first is to establish a definition which is general enough to include the changing forms of empires. This is the case with the definition given by S. M. Eisenstadt, according to whom: an empire is a political system which is strongly centralised and covers a large territory. The centre of that system forms a separate, controlling whole with respect to the remaining areas, and the power is in the hands of the emperor and central offices.[1] Empire may also be defined in general terms as a political organisation which wields power over states (as a "state of states"), where the centre controls the subordinated areas through military, political and ideological means. A characteristic feature of an empire is the existence of internal diversity, coupled with the aspirations of the ruling group to order the world known to that group according to the religious, ideological or political principles developed in the centre. Those aspirations are one of the reasons for the expansiveness of empires.[2]

Such general definitions do not diminish the importance of the second option, which consists in considering a typology of empires and introducing more detailed criteria to distinguish between different forms of empires and variation over time. So, for example, in the historical and political science literature we may find described and defined as distinct: the ancient Imperium Romanum, the medieval Imperium Christianum, early modern seaborne empires, nineteenth century colonial empires, twentieth century totalitarian empires etc.[3] Two opposite theories link empires with the existence of separate world-economies. According to F. Braudel and E. Wallerstein, an empire may be the political expression of a world-economy.[4] R. Kamen and J. Kieniewicz, however, give examples of empires which transgressed the borders of one and mobilised the resources of two or more separate world economies.[5] For example, the Mongolian empire or the Portuguese seaborne empire. Here I would like to discuss the forms of empire functioning in pre-colonial Africa, analyse the features of those organisations and confront them with the definitions of empires current in the disciplines of history and political anthropology.

In the historiography concerning Black Africa, the term *empire* is commonly used, but there is little or no theoretical reflection on the subject.[6] Sub-Saharan Ghana (7–11th century), Mali (13–15th century), Songhay (15–16th century) and Bornu (16–18th century) are all termed *empires* in the literature. Part of the researchers use the term even with respect to political organisations whose territories were much less extensive than those usually recognised as empires and without any clearly discernable distinction between centre and peripheries such as the Bambara states of Segu (17–18th century), the Fulbe state in Masina (nineteenth century), the Tukuler state (nineteenth century) and Oyo (18–19th century), all lying in West Africa. As to other regions of Black Africa, the states referred to as *empires* in the literature include Ethiopia, as well as Luba and Lunda (17–18th century), lying in the Congo Basin, while in East Africa this term is used for Monomotapa (15–17th century).[7]

Most African political organisations known as empires are characterised by:

1. Large area
2. Centralised monarchical rule
3. Presence of a centre, which rules over many ethnic groups with different cultures, economic activities and internal political organisations
4. Successful territorial expansion

Using the term *empire* for such extensive, multi-ethnic and expansive political organisations allows us to distinguish them from another type of African states – with a small territory and either single ethnicity, or with clear domination of one ethnic group. Hence the term is useful and widely used in African studies. However, each of the features of African empires indicated above needs to be discussed and confronted with both the general and detailed definitions of empires.

Unquestionably, a common feature of African empires was their large area. But the term 'a large area' is not precise, for the border between organisations with large and small areas is usually set in an arbitrary way. For example, in the eleventh century the spread of Ghana's territory was about 800 kilometres on the North-South line and 1500 kilometres from the east to the west.[8] The centre of Songhay alone measured in the sixteenth century about 1200 by 800 kilometres, while the whole area of that empire, together with the peripheries, spread for about 1600 kilometres from the north to the south, and for 2400 kilometres from the east to the west. Clearly, these political organisations had undeniably large territories. However, the Fulbe state in Masina, also termed *empire*, measured about 400 kilometres from the north to the south and 450 kilometres from the east to the west. Does such a territorial spread justify the use of the term *empire*? Congo (15–16th century), similar in size to Masina, is termed a state. Hence the scholars' decisions are in this case either arbitrary or result from the presence among the Fulbe of other features characteristic for empires, which Congo presumably lacked.

The territory of each African empire consisted of a political centre and dependent peripheral areas. The central area was governed by monarchs and a centralised administrative apparatus: court dignitaries and provincial chiefs. The dependent peripheries, settled by various ethnic groups, remained outside the centre. Local, dependent political organisations (early state ones, and tribal ones of the chiefdom type) were not destroyed. Even if the conquest involved killing a local ruler who resisted the invasion, the dynasty he was descended from was kept in power. The empire left the new local ruler or chief the freedom to decide how to manage local issues, and only imposed on him the duty to pay tributes, supply military troops and pay homage to the superior ruler.[9] Hence the centralisation of power in African empires did not cover the whole of their territories. Yet this was not solely an African feature. Imperial power with such a construction existed in different epochs, and has been rather typical for empires. Let us cite the example of the twentieth-century Soviet empire, including Russia and other Soviet Union republics as its two-level centre, and states lying outside the territory of the Soviet Union, such as Czechoslovakia, Hungary, Poland, The German Democratic Republic (East Germany), which were dependent, but enjoyed a limited degree of internal independence

African empires differed from similar organisations of later centuries in that they were structures built over dependent early states and tribal chiefdoms. Here I refer to anthropological theories of early states and chiefdoms.[10] According to the most general formulation of Henri Claessen and Peter Skalnik, the early state is a:

> centralised socio-political organisation aimed at regulating the social relations in a complex, stratified society, divided in at least two groups, or emergent social classes – the ruling and the ruled – whose relations are characterised by the domination of the former and tributary duties of the latter; the whole organisation is legitimised by a common ideology, the basic principle of which is reciprocity.'[11]

Comparative studies of early state structures allow us to develop this initial, general definition. Hence an early state is an organisation where the position of the ruler is based on his genealogy, mythical legitimation and the belief of his subjects in his supernatural, sacral power. The aristocracy consists of members of the ruler's family, other members of the ruling clan, and of a few other clans (often related to the ruler's clan) from which the local chiefs are descended. In order to acquire a position in the ruling group and in its hierarchy, an appropriate degree of close kinship to the ruler is necessary. In the early state, the power structures are based on ties of kinship. Social divisions are not based on ownership of land or cattle herds; the ruling group lives off the tribute supplied by the subjects and off spoils. Social differences inside the ruling group, besides being dependent on a person's genealogical closeness to the ruler, follow from the office held and from the value of the goods assigned to a given dignitary out of the resources gathered by the state apparatus. The subject population supplies taxes, tribute and work, and in return, the ruler embraces the population with his care. There is a system of reciprocity in force, but it is imbalanced. Next to the above-mentioned reciprocity system, the ideological basis of early states is constituted by the cult of the ruler and his ancestors.[12]

Although the principle of belonging to the aristocracy through inherited ties of kinship is stable in early states, the composition of the ruling group is not constant. Individuals belonging to privileged clans are elevated to power or moved away from it according to the ruler's will. The dignitaries' power derives from what is delegated to them by the ruler. The fluidity of the composition of the ruling group increases in states where rulers have won the right to appoint commoners to office, as commoners are more obedient and easier to dismiss. This fluidity contrasts with the permanence of local communities, whose basic sociopolitical organisation is not dissolved in the early state, but form the lowest level of management. The local structures within which the dependent population lives are widely varied, and the central authorities do not standardise them – they leave regional, economic and ethnic differences intact, adjust the types of tributes and taxes to these differences, and take local customs into consideration.[13]

The early state is considered and defined not only as a structure but also as a process.[14] This latter approach is concerned firstly with the limits of the early state, that is its beginning and end, and then secondly with the developmental phases of early states, starting with those that are least developed, through those at an intermediary stage of development, to the mature state. Ronald Cohen proposes that a political organisation that is sufficiently centralised to prevent its own fragmentation and to prevent its segments from gaining independence (*fission-antifission*) should be recognised as an early state.[15] H. Claessen and P. Skalnik add that the ability to prevent fission is a manifestation of the centralisation of power. They also raise the issue of there being a time during which an organisation exists in a centralised form, and can be termed a state by virtue of this, but that after the passing of this period the process of fission takes place after all. This additional condition follows from the reversibility of the creation process in many early states. They propose that the difference between a chiefdom and an early state should be considered to be the latter's formation of a legitimised central authority, able to maintain law and order in the area subordinated to it and to prevent – for a certain time – the fission of the organisation (See Chapter 8 in this book for an attempt to develop the antithesis of fission-fusion in a discussion of the reproduction of empire).[16]

The other limit to the early state (the point at which it ceases to be 'early') involves distinguishing between it and a mature state. A number of indicators are proposed, the most important of which might be considered the one formulated by Anatoly Khazanov. He considers early states to be those entities whose organisation contains, at the lower management levels, elements of pre-state communities: traditional village communities and tribes. When these communities disappear and the diversity of traditional, local bonds, dependencies and divisions disappear along with them, the state can be recognised as being mature. Furthermore, passing this barrier makes the process of state formation difficult to reverse, since, in contrast to the early state, the mature state has no organisational structures for people to return to if the state breaks down.[17]

In precolonial African empires, tribal organisation persisted on the lower administrative level – both in the central area and in the peripheries. The tribes were not destroyed – to the contrary, their organisations were used as a lower level of government and tribute collection. The empires were set up over tribal organisations rather than by eliminating them.[18] Hence an important feature of precolonial African empires was their 'early' character in the sense of early state theory. In those empires, the continued existence of tribal organisations and tribal segmentation counterbalanced the centralisation of power, and posed a barrier against full centralisation.

The large territorial spread of those empires resulted from their successful expansion, originating from the central area. However, that expansion was often of a non-durable and temporary character. Though all the empires we know from history broke down after some time and collapsed,[19] a characteristic feature of most African empires was the relatively short period of their expansion and functioning. Sometimes in place of the falling empire another one emerged. This was the case when Ghana was replaced by Mali in West Africa, and when Mali was in turn replaced by Songhay. However, in the seventeenth century the only political organisations operating in the former territories of Ghana and Mali and in the major part of former Songhay territory were chiefdoms. Oyo, Luba, Lunda, Monomotapa all broke down. The only empire characterised by exceptional durability was Ethiopia, which existed until the twentieth century.[20]

The relatively high frequency in the decomposition of African empires can be explained by the persistence of tribal organisations in their structure referred to above. The fragmentation of those empires (analogously to African early state organisations) did not bring about a total disorganisation of social life and anarchy. For each time the function of organising social life was taken over by the chiefdoms, which existed all the time. The imperial structures themselves were transient, but the segments of empires were characterised by high durability. The internal segmentation cannot, however, be seen as the sole reason for the volatility of empires. Ethiopia – an empire, which lasted for many centuries – was also characterised by such segmentation. Another reason for the frequent decomposition of African empires may be sought in the form of their legitimisation.

According to the general definitions of an empire, a characteristic feature of those organisations was the aspiration of the ruling group to order the world in line with the religious, ideological and legal principles developed in the centre of the empire. Empires strove towards a monopoly on the legitimisation of power, establishing the principles of the political system. The imperial centre was at the same time a religious and/or ideological centre. In the Imperium Romanum, the principle ordering the world and justifying the existence of the empire was Roman law, the cult of the emperor and a shared high culture; in the Carolingian empire – according to the imperial ideology – Christianity and the role of the emperor as the man leading the subjects to salvation and converting pagans by force. In the Arab (and later Ottoman) empire, this role belonged to Islam and the notion of the caliphate; in colonial empires, the legitimising idea was the sense of a civilising mission stemming from the belief in the superiority of European civilisation; in the Soviet empire, this role was played by Communist ideology. What were the options and real actions undertaken in that respect by precolonial African empires?

In some of those empires, the rulers referred to local cultures and traditional beliefs. Their legitimisation was based on sacralisation of ruler and of the ruling dynasty.[21] The ruler adopted a role similar to the chief of an extended family towards the whole population subordinated to him. His power over them followed from his bond with the ancestors, from accumulation of prestige accruing from successive generations of leadership. The origins of the ruling dynasty were described and explained in myths passed on by oral tradition, which imbued the rulers with special, magical and supernatural power. This magical and sacral character of power found its reflection in the role of the ruler as the guarantor of the fertility of his country. An expression of that power, as well as a way of calling upon it, were recitals of oral traditions, ceremonies related to the ascension to the throne, insignias, as well as secret incantations and mottos, known to the narrow group wielding power.

As a result, the traditional way of legitimising the authorities of African empires amounted to transferring to the central level the methods used for legitimising the lower level authorities – starting from the chiefs of great families, clans and villages through tribal chiefs up to the rulers of dependent early states. The problem was that legitimisation of the empire did not eliminate those local and group-based (ethnical) legitimisations, but coexisted with them. Legitimisation of the centre had its counterpart in the numerous systems of belief and culture legitimising the individual political segments comprising the empire. As long as the ruler kept achieving military successes and the economic situation was auspicious, the above system of legitimisation of authority and subordination of the peoples included in the empire remained effective. However, military failures or natural disasters might sapp the legitimacy of the central authority and deprive it of its capacity to influence the subjects. Local authorities gained correspondingly in prestige, and the subjects turned to them. The world could well be ordered by the centre, but there were also other orders, which could survive without the central one.

The situation in the African empires whose rulers had adopted Islam, such as Mali, Songhay, Bornu, Fulbe in Masina and in Sokoto, as well as the Tukuler state, was different. Islam, through the introduction of scripture, the development of knowledge systems and the formation of cultural and political elites, constituted a new basis for legitimising hegemonic government. Not only superior rulers and court dignitaries professed Islam – also the dependent, local rulers and chiefs converted. Islam served to join the members of the ruling group coming from different administrative levels, regions and ethnic groups. Hence it acted as a factor unifying the empire.[22] However, the main centres of Islam lay outside Black Africa – in Mecca, Medina and Cairo. None of the Islamised African empires played the role of the centre of the Islamic world. On the contrary, each of them remained on the peripheries of that world. Some attempts at raising the rank of local Islam emerged among the Fulbe in Masina, when in the nineteenth century certain scriptural supplements containing a theory of a West African caliphate were introduced in a local Songhay chronicle Tarikh el-Fettach.[23] The attempt failed when the Fulbe were defeated by the Tukulers' invasion. The centres of the Christian world also lay outside Black Africa. A separate and exceptional case among the Christian states of Black Africa was Ethiopia. The Ethiopian Church created a separate religious, cultural and legal Christian centre. It legitimised the authority of Ethiopian emperors, and justified expansion as well as subordinating the surrounding peoples to Ethiopia. Hence Ethiopia had at its disposal a religious basis for creating an imperial authority.

One more issue remains to be considered: the economic aspect of establishing imperial authority in Black Africa and comparison with the hypothesis seeing empires as a political form of world-economy.[24] Expansion of precolonial African empires was caused, among other factors, by economic stimuli. It was carried out along the routes of interregional and external trade. The thesis of the role of long-distance trade in the creation of African states and empires was formed simultaneously with the beginnings of research on the history of Africa, and is commonly accepted.[25] Many African empires managed to take under their control a network of interregional routes. They also controlled the places where salt, copper and gold were mined, or the main sites where those commodities were transported. The territories of empires often covered different climatic and economic zones, for example, agricultural savannahs and herding steppe zones. However, none of the African empires covered with its reach a whole world-economy. In each of the known examples, African economies controlled by empires were included in world-economies which were larger in terms of both their areas and production volumes. In those larger structures, African economies played the role of peripheral regions. For example from the seventh and eighth century to the nineteenth century the economy of sub-Saharan West and Central Africa was a peripheral area of the Mediterranean world-economy, and the economy of East Africa was a peripheral area of the Indian Ocean world-economy.

This overview of the features of precolonial African empires and their confrontation with the definitions of empire existing in the literature allows us to draw the following conclusions:

1. The term *empire* is used in African studies due to the need for giving a name to the states which were large territorially and multi-ethnically, and to distinguish them from small states.
2. The area of an African empire included the centre and peripheries. The tribes survived both in the centre and in the peripheries as lower levels of the organisation – its segments.
3. The segmentation resulting from the continued existence of tribal and early state organisations counterbalanced the centralisation of power.
4. African empires (except Ethiopia) did not manage to establish separate religious, legal and cultural systems which would have been developed in the centre but would influence the whole area of the empire. As to the traditional culture, the worship of rulers and the imperial dynasty was counterbalanced by the cult of local ruling dynasties. In the case of African Muslim empires, the centres of Islam lay outside them, and in general outside Black Africa.
5. African empires were prone to decomposition and collapse not only due to invasions, but also as a result of internal processes. It was caused by the segmentation of power and legitimacy.
6. A factor which played a large role in the creation of African empires and their expansion were the stimuli created by long-distance trade. However, African empires did not cover within their reach whole, separate world-economies, and their economies played a peripheral role in the world-economies whose centres lay outside Black Africa.

7. Hence in African political organisations termed empire, the imperial features following from the definitions adopted in theoretical research either occurred in an incompletely developed form, or only part of those features had developed, and the others were absent.

In the light of the collected material, among the features of African empires, the most important ones seem to be the incomplete centralisation of power and the rather short durability of their legitimisation, together with a counterbalance to the phenomena of political centralisation and legitimisation of power provided by the continued existence of local centres of tribal and early state authorities and their separate legitimisations.

This type of organisation emerged not only in Africa, but also on other continents. The analogies concern both the processes of their development and their structures. With regard to the history of India, Romila Thapar[26] proposes the terms 'ancient empires' and 'early empires' and claims: 'In the typology of early empires the nature of the relationship between the metropolitan and the peripheral areas is crucial', adding: 'The ancient empires may therefore be examined more usefully in terms of a metropolitan state in juxtaposition with other territories in varying stages of state formation'. On this basis, R. Thapar distinguishes two types of early (ancient) empires. She defines the first of them as follows: 'The earliest empires were those which permitted a wide range of politicoeconomic systems to subsist within their boundaries, and the metropolitan peripheral relationships varied with each system'. The second type 'is distinguished by a smaller range of differentiated systems or alternatively...the more primitive systems of gathering and hunting, pastoralism, barter and primitive agriculture, are marginal to a larger component of complex agrarian structures and commercial networks.'

The second type pointed out by R. Thapar represents in fact two stages of a process where the primitive economic systems were first marginalised, and then completely pushed out and brought to extinction. Moreover, when describing the first type, R. Thapar uses the term *politicoeconomic systems*, while when describing the second one she places a larger emphasis on the difference between the economic systems and disregards the difference between the political systems.

A both interesting and surprising proposal for defining what an early empire was in the light of transformations in the political systems in the area of the East-African Great Lakes region was presented by Edward I. Steinhart.[27] Namely, he recognised the first political organisation – Kitara – as an early empire (or empire), while Buganda, established after the former, as a kingdom (or state). According to E. Steinhart, the process of political transformations in the region followed the course 'from an extensive and loosely-knit "empire" to a smaller and more compact "state"'. E. Steinhart does not see the decomposition of an early empire as a phenomenon of 'decline and fall' of a powerful imperial tradition. In his opinion, this was a process of political development, 'the growth of state power and institutions rather then the decline of "imperial power"'. In this way, according to E. Steinhart, the early empire was characterised by weakness in the institutions of authority and poor internal cohesion.

The recent collective study of ancient (early) empires, edited by Susan E. Alcock, Terence N. D'Altroy, Kathleen D. Morrison and Carla M. Sinopoli,[28] gathered together extensive material originating from different epochs and continents, though lacking examples from Black Africa and Southeast Asia. The authors use the term *early empires* in the study, but they apply it to very different political systems, including those which, in my opinion, exceed the borders of early empires delimited in this paper and in the earlier literature. They examine the Roman Empire together with the modern Spanish Empire in America, and the Portuguese Estado da India. Such a broadly defined type of early empires refers to the whole pre-industrial epoch and is the opposite of the empires of the industrial epoch in the nineteenth and twentieth centuries. This kind of definition is too broad from the point of view of our analysis of African material and the typology of inchoate African empires.

However, the African empires discussed here corresponded to both types of early empires proposed by R. Thapar. An especially relevant feature is the occurrence of 'varying stages of state formation' in the peripheries. Some of those empires (for example Ghana, Luba, Lunda) are comparable with the first type of empires described by that researcher. But others (as Ethiopia, Songhay, Bornu) are comparable with the second type.

If we try to look for European analogies within such a typology, then, most certainly, this cannot be either Imperium Romanum or even the Carolingian empire. True, in both cases there were peripherally located tribal organisations; however, other features of empire were better developed, especially the legitimisation processes and the function of the empire in that respect. The closest European analogue of the early African empires was – in my opinion – the Great Moravian State. The hesitations regarding definition of the character of that political organisation encountered in the literature on the Middle Ages are reflected in the terminology used. In the Czech and Slovakian languages, the term Great Moravian Říše (Reich) is employed, while in German – its counterpart 'Reich' (Das Grosmärische Reich). In French studies we sometimes find Empire or Etat, but most often just La Grande Moravie; in English ones – the Great Moravian Empire or Great Moravia. In Polish it is Państwo Wielkomorawskie, meaning, Great Moravian State. And in Russian, Vielikaia Moravia or Vielikomoravskaia Dierzhava (Empire).[29]

The Great Moravian State was established in the early ninth century and existed for about 100 years, until the early tenth century, when (in 906) it was destroyed by a Magyar invasion. It had a large territory, and included numerous tribal dukedoms (chiefdoms). In its heyday it spread from the territories of the Luzatian Serbs and the Vislanes tribal territory in the north through the tribal territory of Bohemia down to the area of Panonia in the south. The centre of that polity was located in the present Moravian territory. In the peripheral areas, tribal organisations (chiefdoms) operated, headed by local dukes. Their dependence was expressed by paying tributes. The ruler of the Great Moravian State, Rostislav, converted to Christianity. The first churches were built in the centre of the state, and St Method became the bishop of Great Moravia. Starting from that time, the conquests made by that state were combined with the imposition of Christianity on the subordinated tribal dukes, such as was the case with the Vislanes duke. Hence the superior ruler built his rule over the subjects on a base of military power and ideological legitimisation imported from outside[30]. Similarly to the Islamicised African empires, the main religious centres (in this case, Christian ones) were located outside the Great Moravian territory, while the Great Moravian State lay in the furthermost peripheries of Christianity.

The Great Moravian State fell as a result of external invasion rather than internal decomposition. However, a sign of volatility of that Slavic early empire was the fact that no other, analogous organisation was established in central places of the destroyed empire after the conquest. Such an organisation was not established by the Magyar invaders, who about half a century later organised their state in the Panonian lowlands. A separate state was established in Bohemia. In the territories of the Vislanes and the Luzatian Serbs, tribal dukedoms – analogues of chiefdoms – survived, and state organisation developed in those areas in the late tenth century only. Also Moravia itself became again a tribal territory, and the neighbouring states (Bohemia, Poland, Hungary) fought to control it.

Hence we can find analogies to early African empires both in the history of India and in the history of Europe. Such comparisons can be multiplied. They allow us to draw the conclusion that organisations of the early empire types, built over early state and tribal segments, are a common historical phenomenon, which occurs regardless of the chronology, the natural and ethnic environment, or the dominant religious system.

Notes

1. Eisenstadt (1963: 3–5) and (1968).
2. Doyle (1986: 19): 'Empires are relationships of political control imposed by some political societies over the effective sovereignty of the other political societies'; and p. 45: '... it can be achieved by force, by political collaboration, by economic, social, or cultural dependence'. See also Alcock et al. (2001: 2–4).
3. Garnsey & Saller (1987); Folz (1953); Boxer (1969; 1965); Pagden (1995); Kennedy (1987).

4. Wallerstein (1974); Braudel (1979: 42–56); Lubbe (1982).
5. Kieniewicz (1983); Kamen (2003: 561).
6. Tymowski (2006: 18–26).
7. For more extended bibliography see the relevant volumes of the UNESCO General History of Africa: Elfasi & Hrbek (1988); Niane (1984); Ogot (1992); Ajayi (1989).
8. I give the dimensions of African states and empires on the base of the maps from: Mauny (1961: 510, 512, 514); Ajayi & Crowder (1985): maps 24, 28, 29, 35, 37, 39; Tymowski (1996: 450, 454, 466, 608); Tymowski (1979: 255).
9. Vansina (1962); Mair (1977); Claessen (1981); Eisenstadt et al. (1988: 185–96); Tymowski (2005).
10. Claessen & Skalnik (1978); Claessen & Skalnik (1981); Claessen et al. (1985). The term *chiefdom* was introduced to the anthropological literature by Oberg (1955). Other works about chiefdoms: Sahlins (1968: 20–27); Service (1975: 15–6, 81–83); Carneiro (1981); Terray (1984); Skalnik (1983 & 2004); Claessen (1987); Tymowski (1999: 134–39; 2009: 128–32).
11. Claessen and Skalnik (1978: 637–40).
12. Claessen (1978); Claessen & Skalnik (1981); Claessen & Oosten (1996).
13. Khazanov (1978), the issue of local structures, pp. 86–87; Claessen (2002).
14. Skalnik (1978).
15. Cohen (1978), the problem of the organisation's fission, p. 35; Cohen (1981).
16. Claessen & Skalnik (1981:632): 'Limits: Beginning and End of the Early State'.
17. Khazanov (1978: 84–87).
18. Diagne (1967); Tymowski (1999: 144–48; 2009: 137–41).
19. Yoffe & Cowgill (1988); Doornbos (1994).
20. Bartnicki & Mantel-Niećko (1978).
21. Vansina (1962: 325); Diagne (1981), The problems of sacralisation of power, pp. 49–50; Claessen (1981: 63–68); De Heusch (1987).
22. Trimingham (1959; 1964); Monteil (1964); Lewis (1966) and especially Hunwick (1966); Stępniewska (1972); Tymowski (1990).
23. Hunwick (1969); Levtzion (1971); Tall (1972).
24. See notes 4 and 5 above.
25. Polanyi et al. (1957); Bohannan & Dalton (1962); Vansina (1962b); Małowist (1966 and 1967); Meillassoux (1971); Hopkins (1973); Terray (1974); Austen (1987).
26. Thapar (1981).
27. Steinhart (1981).
28. See note 2.
29. Wasilewski (1967); Žemlička (1993).
30. Magna Moravia. Macůrek (1965); Graus et al. (1965).

7

Post-Nomadic Empires: From the Mongols to the Mughals

André Wink

This chapter attempts to throw some light on the study of nomadic empires from the perspective of the long-term (medieval and early modern) history of India. It focuses on what happens to nomads when they enter a sedentary and agricultural realm as conquerors and rulers and then, abandoning their nomadic lifestyle, create what we may call 'post-nomadic empires'. The chapter argues that the Islamic empires created in the Indian subcontinent ('al-Hind') by Turks and descendants of the Mongols, as well as other peoples from Afghanistan and Central Asia, were all of this type: created by people with a recent nomadic past, they were not themselves nomadic in character. These same empires do, however, display a number of characteristic features that continue to link them to their nomadic past. The chapter first discusses the transition from nomadic to post-nomadic empires in this single subregion, then proposes some generalisations about post-nomadic empires and the peculiar condition of post-nomadism.[1]

The historiography of nomadic empires

A student approaching the vast subject of Eurasian nomads and their history for the first time will have no problem finding general introductions to it. There is certainly no shortage of general works on Eurasian nomads, nomadic conquerors and nomadic empires. The beginning student could, for example, turn to a classic work of this genre such as René Grousset's *Empire of the Steppes*.[2] Grousset's book is essentially a survey of the military history of nomads from about the fifth century BC onwards. It highlights the careers of Attila and the Huns, Chingis Khan and the Mongols and of Timur and the Turks – a shortlist of nomadic conquerors who, according to Grousset, are 'in everyone's memory' and are universally recognised to have been a major force in the history of the world until as late as the fifteenth century AD. But he or she could also turn to any number of more recent publications that are basically updates of Grousset's book (which is not say that they are not original in some other respects). Gerard Chaliand's *Nomadic Empires* is perhaps the most recent example of this interesting historiographic tradition.[3] Just the same, none of these works throws much light, if any, on the intriguing problem of how nomadic Turks and Mongols from the Central-Asian steppes came to create the largely agricultural 'Mughal' (Persian for 'Mongol') empire of India.

Historical sociology: nomadic-sedentary interaction

The student who has been introduced to the subject of Nomadic Empires might wish to move on to historical sociology for new insights. There, he or she would find an abundance of general theories which aim to explain the rise and, often seemingly inevitable, decline and fall (or just fall) of nomadic empires. The earliest of such theories, emerging from historical sociology, was also the most interesting and original: the *Muqaddima* or 'Prolegomena of World History' by the fourteenth-century Maghribian historian Ibn Khaldun.[4] It is a theory that recommended itself to many by its sheer simplicity. According to Ibn Khaldun, the pastoral nomadic world of the Bedouin was the womb of political power and military force. This was where the 'wolves' would originate who governed the 'sheep' – until they themselves became like 'sheep' in their turn and would invite a fresh invasion of 'wolves' into the city, thus generating the kind of tribal circulation of elites that Ibn Khaldun saw as characteristic of the southern and eastern shores of the Mediterranean. For Ibn Khaldun, the Bedouin were simply more virtuous, and more disposed to acts of courage, than sedentary people who, after several generations of living in luxury, generally became lazy and used to easy living. This is a mode of reasoning that appears to have been quite common in the Arab world – and it probably still is.

However, even though Ibn Khaldun's theory may well have been applicable to much of the late-medieval Maghrib, it is clear, perhaps even obvious, that it was by no means a universal explanation of the interaction of nomads and sedentary people throughout the Muslim world, let alone the whole world. The Ottoman empire, for instance, contradicts Ibn Khaldun's theory on a number of important points, as Ernest Gellner, among others, has repeatedly pointed out.[5] The Ottoman empire was a stable, strong and long-lived empire by any account, offering the spectacle of a political system of great authority which was not based on the cohesion of a pre-existent tribal group, but relied on a conspicuously non-tribal slave-elite which was recruited on an individual basis – in Gellner's estimate more a Platonic than a Khaldunian solution to the problem of authority.

More specifically, with regard to India, the Khaldunian paradigm of nomadic-sedentary interaction seems ultimately of little value. Considering that India was repeatedly invaded by people of nomadic origin, this may not seem obvious at all. Turko-Mongol writing is pervaded by the fear of the degenerative impact of the Indian environment and its hot and humid climate. Timur's advisers, in the late fourteenth century, held out the following warning: 'Although we may subdue Hind, yet if we tarry in that land, our posterity will be lost; and our children, and grandchildren, will degenerate from the vigour of their fore-fathers, and become speakers of the languages of Hind.'[6]

The problem is that this is not what happened. Three centuries after Timur's invasion of Hind, his descendants were still ruling an empire that was, in the words of John William Kaye, 'the most magnificent the world had ever seen.'[7] In the case of the Mughals – whose very name became synonymous with wealth and power – medieval nomad ferocity or 'vigour' had somehow been transformed into a relatively stable and sustainable, early modern form of political authority over more than a hundred million subjects, most of whom were not even Muslims. Khaldunian historical sociology could not explain this development any better than it could the Ottoman case.

This then seems to lead to the conclusion that in order to understand the nature of nomadic-sedentary interaction it just will not do to invoke one single, simple 'model' (in social science terms). The relationships between nomadic and sedentary societies historically appear to have taken a great variety of different forms, and their nature has always depended on many factors. As Scheidel argues below, nomad power was even crucial in consolidating the Chinese imperial state.

Among these factors, it would be easy to recognise that environmental qualities of both the nomadic and sedentary habitats in question are likely to be among the most important ones. In other words, issues of physical, human and animal geography. But other factors offer themselves for consideration: the level of industrial production, especially of arms and artillery, the degree of monetisation of the economy, the disease situation, the political system, and a host of others. In short, in order to approach the subject better, it would be useful to first abandon the idea that there should be one simple, abstract framework of explanation that fits all situations, and instead move on to actual historical observation and analysis.

The ecology of the Indian subcontinent

Considering India, the first observation to be made is that features of the physical geography of the subcontinent ensure it was historically neither entirely pastoral nor entirely agricultural but a mixture of both. Historically, the Indian subcontinent, to a varying (and, over time, usually diminishing) degree, had its own pastoral economy of sheep, goats and cattle, camels, and even horses, in close association with sedentary village life, but it was mostly unsuitable for the type of 'pure' nomadism that was practiced by the Bedouin of the Arab world or the Mongols of Inner Asia. This is why, over the medieval centuries, the Indian subcontinent never accommodated significant numbers of immigrant Turkish and Mongol nomads. Almost everywhere, it lacked sufficient good pasture land, particularly for the breeding of horses. The nomadic Seljuq Turks, for example, barely touched the outer periphery of India in the eleventh and twelfth centuries. In the thirteenth and fourteenth centuries the Mongols also failed to establish a permanent nomadic presence beyond the western borderlands of Sind and some parts of the Panjab. In this respect, the situation in India was quite unlike that on the Iranian plateau. In the latter area, Seljuq and, more significantly, Mongol conquest brought about extensive nomadisation and, simultaneously with it, the destruction of agriculture on a substantial scale (a phenomenon we also observe in some of the Indian borderlands). It was also unlike the situation in Iraq, where in the thirteenth century pastoral groups of Bedouin made destructive inroads into the breaches left open by the Mongols. Iran and Iraq were unlike India in that both had a relatively low population density per area unit, an arid climate, and an overall ecology that was unfavourable to agriculture; both were profoundly affected on a very broad scale by the repeated invasions of Turkish and Mongol nomads from the thirteenth century onwards. According to John Masson Smith almost a million people and 17 million sheep accompanied the Mongol conquest of an area of Iran and Iraq that was inhabited by only a few million, and of which moreover about two million were massacred or dispersed in the turmoil.[8] Even those scholars who have doubts about the exactness of these figures still readily allow that the two processes of Mongol conquest and migration combined altered the ethnic composition of Iran and Iraq, with the proportion of Turkish and Mongol nomads in the population increasing dramatically.

By contrast, the Indian subcontinent never experienced a 'nomadic conquest' at all. The reason for this is its ecological position at the extreme southeastern end of a continuum that geographers have called the world's largest continuous 'arid zone.'[9] This 'arid zone' extends – with many interruptions and irregularly – from the Atlantic coast and the Sahara, across Suez, to Arabia, the Levant and Iran, and northwards to Central Asia, Mongolia and parts of China. Everywhere, the 'Saharasian' arid zone receives less than 1000 mm (3.28 feet) of rain per year. It includes large areas that were suitable for agriculture but which fall into the same category as the properly arid zone in terms of their relevance for pastoralism and stock breeding.

By the conventional definition used here, nearly half of the Indian subcontinent is arid or semi-arid.[10] The arid zone extends from the Makran, Baluchistan, Sind, and Rajasthan into an eastern direction up to the southern banks of the Ganges near Varanasi, and into a southern direction, into the Deccan plateau and further to Rayalaseema, Kurnool and Cuddapah, and towards the southwest, to the Mysore plateau, ending only in northern Sri Lanka. A quick survey of the modes of pastoralism in this (semi-) arid extension zone in India shows that pastoral variability here has always been high. Most commonly, however, Indian pastoralists were involved in a kind of herdsman husbandry. Herds consisted generally of cattle, sheep and goats, moving up and down hills, or back and forth between seasonally dry river beds, or from monsoon grazing on open lands to the foliage and herbage of forest tracts. In sum, in India the arid and humid areas which served as summer and winter pastures were generally close to each other. Horse breeding was even more restricted, even though there were some good breeding grounds in places like the Kathiawar peninsula.

The implication is that the distribution of Indian pastoralists varied according to the type of pastoralism, animals exploited, and the environment, but that in India genuine pastoral nomadism, while not entirely absent, was always closely associated with sedentary societies and represented a kind of enclosed nomadism. It never constituted an economic system in its own right and it operated over relatively short distances in comparison with the nomadic trajectories in much of the arid zone outside the subcontinent, particularly in Central Asia and the Middle East.

It is in Baluchistan, Sind and the Afghan borderlands that we find the closest approximations to the purely nomadic economies of the arid zone beyond India. But even here pastoral nomadism was limited in terms of autonomy, range and specialisation in stock breeding. A case in point are the Baluchis. These still represented an entirely pastoral-nomadic population when they moved eastward in the eleventh and twelfth centuries under the impact of the Seljuq invasion of Kirman. When they began to spread throughout Makran and Sistan and then moved into Sind, they generally appear to have had very large flocks of sheep and goats, besides excellent camels and black cattle, while their horses were (and still are) rare and small in size, as well as badly tempered. In their domestic arrangements almost all Baluchis remained pastoral nomads, living in clusters of tents made of black felt or coarse blankets, and, more exceptionally, in mud houses, in huts, or in forts. But in actual fact only a small part of the Baluchi population continued to live a nomadic existence. And similar observations can be made about the chief pastoral populations of historic Sind, such as the Jats.

The conclusion, therefore, can only be that the Indian subcontinent has always been ecologically unsuitable for extensive pastoral nomadism, and that this is the main reason why it never invited the mass immigrations of nomadic peoples, complete with herds, that were so characteristic of large parts of Central Asia, Iran and Iraq, and places such as Anatolia, or north-west China.

Straddling the divide between the arid zone and the humid tropics, the Indian subcontinent was however contiguous with the nomadic world of Central Asia, Iran and Afghanistan. Its geographical position ensured that it was within the orbit of the great conquest movements and tribal migrations which character-ised especially the medieval period and which originated among the Eurasian nomadic populations of the arid zone outside of it. But it also ensured that here nomadic people or people with a recent nomadic background always had to adapt themselves to the new environment in which they found themselves. In almost all cases they had to leave their pastoral nomadism behind. Conquests and migrations (often of individuals or single households) occurred, but not nomadisation.

General characteristics of post-nomadic empires in India

We can call the large states that such people of nomadic origin established in India or elsewhere in the sedentary world 'post-nomadic empires' – for lack of a better word – to distinguish them from the more familiar nomadic empires that have existed throughout history. The difference is fundamental. Nomadic empires could only be established by nomads in an environment which is over-whelmingly geared towards pastoral nomadism. Wherever else nomads estab-lished empires (or large political formations), these were not really nomadic but post-nomadic empires because the people who created them, while nomads in origin, had left their pastoral-nomadic lifestyle behind and no longer relied on pastoral nomadism for their subsistence. Post-nomadic empires occurred throughout Indian history. But they were a particularly important phenom-enon in the first half of the second millennium – this being a time when there was a significant shift in the balance of power between nomadic and sedentary societies throughout Eurasia.

If the general distinction between nomadic and post-nomadic empires is unproblematic, we can go on to show that just as there are historical examples of nomadic empires of a considerable variety, there is also a considerable variety of post-nomadic empires – which moreover changed over time. India was by no means the only world region in which post-nomadic empire build-ing was historically important. China provides another interesting and impor-tant set of examples, as does the Maghrib. In summary, we can postulate that Eurasian nomads were agents of change in the sedentary world even if they did not bring nomadism with them. It is just that the changes they brought varied in different places and times along with the nature of the post-nomadic empires they established.

In India we already observe this in ancient times. The so-called 'Shakas' were not only important cultural middlemen (promoting and disseminating other peoples' cultures, be they Persian, Roman-Hellenistic or Indian) but left in India many traces of their own heritage, which long outlasted their own assimilation with the host society: 'Shaka' or 'Scythian' costumes, and the pointed cap or helmet, are on display in the frescoes of Ajanta; and many such cultural influences survived among the peoples of western India. The royal fillet and the cylindrical crown, and certain pieces of jewellery (such as the torque-shaped necklace), thrones in the shape of high armchairs, are also identifiable nomadic imports from Central Asia. In medieval times, however, the role of Eurasian nomads as agents of change in the sedentary world of India became far more important and varied.

First and foremost, even though they left their nomadism behind, the Turko-Mongol groups that made it into India from about the eleventh century AD. onwards brought about a revolution in warfare and military technique that allowed them to impose new patterns of political mobilisation and more effective resource extraction on the peasant population. Arguably, the post-nomadic empires established by the Turks were the first *real* empires in India. In establishing them, the Turks and Mongols were, again, not just cultural middlemen disseminating other peoples' culture – the often mentioned 'Perso-Islamic heritage'– but, due to their geographic position of dominance in the (semi-) arid northwest frontier zone from Afghanistan to the mouth of the Indus, as well as in the steppe lands, acquired a virtual monopoly of the regular supply of good warhorses that the subcontinent could not provide for itself. As inhabitants of the steppes, the Turko-Mongol people in medieval times distinguished themselves by the practice of mounted archery, and this allowed them to prevail over their sedentary neighbours in India as much as in Byzantium, Iran or China.

For this reason Turks and Mongols could bring about a horse-warrior revolution in India even though they did not bring about a pastoral-nomadic one. India, like Byzantium, failed to develop mounted archery. Although horses and horsemanship have a long history here, archery was left to infantry and a relatively small number of elephant riders. The heavy (although never exclusive) reliance on horses and mounted archery by the post-nomadic Turko-Mongol empires is what set them apart not merely from the Indians but also from the Arabs who preceded them in the conquest of the (semi)arid northwest frontier of the subcontinent. The battles of the Arabs in the first centuries of Islam were mostly fought by infantry, supported by archers. But these infantry armies of the Arabs were not recruited from among the nomads but mostly from among the sedentary population of the towns and oases. The relatively minor nomadic element in the Arab armies was largely put to tactical use as light cavalry, especially in raiding excursions. What distinguished the Arab armies was their superior mobility in the desert as well as their ability to concentrate forces over great distances by making use of the camel. The role of the camel was decisive in the early Arab conquests and explains, at least partly, why these conquests did not go much beyond Sind and the arid regions of the Thar Desert. But in spite of the prominent role they gave to the camel, the Arab conquerors were clearly not nomads; neither did they introduce mounted archery to India, nor did they bring large numbers of pastoral nomads along at a later stage for relocation in Sind.

Secondly, post-nomadic imperialism in India did involve a kind of ecological imperialism which was very different from nomadisation. As mentioned before, Turko-Mongol nomadic hordes failed to establish themselves in India on a permanent basis. Only in some very restricted areas, like Binban and the Koh-i-Jud, on the northwest frontier of the subcontinent, did Mongol occupation lead to the (sometimes permanent) devastation of agricultural land or were large tracts of agricultural land turned into pasture to sustain the Mongol cavalry. Post-nomadic expansion never had that effect. But it did lead to important changes in land use nonetheless, and to the predominance of different animals.[11] Normally, post-nomadic empires consolidated themselves in the interstices of the sedentary world, or, to put it differently, they followed the vagaries of India's inner frontier of arid and semi-arid habitats. The new capitals they created were eccentrically located on the interface of the nomadic and sedentary worlds: in Delhi, Devagiri, Warangal, Dvarasamudram, and in places like Bijapur, Golkonda, and Vijayanagara. These new capitals were all located on the fringes of the arid or semi-arid zone and could mediate between sedentary investment and the mobilisation of the resources of military entrepreneurs, merchants and pastoralists.

For this reason, post-nomadic expansion in India led to a dramatic upsurge in importance of the societies of the arid zone and a great increase of the offensive capabilities of mobile warfare. As a result the role of horses, camels and oxen increased considerably in importance and this enhanced the subcontinent's capacity for warfare, transportation and cultivation. But it did not increase the capacity for pastoral nomadism. Furthermore, in this new warhorse military economy the importance of the domesticated elephant was gradually reduced. In the Indian subcontinent, elephants were kept in forested reservations outside the cultivated realm where they needed a transhumance circuit which included both elevated and lowland terrain. Such elephant forests, like grazing lands for horses, stood in a competitive relationship with sedentary agriculture. Over time, with the agricultural realm expanding, the ecological situation of elephants in many parts of the subcontinent had come to resemble more and more that of horses. Horse-grazing, on the other hand, had the advantage that it could be done in non-contiguous areas, which were, moreover, not necessarily excluded from any other use, as elephant forests mostly were. And the mobility of elephants was limited, while they had to be kept in a half-tamed or wild state in forest reservations, and was further impeded by the fodder problem. Horses were more mobile, being always tame, and could more easily be controlled, relocated, concentrated, and deployed over long distances. Beginning with the Turko-Mongol empires in the eleventh century, the disadvantages of the keeping and use of horses relative to elephants were gradually reduced to the point that elephants were bound to become ever more obsolete in warfare. Horses proved to be tactically much more useful in mobile warfare, while elephants could only be deployed statically, in set battles.

Thirdly, the evidence shows that the post-nomadic empires of India were in an almost permanent state of military mobilisation, and that they relied on mounted archers, much like nomadic empires. They were almost equally fluid and indeterminate in their institutional infrastructure, lacking, notably, a clear law of succession or primogeniture. They resorted to the well-known Turko-Mongol practice that J. F. Fletcher called 'tanistry' where male members of the royal lineage and their followers fight among themselves for the throne by war and murder (See further discussion in Chapter 13).[12] The major difference was that the post-nomadic empires did not rely on pastoral nomadism but on agriculture as their means of subsistence. Post-nomadic armies were thus trimmed of their live stock, and unlike the nomadic armies that were mobilised by the Seljuqs or the Mongols, did not move in conjunction with women, children and other non-combatants, while they always appear to have been broken up in smaller contingents and never moved en masse.

The taming of the Mongols

Over the long term, the post-nomadic empires appear to have become more and more structured by factors at work in the sedentary societies they ruled, rather than the other way around. In India the transition from post-nomadic to increasingly agrarian-oriented empires was gradual and never complete. Akbar (r. 1556–1605) made a sustained attempt to tame the Mongol nobility, to turn a loose assemblage of post-nomadic military retainers with a still medieval outlook into a disciplined service nobility, while establishing a rigid court etiquette as a new force of counter-insurgency. The old Mongol/Chaghatay customs of informal fraternising (drinking parties such as are still evident in the *Baburnama*) of commanders and soldiers were abandoned. All nobles received numerical ranks or mansabs and were formally fitted into a quantified status hierarchy which expressed uniformity, discipline and cohesiveness, and which was tightly controlled by the emperor himself.

Akbar put an end to the still commonly practiced 'Code of Chingis Khan.' 'It was the Code (Tora) of Chingis Khan,' wrote Nizam ad-Din in the *Tabaqat-i-Akbari*, 'to massacre or make slaves of all the inhabitants... [of a conquered region]... to utterly destroy many towns and villages and sweep everything clean and clear... to value God's creation as if it was but radishes, cucumbers and leeks.'[13] It can be argued that Akbar himself still practiced the Chingisid code of indiscriminate killing and enslaving during his conquest of the Rajput fortress of Chitor in 1567. The same code was still practiced by some of his generals in the same period. But Akbar allowed merely harmless ceremonial residues of Chingisid customs to survive. He also ordered all cultivated fields to be guarded by orderlies so they would not be trampled upon by the imperial troops, and to pay compensation for any damage that might have occurred.

By the later sixteenth century the Mughal nobility was gradually forced to abandon what was now beginning to be seen as the medieval barbarism of its nomadic Mongol ancestry. To be sure, this civilising process was not really initiated at that time, nor was Akbar the only major historical personality instrumental in advancing it. Numerous Persians and Indians played a similar role at his court. To a considerable extent it had already made headway under the Timurids in fifteenth-century Central Asia and Afghanistan. Nonetheless, it was mostly a sixteenth-century accomplishment of the Mughal Empire under Akbar.

This was still half a century and more before, as Peter Hardy wrote, 'the Mughal courts at Delhi and Agra had become schools of manners and good taste even for opponents and rebels.'[14] In the estimate of the Jesuit Rudolfo Acquaviva, in the sixteenth century 'Akbar and all his men who are Mongols' still had 'not a little of the barbarian.'[15] But a wide gap had by then opened up between the Mughal nobility and the still nomadic Mongols and other 'rude Tartar tribes' of the wild and desolate regions close to the Russian frontier and of Inner Asia. The latter retained their reputation for ferocity and barbarism. Their swarming light cavalry still practiced the predatory style of warfare, sustaining itself in enemy country with the blood of their horses and giving no quarter except to infidels and Shi`ites whom they could sell as slaves.

Akbar's disciplinary drive is above all evident in the realm of revenue administration. Before the sixteenth century the collecting and spending of the land revenue was rather haphazard. The medieval Turko-Mongol rulers conquered and demanded, and killed and enslaved, but had little inclination for audits and paperwork. Akbar however insisted on surveys of resources, records, receipts, and guidelines for action. While in sixteenth-century Europe the increased demands for conscientious bureaucrats installed the bourgeoisie as the main agency of monarchical rule, in sixteenth-century India they brought the Hindu banking and financier castes to prominence. The most prominent representative of this class was Akbar's legendary finance minister Todar Mal. Having been put in charge of scientific surveys and far-reaching revenue reforms, Todar Mal put a growing number of agents in place who developed a new conception of the state as a business enterprise. Akbar thus became the first Mongol with a reputation for bourgeois values, above all frugality. Even leisure activities like the royal qamargha hunt were recast as useful ones. Most strikingly, Akbar became the first Mongol leader who attempted to introduce vegetarianism among the nobility, at least on certain days, in an attempt to 'tame their wolfish nature,' along with attempts to curtail heavy drinking, setting the example himself. Even if Akbar's policies were not entirely successful, they were clearly important steps in the transformation of post-nomadic into agrarian-oriented and sedentary empires.

Conclusion

There is a substantial tradition of scholarship that proclaimed the Eurasian nomads a major factor in the long-term development of the sedentary civilisations surrounding them – China, the Middle East, Russia – but failed to throw much light, if any, on the problem of how originally nomadic Mongols (or Turks) from the Eurasian steppes created the largely agricultural Mughal Empire in India. General theories about the interaction between nomads and sedentary people such as that of the fourteenth-century Arab historian Ibn Khaldun also failed to explain the course of Indian history. This paper draws attention to the 'post-nomadic' character of the empires established by Turks and Mongols in India in medieval times. These empires were founded by people who originally had a nomadic origin but had left their pastoral nomadism behind. The changes they brought about amounted to a revolution in warfare (based on horse warriors) and the imposition of new patterns of resource mobilisation, as well as a form of ecological imperialism that, while different from nomadisation, led to important changes in land use next to the use of animals. What was essential is that the post-nomadic empires of medieval times consolidated themselves in the interstices of the sedentary world and followed the subcontinent's inner frontier of arid and semi-arid habitats. They were in an almost permanent state of military mobilisation, much like nomadic empires, but they did not lead to an increase of pastoral nomadism. Instead they relied on agriculture as their means of subsistence. Subsequently, particularly in the reign of the Mughal emperor Akbar in the second half of the sixteenth century, they became more and more structured by the agricultural societies in which they were established, in the end leading to a single and unified Mughal Empire which was almost entirely agrarian and sedentary in orientation.

Notes

1. For an earlier attempt to come to terms with this problem, see Khazanov & Wink (2001).
2. Grousset (1970).
3. Chaliand (2004).
4. Rosenthal (1958).
5 See, for example, his *Muslim Society* (1981).
6. Davy (1972: 48).
7. Kaye (1880: 646).
8. Smith (1975 and 1978).

9. Hodgson (1974, II: 71).
10. Bryson & Baerreis (1967).
11 See on this issue especially Gommans (1998).
12. Fletcher (1986).
13. Ranking (1990, II: 42–46).
14. Hardy (1972: 17).
15. Correia-Afonso (1980: 56).

8

The Process of Empire: Frontiers and Borderlands

David Ludden

How historians think about empire is important, because the study of empire in all disciplines depends upon historical reconstruction. Historians typically stress particularity, making each empire appear unique, anchored in its time and place, with its own distinct ideas, conditions, institutions and personalities. Yet historians also deploy standard frames of structural analysis which describe each empire as an exemplar of a type of political system, operating coercively, top-down, expanding outward from its central core to dominate subordinate peripheries, running through a lifecycle of birth, growth, decline and death, turning points to identify and explain. These standard features of empire histories facilitate comparison and generalisation about empire as a political form.[1]

The presence of the past

Standard historical thinking also includes the presumption that some empires are most exemplary, and of course, Europeans hold central stage. Ancient Greece and Rome represent classical *imperium*,[2] and modern Europe appropriated the ancients' world-defining powers, so that empires in Africa and Asia appear primitive and parochial in comparison. Karl Marx began to codify Europe's imperial modernity, and Max Weber secured it,[3] as the modern historical profession came into being, in the age of High Imperialism,[4] when comparing imperial Rome and imperial Britain became standard practice (cf. Chapters 2 and 3).[5] Now the United States has entered the club, as metaphoric comparisons with Rome and Britain pose America as the imperial centre of contemporary globalisation.[6]

The Western master-narrative of global modernity has further standardised historical thinking about empire by declaring it came to an end in the twentieth century. In the 1920s, the nation became the norm; after 1945, decolonisation covered the globe with national states. This transition became a pivot of history and empire became a thing of the past, archaic, over and done with, never to return.

But empire escaped history's dustbin when a burst of US imperialism brought the subject back to life. Scholars would now in general seem to agree that empire modelled on imperial Rome and Britain is impossible in a world of national sovereignty,[7] but that under radically new present-day conditions, new forms of empire are feasible.[8] This leads to the proposition that empire is best conceived not as a kind of structure with prime exemplars at all, but rather as a process of adaptive transformation in which people create, assemble, configure, reassemble, renovate and remodel imperial forms of power and authority under diverse, changing circumstances.

Post-colonial studies stimulate this reconceptualisation by showing how empires live in the national present,[9] implying that imperial frontiers extend across boundaries of time into present-day national territory.[10] Recent studies of world history also promote this redirection of research by showing that empires display a vast range of forms and demonstrate adaptive capacities extending well beyond confines of standard models. US empire therefore adds another variant to what now seems to be a virtually boundless set of imperial possibilities, including all variety of modern, premodern, Western, and non-Western empires, all over the world, from ancient times to the present.[11]

Empire is thus acquiring more diverse, expansive histories. David Armitage has for instance described empire's *longue durée* in Europe, arguing, in line with theorists of modern British imperialism,[12] that empire is 'a language of power', which transformed itself repeatedly in Europe.[13] Armitage's premodern Europe moves into a post-colonial present described by Walter Mignolo, who, focusing on Latin America, shows how European empire produced a global language hierarchy,[14] which laid the groundwork for today's globalisation of a neo-liberal imperial civilisation.[15]

Old imperial frontiers not only extend over time to cover today's world, they form borders inside contemporary nations, dividing expansive national elites from defensive, rebellious subalterns.[16] At such borders, imperial contestation and transformation continue, which Mignolo and others engage by locating their research in borderlands.[17] The temporal frontiers of Western imperialism engulf the present, not by reproducing the imperial structures of old, but rather by embedding imperial dynamics of power and authority inside national societies, cultures and economies.[18]

We can visualise this process graphically by imagining that empires are many-layered cakes,[19] which include status, ranks and moving frontiers that become features of nations cut from the cake.[20] The process of empire could therefore continue after empires dismantled themselves post World War II. After cutting up the cake, national elites renegotiated their power positions; they retained what Mignolo calls an imperial episteme.[21] As a result, globalisation today includes many imperial elements, which operate inside nations, in the hands of national elites, and internationally, in the hands of the World Banks global development regime[22] and heavy hands of America's imperial military.[23]

The process of empire

By appreciating their imperial present, historians can better understand empire as a process that entails vast collections of activities, decisions, assumptions and routines, and spatially and temporally shifting aggregations of ideas and motives among individuals who generate imperial forms of power and authority in everyday life, adapting them to changing circumstances. No one controls the process, though the cultural reification of a supreme personality typically helps to legitimate imperial ranks of inequality, honour and respect, and rationalise chains of command that strive to bring people in lower ranks into compliance with the wishes of people higher up. (In this light, it might be useful to think of god as the highest conceivable imperial authority).

In imperial environments, cultural coded ranks of status, honour and privilege coincide broadly with living standards, respectability and fashion. Circles of kinship and sociability form mostly inside ranks. Better-off people higher up tend to congregate in localities higher up the central place hierarchy; and so it goes down to the lowest levels of poverty and marginality. People higher up take their superiority for granted; imperial hegemony entails spreading that assumption down the ranks and out into peripheries, to generate consensus that leaders lead because they are more enlightened, and that better off people naturally have privileges and responsibilities to lead lesser folks. Attributes of superior personal character thus gravitate towards people with superior entitlements to assets of all kinds, notably including health, wealth, beauty, security and education.

Imperial forms of power and authority thus entail systematic patterns of inequality; exhibit a wide range of variation, in many settings, including kingdoms, families, firms, nations and globalisation; and appear in all domains of analysis, including culture, psychology, economics and politics. Though empire need not be spatially expansive, the words *empire* and *imperialism* tend to appear in public discourse during times of expansion and contestation, when hegemony is in the making or under critical scrutiny. Labelling an empire as such occurs by various means, often retrospectively, but the process operates more pervasively than we can appreciate by using evidence only from regimes labelled officially as 'empire'.

That label can also be misleading. It may represent misplaced concreteness, as in the case of the British Empire. The English East India Company's empire in India was not legally part of the empire into which it was incorporated later so as to obscure the Company's role as agent of empire. The Mughal Empire is another telling case, for when and where it prevailed remains debatable: it effectively died in 1706; its forms of power and authority continued to spread and evolve for another century (as we see below); and it ended officially only in 1857.

Official denials of imperial identity can also be misleading. The United States is not officially an empire, but US history makes sense as an imperial process moving through phases of expansion, contraction and transformation.[24] The same is true of India, as we will see.

We should thus deploy the terms *empire*, *imperial* and *imperialism* as analytical terms denoting a kind of power dynamic operating in ranks of systematically patterned inequality, rather than as terms to represent regime ideology or official order. Two influential recent studies apply this principle effectively: P. J. Cain and A. G. Hopkins use it to account for centuries of adaptive transformation by British imperialism,[25] and Michael Hardt and Antonio Negri use it to theorise empire as an amorphous field of class power with no fixed institutional form that organises contemporary global capitalism.[26]

The centrality of margins

Empire looks different from different angles. A useful conventional contrast is between centre and periphery. Imperial historians typically look out from centres of supremacy, as do Cain and Hopkins, whose main concern is in fact to re-centre British imperialism by focusing on expansive adaptations by 'gentlemanly capitalism' based in The City financial district of London. This centre-outwards approach speaks to a general desire to account for 'the big picture', to embrace all imperial centres and peripheries in one framework, as Hardt and Negri also endeavour to do. In the big picture, logics of power expanding outwards from centres provide keys to empire, and each empire appears to be a distinct entity with its own identity and history, visible most clearly, and documented most accessibly, in its highest ranking central places.

Most people experience, visualise and engage the process of empire in frontiers and peripheries, however. Most of the process occurs in places and among peoples where hegemonies are taking shape and being challenged, as material conditions change, compelling adaptive transformations that define empire as process. When the process rather than structure of empire becomes the subject of historical study, peripheries become central sites for research.

This shift in focus generates practical problems. Because activity on peripheries occurs at low levels of imperial authority, it is by definition least important for people with the most power; as a result, it typically seems to comprise mere local minutiae that often escape elite knowledge entirely. Borderlands and frontiers may be critical sites where empire adapts sensitively and diversely to new conditions, but being far from elite minds, they remain marginal, and their documentation disposable.

Imperial knowledge is hierarchical, giving precedence to people and places with higher ranks. Historians work in archives constructed accordingly, and historical work on the margins risks obscurity because it cannot reveal the big picture. On the margins, we find instead minute details about the process of empire in local environments. To appreciate the centrality of imperial margins, we must read imperial evidence against the grain of its knowledge hierarchies, which construe empire as being built only by high-level elites.[27]

On peripheries, moreover, various imperial histories mingle in borderlands where spatial and temporal frontiers overlap. Military, political, institutional, cultural, linguistic, ethnic, social and economic frontiers move spatially and temporally at their own pace, so that empire cannot be contained within definite parameters. In elite views from the apex of empire, each regime has its own place in space and time; but on the margins, empire typically includes contending, intermingled imperial histories, encoded in various languages.

Thus in borderlands, 'the language of power' can be multiple, creolised and available only in translation or indirectly; archives are typically polyglot, dispersed, obscure and contradictory. Obvious examples of such imperial borderlands appear today in Iraq and Afghanistan, where the expansive frontiers of imperial Ottomans, Mughals, British, Russians and Americans overlap in localities where imperial transformations constitute much of what we call local history. Appreciating this imperial present suggests how localities in borderlands might reveal critical dynamics of empire.

Imperial dramas

Archives in India and Bangladesh contain large folio manuscript volumes called District Records, penned in English by local East India Company scribes to preserve correspondence into and out of district offices, during the century after 1770. These letters to and from each District Collector, compiled and bound chronologically, document the lowest level of Company official activity and display minute local dynamics of imperial discovery, translation and adaptation to changing circumstances.

District Records run to hundreds of volumes for each district of Company territory in Bengal and Madras Presidencies. I have used them to analyse the formative period of British India, 1770–1820, in Sylhet[28] and Tinnevelly[29] districts, which provide my comparative case studies here. Each is the farthest district from its presidency capital, Calcutta and Madras respectively, and in both, District Records initially describe the Collector setting up office and gathering information on his roughly 5000 square miles of territory, taken from Mughal successor states on Mughal frontiers (Figure 2).

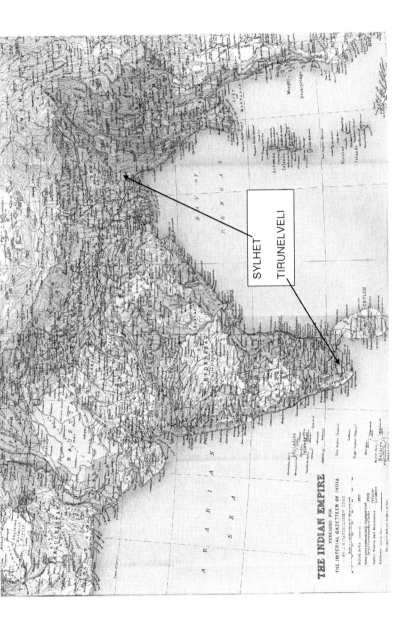

Figure 2 British India, showing Sylhet and Tinnevelly

Source: Imprint by The Imperial Gazetteer of India. Prepared by J. G. Bartholomew, Oxford: Clarendon Press, 1909 (Available at http://dsal.uchicago.edu/maps/gazetteer/images/gazetteer_frontcover.jpg)

The records depict imperial dramas in obscure rustic places, where Collectors live and work with a small local staff, serving the Board of Revenue in the Presidency capital and Company stakeholders in far-off London. Letters move up and down the ranks, over great distances, mostly by ship, depicting official action and its changing context, describing everything from masonry and stationery to travel, farming, trades and exchange rates. The drama of changing local contexts depicts local people building the imperial stage, feeding and clothing its actors, and conditioning imperial decisions, prospects, impact and adaptability locally.

From the outset we see the Collector recruiting locals to build the regime. He expects them to support him because he has legitimately acquired his authority. His legitimacy is crucial. Authority had passed from one previous regime to another; this continuity sustained the power of local elites across regime transitions, and local elites in turn sustained each regime in succession. With this in view, our Collectors seek to forge another successful regime transition.

In India, it is an old story. The Company wants to keep it moving. So have state authorities ever since. The past shapes the future: investments made under past regimes in the productivity of local economies and in the power of locals to control local resources pay dividends for future generations. The hinge between past and future is the reconstitution of local ranks of inequality under one regime after another, the adaptive transformation of imperial power and authority. Each new regime must work with what it finds locally, and what it finds depends on older regimes. Old imperial frontiers thus move across boundaries of time, creating borderlands among overlapping regimes.

As the process of empire moves from past into future, Collectors mediate between the highest and lowest levels of authority. They revise orders handed down from above to suit their ongoing engagements with locals, who explain how things are done locally. We can hear local informants whispering in the Collector's ear as he tells his superiors what local people are doing and how he is most respectfully adapting the imperial script to make it work locally. Languages of empire are not only English but the Mughal's Persian and the Bengali (in Sylhet) and Tamil (in Tinnevelly) of regional regimes.

The Collector's measure of success is simple. His career advancement up the ranks depends on his ability to maximise net tax receipts moving up the ranks into urban treasuries. To achieve this goal, he must collect taxes and build institutions to secure and increase taxation with minimum assistance from above and keeping costs to an absolute minimum.

Penurious frontiers

Penury on East India Company frontiers is typical in India. It makes sense as a general feature of empire because of the low rank of frontier sites and officials.

Imperial priorities gravitate toward higher interests and higher purposes. (Again, divine authority comes to mind.) Exalted elites make big decisions about resource allocation. Empire concentrates on channelling wealth up the ranks, not down. Higher-ups want frontiers to take care of their own incorporation as productive peripheries. The less frontier problems burden elites at the centre the better.

And yet, incorporating frontiers always requires some investment by people in high places. When, why, where and to what extent and effect such investments operate shapes the process of empire as a whole: it largely determines the character of relations between centres and margins, in part by promoting imperial prosperity that spreads the wealth among the ranks.

Imperial investments must travel imperial space that is horizontal (geographical distance) and vertical (status ranks), where investors change in their relative influence as we move out from central places to margins and down the ranks into peripheries and frontiers. At imperial centres, high level elites live, work and have the most influence; peripheral people have little to say, and frontier people, almost nothing. On peripheries, central control is weakest; empire is disparate and dispersed; locals have the most influence. And outside the firm grip of empire, frontiers are peripheries-in-the making, whose trajectory of incorporation remains uncertain.

Major policy decisions about imperial investment occur among elites in high places, but the cause and effect of investment arise on margins. Some kinds of frontiers are easy and cheap to incorporate; others require expensive war and infrastructure. Some investments find loyal subordinates, others spawn rebellion. What types of investments occur, when and where, and what impact they have differ from place to place and time to time: investing in staff, governance, war, education and economic development may have various results depending on methodology and local conditions.

As a general rule, elite investments flowing outward from centre to margins increase imperial unity and standardisation, and thereby reduce local autonomy and diversity. China and India provide useful examples. Imperial China invested much more heavily to propagate a system of centralised ethnic, linguistic, bureaucratic command and control. Imperial India invested much less. The Company followed the Indian pattern. After 1857, the British Crown increased investments, producing the most unified empire ever in South Asia; after 1947, national regimes invested still more; but effects of penurious frontier imperialism remain visible today. In China, the centre structured empire on peripheries; in India, frontier penury spawned imperial localism.[30]

Frontier imperialism

Thus we can propose two types of imperial processes. One, we can call imperial fusion: it propagates a standard pattern of power and authority using heavy central investments to incorporate peripheries in a unitary framework of centralised imperial management. The other, we can call imperial fission: propelled by frontier activists, it spreads much more independently of central command and control. Imperial fusion pushes coherently outward from core areas. Imperial fission pulls in various directions, as local activists running here and there drag central authorities into frontiers to protect investors and pursue opportunity.

Imperial fission predominates in southern Asia, from Mediterranean to Pacific, where the innovative replication of imperial order produced peripheries where locals retain substantial control (See Chapter 6 for such processes in the tribal societies of Africa).[31] Central investments on the margins typically seek to confirm imperial ranks and secure elite loyalty without forcing minute local obedience to central dictates. Fissiparous empire adapts itself to environments of extreme local diversity, as new regimes incorporate bits and pieces of old regimes; it absorbs and valorises local diversity – of language, ethnicity, culture, religion and locality (e.g. India's famous 'village communities') – within elaborately ritualised, symbolic unity, such as we find in Buddhist, Hindu and Muslim empires.[32] ('Unity in Diversity' has also been India's national motto.)

Penurious frontiers typify fissiparous empire and spawn local imperial activism. The English (but not the French or Dutch) East India Company fit this pattern. The English Company did not strive to produce British colonies, did not articulate a centralised process of imperial fusion. It was a frontier enterprise controlled by investors who operated in borderlands between globally expansive seaborne merchant capitalism and Indian imperial territorialism. In these borderlands, local decisions, not centralised elite imperial plans, moved empire from past to future.

The Company's frontier activists leveraged their influence in London to drag the British state into Indian frontiers, as the Company depended for profits on weak British state control over Company operations. Deeply invested as it was in India's already penurious frontiers, the Company reproduced them once again in English terms, and frontier penury thus continued to give local elites mighty leverage in determining the future of imperial patterns of power and authority throughout the Indian countryside.

The Company's success stretched and stressed British priorities at high levels, raising loud complaints in London, where exalted elite decisions to incorporate India into a truly British empire stripped the Company of its frontier autonomy slowly but steadily, from 1784 to 1857. During this long transition, a centralised British imperial fusion did embrace India, but long before 1857, frontier imperialism had established a plethora of distinct local forms of imperial order, in peripheries like Sylhet and Tinnevelly.

Imperial borderlands

Each frontier site incorporated into peripheries of British India occupied spatial and temporal borderlands formed by India's long history of imperial fission. Fissiparous empire had dispersed imperial activists into unruly Indian frontiers for many centuries. Aspiring rulers sent commanders with armies out to collect what they needed to sustain new regimes, granting them powers to bestow imperial honours and protection on locals who supported them. Open land was abundant and implacable foes typically fled rather than submit. Frontier rulers and escapees then launched their own dynasties, striving to subordinate recalcitrant elements, extend dominion over open areas and conquer neighbours. The result was countless breakaway regimes and localised imperial environments where elite power to control land, labour and capital attached itself to numerous regimes in succession, often to more than one at a time.

No single empire, not even the British Empire, ever embraced the whole subcontinent, yet imperial India displays a clear spatial order. Its epicentre is the Indo-Gangetic river basin, India's imperial heartland, stretching from the western mountains above Punjab to the eastern mountains above Bengal. For a thousand years, until the seventh century, empire moved along Indo-Gangetic trajectories from east to west. Then for the next millennium, it travelled from west to east. And then, in the eighteenth century, it marched again from east to west: the Company's imperial capital became Calcutta, in the east, and the last British capital sat on the site of the old Mughal capital, in the west, in New Delhi, where India's capital remained after independence.[33]

In the sixteenth century, Mughal emperors built an empire marching from Afghanistan to Bengal. The Mughals brought significant centralised order by commanding huge armies that kept frontier aspirations in check. Mughal fusion worked until the eighteenth century, when fission followed, as the centre weakened: regional regimes became independent and regional regimes built on Mughal patterns spread in all directions.[34]

During the period of Mughal fission, the English Company established itself in Mughal peripheries on the coast, expanded into the Mughal interior, took Mughal territory, and attacked Mughal frontiers. Frontier wars continued until Britain's Indian empire emerged in full territorial form after 1870.[35] The Company's first great surge of territorial expansion came during British wars against revolution in Europe and America, between 1770 and 1820, when British India took shape and the Company enforced strict penury on frontiers.[36] This formative period is our concern here.

Sylhet lies on the far eastern margin of Indo-Gangetic imperial space, in northeast deltaic lowlands, on borderlands embracing tropical mountains above, where no Indian empire ever held sway until British conquest after 1820. Sylhet first took shape as a region when it became a frontier piece of the Mughal Empire in the seventeenth century. Its frontier status remained during Mughal fission as Mughal order spread under Nawabs who ruled eighteenth century Bengal. A clear indication of its continued frontier status was the absence of imperial coinage when the first resident English Collector arrived in 1784, 20 years after the Company acquired Bengal from the Nawab. Then, Sylhet's only commercial coin was the cowry shell, acquired in circuits of sea trade around the Bay of Bengal. Until 1784, no state revenue had left Sylhet for imperial centres outside, and even then it could only do so by being converted expensively into Company rupees.[37]

Indo-Gangetic Empire never controlled the Indian peninsula; rather, fissiparous empire dispersed frontier activists from north to south who adapted northern imperial forms to southern environments. Mughal imperial order spread south from the sixteenth century and reached the far south in the eighteenth century under Mughal successor states in southern regions already endowed with old imperial institutions.

Tinnevelly was one of those southern regions, at the tip of the peninsula, in the farthest south, where fissiparous imperial forms built around Hindu kings and temples were established in the first millennium, as all over the peninsula, concentrated in river valleys. Empire in Tinnevelly centred on the Tambraparni River; constantly enriched by coastal trade, it absorbed many immigrant settlers over the centuries. Its fissiparous Hindu imperial order remained intact even when it became a periphery of a Mughal Nawab's domain in 1740, when tax payments began travelling for the first time ever, in Mughal fashion, up the coast to the Nawab in Madras. The Company subordinated and then replaced the Nawab to form the Madras Presidency after 1770.

Violence and repression

During the period 1770–1820, Sylhet and Tinnevelly were frontier borderlands where the Company Empire occupied Mughal and Hindu imperial spaces. These two districts represent two among many variants of frontier incorporation into peripheries of British India. Having acquired both from Mughal successors, the Company built its legitimacy in both on Mughal authority and precedence, adapting Mughal forms to new purposes, above all, to the increase of taxation flowing to Presidency capitals. Locally, most people who had controlled land, labour, capital, information and skills under the old regime continued to do so, and many expanded their horizons under early Collectors who depended on them to secure the revenue. Mughal forms of imperial order survived under Company authority, inside Company territory, infusing and mingling with novelties introduced by the Company, most notably, with a radically new discourse on private property in land.

In both districts, frontier turbulence forced Presidency elites to invest reluctantly in military operations, dispatching armies that accomplished their violent mission in 1791 (in Sylhet) and 1802 (in Tinnevelly). In both cases, local violence was an expression of opposition to innovation. Novel imperial intrusion into local patterns of power and authority triggered violent reactions in strict proportion to the challenges they posed to local elites: where there was no threat, the transformation of old imperial forms went smoothly, with no violence; where there was some threat, violence erupted among local rivals; and where there was major threat, organised attacks on various participants in the new regime, officials and civilians, triggered military repression.

Following this pattern, there was much more violence overall in Sylhet, where Mughal authority had left locals mostly to themselves, and much less in Tinnevelly, where local authority had depended upon transactions up and down imperial ranks for a thousand years. But in both, serious violence erupted as Collectors sought to expand a new imperial order across borderlands of fissiparous empire and its spotty spatial expanse.

Innovations that irritated local politics derived from the Collector's basic function, to collect revenue. Collectors demanded more tax more frequently than ever before, from more people. They changed the style of tax transactions, demanding payment in return for state recognition of what they understood as land ownership rights. Failure to meet the Collector's tax demand, in stipulated form, at his set time, justified his revocation of rights to land. All of a sudden, a state official was demanding more taxes, on more rigorous terms, and threatening more dire consequences for noncompliance.

In the Mughal imperial order and among Hindu contemporaries, payments that travelled up the ranks from the lowest to highest levels were integral components of the ranking system that constituted authority at each level. Tax and tribute went up the ranks and honour came down, forming the cultural substance of imperial territory. Transactions between men who gave and received payments formed ritual moments of recognition that dramatised and constituted their respective ranks. Such moments emerged amidst the everyday politics of haggling and negotiation that engaged all participants in the nitty-gritty of on-the-ground local realities.

In aggregate, therefore, flows of wealth in imperial space represent the ups and downs of empire. More revenue moving more routinely from lower to higher ranks represents centralising imperial fusion. Diminished revenue at the centre indicates fission. For instance, in eighteenth-century Bengal, the Nawab's increasing independence from the Mughals appears in his failure to remit cash to Delhi, despite formal ritual acceptance of Mughal authority.[38]

Imperial frontiers are marked by gaps and limits in the flow of wealth and in the grid of personal ritual relations of rank among men who constitute empire.[39] Imperial fusion expands and tightens the grid. Fission breaks it up. Its separate pieces might be woven together again and again, but some are more difficult to suture, and others impossible. Frontiers include people who refuse to participate in any kind of imperial ranking whatsoever, who live entirely outside domains of imperial culture.

Eighteenth century Sylhet was frontier space. Even its productive agrarian lowlands had few people who had ever paid taxes with any regularity to any imperial authority. Its coin served no imperial purpose outside Sylhet. And on its margins, hill people and shifting cultivators had fought and fled all the local activists spawned by Indo-Gangetic imperialism over the centuries; they lived outside the pale.

Tinnevelly was, on the other hand, an old imperial region, whose richly irrigated river basins had a venerable system of taxation replete with rituals that confirmed ranks at all levels. Its metal coins bore the imprint of empire. It became a solid periphery when river valley elites began sending taxes to Madras after 1740. Even so, centuries of frontier colonisation had established warlords outside the river valleys who resisted imperial subordination: their independence typified fissiparous empire all over the southern peninsula; their payments up the imperial ranks had the quality of contested tribute, not routine taxation.[40]

Company Collectors in Sylhet and Tinnevelly followed a single central directive from London, passed down through Calcutta and Madras: send more money! They focused their work on increasing the number of local elite men who would pay more cash taxation for state protection of their local rank. The Company defined the ranks in terms of 'land ownership', but their real meaning was broader. Collectors effectively sold certificates of 'property rights' that bolstered local prestige in all its social, economic, cultural and political complexity. Each Collector recruited local men to support the new regime with the assurance that paying more taxes more regularly would guarantee state support for their control over village land, labour and capital.

In Sylhet, such guarantees did not mean much, initially, because relatively poor Sylheti rustic elites did not depend on higher authority for control over local resources. In Tinnevelly river valleys, however, urbane elites built their wealth and stature on such dependency.[41] So initially, Company revenue in Sylhet was meagre, while in Tinnevelly it flowed amply. To increase revenue in Sylhet, Collectors had to exert force locally at every turn, to convince men of means they would benefit from joining the imperial ranks, while in Tinnevelly river valleys, men with assets to invest rushed to acquire new certificates of privilege.

On their old imperial borderlands, however, Sylhet and Tinnevelly look more alike. For they both spawned revolt. Where Mughal order had reached its limit, in localities ruled by martial ethnic groups determined to retain independence, Company armies had to kill enemies of the new order. In both cases, the Company and its allies called these enemies barbarians and imagined they engaged in conspiracies to thwart the advance of civilisation; this idea justified the kind of extreme brutality that was commonplace under Western imperialism. War's outcome was also similar in one respect: Company revenue soared thereafter, as more local men paid to confirm their local authority. Troops marching around these districts waging wars that everyone knew about had a profitable demonstration effect outside zones of violent conflict.

The process and outcomes of war were also quite different in each case, however. In Sylhet's northern margins, the Company faced enemies in what later came to be called 'tribal societies', who never engaged in rituals of ranking with any imperial authority. These Khasias were literally outside the pale. They spoke languages unintelligible to imperial elites at all levels. They were not Muslim or Hindu, but animists. They lived on external frontiers of fissiparous imperial expansion.

The goal and outcome of war in Sylhet were to exclude Khasias from the imperial lowlands of Bengal, to prevent further infiltration and miscegenation, which had blurred boundaries of imperial order. The Company did not actually win the 1791 war; it rather ended it by drawing a border between lowlands it could conquer and highlands it could not (a border that remains today, separating India and Bangladesh). Inside the new border, in the lowlands, Sylhet Bengalis paid taxes to acquire land taken away from a formerly mixed population of Bengali-Khasias, who disappeared from history.

In Tinnevelly, war erupted at old territorial borders inside fissiparous empire, where Hindu warrior chiefs called Palayakkars established themselves in territories controlled by caste brethren. These rebels were caste Hindus; they spoke Tamil; they understood the logic of imperial ranks; and they rejected demands of the Company and its ritual implication of rigorous subordination. In this context, Company conquest in 1802 represents a moment of imperial fusion. Nevertheless, fission continued in a new guise, as the Company bestowed zamindari landed estates on Palayakkars under laws that distinguished their domains from localities under direct British administration. The political distinctiveness of old Palayakkar territories continues to this day.[42]

Conclusion: the reproduction of imperial forms

How might all this affect how historians think about empire in general? Let us begin with frontier turbulence and repression. In imperial history, they represent resistance to empire facing the force of imperial expansion. In national history, they represent indigenous subaltern struggles against alien imperial domination, won or lost.[43] In world history, they typify transitions to a new dominant order during the advance of civilisation, progress and modernity.

Historical thinking about all these processes tends to buttress structural approaches to empire, its opposition, its space and time. The result is a two-sided reality with clear lines separating opponents, territories and time periods, which scholars can study from either side, or, like Mignolo, in their borderland. Structural dichotomies make political struggles amenable to military metaphors, which Antonio Gramsci extended into class analysis, where they entered post-colonial and subaltern studies. And in the world of real-life politics, where scholars deal constantly with partisan dichotomies, we who oppose inequity understandably identify with oppressed peoples.[44]

Structural dichotomies thus make good sense. They are useful. They present historical studies with clear either-or, this-or-that choices between empire and nation, unity and fragmentation, dominance and rebellion, collaboration and resistance, loyalty and betrayal, progress and stagnation, continuity and rupture, and such. Such oppositions allow analysts to draw clear lines between contending forces, to inscribe borders among definite territories and to define periods of history that follow in succession. The result is appealing neatness: then there was empire, now there is nation; here is domination, there is resistance; they have one history, we have another.

Yet turbulent frontiers in early-modern India indicate that such dichotomies obscure historical complexity whose elaboration can serve useful political as well as academic purposes. The first step is to rethink what we want to explain.

If we want to explain British India, we can stay in a world of dichotomy. For as Cain and Hopkins clearly argue, explaining British imperialism requires that we focus on Britain's national interior and its imperial exterior, that is, on the expansion of British power out from its core into peripheries. And on the Indian side, British Empire stands inherently opposed to nationhood.[45] Both terms in 'British India' acquire their meaning by their analytical opposition. The moment of national separation in 1947 dramatises an eternal structural reality deeply embedded in historical studies.[46]

If however we seek to explain the process of empire in areas embraced by British Empire and by India, we can escape structural dichotomies. We can shift our attention and range widely across imperial spaces, avoiding border guards who defend the rigidly bounded territories of national and imperial histories. We can live and work in different kinds of geographies and temporalities.

Most critically, we see that British imperialism did not introduce empire into India, and that Indian nationhood did not end the process of empire, which continues today, moving from past to future. Locating historical analysis in a world where empire is not archaic but a living force in everyday life, we see the process of empire as including a vast array of long- and short-term local, regional and global transformations, which embraced India and Britain variously at different moments and periods, as spaces of empire shifted shapes during the expansive history of what we now call globalisation.

In that context, turbulence and repression on imperial frontiers appear as dynamic elements in the adaptive transformation of imperial power and authority, the historic reproduction of imperial forms. Sylhet and Tinnevelly indicate that local events on imperial margins may hold keys to understanding the process of empire as a whole.

These cases indicate that the process does not necessarily entail top-down imposition by elites at high echelons of imperial structures that force localities into a standard grid. Some parts of the world, like China, and some times, like 1791 and 1802, dramatise elite efforts to mold obediently standardised peripheries. Even in China, however, such moments of fusion pass and give way to localised imperial fission.[47] In southern Asia, imperial fusion accelerated after 1857 and 1947, but fissiparous empire is the norm and remains the dominant modality of imperial transformation.[48]

Frontiers are places and time where empire strives to incorporate people into orderly peripheries. Frontiers often lie inside older imperial territories, whose borderlands thus overlap spatially and temporally with new domains of imperial expansion. Violence and repression on Company frontiers arose in direct proportion to the disruption that imperial innovation posed for old ranks in borderlands. When the Company pushed its frontiers of control beyond peripheries of older regimes, changing the ranks of imperial authority, it faced violent opposition, which it met with repression, which in turn produced a new order, adjusting imperial ranks without destroying them, allowing fission to proceed under official policies of fusion.

This account of the reproduction of imperial forms holds some simple lessons not only for historians but for scholars of empire in today's world of neo-liberal globalisation. One is that empire is obsessed with rank. By ranking peoples, places, cultures, traits, technologies, levels of development and such, the ritual discourse of empire forms a many layered cake of imperial institutions, titles, officers, locations and participants, which provides a grid for upward social mobility as it channels wealth upwards to higher levels of power and authority, thereby enforcing, valorising and naturalising inequality. Today the World Bank, Wall Street and US Treasury stand in apex imperial positions like those enjoyed by the Bank of England and City of London a century ago.[49]

Second, these two comparative case studies indicate that empire, though essentially territorial, and thus focused intently on controlling resources inside specific spaces, is also inherently mobile.[50] Empire creates boundaries for territorial control – including national borders – as it also expands, contracts and shifts spatial configurations over time. Military power, economic wealth and ritual activity move around constantly in structured imperial circuits of space, to show the flag, suppress rebellion, impress neighbours and rivals and move the assets on which empire depends into the hands of people in places endowed with superior entitlements.[51]

Third, we see here that imperial space and time are shifting and uneven. Power concentrates in core, central areas, where wealth accumulates most.

Wealth and power move along routes among core sites, connecting elites from all ranks, from empress to villager, White House to slums and refugee camps. Centralising powers fade over distance and down the ranks, however, as places become more costly and less valuable to incorporate, while opponents and 'others' proliferate.

Fourth, we can see imperial fusion as the ideology of centralising elites, even as fission pervades many frontiers and peripheries. Imperial time and territory are alike most rigidly defined by centralising authorities, including those who create national histories, which portray the moment of independence as the end of empire. On imperial margins, the complexity and ambiguity of historical time and space appear more clearly, and fission is more ideologically attractive. In this light, it is reasonable to argue that increasing economic inequality globally and in most nations today is a result of imperial fusion driving more wealth up the ranks under neo-liberal policy regimes around the world.[52]

Fifth, we can now imagine geographies of empire where inhabitants live both in strictly bounded territories and also, at the same time, in changing patchwork spaces composed of connected, ranked sites of empire strung along routes of mobility and surrounded by unruly areas outside imperial ranks. We should thus not imagine that we must choose between a world of national histories and of imperial self-reproduction. Analysts need not find a stable, singular subject position. For empire is about dynamic relationships; its complexity evades methodological individualism; and any fixing of one's location or identity invites interrogation as a transaction with empire.

Last but not least, we can conclude that old histories of obscure places like Sylhet and Tinnevelly hold little promise when empire is conceived as structure, but considerably more when we think of empire as a process. Thus the extreme scarcity of localised, long-term studies of empire indicates the continued dominance of historical thinking that tosses empire into the dustbin by making the nation empire's eternal other and its permanent successor as a global frame of legal authority, political identity and historical understanding.

Notes

1. Burbank & Cooper (2010) traces the variability of the 'imperial form' across millennia and continents.
2. For a wonderful account of the relationship between Western imperialism and Eurocentric history, see Blaut (1993). See also Chakrabarty (2000).
3. O'Leary (1989); Ludden (1993).
4. Novick (1988).
5. Bryce (1914).
6. See Ferguson (2003 and 2004); Murphy (2007). One of the most interesting recent contributions to this literature is by Michael Rose, a retired British Army general who commanded United Nations forces in Yugoslavia in 1994–1995, who concludes

his *New York Times* Op-Ed piece ('How a Revolution Saved an Empire,' July 5, 2007, A-13), by saying, 'Today, of course, the United States finds itself in much the same position as Britain in 1781. Distracted and diminished by an irrelevant, costly and probably unwinnable war in Iraq, America could ultimately find itself challenged by countries like China and India. Unless it can find a leader with the moral courage of Pitt, there is a strong probability that it will be forced to relinquish its position as the global superpower – possibly to a regime that does not have the same commitment to justice and liberty that the United States and Britain have worked so hard to extend across the world over the past two centuries.'

7. Layne & Thayer (2007).
8. See Harvey (2003), and Hobsbawm (2008).
9. See Burton (2003) and also Prakash (1995).
10. Loomba (1998).
11. See Burbank & Cooper (2010). Arundhati Roy (2004) considers the United States and India as interlocked imperial nations in *An Ordinary Person's Guide to Empire.*
12. Cohn (1985); Viswanathan (1989).
13. Armitage (2000: 29–35).
14. Mignolo (2000).
15. Ibid.
16. Baruah (2005) (the preface to second edition, 2007, cites Mignolo explicitly).
17. Ludden (2002).
18. See for instance Dirks (2001).
19. Danzig (1969).
20. Bailyn & Morgan (1991).
21. Mignolo (2000). See also Memmi (1965) and Nandy (1983).
22. Goldman (2005); Ludden (2006a and 2005).
23. Johnson (2004); Katsenstein (2005).
24. See Kaplan & Pease (1993).
25. Cain & Hopkins (2002: 54ff.).
26. They evoke the difference between old and new imperial forms by distinguishing old 'imperialism' from the new 'empire' of late capitalist globalisation, anchored in the United States without being a definitively US Empire. See Hardt & Negri (2001).
27. A good example is Guha (1963).
28. Ludden (2003).
29. Ludden (1985).
30. Extending this comparison to embrace Britain and America yields the observation that ethnic settlement patterns indicate levels of imperial investment. The British and Americans produced the most densely integrated peripheries where white settlement predominated. The extent of white settlement became an index of imperial integration, as did that of Han Chinese. By contrast, British India had a tiny elite composed of British and Indian ethnicities, held together primarily by shared English education. Empire's major investment in India was in schooling its elite. This strategy remained in force among imperial powers after national independence, not only in South Asia but also globally, as the education-based logic of British imperial investment was adopted by the Americans under the Fulbright programs and many other public and private initiatives.
31. To continue the line of reasoning in the previous note, fissiparous empire would be typified by small educated elites skilled in the adaptation of empire to various localities and circumstances. This pattern fits India from ancient times and also the

imperial project of global capitalism, of which India is today a more useful exemplar than China, where imperial fusion remains dominant despite China's national integration into the world economy of contemporary globalisation.

32. Literature on state formation in Asia is of course too vast to summarise or discuss here, but useful work on what I call 'imperial fission' includes Kulke (1993), Stein (1980) and Wink (1990). See also Kulke (1982).
33. Schwartzberg (1978).
34. Richards (1993).
35. A succinct account of the whole imperial process is in Ludden (2002: 127–36). More details on regions appear in Ludden (1999). The final territorial form of British India described the geographical frame of Indian national identity: see Goswami (2004).
36. Cain & Hopkins (2002: 62–104).
37. On the early modern cowry shell economy, see Perlin (1993: 152–63, 270); Hogendorn & Johnson (1986); and Wicks (1992: 28–72).
38. The classic account is Calkins (1970).
39. For a view from the centre, see Blake (1979) reprinted in Kulke (1995: 278–304).
40. On territorial partitioning in southern India, see Ludden (1996).
41. On eighteenth-century urbanity in Tinnevelly, see Ludden (1995 and 1990).
42. Ludden (2000c).
43. Classic accounts of subaltern resistance to Western imperialism are Scott (1976) and Guha (1983).
44. See Ludden (2002).
45. A classic statement is Chandra (1979).
46. The comprehensive erasure of empire from post-1947 India is beautifully captured in Chandra et al. (2000).
47. White III (1998).
48. See Ludden (2006a and 2005).
49. Compare Cain & Hopkins (2002) and Goldman (2005).
50. See Ludden (2003b).
51. Ludden (2002d). On the process of entitlement, see Sen (1981) and Ludden (2002c).
52. Ludden (2006b).

9

The Emblematic Province – Sicily from the Roman Empire to the Kingdom of the Two Sicilies

Giovanni Salmeri

'Prima omnium, id quod ornamentum imperii est, provincia est appellata (She was the first to receive the title of province, the first such jewel in our imperial crown)'.[1] With these words Cicero (106–43 BC) depicts Sicily in the *Verrines*, emphasising what was to be the island's condition – *naturaliter provincialis* as it were – for most of its subsequent history up to the Unification of Italy (1861). This condition, implying the absence of political autonomy, has meant that starting from *De rebus siculis* by the Dominican Tommaso Fazello, published in Palermo in 1558,[2] and for at least the next two centuries, the historians hailing from the island tended to view their past as a succession of invasions, beginning with the Sicani and Sicels and proceeding with the Greeks, Carthaginians, Romans, Vandals, Byzantines, Arabs, Normans, French and Spanish. No one invading power was given priority, even though the Greek period and the Norman reconquest of the island for Christendom were recognised as being particularly important.[3] As a corollary to this interpretation, Fazello found it very difficult, if not impossible, to identify and define the Sicilian people. He could really do no more than speak of their collective *mores*, namely the customs which took root and developed under the successive invasions.[4]

This vision of the history of Sicily – dominated by that fatalism which often characterises peoples long held in subjection – also transpires in some of the sentiments of Don Fabrizio Salina in Lampedusa's novel *Il Gattopardo* (*The Leopard*) published in 1958.[5] Yet Arnaldo Momigliano[6] was surely mistaken in affirming that this was the sole and largely consensual approach to the island's past. There were in fact intellectuals – jurists for the most part, but not only – who, particularly under Spanish rule in the seventeenth century, proved able to go beyond the schematic interpretation of Sicily's history as a succession of invasions.[7] Their reflection on the island's condition as a province in the Roman period made for a more dynamic vision, for its submission to the central power was seen not as an immutable reality but as something that was potentially, as indeed proved the case, subject to negotiation and transformation.[8] Such a notion of province proved very useful to Sicilian jurists when it came to theorising, or indeed one might say inventing, the role of their homeland in the context of the Spanish Empire.

In relation to all this it is important to stress that Sicilian intellectuals, as we shall see, found an indispensable aid to their reflections concerning the island's provincial dimension in Cicero's orations against Verres. Dealing with the same geographical context, the speeches were read and culled for direct and specific political instructions and claims. This gives the Sicilian dialogue with its classical past a particularly intense hue even compared to the rest of Europe at that time, where a lively use of the Greek and Roman texts more often bore a clear rhetorical or antiquarian stamp. Thus the *Verrines* were taken as a model for the prosecution of corrupt governors by Edmund Burke in the trial of Warren Hastings (1789–1794) – the first Governor-General of Bengal – before the House of Lords.[9] To the Sicilians, however, the *Verrines* were more than a rhetorical model, they represented a political programme.

In this chapter with the aim of appraising the provincial condition of Sicily in the long term, we shall start from the genesis and first two centuries of the Roman province. We shall go on to consider how the province was idealised in Cicero's *Verrines*, and conclude by considering the wholly political use which Sicilian intellectuals in the seventeenth and eighteenth centuries made of their reflections concerning the provincial experience of the island in Roman times.

The Roman Province

In the preface to his account of the First Punic War (264–241 BC), the Siceliot historian Diodorus of Agyrium asserted: 'Sicily is the noblest of all islands, since it can contribute greatly to the growth of an empire (*pros auxesin heghemonias*)'.[10] Written with lucid retrospect in the second half of the first century BC, when the processes of Roman expansion in the Mediterranean and organisation of conquered territories into provinces were well on the way to completion, these words attribute to Sicily a primary role in the formation of the Roman Empire.[11] In fact, the island became the first Roman province at the end of the First Punic War, and would serve as both an important base in the conquest of Africa and a sort of laboratory in which Rome experimented with forms of domination that it was subsequently to apply in the lands brought under its rule.

Rome's arrival in the island was motivated by an appeal for help from the Mamertines, mercenaries from Campania who had been hired by King Agathocles to fight in Sicily and since 289 BC had installed themselves in Messana, as a base for their raids on the surrounding lands. Hieron, the new strong man in Syracuse, rose against the Mamertines and defeated them in

265 BC, securing the title of King in his city, but failed to drive them out of Messana. Anxious to guard against further attacks, the Mamertines appealed for help first to the Carthaginians and then to the Romans. The unexpected upshot was that, having withdrawn from Messana, the Carthaginians came to an agreement with Hieron. This marked the beginning of the first Punic War, and also of the expansion of Rome beyond the Italian peninsula.[12]

Thus the Roman invasion of Sicily followed the classical pattern of the request for help made to a great power by one of two sides engaged in conflict – a model Rome was to conform to on other occasions, especially in the Hellenistic East.[13] Nonetheless the Mamertines' appeal does not in itself seem sufficient to account for the Roman operation in Sicily, nor indeed for its spectacular success. To explain both aspects adequately we must bear in mind that Rome had been maintaining relations with the variegated world of southern Italy for many decades – both with the Italic populations and with the Greek cities – and had thereby acquired the control of a number of diplomatic and military 'tools' that were to prove of service in Sicily. Moreover, since the end of Pyrrhus's expedition, terminated at Beneventum in 275 BC, Rome had become the hegemonic power in southern Italy, and in 270 BC had taken direct action at Rhegium, across the Straits, to free the city from a band of mercenaries and return it to its inhabitants.[14]

After the arrival in Sicily with its legions from Southern Italy, Rome set about pillaging the territory controlled by Syracuse. In a fine example of 'Realpolitik',[15] Hieron II abandoned the alliance with Carthage and came to terms with Rome, thereby maintaining possession of his kingdom.[16] Having no further worries about Syracuse, Rome could concentrate on combating Carthage, with which it had hitherto maintained relations of *amicitia*,[17] but which had come to represent a threat to Rome's sphere of interest. Following a war that lasted more than 20 years[18] and after several centuries of occupation, the Carthaginians were forced out of Sicily in 241 BC.[19]

Having acquired extensive territory in western and central-southern Sicily, Rome now faced the problem of administering it. This was its first conquest outside Italy, and despite the possibility of naval contacts across the Tyrrhenian Sea, the island was still too far from Rome for it to be controlled using the tried and trusted systems employed in the peninsula itself, namely the formation of alliances, the imposition of military obligations, the confiscation of territory and the foundation of colonies of Roman citizens.[20] So it was that western Sicily became Rome's first province,[21] possibly taking the previous system of government under the Carthaginians as a model;[22] and in 227 BC Rome sent a specially designated praetor to rule the island,[23] thereby inaugurating, together with his counterpart designated for Sardinia in the same year, the seemingly endless list of provincial governors that were to succeed each other through to the demise of the Roman Empire.

If the western half of the island was forced to come to grips with the details of provincial rule, in the eastern half the kingdom of Hieron II flourished above all in Syracuse and certain minor cities.[24] Holding faith with Rome through to his death in 215 BC, the sovereign secured a long period of peace and calm for his lands, which proved a particular boon for agriculture. His subjects were required to pay tithes in kind, above all in grain, a system that was later to be known in Sicily, after the king, as the *lex Hieronica*.[25] The tithes, and the profits made from sale of the produce, not only went to subsidise the prosperity of the court; they also ensured the prestige of the sovereign in the Greek world, through the donations sent to sister cities in times of need, and financed the substantial building policy that characterised not only the capital but also the other cities in the small kingdom.[26]

The death of Hieron spelt the end of the heyday of Syracuse: his heir, Hieronimus, chose to abandon the alliance with Rome in 214 BC, which led directly to the conquest and plunder of Syracuse by the consul M. Claudius Marcellus, after a long siege, in 211 BC.[27] For the first time in its history Sicily came under a single power, and this was indeed a matter of great moment for the island: in the long term this favoured processes of integration that had never previously been possible.

Following the same line it would pursue in the Hellenistic East, Rome aimed above all to make the greatest possible profit out of the island, and showed no inclination to force its own language and customs upon it.[28] Jonathan Prag makes the very interesting point that 'Roman rule in Sicily entailed the continuity, indeed the encouragement of traditional norms, in the form of local military activities and their institutional concomitants, in particular the *gymnasion*.'[29] In terms of language, just as Greek had become the idiom of the local population of the Sicels in the eastern part of the island from the end of the fifth century BC, so it made its way into the former Punic area, and the Greek artistic and cultural traditions began to enter the common heritage. In the last two centuries BC, one can really continue to speak of Punics, Elymi and Sicels when dealing only with religion and mythology.[30]

The Romans seemed unperturbed by the fact that very little Latin was spoken in Sicily, or by its almost total Hellenisation, which had clearly been favoured by administrative unification.[31] On the contrary, they took a very keen interest in the island's grain production, which seems to have become the focus of the province's organisation after the conquest of the kingdom of Hieron II.[32] Syracuse was the residence of the governor. The staff of the Roman government included two quaestors, with specific financial competence, one based at Lilybaeum in the former Punic area and the other at Syracuse.[33] A point to stress here is that, whereas in the Republican period Rome adopted a policy of foundation of colonies throughout the Italian peninsula, this was not the case in Sicily. The island therefore experienced no upheaval in its ethnic, social and, indeed, economic situation as a result of the introduction of compact groups of new residents.[34] The island's first colonies were established by Augustus and, as in other provinces in the Greek world, they often served to punish and control localities which the *princeps* considered dangerous.[35]

As for the island's cities, on the whole they continued to enjoy a fair degree of freedom in the administration of their internal affairs.[36] Rome merely introduced a sort of hierarchy, in practice based on how they had behaved during the Punic Wars:[37] in particular, Messana and Tauromenium were distinguished as *foederatae civitates*,[38] receiving the privilege of exemption from every form of contribution, while five other *civitates* – whose citizens were not obliged to pay tithes – were *sine foedere immunes ac liberae*.[39] A large proportion of the Sicilian cities, whose populations consisted essentially of small and medium landowners, fell into the category of *civitates decumanae*,[40] which meant that their inhabitants were subject to the payment of a tenth of their agricultural produce – and grain in particular – and it was this that most patently symbolised their submission to Rome.[41]

The system known as the *lex Hieronica*, which in all likelihood the Romans had adopted in western Sicily right from the official beginning of the province,[42] was maintained in eastern Sicily[43] also after the fall of Syracuse. This decision was taken by the consul M. Valerius Laevinus, who arrived from Rome in 210 BC, stayed on as proconsul in 209 and 208, and can be considered one of the first, if not in fact the first, Roman senator expert in Greek affairs.[44] On the island, in particular, Laevinus seems to have grasped the full potential of the form of taxation successfully applied by Hieron II. The tithes served essentially to guarantee the city of Rome a regular supply of grain. Moreover, the use of Sicily as a granary[45] brought about and fostered, in the medium term, the radical changes in Italic agriculture that saw the prevalence of slave labour in farms, with a particular emphasis on such remunerative cultivation as olives and vines as well as sheep-farming.[46] While Rome may not have set out to impose a monoculture system on Sicily based on grain-production, this was in fact what happened to meet its demands as an imperial power.[47]

Some 60 years after Laevinus, the Sicilian scene was shaken up by the Roman destruction of Carthage in 146 BC and the subsequent creation of the province of Africa. Flocks of *equites*, bankers and tradesmen of mainly Italic origin were drawn to the new province and its cities by the urge to exploit all the resources without delay. Situated as it was on the route from Italy to Africa, Sicily found itself included in the economic circuit activated by this new state of affairs,[48] and a fair number of *equites* and *Italici* arrived in the island.[49] Their investment of capital in the formation of *latifundia* and introduction of large contingents of slaves – made available by the conquest of Carthage – for use primarily as shepherds, upset the island's relatively static economic and social structures, paving the way for the two slave wars of 135–132 and 104–100 BC.[50] Nevertheless, the impact of these events did not go so far as to affect Sicily's basic role as granary province, nor the prevalence of small and medium landowners.[51] Neither was the situation of the island greatly affected by the misappropriations and theft practised by Gaius Verres, who was *propraetor* from 73 to 71 BC,[52] and who, thanks to Cicero's orations against him, became the prototype of the 'bad' provincial administrator.[53]

It would be too lengthy here to go into the trial of Verres, held before the *quaestio de repetundis*[54] in 70 BC with Cicero as prosecutor,[55] but for the purpose of this chapter it should not be passed over that representatives of the province played an active role in the trial. Although there had been other cases of governors of Sicily being accused and indeed sentenced for embezzlement, this was the first time Sicilians had been among the protagonists.[56] Realising that the days were numbered for the Sullan order under which Verres had benefited and that Cn. Pompeius was emerging as the new main player in the politics of the imperial capital, they approached Cicero to act as prosecutor before the court,[57] well aware not only of his ties with Pompeius, who in the year of the trial was consul together with Crassus, but also that in the following year Cicero himself would be *aedilis*.[58] All this, as well as Cicero's brilliant conduct of the prosecution, must have played its part in the trial's rapid conclusion, with the collapse of Verres' defence and his subsequent flight into exile already after the first part of the trial, related with the *actio* I of Cicero's speeches. The more copious *actio* II, one of the masterpieces of Latin eloquence, was never pronounced, but only written after the victory to publicise and celebrate Cicero's triumph in court.[59]

As for Sicily's role as principal grain supplier to Rome, it began to totter with the secession of the island accomplished by Sextus Pompeius – contending with the heirs of Caesar – who blocked the shipping to the City of tithes of grain from 43 until 36 BC, when he was defeated by Octavian. Shortly afterwards, the arrival in Rome of the Egyptian grain tribute, following the defeat of Antony and Cleopatra at Actium in 31 BC, helped to make the Sicilian deliveries less significant.[60] It is indeed for this reason that the year 30 BC has been indicated as the closing date of the period that began in 210 BC and saw Sicily as the supply province par excellence.[61] At the administrative level, the end of this epoch was marked by Augustus's abolition of the fiscal system of tithes and its replacement with a *stipendium*, as was the practice in other provinces.[62]

Sicily was thus released from the condition of economic dependence, which, on account of the obligation of paying tithes, had resulted in an agriculture based predominantly on wheat. The new situation allowed the island not only to differentiate its agricultural production and make ample room for the more profitable cultivation of vines and olives as well as grazing, but also to renew its commercial links with other regions of the Mediterranean and in particular North Africa.[63]

Cicero on 'Courtesy' and 'Utility'

To sum up, we can draw on the approach taken by Hardt and Negri in *Empire* distinguishing between 'command',[64] its objective being general control of the multitude through the application of tools such as military power and communications, and 'administration'[65] which aims at solving specific problems one by one, without following any broad guidelines, the criterion for success being local efficacy. As for 'command', the hallmark of 'province' on Sicily in the Republican period was above all its use as *cella penaria rei publicae* and *nutrix plebis romanae*, 'food store of the Republic and nourisher of the Roman population.'[66] While at the level of *histoire événémentielle* a manifestation of Rome's 'command' in Sicily can be seen in the harsh military repression – with the despatch of consuls and legions – carried out on the occasion of the two slave revolts, which took place in the second half of the second century BC,[67] the 'administration' was left in the hands above all of local officials and seems to have had a vast scope in Sicily. As in the rest of the Greek world, Rome did not intervene in any significant way to transform the political structures in the island's cities, and showed no inclination to impose its own language or customs.[68]

But what sort of idea the Romans had, or rather, formed, of their dominion on the island? In answering this question Cicero's *Verrines* can be of some help, provided we do not lose sight of the fact that the orator had various reasons for presenting an idyllic picture of relations between Rome and Sicily. Above all this enabled him to depict Verres's behaviour as being all the more blameworthy for having, as governor, played havoc with an arrangement that was mutually advantageous for both Sicily and Rome.[69] Thus, in the passages from the *Verrines* we shall look at, the island's provincial condition is seen to be subjected to a process of ideologisation aiming to present it as unique and exceptional.

At the beginning of the *actio* II Cicero says: 'Before I speak of Sicily's distresses, I feel that I should say a little of the high position of that province, of its antiquity, and of its practical importance. Your attentive consideration, due to the interests of all our allies and all our provinces, is especially due, gentlemen, to those of Sicily, for many strong reasons, the first of which is this, that Sicily was the first of all foreign nations to become the loyal friend of Rome (*primum quod omnium nationum exterarum princeps Sicilia se ad amicitiam fidemque populi Romani adplicavit*). She was the first of all to receive the title of province, the first such jewel in our imperial crown. She was the first who made our forefathers perceive how splendid a thing foreign empire is. No other nation has equalled her in loyal goodwill towards us'.[70] A little further on he adds: 'From this province therefore it was that our forefathers took that great step in their imperial career, the invasion of Africa: for the great power of Carthage would never have been crushed so readily had not Sicily been at our disposal, supplying us with corn and affording safe harbourage to our fleets'.[71]

In speaking in this way Cicero – well aware of the importance attributed by the ancients to being the first to find, invent or reach something (let us think of the famous *protoi heuretai*) – extols the status of Sicily as Rome's first province (*prima omnium, id quod ornamentum imperii est, provincia est appellata*[72]) and its loyalty, leading to the useful role it played in Rome's imperial expansion. Two further passages continue in the same vein: '[...] our relations with the province for all purposes were always such that we looked upon her various products not as growing on their soil, but as already added to our stores at home. When has she failed to pay us punctually her tribute of grain? When has she not spontaneously offered us what she believed we wanted? When has she refused to supply what was ordered of her? Cato Sapiens called her in consequence "the state's storehouse, the nurse at whose breast the Roman people is fed"([...] *ille M. Cato sapiens cellam penariam rei publicae nostrae, nutricem plebis Romanae Siciliam nominabat)*'.[73] After a few more remarks, Cicero concludes his case by stating: 'Our tributes and our provinces constitute, in a sense, so many properties for the Roman people; and thus, just as you, gentlemen, gain most pleasure from such of your estates as are close to Rome, so there is something pleasant in the nearness of this province to our city ([...] *sic populo Romano iucunda suburbanitas est huiusce provinciae)*'.[74]

With this insistence on Sicily's constant support for Rome, Cicero provides further evidence for the image of the ideal province which, thanks to its *suburbanitas*, stands almost as Rome's 'back garden'.[75] The penultimate citation dwells specifically on the effect that the island's immediate readiness to come to terms with Rome had on the system for taxation of its territory: 'Let me remind this Court of the differences in the system of land taxation between Sicily and our other provinces. In the others, either a fixed tax has been imposed, which is called a "tribute", as for example that imposed on the Spaniards and most of the Carthaginians, which may be considered as the reward of victory and penalty of defeat; or else the taxation system is regulated by censors' contracts, as in Asia under the Sempronian Law. But to the Sicilian cities we granted conditions of trust and friendship by which their old rights were maintained, and their position as subjects of Rome remained the same as it had been under their own rulers'.[76] Essentially – Cicero argues – Rome retained the system of tithes in force under Hieron II unchanged in Sicily[77] as a sign of respect, rather than a matter of self-interest. This was undoubtedly a stroke of genius, in which the orator transformed the deployment of an instrument of command into a gesture of courtesy.

Quite apart from every form of idealisation, which was probably designed to establish a collaborative vision of the empire, Cicero was in any case well aware of the *utilitas*[78] and fundamental importance of the island as principal supplier of grain to Rome. Indeed, he points out: 'You must all know, gentlemen, that so far as the interests of the Roman state are concerned, the general utility and advantage of our province of Sicily is mainly derived from the grain which it sends us; its other contributions are useful to us, but this one is the food we live on'.[79] Here he is indeed 'telling it straight', in spite of the highly rhetorical context.

Sicily in the Spanish Empire: a comparison

From the sixteenth to the eighteenth centuries the Sicilians found themselves in a position of administrative and tributary subordination to sovereigns residing now in Madrid, now in Turin, now in Vienna, now in Naples, represented *in loco* by a viceroy, and whenever thoughts turned to their ancient history, they were inclined to focus their attention on the Roman period when the island was a province, rather than the Greek period when it was torn by strife between its free cities.[80] This was the case above all during the nearly two centuries when they were part of the empire of the Spanish Habsburgs, from 1516 to 1700. Not only did the 'political imagination'[81] of the Sicilian ruling class and intellectuals nurture itself on Roman history and political thought, it also elaborated a profound reflection on the provincial role of their island under the Romans which proved of no little significance when it came to negotiating a position of privilege within the Spanish Empire and defending their rights. It is not hard to imagine that the *Verrines*, in which Cicero presented Sicily as the ideal province, had a fundamental contribution to make in this direction.

We find illuminating material as early as the seventeenth century, in the *Instrucción para el príncipe Filiberto quando fue al virreynado de Sicilia* written by the jurist from Palermo Pietro Corsetto in his capacity as regent of the Supreme Council of Italy in Madrid. The text was drafted at a crucial moment for the Spanish Empire: 1621, the year which saw the demise of Philip III and succession of Philip IV, and also the establishment of the regime of the Count-Duke of Olivares. Taking the side of Olivares, in his *Instrucción* Corsetto exhorts the new viceroy Emanuel Philibert of Savoy to make moderate use of his power, and describes what he holds should be the role and treatment of Sicily within the Spanish Empire.[82] Corsetto believes that his fellow Sicilians had deserved to be treated like sons by their king since, after the Vespers of 1282 and expulsion of the Angevins, they had quite freely placed themselves in the hands of Peter III of Aragon through the affection and gratitude they felt for his wife, Constance, of Norman descent. Moreover, as the first province of Aragon, Sicily constituted 'the gateway by which the Spanish came to conquer Naples, from whence came also the title and state of Milan'.[83]

With these reflections on the expansion of Spain in the Mediterranean, which saw Sicily in a leading role, Corsetto can hardly help also pointing out that 'the same thing happened with Sicily to the Romans as Cicero explains in the *Verrines*, and certainly the two appear as parallel lines'. Just as Sicily bestowed itself upon Aragon, so once before, in the words of the Roman orator, 'omnium nationum exterarum princeps [...] se ad amicitiam fidemque populi romani adplicavit (she was the first of all foreign nations to become the loyal friend of Rome).' Just as Sicily remained ever obedient to the Spanish sovereigns, so it had formerly given the Romans a taste of 'quam praeclarum esset exteris gentibus imperare (how splendid a thing foreign empire is)' and was the only one to show unfailing *fides* and *benevolentia*, loyalty and goodwill. And just as the Spanish had embarked on the conquest of Italy from Sicily, so the Romans had had the fortune to conquer Africa and subsequently become masters of the world by passing through the same outpost.[84]

Concluding this extended parallel, and confident in the primacy the Roman orator ascribed to Sicily among all the Roman provinces, Corsetto renews his plea that 'the Sicilians be treated as sons, and not as slaves, and that justice be administered among them according to those laws by virtue of which they had entrusted themselves of their own free will to the crown of Aragon'.[85]

A decidedly broader perspective on relations between Sicily and Spain was taken by the jurist from Catania, Mario Cutelli.[86] Indeed, the commentary to the various laws set out in his *Codicis legum sicularum libri quattuor* of 1636 constitutes a weighty assessment of imperial power. In particular Cutelli offers an original interpretation of the moral reform which the Count-Duke of Olivares brought about in Spanish policy; making constant reference to Tacitus and Seneca, he exposes the degradation of the Sicilian ruling class of his age, which he portrays as wallowing in luxury, exploiting the *plebs*, *the common folk* and, worst of all, devoid of any sense of public duty and the state. His dream was that these nobles might undergo moral and political regeneration and that they might once again dedicate themselves to wise and good government.[87] But, if Cutelli's authorities are the moralists Tacitus and Seneca in such matters as the relations between monarch and ruling class, between monarch and people, and between ruling class and people, for more concrete issues like Sicily's grain production and its fundamental importance for the economy of the Empire, the jurist looks to Cicero and the *Verrines* and, secondarily, to the geographer Strabo.[88] Both authors provide him with the terms of comparison to assess the depopulation of the Sicilian countryside in his time, while the Roman orator, with his prosecution of Verres, surely contributed to the violent invective that Cutelli launches against excessive taxation, denounced as being responsible for the revolts and intestine wars that plagued the provinces. 'And one should not place too much trust in obedience, for danger invariably arises when the burdens have grown enormously, and even those who care little about such matters feel that there is nothing for it but to rebel.'[89]

Following Corsetto and Cutelli, throughout the seventeenth century the period of Roman domination in Sicily continued to provide food for thought for the island's jurists, intent on guiding the viceroy's governing hand and interpreting the legislation of the Spanish monarchs. In the eighteenth century, even after the departure of the Spanish, the centuries of Roman presence in Sicily continued to be the main field of interest for intellectuals, and above all historians. One particularly significant figure is Baron Giovan Battista Caruso,[90] who in 1716 published the first volume – dedicated to the ancient world – of his *Memorie istoriche di quanto è accaduto in Sicilia dal tempo de' suoi primieri abitatori sino alla coronazione del re Vittorio Amedeo.* Without dwelling on the periods he spent studying in Rome and Paris, here it is important to stress the key role in the origin of his work played by the end of Spanish domination and the coronation of an Italian, Victor Amadeus II of Savoy, as King of Sicily at the end of the War of the Spanish Succession in 1713. This development prompted Caruso to abandon his scholarly researches and set about writing a general history of Sicily, which he dedicated to the son of Victor Amadeus, Charles Emanuel. Showing a keen civil and political sense, in the *Proemio* he expresses the hope that a knowledge of the island's past would bring the young man to closer acquaintance with his future subjects.

As for the Roman conquest of Sicily, the historian has no qualms in admitting that it was thanks to this that, in spite of the loss of its liberty, the island rapidly gained its unitary identity: 'When Sicily had been brought under the yoke by the victorious arms of the Roman Republic, its peoples lost the ancient glory of sovereign command and the liberty they had enjoyed. But, although at first they did not take readily to the foreign dominion of Rome, they gained in exchange that tranquillity and peace which for too long they had been denied. Sicani, Sicels and Greeks, who had formerly lived in discord [...] and almost always in enmity, under the new government came willy-nilly to form one whole'.[91] Statements such as these on the Romans were the outcome of searching reflection on their rule in Sicily and its deepest significance, for Caruso had no doubts about the degeneration of the slave wars and the depredations of governors like Verres.[92] Something of the sort had also occurred in the times of the hated Spanish domination, but it was with Rome that Sicily first achieved unity, and then under Augustus and the Antonines that it was able to enjoy centuries of peace and sound government.

This interpretation of Roman rule in the island was subscribed to by all the Sicilian intellectuals who took an interest in history and law in the eighteenth century. We can note in particular the radical version supplied by the jurist from Girgenti Vincenzo Gaglio, in 1776, in a study bearing the intriguing title: *Problema storico, critico, politico se la Sicilia fu più felice sotto il governo della repubblica romana o sotto i di lei imperatori?* (*Historical, critical and political problem: was Sicily happier under the government of the Roman republic or under Rome's emperors?*). In this text Gaglio takes a thoroughly dim view of the Republican period, when the island offered up its grain and in return was plundered by the governors. Drawing explicitly on Locke and Beccaria, he also stresses how the Sicilians' right to property, in terms of both their persons and their goods, was forever being abused under Verres.[93] With Augustus, on the other hand, conditions decidedly improved on the island: the right to property was guaranteed to all;[94] moreover, in order to revive the fortunes of Sicily after the war against Sextus Pompeius, the emperor rebuilt cities like Syracuse and set about founding numerous colonies. Gaglio also sees all the other emperors down to Diocletian, and in particular Hadrian, as friends to Sicily, working for the island's well-being: to the provinces in short, as the Scottish philosopher Hume held, the government of one proves more advantageous than the government of many – the government of a prince rather than of a republic.[95] For his part, Gaglio concludes his text with the observation that he is happy to live in his native Girgenti under a wise sovereign, namely the Bourbon Ferdinand III, son of Charles, resident in Naples.[96]

Conclusion

Up until the end of the eighteenth century, then, in their dealings with the central power Sicilian intellectuals and the ruling class – using also the Roman precedent – sought to obtain privileges and safeguard their rights, limiting external interference, according to the model which, *mutatis mutandis*, is splendidly exemplified by the ruling class and the sophists and rhetors of the Greek provinces in the Roman Empire.[97] Without going into a comparison between the two situations, here I can just recall that, in the first three centuries AD among the Greek aristocrats and intellectuals, nobody ever rejected the power of Rome, or believed that their world could be governed by anyone other than the *basileus* based in Rome.[98] In Sicily, through to the end of the eighteenth century, the ruling groups maintained the same type of unconditional acceptance of the Habsburg Empire of Spain or Austria, and rule from Turin or Naples, without rejecting the provincial condition of their homeland.

It is possible to detect a change of outlook in the *Viaggio in Grecia*, published in 1799 by Saverio Scrofani, an agronomist and economist hailing from Modica, who had spent periods in Florence, Paris and Venice and had travelled through Greece and the Levant.[99] He depicts Sicily as a Greek land *par excellence*, while the provincial experience under the Romans, which had been so important up until the 1770s, is not mentioned. Scrofani addresses his fellow islanders in these terms: 'Outsiders (foreigners) laugh at you, but they do not know you: they may be able to examine, measure and describe the works of the Greeks, but you are capable of imitating them. Remember that in the ancient rusticity you were the only ones who passed on to Europe the arts and sciences, and who knows, if you will not prove the only ones to preserve them from the impending barbarianism. Show yourselves worthy of your origins: the fire which has infused genius in the land of Empedocles, Gorgias, Archimedes and Theocritus has not yet been extinguished'.[100]

The passion for his homeland evinced in this passage developed in the years Scrofani spent far from Sicily, when his dealings with both Italian and foreign intellectuals helped him acquire a clear national physiognomy. At a time when Hellenism was undergoing a marked renaissance,[101] he could not have chosen better than his island's Greek past: rescued from oblivion above all by German scholars and poets, Winckelmann and Goethe *in primis*,[102] it took on not so much an aesthetic character as an ethical and political significance, becoming a patent of nobility *vis à vis* the rest of Europe and, even more, a patrimony of values which could stand the island in good stead during storm-tossed times.

After Scrofani the island's intellectuals came to value Sicilian Hellenism and the glorious history of its free cities, in a predominantly political vein. It became one of the most significant instruments for laying claim to forms of autonomy in a world in which, in the aftermath of the French Revolution and the Napoleonic period, not only the reality but also the notion of empire was undergoing profound changes, and the formation of national states was getting under way.

In this respect the appearance of the treatise *Sulle antiche e moderne tasse della Sicilia* had a certain significance. It was the work of the lawyer Giuseppe Emanuele Ortolani and was published in Palermo in 1813, the year Ferdinand III – then only King of Sicily, since the throne of Napoli was occupied by Murat – ratified the Constitution voted by the Sicilian Parliament in 1812. In the historical résumé with which he prefaces his treatise, Ortolani passes over the Romans altogether and talks about the 'epoca Grecosicula (Greco-Sicel epoch)', saying that 'Sicily could be justly proud' of it.[103] When he comes to the heart of his subject, he shows no compunction about denouncing Roman rule for reducing the province to a 'skeleton'.[104] Gone indeed are the times of Corsetto and Gaglio.

Following the unification of Naples and Sicily in a single kingdom in 1816, and above all after the harsh repression of the Sicilian uprisings in 1820,[105] the anti-Roman spirit of the Sicilian intellectuals was reinforced, taking on a barely dissimulated anti-Neapolitan significance. 1823 saw the appearance of Domenico Scinà's *Discorso intorno ad Archimede*. As well as extolling the originality of the mathematician's achievement, this treatise makes much of the readiness with which, overcoming deep-lying prejudice *vis à vis* the practical applications of science, Archimedes had placed his knowledge at the service of his birthplace, Syracuse, which in the years 213–211 BC was besieged by the Romans, and devoted himself to producing a whole range of engines of war.[106] With his status as a true symbol of Sicilian resistance to Roman violence, Archimedes became a fundamental figurehead for the local intellectuals who, after 1820 and under the leadership of Scinà, sought to affirm the autonomy of the cultural and political traditions of their homeland.[107]

Having turned its back on the provincial model which, up until the last decades of the eighteenth century, had oriented its dealings with the empires and kingdoms to which it was in practice subservient, Sicily entered the century which was to see the emergence of the modern nation state relying confidently on the tradition of its Greek cities. In a word, Sicily was looking for the autonomous space of its own that, in due course, in the face of many difficulties, it was to find within the Italian nation state.

Notes

1. Cic., *2Verr.* 2.2. All the excerpts from *Verrines* quoted in this chapter are given in the translation of L. H. G. Greenwood (Loeb Classical Library). Greek and Latin texts are referred to by the standard abbreviations as given in the *Oxford Latin Dictionary* and Liddell & Scott, *Greek-English Lexicon*.
2. On *De rebus siculis*, one of the most significant works of the Italian antiquarian historiography of the sixteenth century, see Salmeri (1998: 265, 270, 272).
3. See Momigliano (1984: 115–17); La Rosa (1987: 703–04); Ceserani (2000: 175–76).
4. La Rosa (1987: 704).
5. 'For over twenty-five centuries we've been beating the weight of superb and heterogeneous civilisations, all from outside, none made by ourselves, none that we could call our own' (trans. A. Colquhoun). See Said (2006: 91–114).
6. See note 3 above.
7. See section below on 'Sicily in the Spanish Empire: a comparison.'
8. On this matter in general see Forsén and Salmeri (2008: 4–7).
9. 'We have all in our early education read the Verronean [*sic*] orations. We read them not merely to instruct us, as they ought to do, in the principles of eloquence, to instruct us in the manners, customs and Laws of the ancient Romans, of which they are an abundant repository, but we read them for another motive for which the great Author published them, namely that he should leave to the world and the latest posterity a monument by which it should be shewn what course a great public Accuser in a great cause ought to follow, and as connected with it, what course Judges ought to pursue in such a cause. In these orations you see almost every instance of rapacity and peculation which we charge upon Mister Hastings. Undoubtedly too many Roman and English Governors have received corrupt gifts and bribes under various pretences [...]' (Speech in Reply, 16 June 1794): Burke (2000: 662–63). On the trial of Hastings, as a comparison for that of Verres (notes 55–59 below), see Holm (1898: 439–47). Ciccotti (1895: 224, 226) too, in discussing the trial of Verres and Cicero's orations, makes some allusions to the trial of Hastings.
10. Diod. Sic. 23. 1.
11. On the formation of Diodorus' historiographic perspective, see Corsaro (1998) and Corsaro (1999).
12. Gabba (1990: 58–61). See also Eckstein (1987: 73–101); Lazenby (1996: 43–48); Hoyos (1998: 33–93).

13. Eckstein (2008: 220–46). Gruen (1984: 86–131) discusses the requests from the Hellenistic states to Rome asking for the resolution of disputes and settlement of contesting claims.
14. Musti (1988: 537–42); Gabba (1990: 55–58).
15. See Eckstein (1980: 200) and (2006: 167).
16. Polyb. 1. 16. 5–9. In favour of a formal alliance between Hieron II and Rome (263 BC), see Gabba (1990: 61); Serrati (2000: 116). More plausibly Gruen (1984: 67) excludes that 'the two were now bound in alliance on the model of the Italian *foedera* [...]'. In this perspective see also Eckstein (1980: 184–92) and (1987: 115).
17. Polyb. 1. 62. 8, 3. 22. 4, 3. 24. 3. See Gruen (1984: 59–61).
18. Gabba (1990: 62–65); Lazenby (1996: 61–170).
19. On the Carthaginian presence in Sicily, see Hans (1983: 119–53); Huss (1985: 93–148, 156–66, 176–203, 207–15).
20. Crawford (1990: 96).
21. Cic., *2Verr.* 2. 2.
22. Carthaginian dominions on the island were given the names of *epikrateia* (especially Diod. Sic. 16. 82. 3 who refers to the treaty of 339/38 BC between Syracuse and Carthage) and *eparchia* (especially Polyb. 1. 15. 11 and 1. 17. 5), a term commonly used to designate the Roman provinces in Greek sources: see Hans (1985: 119). With respect to the organisation of the fiscal system of their first province, Pinzone (1999: 23–36) believes that from the outset (227 BC) the Romans adhered to the model of the so-called *lex Hieronica* (see note 25 below), but see Serrati (2000: 123–25).
23. Brennan (2000: 91–92); Gabba (1990: 65). On the possible forms of government of the province between 241 and 227 BC, see Crawford (1990: 92–94).
24. On Hieron II and his kingdom, see Berve (1959); De Sensi Sestito (1977); Lehmler (2005). Among the minor cities there were Akrai, Leontini and very probably also Tauromenium (Carbè, 1995).
25. Cic., *2 Verr.* 2. 32 and 3. 14–15. On the *lex Hieronica* and its application by the Romans, see Pinzone (1999: 1–23) (with ample bibliography), Genovese (1999) and, more recently, Andreau (2007); Bell (2007a); Bell (2007b); Dubouloz (2007). Mazza (1980–81: 300–04) – following Rostowzew (1910a, 233) – tends to maintain that the so-called *lex Hieronica* was based on the fiscal regulation of the Hellenistic kingdoms, in particular that of the Ptolemies. Whereas De Sensi Sestito (1977: 156–58) tends to credit Hieron II with a degree of originality.
26. Salmeri (2004: 261–62); Campagna (2004); Portale (2004).
27. Eckstein (1987: 135–55).
28. See Salmeri (2004: 262–63); Adams (2003: 545).
29. Prag (2007b: 69).
30. Salmeri (2004: 259–61, 267–71). See also Willi (2008: 17–18, 40–46).
31. On the characteristics of Sicilian Hellenism during the Republican period, see Salmeri (2004: 263–74).
32. Liv. 26. 40 and 27. 8. 13–19. See Mazza (1980–81: 313–17); Gabba (1986: 72–73); Gebbia (1999); Soraci (2003).
33. For an explanation of the presence of two quaestors in Sicily, see Pinzone (1999: 9–11).
34. Gabba (1986: 73); Salmeri (2004: 266).
35. Salmeri (2004: 274–77).
36. On the tendence of Rome to conserve the existing civic structures (fulfilling a basically administrative role) in the areas of the Greek world which came under its control, see Salmeri (1991a, 570–71).

37. See Pinzone (1999b and 2000). Pinzone (1999b: 468–470) is right to exclude from the hierarchy created by the Romans in Sicily the *civitates censoriae*, usually placed on a lower rung, and in any case never mentioned by Cicero in the *Verrines*. *Contra*, Genovese (1993) does not call their existence into doubt.

38. Cic., *2Verr.* 3. 13. Also Netum was a *civitas foederata* (Cic., *2Verr.* 5. 133), but subject to forms of contribution, at least at the time of the *Verrines*.

39. The five *civitates* were the *Centuripina, Halaesina, Segestana, Halicyensis, Panhormitana* (Cic., *2Verr.* 3. 13).

40. Ibid.

41. Gabba (1986: 73).

42. See note 22 above.

43. See note 25 above.

44. Before his mission in Sicily Laevinus had held command in Macedonia from 214 to 211 BC and, subsequently, he was to be sent by the Roman state to Pergamum in 205 BC, see Salmeri (2004: 265–66).

45. See Cic., *2Verr.* 2. 5 ('Itaque ille M. Cato Sapiens cellam penariam rei publicae nostrae, nutricem plebis Romanae Siciliam nominabat (Cato Sapiens called her in consequence "the state's storehouse, the nurse at whose breast the Roman people is fed")'); 3. 11.

46. Gabba (1986: 74).

47. Salmeri (2005: 196).

48. Salmeri (1986: 399–400).

49. Diod. Sic. 34–35. 2. 1 e 2. 27 [*FGrH* 87 F 108 (Posid.)], see Coarelli (1981: 10). For a list of the *equites* present in Sicily in the Republican period, see Fraschetti (1981: 66–71).

50. See Urbainczyk (2008: 10–14, 20–21, 38–46, 54–60).

51. Gabba (1986: 75–76); Salmeri (1986: 401); Salmeri (2004: 271–72).

52. See Wilson (2000) who refers to 'much of Sicily flourishing at the time of Verres' governorship' (p. 160). See also Perkins (2007: 33–34) On Verres as *propraetor*, see Prag (2007c: 305).

53. On the *Verrines*, see recently, Prag (2007a); Dubouloz and Pittia (2007); Lintott (2008: 81–100) For Verres as prototype of the 'bad' administrator, see note 9 above.

54. Court established to secure compensation for the illegal acquisition of money or property by Roman officers serving abroad.

55. See Lintott (2008: 81–100).

56. Cic., *2Verr.* 2. 8 and 155.

57. Cic., *Diu. Caec.* 27, 63. One should not forget that Cicero had been *quaestor* in Sicily in 75 BC, see Prag (2007c: 304–05).

58. Lintott (2008: 87).

59. Ibid.: 94.

60. Salmeri (1986: 402 and n. 28).

61. Gabba (1986: 78). Nonetheless even during the Imperial age Sicily never stopped producing and sending grain to Rome, see Salmeri (1986: 410–12); Pinzone (1999: 188–90).

62. Rostowzew (1910b: 152–53). While this was long the *communis opinio*, see Pinzone (1999: 173–206) who dates the introduction of a form of *stipendium* in Sicily to the first year (57/56 BC) of the *cura annonae* of Cn. Pompeius, lasting five years. Brunt (1981: 162) expresses doubts on the stipendiary condition of Sicily in the Imperial age.

63. Salmeri (1986: 402).
64. Hardt and Negri (2000: 344–48).
65. Ibid.: 339–344.
66. See note 45 above.
67. See note 50 above.
68. See notes 28, 31 and 36 above.
69. On Cicero's 'construction' of the image of Verres and the Sicilians, and more generally the rhetorical dimension of the *Verrines*, see recently Tempest (2007); Steel (2007). See also Vasaly (1993); Steel (2001).
70. Cic., *2Verr.* 2. 2.
71. Ibid. 2. 3.
72. See note 1 above.
73. Cic., *2Verr.* 2. 5.
74. Ibid. 2. 7.
75. On *suburbanitas Siciliae*, see Sartori (1983).
76. Cic., *2Verr.* 3. 12.
77. See notes 42–43 above.
78. See Gebbia (1999).
79. Cic., *2Verr.* 3. 11.
80. This topic is extensively discussed in Salmeri (1991b). See also Gallo (2006).
81. Pagden (1998).
82. The text of the *Instrucción* can be found in Sciuti Russi (1984: 57–113). On Corsetto and his activity, see Sciuti Russi (1984: xliii–lxxxiv).
83. *Instrucción*, in Sciuti Russi (1984: 67–69).
84. Ibid.: 69–70. The citations of Cicero are from *2Verr.* 2. 2–3.
85. *Instrucción*, in Sciuti Russi (1984: 70). On Roman acceptance of local norms and customs in Sicily and more generally in the provinces of the Greek world, see section on 'The Roman Province' above.
86. On Cutelli, see Giarrizzo (1989: 290–96); Sciuti Russi (1994).
87. Sciuti Russi (1994: 19–28).
88. Cutelli (1636: 154–55).
89. For the citation, see Salmeri (1991b: 279).
90. See Condorelli (1982: 81–95); Giarrizzo (1989: 385–92).
91. Caruso (1875: 458).
92. See Caruso (1875: 500–08).
93. Gaglio (1776: 54–55).
94. Ibid.: 107.
95. Ibid.: 250–52. On Gaglio's reading of Hume, see Giarrizzo (1989: 465).
96. Gaglio (1776: 272).
97. This model is already clearly formulated in Salmeri (1982), above all in opposition to scholars (e.g. Gabba, 1959; Bowersock, 1969; Jones, 1978) who present the Greek intellectuals and ruling class in an excessively subordinate position, in political terms, *vis à vis* the Roman Empire. Thereafter, see especially Swain (1996) and Veyne (2005).
98. Salmeri (1982: 112–13).
99. See Zapperi (1962); Giarrizzo (1970); Diaz (1989: 54–61).
100. Scrofani (1988: 199).
101. Tsigakou (1981); Constantine (1984); Marchand (1996); Clogg (2003); Hamilakis (2007: 57–123).
102. Salmeri (1991b: 275–77); Cometa (1999); Salmeri (2001).

103. Ortolani (1813: 6). In using the phrase 'epoca Grecosicula' (Greco-Sicel epoch), above all in the early decades of the nineteenth century, Sicilian scholars and historians referred to the Greek presence in the island up to the third century BC. The term 'Sicel' distinguished this reality from all the other Greek experiences throughout the Mediterranean, presenting it as benefiting from the contribution of the local peoples.
104. Ortolani (1813: 15).
105. See Romeo (1973: 161–70).
106. See Scinà (1823: 56, 70–71, 97, 115–16).
107. Salmeri (1992: 51–52).

Part III
Comparative Histories

10

Lord of All the World – The State, Heterogeneous Power and Hegemony in the Roman and Mughal Empires

Peter Fibiger Bang

> When I became emperor it occurred to me that I should change my name lest it be confused with the Caesars of Rum. An inspiration from the beyond suggested to me that the labor of emperors is world domination (jahangiri), so I named myself Jahangir and made my honorific Nuruddin [light of religion] because my accession occurred … at a time when the world was being illuminated.
>
> Jahangir, Mughal emperor[1]

Behind these observations was the ruler of the Mughal Empire between 1605 and 1627, Jahangir. The quotation is taken from his memoirs penned during the period of his reign and explains how he adopted the name under which he is known to history. The style is terse, the contents unexpected and pregnant with questions. In Jahangir's reflections on 'World Rule' and providentially ordained government we see the confluence of three traditions of statecraft normally thought of as separate: Mughal, Ottoman and Roman imperialism. Within the space of a few lines, the problem of the character of universal empire appears as a question of similarities between Rome and the so-called Oriental despotisms of the Mughals and Ottomans. The emperor of Hindustan is found actively seeking to distinguish himself from a league of 'Caesars'. The said 'Caesars of Rum', of course, were not the original Roman, but the Ottoman sultans, two of which had in previous generations held the name Selim, just as Jahangir had been named Salim at birth. 'Caesar', in turn, had been added by the Ottomans to their titles after the conquest by Mehmed II in 1453 of Constantinople, the old, and by then dilapidated, capital of the Roman Empire. As *Kaiser-i-Rum* Mehmed immediately moved his seat of government to his new won city and began restoring it to its former glory as the centre of a far-flung Mediterranean empire. Only from this time-honoured position, the meeting place of two continents, could the Ottomans hope to follow in the footsteps of the Romans and convincingly aspire to a universal dominion, as we read in the account of Kritovoulos, a contemporary Greek to join Ottoman service.[2]

Latin Christianity, however, was less convinced by the Ottoman claim to have won the Roman succession than horrified by the Muslim conquest of the old Christian metropolis of Constantine. Calls for a crusade to drive out the Ottoman infidel were repeatedly sounded. Pope Pius II, also known as the humanist scholar Aeneas Silvius Piccolomini, made it a key concern of his pontificate to organise a campaign to recapture Constantinople from Islam: 'He died in 1464 on his way to Ancona, to bid God-speed to a crusade that never assembled'. In Russia, the state and church used the fall of Constantinople as a pretext for proclaiming the transfer of the Roman imperial and patriarchal succession to Moscow.[3] Either way, the heritage of Rome was claimed to belong properly within Christendom. This view has continued almost unchallenged to our times. Rome has normally been taken to belong to the West whereas Muslim empires have been firmly located in the Orient. They have been understood as worlds apart in a very fundamental sense, even though the Ottomans occupied a large part of the previously Roman Mediterranean world.[4]

It is, in fact, quite remarkable that, a few notable exceptions apart (e.g. Chapter 12 in this book), there has hardly been any sustained attempts to compare the world of Rome with that of the great pre-industrial Muslim empires.[5] Rome has no real parallel in later pre-industrial European history. At its height, the writ of the Roman Caesar ran from Scotland to the Euphrates. The Roman experience surpassed anything known to later European rulers and only finds suitable comparisons in pre-industrial empires equally based on the conquest and taxation of wide agrarian territories of similar dimensions such as the Muslim polities of the Middle East and India and the various Chinese dynasties.[6] Nonetheless, the idea of world rule has until recently been treated as something peculiar to Oriental societies and foreign to the core of Roman culture.[7] It was traditionally understood as an expression of the form of government, Oriental despotism so-called.[8]

With roots in hostile Hellenic accounts of the Persian Great King, the theory of Oriental despotism has had a surprisingly long run for its money in modern historiography, since it was first given systematic shape by Montesquieu. The blatant hyperbole of imperial claims to universal hegemony was seen as an expression of brutal despots who enjoyed absolute power and kept their wretched subjects in an iron grip of fear, plunder and oppression.[9]

Yet, this understanding of universal empire militates against common sense. As Voltaire wryly remarked about the Great Mughals: 'It is difficult to understand how sovereigns who could not prevent their own children from levying armies against them, should be so absolute as some would like to make us believe.'[10] What frequently strikes the modern observer is precisely the weaknesses of these allegedly omnipotent monarchs who in governing extensive dominions, and claiming hegemony over even more, liked to pose as rulers of the world. In practise, they lacked the absolute power ascribed to them by legend completely to overwrite and dominate established social relations. Government was more often than not thinly spread on the ground. To function, these empires had to negotiate, compromise and strike alliances with established elites and tolerate the continuation of established customs. Vast agrarian empires both seem weak and strong at the same time. The basic problem for comparative history, in short, is how to reconcile the hyperbole of the claim to universal rule with a notion of power as layered and shaped by historical compromise (see also Chapter 4 in this book).[11] After all, the Ottomans aspiring to the leading position within the Islamic world, still bothered to assert the venerable Christian title of the now defunct Caesars. By the turn of the seventeenth century, the world of agrarian empires was an old one; it was the product of very many centuries of state formation; and governmental power was constituted by multiple, historically deposited, layers of imperial statecraft.

This chapter explores the character of universal lordship through comparison of examples from the Roman and Mughal empires. The following section offers a basic world history framework for comparison of agrarian universal empires. Next the argument moves on to examine in detail the character of the notion of world rule as embodied by the Roman and Mughal emperor. The claim to universal hegemony enabled expansionist imperial powers to comprise and manage very diverse territories and, in terms of political organisation, composite and heterogeneous realms. Most modern theories of the state, however, are predicated on a unitary conception of statehood stressing sovereignty, homogenised bureaucratic rule and national unity. The last section of this paper points out that this notion of the state was in fact coined in express rejection of universal empire. When dealing with such empires, we therefore have to seek behind these modern notions. Unitary states, historians have become increasingly aware, are a relatively recent phenomenon. Students of early modern Europe now speak instead of the composite or conglomerate state. Yet compared to these, the situation of Mughal and Roman government was different. Their vast territories afforded them with sufficient resources to build up strong centralised capacities without having to tolerate and foster the consolidation of strong provincial autonomous bodies, nor the need to impose tight controls across very diverse provincial societies; in the day-to-day affairs these were left to govern themselves. Universal empires, like the Mughal and Roman, combined the creation of strong central institutions with the continued existence of a very indirect form of rule.

Agrarian empire, global history and Middle Eastern state formation

Comparative studies are frequently met with the objection that every cultural tradition is unique. That is, of course, undeniable; but only in a limited sense.

Cultures, as they come to expression in language and products of art, obviously develop individual idioms. No one could mistake the Persian literature and monumental architecture of the Mughal Empire for the comparable creations of the Roman world. But that is not all there is to it. Societies are not solely determined by their particular philologies and their cultures have not usually developed in isolation. Technologies, ideas and forms of organisation have been borrowed and emulated endlessly through history. Sometimes processes of cultural diffusion took place as direct transfers. These can occasionally be studied with great precision such as for instance the reception of Platonic and Aristotelian philosophy in the Arab world. But cultural transfer and adaptation always involves a creative process, even when restricted by fixed texts. It is, therefore, a process which historically has involved much more than exact copying. Cultural similarities are not necessarily the products of peaceful imports and direct transfers. The three C's, competition, confrontation and conquest have been strong forces in spawning emulation and creating a broad convergence of institutions between societies with diverging religious, literary and linguistic conventions.[12] The tradition of statecraft which began to develop in the Middle East during the Bronze Ages and gradually expanded to take in more and more areas, is precisely an example of such a process of broad emulation.[13] Military confrontation, conquests, repeatedly followed by liberation and reconquests explain why similarities in institutions of government which can be observed between societies widely distant in time and place, should not be dismissed as merely superficial and unimportant.

The process of state-formation originating in the Middle East regularly culminated in the creation of large agrarian or, as it was called in the introduction to this book, tributary empires based primarily on the taxation of vast peasant populations.[14] For reasons of convenience, we may roughly distinguish two phases. The ancient moved into a higher gear with the formation of the Assyrian Empire, then Achaemenid Persia followed by Alexander's conquests. It culminated in the emergence of Mediterranean Empire under the Romans, a Middle Eastern under the Parthian and later Sassanid dynasty and the more hazy and shifting Indian/Central Asian polities of the Mauryan Empire, the Greco-Bachtrian Kingdom and the Kushan Empire. The second phase took its beginning in the seventh century when Islam emerged as the dominant force in the Mediterranean and Middle East and for a while united these two parts of the old world under the Umayyad and 'Abbāsid Caliphs. Several Muslim imperial polities followed before the whole thing culminated, after an infusion of Mongol statecraft, in the sixteenth and seventeenth centuries with the Ottoman, Safavid and Mughal empires spanning the old world from the Balkans to the Indian subcontinent.[15] Similar processes spawned the development of a parallel imperial tradition in China with the formation of the Qin/Han Empire (see Chapter 11). The Chinese tradition of statecraft, though, was never completely independent of the rest of the old world. Conquests into the Tarim Basin, the influence of Buddhism and repeated confrontation with the nomads of Central Asia, among other things, ensured a degree of contact. The Mongols and their heritage, for example in the Qing dynasty, created a broad convergence between the 'Celestial Empire' and the Muslim dominions.[16]

Universal empire

The notion of universal rule was one of the currencies of power which served this world of agrarian empires in one form or other and helped shape the style and institutions of government. It was a strategy of power that geared the state to expansion and absorption of conquered foes. This came to expression in the idea of the imperial ruler as not merely a king, but *the* king of kings.[17] The title dated far back in the Middle East and was adopted by the Achaemenid monarch as he subjected most of the ancient world to his overlordship. He presented himself as universal ruler and through various linguistic mutations the title of Shahanshah, the king of kings, survived as a standard ingredient in Persian traditions of kingship down through the centuries.

As Babur, of Turkish and Persian cultural outlook, descended upon India from Afghanistan to lay the foundations of the Mughal Empire in the early sixteenth century, the new Perso-Indian dynasty also styled and conducted themselves in the manner of a Shahanshah. We have already encountered how Mughal rulers toyed with the idea of world rule or domination.[18] They paraded themselves as the descendants of the world-conquering Tamerlane.[19] They were Timurids and took pride in the great variety of peoples that flocked to their throne in respectful submission, paid homage and brought precious rarities as gifts from all the over the world. Muslim nobles, Hindu princelings, sages and saints, Jesuit missionaries from Portugal, Dutch and British trader ambassadors, all formed part of the gaudy spectacle that was the Mughal court.[20] The Timurid emperors were keen not to be taken as the inferior of anyone. They rivalled the Ottomans for the position of pre-eminence within Muslim civilisation. As the Ottoman Sultan claimed the title of Khalifa, the universal leader of Islam, so did the Mughals. To bolster this claim, they took care, at least in some periods, to organise the annual Hadj, the pilgrimage, from India and sent lavish gifts to adorn and enrich the holy places.[21] Diplomatic relations with their Ottoman rivals, on the other hand, never achieved stability and permanence. Each ruler found it difficult openly to recognise the equality of the other dynasty. The Mughals, for instance, pointed out that the Ottoman sultans had received their realm in vassalage at the hands of Tamerlane or Timur after they had been overcome in battle. Diplomatic correspondence reveals the ruling houses trading carefully modulated insults. For example, Mughal monarchs would style themselves as Khalifa while deliberately omitting the same title when addressing their Ottoman peers in more mundane terms merely as 'possessor of the empire of Alexander', 'Caesars of Rum' or 'Glory of the Caesars'.[22]

The diplomatic history of the Roman Empire contains a strikingly similar episode. With the establishment of imperial monarchy by Augustus, the only power left to rival the might of Rome was the Parthian empire. Clashing over the right to appoint the king of Armenia at the beginning of our era, Augustus is reported to have sent the Parthian ruler, Phrataces, a letter 'without the appellation of king', even ordering the opponent to lay down his royal title. The Roman ruler claimed superior authority. Following the pattern already familiar from Mughal-Ottoman diplomatic correspondence, Augustus received an insulting letter back styling him merely as 'Caesar', his family name, while Phrataces spoke of himself as the 'king of kings'.[23]

Effectively, in other words, Augustus contended with the Perso-Parthian monarch for the position as the true 'king of kings' of the ancient world. Nonetheless, Greco-Roman political discourse was avidly opposed to the Persian tradition of kingship. Greco-Roman civilisation had developed on the fringes of the Middle Eastern tradition. Here, the Persian 'Shahanshah' became a very controversial and much hated figure. Immortalised in the pages of Herodotus, the victory achieved by a coalition of Greek city-states over a series of invading Persian armies in the early fifth century BC was to be a formative experience in the creation of Hellenic culture. The Persian Shahanshah, or Great King as the Greeks usually called him, was vilified as the quintessential tyrant and archetypal enemy of Hellenic liberty and culture.[24] The Romans, by tradition averse to anything royal, took over this image of their archenemy on the eastern fringes of the empire. Accusing a Roman ruler of behaving in Persian fashion remained a term of abuse throughout antiquity.[25]

Augustus, however, could draw on other more acceptable models. Alexander the Great, the conquering hero of Hellenism was a more suitable, if not entirely flawless, ideal.[26] Having defeated the Persian Great King, Alexander went on to expand the Achaemenid world empire, surpassed anyone who had gone before him and became a Greco-Roman version of the 'king of kings'. He was truly a fit standard on which to measure greatness, a worthy role model to rival. The Roman conquerors took Alexander to their hearts as they rose to dominate the Mediterranean world. It is no coincidence that most of our written sources for the life of Alexander date to the Roman period. Pompey, the Roman conqueror of the East, late-republican magnate and proto-emperor, even adopted the cognomen 'Magnus' and invited comparisons with the Macedonian adventurer.[27] An anecdote, true or false, later circulated of Caesar that in his early 30s he had wept at the sight of a statue of Alexander during a visit to the temple of Hercules at Gades. By that age Alexander had won himself the world, whereas Caesar had as yet achieved little of note.[28] When Augustus had finally defeated his rival Antony and in the same move conquered the Egypt of Cleopatra, he made sure to visit the grave of Alexander during his stay in the royal capital wearing the name of the Macedonian conqueror. However, when asked whether he would also care to see the graves of the Ptolemies, Augustus is reported scornfully to have rejected the proposal. He had 'come to see a king, not a row of corpses'.[29] The Roman Imperator was a world ruler, not a mere king.

The title of king, however, let alone king of kings, was to remain controversial in Roman state ideology. It had become a firmly established symbol of tyranny and oppression of the aristocracy. Princeps, therefore, meaning first among equals, became the Roman term used to denote the position of the sole ruler. The title, however, was never included in the formal enumeration of the emperor's offices and honours. In constitutional terms, princeps was an informal, but nonetheless well-established, expression.[30] It was intended by the emperor to signal respect and will to peaceful coexistence with his aristocratic peers; he was still one of them. But these were matters of court etiquette and misled no one. The Roman Princeps was more than a mere human. He wore the name Augustus to invest his person with a sacred, elevated and solemn authority. The Princeps was a Shahanshah in all but name.[31] On festive occasions versatile poets might even exuberantly flirt with this idea: 'Greatest of censors and princeps of principes'.[32] The Roman emperor already exceeded everyone else and did not need to further bolster his authority with the name of king, as Suetonius in his biography make the courtiers remind Caligula horrified at the emperor's alleged thoughts of changing the principate into an openly declared monarchy.[33] The image that encounters the reader from the idealised account of Augustus' life and reign which was publicised on bronze tablets in front of his Mausoleum, is nothing so much as that of a universal monarch. This was also how the account was presented to the provincial elites of Asia: 'The accomplishments of the divine Augustus by which he subjected the whole world to the rule of the Roman people'.[34] The account then goes on to list the great conquests and military victories of the deceased monarch. Like Alexander, Augustus is depicted as receiving numerous embassies from near and far, bringing peoples hitherto barely known to the Romans within the orbit of their power. Even the Parthians are portrayed as accepting submission and receiving their kings from the hands of Augustus; and Alexander's exploits are matched by the reception of Indian embassies, actually from Ceylon to be more precise.[35]

It is, in other words, a mistake, though it has often been made, to consider the basic idea of the Principate as fundamentally incompatible with the idea of a universal emperor. Rather, it was an expression of a problem which universal emperors had in common. These rulers were patrimonial lords. They were the leaders of an aristocratic society and had to use their own means and vast extended household to provide the basis for developing a state-administration (see also Chapter 13).[36] A prominent feature of Augustus's account of his exploits is the, to some extent inflated, claim to have complemented the income from imperial taxes with his own means to finance governmental activities.[37] From an aristocratic point of view, it was paramount not to be excluded from participating in government activities. Access to these was crucial for the preservation of privilege and expansion of wealth. Emperors, and kings for that matter, were therefore generally confronted with a strong demand not to withdraw, either from society in general or from aristocratic circles in particular. The emperor should remain accessible, avail himself of the council and services of the 'best men' and not withdraw to the dark corridors of his palace and leave the government in the hands of his slaves, eunuchs and other personal dependants.[38] Government of the empire had to remain open, if you like, for the exercise of influence and the distribution of favours. The Roman historian Tacitus, as always with a sharp eye for the workings of power, put the matter straight. In his account of Tiberius' administration of justice, he censured the emperor for refusing to bend the rules in favour of the high and mighty: 'As a result of his presence, many verdicts were recorded in defiance of intrigue and of the solicitations of the great. Thus, while equity gained, liberty suffered'.[39]

The title of princeps was a token of the emperor's intention of respecting aristocratic privilege and political rights. As Augustus famously declared, he only surpassed his peers in 'authority', not legal powers when he took on Republican magistracies.[40] It was a declaration that imperial government was not exercised for the monarch's personal benefit and that the aristocracy was invited to share in his rule. Symbolically this also came to expression in grand gestures such as declaring the palace a 'public house'.[41] The emperor was accessible to everyone. That most famous of all Roman monuments, the Colosseum, was also in some sense a result of this ideology. Opened in AD 80, it was part of the propaganda to consolidate the new Flavian dynasty after the Julio-Claudians. The fallen emperor Nero had been constructing in Rome a vast palace, a 'golden house'. This was now cancelled. Rome was not to be converted into the dwelling of only one man, it was said. Instead, the lake of the great palatial park was chosen as a site for constructing a huge monument where the emperors could entertain the population of the capital and allow the Romans to share in the bounty of empire.[42]

The theme of accessibility features no less prominently in Mughal statecraft, though the symbolic articulation is slightly different. Listen to Sir Thomas Roe, the English ambassador to the Mughal court in 1616: 'I went to court at four in the evening to the durbar, which is the place wher the Mogull sitts out daylie to entertayne strangers, to receive petitions and presents, to give commands, to see and to bee seene'.[43] Visibility and accessibility were central to the Mughals' exercise of power. The day of business was structured around a series of appearances and audiences.[44] In the morning the emperor would appear in the Jaroka window of his palace to be seen by his subjects assembling outside the ramparts. Later in the day would follow a number of durbars or audiences, the first of which we heard Roe describe. This was where the Mughal would meet with the great nobles in his service and be open for petitioners approaching his throne from far-flung places. The accessibility of the emperor was given symbolic and ritual expression in palatial architecture. In the Red Fort of Delhi, the Hall of Public Audience was constructed in a way to make the emperor face towards the centre of the city while sitting on his throne receiving petitioners.[45] Likewise, Jahangir recalls how he ordered a chain to be hung from his palace in Agra with golden bells attached to it. Had anyone failed to receive justice, he could in theory ring the bells to call the attention of the emperor to his problem. The imperial throne was to be a place of refuge, an anchor of justice and the moral order of society. Here the lamb could lie down safely beside the lion.[46] The idea of the emperor as offering his subjects a kind of asylum is also known from Roman history where the statues of the emperors were generally recognised as places of sanctuary.[47]

Imperial accessibility meant more than sharing power with just one aristocratic group. As Chris Bayly has recently insisted, the universal aspirations of emperors also necessitated embracing, from a position of aloofness, a diversity of cultural traditions; the justice of the emperor was for all his loyal and deserving subjects. The Great Mughal could not simply make do with appealing to the group of Muslim nobles who had provided the basis of the original conquest. His empire comprised a patchwork of different ethnic and religious communities, including different varieties of Islam and a majority population showing allegiance to one or more of the many cults contained within the broad framework of Hinduism. The emperor needed, to a greater or lesser extent, to practice government in an ecumenical and syncretistic spirit.[48] Some of the Timurids took great care to seek council from the representatives of the many different beliefs and religions existing within their realm, including Hindu pundits, Jain gurus and Portuguese Jesuit missionaries. The court also sponsored various Hindu ceremonies, temples and festivals. The Great Mughal was not only the head of the *umma*, he also acted as a patron of other ethnic and religious communities – sometimes with greater success than at other times. The attempts of the Great Mughals to appoint the leaders of the Sikh religious sect met with only limited success. The Hindu warrior aristocracy, the Rajputs, on the other hand, seem to have appropriated their Muslim overlord within their own religious and cultural traditions. In Rajput poetry we encounter the Great Mughal, Akbar, as an incarnation of their Hindu warrior hero and god Ram. The Jain sect also claimed and sported the support and patronage of the Mughal emperors.[49] The position of the emperor was a complex and heterogeneous construct.

Universal imperial power, in other words, was composite. There was a constant pressure on and need for the emperors to pay respect to the different traditions of culture and privilege within their far-flung territories. When Alexander began to adapt his monarchy to the Persian traditions prevalent in most of his newly won territories, the Roman senator and historian Arrian explains, it bred dissatisfaction among his Macedonian nobles. They had no intention of beginning to pay homage to their king after the Persian fashion:

> Will ... you put this dishonour on the Macedonians, or will you yourself make a distinction once for all in this matter of honours and receive from Greeks and Macedonians honours of a human and Greek style, and barbarian honours only from Barbarians? But if it is said of Cyrus, son of Cambyses, that he was the first of men to receive obeisance and that therefore this humiliation became traditional with the Persians and Medes, you must remember that this very Cyrus was brought to his senses by Scythians, Darius too by other Scythians, Xerxes by Athenians and Lacedaemonians.[50]

An insensitive drive towards uniformity would rarely have been tolerated; it would only have served to breed discontent, cause resistance and, in the last instance, provoke rebellion.

Emperors had little choice but to follow along and handle different groups in different ways. Just as Mughal rulers had to broaden their appeal and patronage to include aristocratic groups outside their original fold, so did the Roman emperors. The Caesar was a Princeps to the senatorial aristocracy. But the governmental institutions carried over from the Roman Republic were not designed to serve the empire at large, only the Roman city-state, and did not really provide for the provinces. The Greek provincial aristocracy, entrenched in most of the eastern Mediterranean, seems to have cared little for the niceties of the Roman republican constitution. Instead, they treated the emperor simply as a king and appropriated him within their own cultural traditions.[51] In their view, the Roman emperor was to keep the world in its proper order. That meant strengthening the position of the Hellenic land-owning aristocracy and preserving its traditions with a minimum of interference. The Philhellenic policies of Nero, for instance, found an ambiguous reception among the Greek élites. Rearranging the calendar of the great religious festivals in order for the emperor to participate in the various sport, musical and theatrical contests during a tour of Greece did not constitute good government in their eyes. Quite the reverse, the emperor had forgotten the dignity of his office while only creating confusion in the Greek world. A good emperor should know how to respect the different roles which had to be filled by him as monarch and them as his loyal Greek aristocracy.[52]

Most Roman emperors were more discerning than Nero and attempted with greater success to sponsor and appeal to various provincial cultural and religious traditions. Hadrian even created a Panhellenic league, centred on his newly erected complex of temples to the Olympian Zeus in Athens, which was intended to strengthen connections between the top echelons of the Greek-speaking élites of the Aegean world.[53] In Egypt, where Augustus, at the time of conquest, had become king while simultaneously only a magistrate at Rome, as Ronald Syme observed, the powerful groups of priests were curtailed.[54] But the new rulers continued to sponsor the temples. Many of the vast temple complexes in unmistakably Egyptian style still visible, such as Dendera and Kom Ombo, were to a large extent constructed during the reign of the emperors. Almost every Caesar until the time of Constantine is attested in hieroglyphic inscriptions wearing the time-honoured title of Pharaoh and many are still found depicted in Egyptian-style reliefs.[55] The Jewish elites also appealed for imperial protection and expansion of their rights and privileges. The successors of Augustus, according to Philo, a Jewish member of the Alexandrian upper classes, should follow the example set by the first emperor 'in confirming the native customs of each particular nation no less than of the Romans'.[56] Emperors responded by sponsoring the cult in the temple of Jerusalem where daily sacrifices were performed in their name until the fateful rebellion which ended in the sack of the city and the destruction of the sanctuary by Titus in AD 70. The position of the Roman emperors was as composite an amalgam as later that of the Mughals.

A letter from the emperor Claudius to the Alexandrians, published by the Roman prefect of the province of Egypt, brings out the complex and heterogeneous reality of universal imperial power with particularly clarity: 'Lucius Aemilius Rectus declares: Since at the reading of the most holy and the most beneficent letter to our city, the whole city could not be present because of its large population, I thought it necessary to publish the letter in order that, man for man, as you read it, the greatness of our god Caesar might be an object of wonder to you…'.[57] The letter from the 'god Caesar' was a reply to a request to grant him a wide variety of honours in Alexandria. Most of these Claudius accepted, 'but a priest for me and erection of temples I reject, not wishing to be offensive to the men of my time and judging that temples and such things should be reserved and granted by every age to the gods alone'. To accommodate republican tradition in Rome the emperor declines the establishment of a cult to him in Alexandria, yet the supreme imperial authority in the province responds to local sentiment by calling Claudius a god. Universal hegemony presents a heterogeneous form of state.[58] Though claiming world hegemony, universal empires did not require a uniform, generalised form of power; they gloried in diversity (cf. Chapter 1, pp. 2–3). Listen to Eusebius on Constantine:

> There were constant diplomatic visitors who brought valuable gifts from their homelands, so that when we ourselves happened to be present we saw before the outer palace gates waiting in a line remarkable figures of barbarians,

with their exotic dress, their distinctive appearance, the quite singular cut of hair and beard; the appearance of their hairy faces was foreign and astonishing...For men of Blemyan race, and Indian and Ethiopian...could be seen...Each of these in their turn...brought their particular treasures to the Emperor, some of them golden crowns, some diadems of precious stones, others fair-haired children, others foreign cloths woven with gold and bright colours, others horses, others shields and long spears and javelins and bows, showing that they were offering service and alliance with these things to the Emperor when he required it.[59]

Irregular power and state segmentation

To handle all this diversity, the emperor was often thought of in bodily and familial terms. He might be likened to a head with the empire constituting the body and limbs. Each individual part could then be seen as performing the particular function in the imperial body politic for which it was suited. Another image was that of the shepherd and his flock; and the father and his children. Common to these images was the notion of the emperor as enjoying some kind of mystic union or affinity with his subject peoples. Modern political theory, on the other hand, developed in express opposition to this conception of authority during the sixteenth to eighteenth centuries. Locke, for instance, dismissed the patriarchal notion of the ruler as a 'strange kind of domineering Phantom', and prior to that Grotius had rejected the whole idea of universal empire as contrary to reason, it was a 'stultus titulus'.[60] It is probably not entirely by coincidence that one of the most glowing defences of universal empire to appear in the seventeenth century was written by the mystic visionary, the Dominican friar Tommaso Campanella. In the *De Monarchia Hispanica* he called on the Spanish king to unite Christendom in a new world empire. The programme reveals a highly developed sensibility towards the delicate dilemmas of imperial rule; it combines an understanding of the need to foster imperial unity through a programme of gentle and patient hispanisation with an insistence that the monarch restrain himself and adjust his laws to fit local traditions. 'It is necessary that law should conform to custom', he advised.[61]

Most Roman and Mughal historians will recognise the image of a polity where the gradual promotion of an élite high culture is balanced by the continued need to show respect for provincial and local diversity.[62] Yet, in the recent most full-length study of Campanella, this is precisely what caused the author to object: 'Campanella's treatment of laws proves disappointing. Given his pronounced commitment to hispanisation, one is surprised to discover an apparent missed opportunity to achieve greater coherence and equivalence among the parts'.[63] The disappointment of Campanella's commentator here is a symptom of expectations generated by modern notions of the state and authority. These were shaped around a vigorous programme of harmonisation of local particularism and strong unification. A proper state is a unitary polity defined by key concepts such as sovereignty, monopoly of violence and nationalism. The doctrine of sovereignty, as developed by Bodin and Hobbes to prevent internal dissension and conflict within their respective kingdoms in the future, dictated the indivisibility of political authority. The state had to transform itself into an awe-inspiring Leviathan, a great leveller which would destroy all other competing loci of power in society.[64]

With their far-flung territories, great ethnic variety and composite structure of power, universal empires are difficult to fit into the mould of the unitary state. Sovereignty was often layered, most notably, but not solely through the inclusion of client-kingdoms; an effective monopoly of violence was impractical given the huge distances involved and the small size of the governmental apparatus, dreams of national unity, not even thinkable. In a sense, universal imperial power defies modern concepts of the state. This was, by the way, obvious from the very beginning. Bodin spent considerable time on an inconclusive analysis of the Roman principate. Where was sovereignty located in constitutional terms?[65] Legal historians, steeped in the modern paradigm of the state, have been occupied by this problem for centuries and have produced an enormous body of literature without reaching a firm conclusion. Among the proponents of the new 'political science', it was the German lawyer and historian Pufendorf (1632–94) who best realised the implications of the new conception of statehood. He insisted that not all states could be reduced to the principles of the new political doctrine, these had something irregular about them. The notion of a universal Roman empire was one such irregular body, 'irregulare aliquod corpus, & monstro simile'.[66]

However, to Pufendorf irregular states represented a residual category; they never really attracted much attention in the development of modern political science. Everything was set towards greater uniformity. This means that historians of great pre-industrial polities have, to some extent, been faced by a dearth of models, and study has focused on the central, official structures of the imperial states.[67] But during the last decades interest in irregularities have been gaining ground. Historians are now increasingly aware that homogenous states, even if never perfect, were only a relatively late development. In early modern European history, the 'composite' or 'conglomerate' state has moved high up on the agenda.[68] But, for the student of universal empires, the European composite state carries certain limitations as a model. It had developed as much as a result of dynastic alliances as of conquest.

The empire of Habsburg Charles V (1500–58) provides the most suitable illustration.[69] As the culmination of a number of fortunate marriage alliances, the crowns of Spain, Naples and extensive possessions within the Holy Roman

of universal imperial government. From the reign of the Mughal Emperor Aurangzeb is reported an episode concerning the flogging and subsequent death of an ascetic of a militant Sikh order. A flag publicising a warning to the emperor had been put up at the chief police officer's podium in Delhi under the cover of night. The incident was reported to the Emperor who ordered the culprit caught. Always suspicious of dissidence among the religious sects, state officials activated their intelligence channels, searched for the perpetrator, arrested an ascetic militant Sikh and had him severely punished. The rationale behind this way of conducting government, as has recently been observed by Chris Bayly, was not to achieve routine bureaucratic regulation of subjects' lives, 'rather this was a system of watching infractions of morality or royal right. It was designed to cajole the subject into godly submission, rather than to mount a constant policing as some nineteenth century European states attempted to do'. This was rule by example rather than systematic and methodical enforcement of the law.[84]

From the Roman province of Bithynia-Pontus comes the evidence of the letters of the governor Pliny who had been sent on a mission of restoration after the social order of the province had been disturbed. In the most famous of the letters, Pliny treats the question of Christians in the province.[85] The imperial authorities suspected the loyalty of practitioners of the Christian faith because they refused to participate in the regular civic cults (including the imperial). But this did not normally give rise to a general policy of persecution. The peace of the province, however, had been broken. Any kind of organisation which might be suspected of breeding dissension was a potential problem. The gathering of social 'clubs' was banned. People had therefore started to report possible Christians to the governor. Pliny, however, is careful to act with restraint and is confirmed in this policy by the emperor: 'These people should not be hunted out; if they are brought before you and the charge against them is proved, they must be punished. But in the case of anyone who denies he is a Christian, and makes it clear that he is not by offering prayers to our gods, he is to be pardoned as a result of his repentance however suspect his past conduct may be'.[86] Only open defiance, in direct confrontation with the imperial authority was to be punished. Examples had to be set to restore provincial order. But there was to be no witch-hunt with anonymous allegations and the imperial government being dragged down into impenetrable local conflicts. This would only breed further conflict and dissension. But that was not the idea. The objective was to restore provincial society to its previous state where it had been able to run itself with a minimum of intervention from the imperial authorities, and where, as we learn from the others letters, rules and regulations were regularly bent and allowed to lapse to suit present concerns.[87] The law of empire was only enforced sporadically. Government had to economise and use its means selectively. When things fell foul, it had to demonstrate its will to act, set an example and send the message to provincial society that, as

Claudius reprimanded the Jews and Greeks in Alexandria: 'I simply tell you that unless there is an end to this destructive and remorseless anger of yours against each other, I will be forced to show what kind of a person a benevolent Leader can be when he has been turned to justifiable anger'.[88]

Notes

1. *The Jahangirnama: Memoirs of Jahangir, Emperor of India*, translated, edited and annotated by Wheeler M. Thackston (Oxford 1999): 22. Translation slightly modified, Thackston writes 'Caesars of Anatolia', Anatolia being used for Rum, etymologically, in other words, the East Roman Empire. Note in classical Latin that Caesar was pronounced 'kaisar', the form under which the title was used in Persian. The title of the chapter gestures to Pagden (1995), a book dedicated to studying how modern notions of colonial empire developed out of and in opposition to older ideas of universal empire. This contribution, however, focuses precisely on the latter. References to Greek and Latin classical texts are given by author name and the standard divisions into books and chapters (where necessary preceded by the title of the text or a standard abbreviation according to the *Oxford Latin Dictionary*, Liddell & Scott, *Greek-English Lexicon* or the *Checklist of Greek and Roman Papyri*.) The contents of this chapter have been presented to audiences in Copenhagen, Florence, Princeton, Bristol, Charlottesville and Cambridge and I am thankful for helpful comments, lively discussion and hospitality on these occasions. I am also much obliged to Muzaffar Alam for discussing questions relating to Persian with me and to Peter Garnsey, Patricia Crone and John Hall who have all read earlier versions of this text and helped me improve it in numerous ways.
2. Kritovoulos, *History of Mehmed the Conqueror*, trans. C. T. Riggs (Princeton 1954), Book I, 57–87, 193–95; II, 1–8 and 53–56; Goffman (2002: 51–54, 107).
3. Runciman (1965, chapter 12), quotation from p. 167.
4. Cf. Wiesehöfer (2006: 13) on the marginal position of the Middle East in general within the horizon of mainstream classics.
5. In addition to Wickham, Chapter 12 in this book and (2005), see Haldon (1993), Saller (1982: 191 and 205) and now Bang (2008).
6. Scheidel (2009), Mutschler & Mittag (2009) and Whittaker (1994) represent pioneer efforts to foster comparisons between Roman and Chinese history.
7. Nicolet (1988) (Engl. Trans. 1991 as *Space, Geography and Politics in the Early Roman Empire*), followed by Whittaker (1994), marked a new departure.
8. The tension between Greco-Roman city-state, based on law, and Oriental despotism in descriptions of the Roman monarchy is a regular trope, for example Bleicken (1995, Bd. 1: 79–99).
9. Wittfogel (1957) is the modern classic. Montesquieu (1759), Part 1, Book 3, chapters 8–10 and Book 8, chapter 21.
10. Voltaire (1963) (first publ. 1756), chapter 194 (translation by this author).
11. Kafadar (1994).
12. Elias (1997, Vol. 1: 9–75 and Vol. 2) for a fundamental discussion of the importance of competition and conflict for creating convergence between societies and social groups. McNeill (1982) is a forceful demonstration of this principle as a vehicle of world history.
13. Goody (1996); Wilkinson (1995). See Crone (1989) for an attempt to identify such broad similarities.

14. For the basic family resemblance of these agrarian empires, see also Haldon & Goldstone (2009) and Howard (2007: 165–66), noting that the Ottomans should be seen on a family background of agrarian empires reaching back to antiquity.

15. Needless to say this is only intended as a rough and incomplete historical sketch. For our 'second' phase, Hodgson (1974) remains a valuable guide; On the first, Fowden (1993) is a brilliant and refreshing essay; Morris & Scheidel (2009) comprises a number of illuminating analyses.

16. Islamoğlu & Perdue (2009); di Cosmo (2002); Lewis (2007).

17. Schäfer (1974) surveys the career of this notion during antiquity.

18. Cf. M. Cleveland & E. Koch, *King of the World. The Padshahnama. An Imperial Mughal Manuscript from the Windsor Castle*, with a new translation by Wheeler M. Thackston (London 1997).

19. Balabanlilar (2007).

20. *Jahangirnama* (trans. Wheeler M. Thackston, Oxford 1999), constantly depicts Jahangir being presented with the best loot, the most spectacular wonders, the choicest artworks and the most accomplished artists, for example pp. 220–21, 231, 243, 251. To his throne the whole world was drawn, every variety of person, from learned sheiks to exotic Europeans, cf. painting reproduced on p. 259. A theme of Roe's journal of his embassy to Jahangir's court is the constant requests and enquiries from the emperor as to what gifts Roe could bring him from England: rare dogs, a special horse, a miniature painting (William Foster (ed.), *The Embassy of Sir Thomas Roe to India, 1615–19* (Oxford, new rev. ed. 1926), pp. 160, 130, 188–90 and 222–26).

21. Pearson (1996, chapter 5).

22. Farooqi (1989, chapter 5). Hammer (1830) brings in the appendix translations of a number of letters exchanged between the Mughal and Ottoman courts. Letters 2–4 show both sides engaging in a symbolic battle over pre-eminence by careful manipulation of titulature and comparison of territories and conquests. See further, Alam & Subrahmanyam (2007, chapter 7).

23. Dio Cassius 55, 10, 20. Sommer (2005: 66–78) for a recent discussion of Roman Parthian/ Sassanid relations which is also revealing of our general problems in handling the notion of universal rule. Roman emperors, of course, knew full well that they could not command the Parthian monarch the same way they could some of their subject client-kings. But did that make them recognise him as equal, as Sommer concludes on p. 66? Only in a very limited sense; they were the sole power able to rival the Roman Empire, but only 'in a way' as Strabo observed (*Geography* 11, 9, 2). The Roman emperors continued to harbour ambitions of following in the footsteps of Alexander; their legions pressed on in the East in pursuit of further conquests. Trajan made it briefly to the Persian Gulf even if his efforts were dashed in the end. Given the chance, Roman emperors would intervene in the Parthian succession. Recognition did not quite mean equal, at bottom the conception of sovereignty was hierarchical. Rome was *caput mundi* (head of the world), but the Parthians ruled in Persia. As Sommer also observes (p. 68, n. 82), both sides strove to claim a sort of 'Tributsoberherschaft', even if only symbolical. See further Canepa (2009). De facto recognition did not preclude claims or aspirations to pre-eminence. As descendants of Timur, who had defeated and reduced the Ottoman sultan to a tributary, the Mughals could see themselves as superior to the rulers in Constantinople and at the same time recognise them as independent.

24. Isokrates, *Oration 4* (*Panegyricus*) parades most of the stock themes of the anti-Persian Greek discourse. Writing some generations before, Herodotus, for example book 7, is more nuanced, less absolute in his contrast between the despotic Great King and the free Greeks. Hall (1989), for a basic treatment of the Greek 'construction' of Persia.

25. For example Seneca, *De Ira* III, 16–21; Lactantius, *De Mortibus Persecutorum* 21, 2. Alföldy (1970: 6–25) offers a fundamental discussion. More recent treatments of the Greco-Roman image of Persia include Lerouge (2007) and Drijvers (2006).

26. Cf. Plutarch, *On the Fortune of Alexander* I (*Moralia* 326D-345B) for a laudatory version of the meaning of Alexander for Greco-Roman civilisation; Spencer (2002) and Kühnen (2008) are two recent discussions bringing out the complexity and polyvalence of the Alexander myth in Roman politics.

27. Plutarch, *Pompey* II, 1–2; XIII, 4–5; XLV-XLVI.

28. Suetonius, *Caesar* 7.

29. Suetonius *Augustus* 18, 1 (Robert Graves' translation in 'The Twelve Caesars').

30. Mommsen (1887, II, 2, 774–76) is still basic on such matters; Syme, *The Roman Revolution* (Oxford 1939) is classic and remains a valuable analysis. Winterling (2003) and Pani (2003) offer illuminating discussions of the built-in tensions of the principate. Lendon (1997) provides a full-length study of the central importance of the exchange of honour for the functioning of Roman monarchical rule.

31. Cf. Lo Cascio (2000: 16) describing the Roman principate as a mixture of the principle of the city-state and the principle ultimately of the Persian monarchy.

32. Martial *Epigrams* VI, 4, 1: 'Censor maxime principumque princeps.'

33. Suetonius *Caligula* 22, 1–2. Cf. Fowler & Hekster (2005: 20–22 (on mutual royal rivalry as important in shaping the construction of kingship) and p. 36: 'In both Roman and Parthian worlds, in important but contrasting ways, Achaemenid Persia continued to determine the royal agenda').

34. *Res Gestae Divi Augusti* (trans. Sherk, 1988: 41). The bronze plaques in Rome have long since been lost, but the inscription is known from the copy engraved in Latin and parallel Greek translation on the walls of the temple of Roma and Augustus in Ancyra, modern Ancara.

35. *Res Gestae Divi Augusti* chapters 3–4, 25–30 (military conquests), 31–32 (embassies).

36. On the patrimonial aspects of the Roman emperor: von Premerstein (1937); Millar (1977); Saller (1982); Lo Cascio (2000: 97–174). On the Mughals: Pearson (1976); Blake (1979).

37. Veyne (1976: 451–75) and further pp. 534–68 for a discussion of the character of the Roman imperial household.

38. Pliny *Panegyricus of Trajan,* chapter 48–49; *Dio* Cass. Lxxiv 3,4; Herodian I, 2, 4.

39. Tacitus *Annales* I, 75, with MacMullen (1988: 133).

40. *Res Gestae Divi Augusti* chapter 34.

41. Pliny *Panegyric of Trajan* 47, 4; *Dio* Cassius Lxxii 33, 2.

42. Suetonius *Nero* 39, 2 and 31.1–2; Martial *Liber de spectaculis* for a set of poems celebrating the opening of the Colosseum, no. 2 reflects the Flavian propaganda directed against Nero; Griffin (1984: 133–40). For the point in general, see the discussion of Hekster (2005).

43. *The Embassy of Sir Thomas Roe to India, 1615–19 As Narrated in his Journal and Correspondence,* ed. Sir William Foster (Oxford, 1926): 84–85.

44. Described in idealised form at the turn of the sixteenth century by the high-ranking courtier Abu'l Fazl in the *Ain-i-Akbari,* book I, chapters 72–74 (trans. Blochman & Jarret, Vol. 1, Calcutta 1873).

45. Asher (1992: 193); Koch (1994: 143–65).

46. *Jahangirnama* (trans. Wheeler M. Thackston, Oxford 1999: 24, with facing reproduction of a miniature painting showing Jahangir with the chain of justice and standing on a globe where a lion lies peacefully next to a lamb while the emperor is shooting arrows at poverty).

47. Price (1984: 192–3).
48. Bayly (2004: 29–36, 42–4).
49. Prasad (1997: 97–108); Ziegler (1978); Richards (1993: 21–4, 34–40 & 177–8).
50. Arrian *Anabasis* IV, 11, 8–9 (Cleanthes rebuking Alexander's attempt to introduce proskunésis as the general way of paying homage to the emperor, translation by Brunt in the Loeb Classical Library).
51. This was the basic insight at the heart of Millar (1977).
52. Cf. the Hellenic sentiments given voice in Philostratus, *Apollonius of Tyana* V, 7 & 10. Swain (1996) and Whitmarsh (2001) for basic surveys and discussion of the cultural response of the Greek elites under the emperors. Most recently, Madsen (2009).
53. Spawforth & Walker (1985–86). Boatwright (2002).
54. Syme (1939: 273). Caponi (2005: 98–99 & 152–4), partly redresses the old interpretation of the relationship between Roman conquerors and Egyptian temples. Some land-incomes were undoubtedly confiscated, but the temples continued as highly privileged institutions in provincial society.
55. Grenier (1995). Further Herklotz (2007).
56. Philo, *Legatio ad Gaium* 153 (ta patria/translation modified from F. H. Colson in the Loeb Classical Library) & 157 (sponsorship of Jerusalem cult).
57. Bell (1924) is the basic edition of this Greek text, with commentary and translation. Harker (2008: 25–28) for a recent discussion. The document is preserved in a rather carelessly executed copy. Harker uses this as a basis for his claim that the text may have been re-edited to suit Alexandrian interests, but only with respect to certain Jewish claims and rights. However, that is speculation. I see little reason to doubt the basic veracity of the letter as it is preserved. Comparison with documents regarding this case reported by Josephus in *The Jewish Antiquities* (19, 279–85) reveals what to expect if the contents of the letter had indeed been tampered with or re-edited after its publication by the governor. Be that as it may, the basic documentary character of the text is not in doubt.
58. Cf. Flaig (1992) who also sees the Roman emperorship as composite, based on obtaining accept from various discrete constituencies. His analysis, however, is primarily centred on Rome. For the empire, it was no less important to solicit the cooperation of diverse regional elites.
59. Eusebius *Vita Constantini* IV, 7, 1–2, translation from Cameron & Hall, *Life of Constantine* (Oxford 1999), pp. 155–56. In their commentary *ad loc.* they see nothing but clichés, wrongly I think. There was a reason that people continued to repeat these themes down through the centuries. More generally, see Bayly (2004: 34).
60. Locke (1988: 145) (*First Treatise on Government*, §7); Grotius (1913, p. 387): 'Vix adderem stultum titulum esse quem quidam tribuunt Imperatori Romano... (*De Jure Belli ac Pacis*, II, 22, 13).' Pagden (1995) traces how modern theories of statehood, empire and society developed in opposition to the notion of world rule.
61. Campanella (1653, chapter XI, p. 69): 'Deinde lex consuetudine conformis sit necesse est'.
62. Cf. Woolf (1994); Alam (1991, chapter 5).
63. Headley (1997: 217).
64. Hobbes (1996: 117–29) (*Leviathan*, chapter 17–18); Bodin (1986, Vol. 1: 179–228=*Les Six Livres de La République,* book 1, chapter 8); van Creveld (1999, chapter 3).
65. Bodin (1986, Vol. 1: 205–09; Vol. 2: 27–30=*Six Livres de La République*, Book 1, chapter 8, Book 2, chapter 1.).
66. Pufendorf (1910) (*De Statu Imperii Germanici*, chapter 6, 9). This famous sentence was written with respect to the Holy Roman Empire or *Reich* in the decades after

the Thirty Years War which had effectively destroyed whatever hopes the Kaiser had left of controlling his patch-work realm. However, to Pufendorf it was not simply the (failed) Holy Roman Empire of his own day which represented an intellectual problem; it was the very idea of a universal Roman Empire, in whatever form, which constituted an irregular challenge to the theory of indivisible sovereignty, cf. Pagden (1995: 107). Even the classical Roman Empire had a latent irregularity in its construction. The republican constitution which many celebrated as a perfect mix, was in fact rather an irregular body, Pufendorf (1675: 501) concluded in the essay *De Forma Reipublicae Romanae*; its internal tensions ushered in 'a badly formed monarchy whose faults finally threw down the massive, but feeble edifice in miserable ruin' (p. 512, my translation of the Latin text). In his main work, *De Jure Naturae et Gentium,* Pufendorf also included a discussion of the potential irregularity and instability of the Roman imperial monarchy which due to its military base always threatened to break down in division and civil war (book 7, chapter 5, § 15; pp. 687–89 in Pufendorf, 1998, Bd. 4, 2).

67. Cooper (2005) for some critical observations on the relationship between modernist theory and its failure to account for the longevity and continued social dynamics of empire and imperialism through most of history: empire constituted a very real rival or alternative to nation-states until quite recently.

68. Elliott (1992); Gustafsson (1998).

69. Koenigsberger (1971, chapter 1) for an excellent treatment of the varied empire of Charles V.

70. Francisco de Victoria, *De Indis* II, 1 (translation from p. 255 in Vitoria, 1991); For the Latin text, see Vitoria (1917, 236).

71. Victoria *De Indis* II, 1: Item nec Regnum Hispaniae est subiectum Imperatori, nec Francorum ... See Muldoon (1999, chapter 6) for a discussion.

72. In a thoughtful, but dense study Peter Eich (2005) has suggested to use the early-modern forms of patrimonial monarchy as offering parallels to the Roman imperial monarchy. Much can undoubtedly be learned from such a comparison, but at the same time these monarchies were part of a different process of state-formation than the agrarian empires.

73. Cf. for example the conclusion of Deininger (1965): the provincial councils of the Roman Empire did not function like parliaments.

74. Cf. Cohen and Lendon (2011).

75. Lockhart (2007: 163–69).

76. The literature is staggering, some influential interpretations: Bayly (2004, chapters 3–4 and 6–7); van Creveld (1999); Tilly (1992); Brewer (1988); Gellner (1988, chapters 5–6); Mann (1986, chapters 13–14); McNeill (1982).

77. Mann (1986, chapters 5, 8 and 9). Lieven (2001: 138–48) for an illuminating comparison of the changing balance of power between a Russian state pursuing a vigorous programme of intensification and modernisation and a more extensive Ottoman form of territorial control.

78. Eisenstadt (1963: 26–28).

79. Plutarch, *Philopoimen*, chapter 5.

80. Stein (1985: 387–413). Stein imported the notion of state-segmentation from the anthropological literature on Africa, but transformed the concept to apply it to societies with a firmer agrarian base and more elaborate and stable religious and political institutions than those discussed by Tymowski in Chapter 6.

81. Luttwak (1976) on the economy of force.

82. Hasan (2004); Alam (1986), on the importance of local landowners for running the Mughal empire. For Rome, Garnsey & Saller (1987, chapter 2) is fundamental ('government without bureaucracy'). More recent, for example Brelaz (2005).
83. Cf. the study by Meyer-Zwiffelhoffer (2002) stressing how the Roman provincial governor did not so much directly administer his province as respond to appeals, complaints and requests from the subject population.
84. Bayly (1996: 19–20), citation p. 19. See Peachin (2007) for a discussion of the 'power of exempla' in Roman government.
85. Plinius *Epistuale* X, 96.
86. Plinius *Epistulae* X, 97, 2 (Trajan to Pliny, trans B. Radice in Loeb Classical Library): Conquirendi non sunt; si deferantur et arguantur, puniendi sunt, ita tamen ut, qui negaverit se Christianum esse idque re ipsa manifestum fecerit, id est supplicando dis nostris, quamvis suspectus in praeteritum, veniam ex paenitentia impetret. See in general, MacMullen (1966: 155–56, 176–77).
87. Lapse of rules, for example, Plin. *Ep.* X, 114 + 32, economising of governmental resources, for example *Ep.* X, 20.
88. *P. London* 1912, ll. 79–82 (Letter of Claudius to the Alexandrians in AD 41, trans. cited from Sherk (1988) no. 44).

11
Fiscal Regimes and the 'First Great Divergence' between Eastern and Western Eurasia

Walter Scheidel

Early state formation in East Asia and Europe: from convergence to divergence

In the most general terms, state formation in eastern and western Eurasia unfolded in similar ways from the late second millennium BCE into the early first millennium CE.[1] In both cases, large Bronze Age states collapsed into hundreds of small polities (in the Iron Age East Mediterranean and in Spring-and-Autumn China) that were subsequently consolidated into unified political-military systems in which a small number of major powers competed for dominance (in the Mediterranean in the last eight centuries BCE and in Warring States China). This process culminated in the creation of core-wide empires that lasted for several centuries (the mature Roman empire and the Qin-Han empire). The institutions of the late Roman empire in the fourth to sixth centuries CE resembled those of the mature Han empire much more closely than those of any of the earlier western states had resembled those of earlier eastern states: in this sense we may speak of *convergent* rather than merely roughly parallel development. Abiding differences can be identified in the spheres of military and ideological power, with stronger marginalisation of the military and closer ties between political and ideological power (Legalism-Confucianism) in Han China compared to the Roman Empire. However, even in those areas some convergent trends did eventually emerge, such as warlordism in the late Han, Three Kingdoms and Western Jin periods, and the attempted cooptation of Christianity by the late Roman state. Moreover, both states ended in similar ways, with their more exposed halves (the west in the case of Rome, the north in China) being taken over by semi-peripheral 'barbarians' and turned into a handful of large but unstable successor states that relied to varying degrees on existing institutions of government (Goths, Franks, Vandals and Lombards in the West, the so-called 'Sixteen Kingdoms' in northern China), while traditionalist regimes survived in the other halves (Byzantium and five of the 'Six Dynasties' in southern China, respectively).

By the sixth century CE, these trends finally began to diverge. At that time, attempts to regain lost Roman possessions in the western Mediterranean succeeded only in part, and in the following century the East Roman state faced near-fatal assaults by Persians, Avars and most importantly Arabs. Despite the tremendous scale of their initial successes, the Arabs were unable to create a stable ecumenical empire. Political fragmentation throughout western Eurasia increased during the late first millennium CE, most notably in Christian Europe where states gradually lost the ability to control and tax populations and sovereignty de facto came to be shared among monarchs, lords, local strongmen, semi-independent towns and clergy. The (re-)creation of centralised states was a drawn-out process that primarily unfolded during the first half of the second millennium CE but in some cases took even longer, creating a cluster of polities in which balancing mechanisms prevented the creation of a core-wide empire. Instead, intense interstate competition, internal social and intellectual upheavals, the creation of new kinds of maritime empire, and (eventually) technological progress, gave rise to the modern nation state. In sixth-century CE China, by contrast, imperial reunification restored the bureaucratic state that largely succeeded, albeit with substantial interruptions, in maintaining a core-wide empire under Chinese or foreign leadership until 1911 CE. In some ways, the People's Republic today is merely the most recent reincarnation of this entity.

Fiscal regimes and state power

Any attempt to explain this post-ancient divergence must address two distinct but related issues: the survival and reinvigoration of the centralised state as the dominant form of political organisation in China as European (and to some extent also southwest Asian) states entered a prolonged phase of diminished capabilities, and the restoration of unified political control within an area that was broadly coextensive with preceding core-wide empires, a goal that was accomplished in China but not in Europe or southwest Asia.[2] In this chapter, I focus on the role of fiscal regimes in determining state strength in this period. After a brief look at the tax systems of the Roman and Han empires I introduce a recent model of change in post-Roman western Eurasia and then suggest ways of interpreting developments in post-Han China within the framework provided by this model.

Convergence: imperial taxation

In China during the Warring States period, land taxes are recorded from the sixth century BCE onward in connection with the expansion of military capabilities. At the same time, census registers became common, enabling rulers to count people and assets at the level of individual households.[3] The Roman republican state likewise combined taxation of private property (*tributum*) with mass levies of infantry.[4] Centralisation in China gave rise to an at least nominally uniform tax system across the unified empire of the Han dynasty whereas the Roman conquests produced a bundle of regions in which local tax regimes prevailed or had to be introduced ad hoc by the new ruling power. Thus, although the degree of actual uniformity in China should not be over-estimated, there can be no doubt that standardisation proceeded much more slowly in the West. While regular provincial censuses commenced under the monocratic regime of Augustus, fiscal regimes continued to vary across the empire. Not until the late third century CE did the central government seek to impose standardised modes of registration and taxation across its realm. In both systems nominal tax rates were of the same order of magnitude.[5] Land taxes (at 10–20 per cent of yield in Rome and 3–7 per cent of yield plus an annual property tax of 1.2 per cent in Han China) dominated and poll taxes were common (throughout China and at least in some Roman provinces), accompanied by a host of more specific exactions such as taxes on legacies and slave manumissions in Rome or taxes on vehicles and monopoly fees on iron and salt production in China. Civilian corvée labor was required at both ends of Eurasia, though more consistently so in China as a legacy of the Warring States system of mass mobilisation. Military service, nominally a widespread obligation under the Western Han and in the later Roman Empire, could be commuted into cash payments, as were various Roman taxes in kind. Levies on trade provided further revenue: Han merchants were taxed at higher rates than others, and internal and external tolls were known in both empires. Roman cities, more autonomous than their Han counterparts, collected their own municipal taxes and dues.[6] Fiscal demands coincided with growing monet-isation and monetary standardisation: both the Roman and the Han currency systems expanded massively in this period, and a government document from one Han province indicates that by the end of the first century BCE a strikingly large proportion of revenue was collected in cash.[7]

The principal beneficiaries were the functional equivalents of the 'state class' of the early Arabic empires discussed in Chris Wickham's chapter. In the mono-cratic Roman state, this group was made up of the central court, the military and, in late antiquity, salaried 'civilian' officials, as well as of local elites involved in tax collection.[8] In Han China, civilian administrators – both career bureau-crats and eunuchs – may have benefited most, although the military at least at times absorbed considerable resources as well. In both environments hun-dreds of thousands of individuals depended on tax revenue to make a living: some 300,000–600,000 soldiers in the Roman empire eventually joined by over 30,000 salaried administrators; some 120,000–150,000 administrators, perhaps 100,000 state slaves, and an indeterminate number of soldiers in Han China.[9]

The emphasis on local and regional administrative staff in China and on the frontier military in the Roman empire suggests that a larger share of state revenue was expended locally in the former than in the latter polity and that the Roman system was consequently more vulnerable to disruption in so far as its survival depended more strongly on the integrity of the whole whereas Chinese state institutions may have been more fractionable.[10] What the two systems had in common was that prolonged ecumenical peace enabled local elites to extend their property-holdings and patronage and in so doing increasingly sheltered taxpayers from the reach of the state. Both the Eastern Han and even more so the Three Kingdoms and Western Jin periods in China and the western late Roman Empire witnessed intensifying competition between the extraction of tax and the collection of rent, with rent crowding out tax.[11] The dissolution of the united empires thus coincided with a weakening of their tax systems that both contributed to and was driven by the erosion of state power.

Divergence: Western Eurasia

Chris Wickham has developed what one might call a 'fiscalist' model of state formation in post-ancient western Eurasia.[12] The 'strong' Roman state (which counted and taxed a demilitarised civilian population in order to support a large standing army) was succeeded in part by states that maintained systems of taxation and salaried armies (the East Roman and early Arab states) and in part by weaker or weakening states whose rulers gradually lost the ability to count and tax their subjects (the Germanic successor states in the west). In some marginal areas, state institutions collapsed altogether, most notably in Britain. In 'strong' states with registration, taxation and centrally controlled military forces, rulers enjoyed greater autonomy from elite interests, and elites depended to a significant extent on the state (for offices, salaries and indirect benefits) to establish and maintain their status. In 'weak' states, elites relied more on the resources they themselves controlled and enjoyed greater autonomy from the rulers. In the absence of centralised tax collection and coercive capabilities, the power of rules depended largely on elite cooperation. From the perspective of the general population, local elites rather than state rulers dominated, and feudal relationships were a likely outcome. At the same time, in the absence of trans-regional integration that is characteristic of 'strong' states, elites tended to be less wealthy. These conditions also had profound consequences for economic performance, eroding interregional exchange in and among 'weak' states. Over time, even the relatively 'strong' post-Roman successor states witnessed a decline of state taxation and salaried military forces, most notably in seventh- and eighth-century CE Byzantium. The Umayyad Empire also suffered from the regionalisation of revenue collection and military power.[13]

In this context of fiscal decline and decentralisation of political and military power, it became harder to maintain state capabilities (especially in the military sphere), economic activity was curtailed, and the prospects for the restoration of a stable core-wide empire were poor. Eventually, even the Abbasid Empire splintered into a number of regional successor states, and attempts by Charlemagne and the Ottonians to set up larger empires in northwest Europe proved short-lived. In different parts of Europe, the success of subsequent efforts to stem the erosion of the state and to restore central state capabilities varied greatly in terms of speed and scope.[14] In the Eastern Mediterranean, only the Ottoman Empire eventually achieved historically high levels of central state control.[15]

Divergence: China

I hope to show that Wickham's explanatory framework can fruitfully be applied to account for developments in early medieval China that differed signally from conditions in western Eurasia.[16] Modern narratives of the principal northern successor states in fifth and sixth centuries CE consistently emphasise the gradual restoration of Han-style governmental institutions that enabled rulers to count and tax an increasing proportion of their subjects, curb elite autonomy and mobilise growing resources for military efforts that eventually resulted in imperial reunification.[17] The actual degree of government control at different times during the Period of Disunion (317–589 CE) is hard to determine empirically. If we accept reported census tallies as proxy evidence for the strength of the central authorities,[18] it appears that the collapse of the Han regime resulted in a dramatic relaxation of centralised control. Census tallies for the second century CE range from 9.2 to 10.8 million households with 47.6–56.5 million residents. Reported totals of c. 1.7 million households in all the Three Kingdoms combined (c. 240s/260s CE) as well as the Western Jin tally of 2.5 million for the entire empire in 280 CE are therefore clearly defective.[19] Even if the latter were indeed a tally of taxable households only, it would primarily reflect the state's inability to tax a large majority of all existing households. Three centuries later, by contrast, census quality had greatly improved. In the late 570s, the northern states of Northern Qi and Northern Zhou together counted 6.9 million households with 29 million residents, and 20 years after the absorption of the Chen state in the south the tally had risen to 8.9 million households with 46 million individuals (609 CE), close to Eastern Han levels.[20] These figures indicate that – at least – by the sixth century CE, the northern successor states had reattained a capacity to count and tax the general population that was roughly comparable to that achieved by the intact Han state.

This impression is reinforced by references to the deployment of very large military forces by these states, such as 170,000 soldiers in 575 CE, 145,000

subjugated Chinese: the former ruled and performed military service while the latter farmed, paid taxes, and provided corvée labor.[32] This distinction was upheld by the Tuoba Xianbei whose Northern Wei state for the first time re-united northern China in 439 CE. In the west, Germans received shares of land on which they settled.[33] In addition to this entitlement and benefits that might accrue from continuing military service, the newcomers were at least initially formally distinguished from the local populations: for instance, the Ostrogoths in Italy did not assume Roman citizenship and were therefore unable to hold civilian offices; they may also have been subject to separate laws.[34] In North Africa, religious affiliation separated the Vandals from local mainstream society. In the more durable successor states of Visigothic Spain and Francia, however, Germans and locals merged over time: by the late seventh century CE, everybody in northern France was considered a Frank. Unlike in northern China, this did not seem to require formal decrees by the rulers.

From the perspective of Wickham's revenue-centred model, the replacement of imperial courts and professional armies by foreign conquest elites assumed crucial significance only if it entailed changes in compensation practices: if new administrators and military forces had continued to receive government salaries derived from generalised taxation, a 'strong' state might readily have been maintained. The Umayyad state, with its elaborate system of stipends for soldiers and their descendants, illustrates this principle, at least at the regional level – although in that case, the crucial element of central control had already been lost (see further Chapter 12). However, if the foreign conquerors had been given land allotments (or guaranteed stipends from land allotments owned or cultivated by others), the state's motivation for persevering in population registration and direct taxation might have been greatly diminished. To varying degrees, this latter scenario seems to apply to the Germanic successor states.[35] If these polities were weakened by the settlement of the original Germanic immigrants on the land and the consequent erosion of population registration, taxation and ultimately centralised government control (and similar features can be observed in the East Roman state after the mid-seventh century CE), we must ask whether the Xiongnu and Xianbei elements who had come to control northern China from the early fourth century CE onward were supported in ways that were more conducive to continuing fiscal activities and the maintenance of mechanisms that connected the central government with local communities.[36]

Comparative evidence from later periods suggests that conquest by steppe populations repeatedly coincided with the maintenance of state taxation. In the tenth century CE, the conquest state of Liao set up a dual system with separate laws for the Qidan (that is, the steppe conquerors) and the Chinese, and strictly separated the Chinese administrative apparatus (with its civil service examinations) from the politically dominant Qidan community. Subsequently, the Jin regime of the Jurchen (that is, the next wave of steppe conquerors) continued and expanded the Liao pattern of dual institutions. When the Jurchen population moved into northern China in the first half of the twelfth century, all families were given land and oxen for farming, and elite members received hereditary offices, serving as civilian and military leaders. The latter enjoyed increasing wealth, while the fighting capacity of the Jurchen commoners supposedly declined. However, no feudalisation occurred, and rulers were on occasion even able to implement centralising reforms. In the Yuan period, Mongols who had moved to China were assigned appanage lands (farmed by locals) to sustain them. Mongols did not normally reside on these lands and could even sell them. In the imperial administration, the practice of dual staffing paired Chinese officials with Mongolian supervisors. In all these cases, the conquerors were committed to preserving Chinese institutions of administration.

To return to the Period of Disunion, the fourth- and fifth-century CE practice of forcibly relocating large numbers of subject Chinese to the political centres of the various northern successor states suggests that their labor was required to support not just the courts but also the attached foreign *guoren* populations. At first sight, this system of concentrating and exploiting civilians in the capital regions and controlling outlying areas with the help of local fortress chiefs may not seem readily compatible with the concurrent maintenance of institutionalised statewide bureaucratic structures and the survival of centrally supervised population registration and taxation at the district level. Ray Huang notes that if left to their own devices, the leaders of coalitions of these local self-defence units might have turned into feudal lords but that this development was aborted by government raids on these settlements that deprived leaders of their 'semi-formed local autonomy'.[37] In this case, however, the presence of a strong and highly mobile central army in the form of Xiongnu and Xianbei cavalry units under the direct control of rulers may have been a critical factor. Germanic rulers do not normally appear to have maintained centrally deployed standing military forces beyond royal bodyguards (a royal slave army in sixth-century CE Visigothic Spain is a telling exception), and rulers increasingly relied on armies raised through the intermediation of their lords. Later recourse to mercenaries was motivated by growing problems with this process.[38] In China, by contrast, developments in the military sphere tended to increase state power. Kenneth Klein has argued that centralisation was in part driven by the pressure exerted by the Rouran in the steppe, which caused the Tuoba rulers of Northern Wei to set up frontier garrisons, thereby mimicking the behaviour toward steppe peoples conventionally displayed by the imperial agrarian state.[39] Later on, conflict between the Tuoba regimes of Western Wei/Northern Zhou and Eastern Wei/Northern Qi likewise precipitated the creation of enhanced mobilisation mechanisms, especially in the former entities where a relative scarcity of Tuoba forces encouraged the military mobilisation of large numbers of Chinese who had previously primarily been employed in logistical and support functions. The powerful 'Twenty-Four Army' system that eventually facilitated imperial reunification was the main fruit of these developments.[40]

The successful preservation of centralised military capabilities and of at least rudimentary administrative institutions was a vital precondition for the eventual resurgence of a 'strong' state in northern China. In 485 CE, the Northern Wei court sought to introduce an Equal Fields system, with standardised land allotments to individual households. This measure was accompanied by the designation of prominent villagers charged with the verification of census registers and the supervision of tax collection. More generally, the measures reported for the sixth century CE, especially for the Northern Zhou regime, reflect a state with considerable capabilities which used them to expand them even further.[41] All of this raises the question of how much rulers had to rebuild from scratch and to what extent state control had always been maintained at the local level, even in times of upheaval.[42] This is a key problem of the history of this period and calls for further investigation.[43]

Notes

1. For more detailed discussion, see Scheidel (2009a) and in preparation. This chapter has grown out of the 'Stanford Ancient Chinese and Mediterranean Empires Comparative History Project' (www.stanford.edu/~scheidel/acme.htm).
2. For a discussion of the latter issue, see Scheidel (forthcoming b). Cf. also Adshead (2000: 54–71); Lieven (2001: 33–39). I label this process the 'First Great Divergence' to distinguish it from the concept of the 'Great Divergence' (between Europe and the rest of the world, most notably China, during the last two centuries) popularised by Pomeranz (2000). The extent to which this 'First Great Divergence' – in the sphere of state formation – laid the foundations for the modern 'Great Divergence' – in terms of economic development – is a key question of world history.
3. Lewis (1990: 58–61, 91).
4. For example, Nicolet (1980: 49–109, 149–206).
5. For convenient surveys of the evidence, see Nishijima (1986: 595–607); Ausbüttel (1998: 74–94). For a discussion of the scale and distribution of state revenue and expenditure, see Scheidel (forthcoming a).
6. See now especially Schwarz (2001).
7. Duncan-Jones (1994); Scheidel (2009b). For the revenue record of Donghai commandery (dating from c. 10 BCE) found at Yinwan in 1993, see Loewe (2004: 60) (c. 80–90 per cent paid in cash).
8. In the Principate, the military is thought to have absorbed perhaps two-thirds to three-quarters of state revenue (Duncan-Jones, 1994: 45; Wolters, 1999: 223). I put 'civilian' in quotation marks because of the military habitus of the late Roman proto-bureaucracy. For the rise of centralised patrimonial bureaucratisation in the Roman empire, see especially Eich (2005). For the role of the elites, see briefly Wickham, in this volume. For the functional definition of the *honestiores* as the Roman 'political class', comprised of aristocrats, local elites and veterans, see Scheidel (2006: 42–43).

(Active soldiers also belonged to it de facto if not de iure.) Due to republican traditions, the population of the Roman capital (or, later, capitals) enjoyed entitlements in the form of food subsidies that lacked an equivalent in China: for a comparison of welfare practices in Rome and Han China, see now Lewis (2009).

9. Rome: Rankov (2007: 71); Elton (2007: 284–85) (soldiers); Palme (1999) (officials). Han China: Loewe (2004: 70–71) (officials); Nishijima (1986: 593) (slaves); Loewe (2006: 59, 62–65) (soldiers).

10. This is supported by the Donghai records from c.10 BCE according to which in a given year 55 per cent of the tax revenue in cash and 81 per cent of tax grain had been expended by the commandery administration, presumably within the commandery itself: see Loewe (2004: 60). Compare Wickham's analogous argument about the Umayyad and Abbasid empires, in this volume.

11. Rome: Wickham (1994: 19–30, 50–51). China: Ebrey (1986: 617–26); Lewis (2007: 111); and cf. more generally Balazs (1964: 101–25); Chao (1986: 103).

12. Wickham (2005). This summary is indebted to Sarris (2006).

13. For the latter two polities, see especially Haldon (1997) and Kennedy (2001), as well as Wickham, in this volume.

14. See especially Levi (1988: 95–144); Tilly (1992); Spruyt (1994); Ertman (1997); Glete (2002).

15. For example, Imber (2002: chapter 5).

16. For Wickham's own earlier views on state power in China, see Wickham (1994: 51–56).

17. See especially Pearce (1987), and more concisely Graff (2002: chapter 5) and Lewis (2009, chapter 3).

18. It would be wrong to assume that census totals from this period primarily document demographic conditions. Although it is likely that war and crises caused significant demographic losses through death and migration, the record contains sudden massive fluctuations that cannot possibly reflect reality: the best examples are shifts from 10.7 million households in 157 CE to 1.7 million (composite figure for all polities) in 264 CE; from 4.2 million (ditto) in 580 CE to 8.9 million in 609 CE; from 8.9 million in 755 CE to 1.9 million in 760 CE (!); and from 4.5 million in 996 CE to 7.4 million in 1006 CE and on to 9.1 million in 1014 CE (see Bielenstein 1987: 12, 15, 17, 19–20, 47). These observations suggest that census tallies are best used as an index of state strength rather than as straightforward demographic evidence.

19. Bielenstein (1987: 12, 15–17).

20. Bielenstein (1987: 1987: 17–19). Cf. also Graff (2002: 127) and 136 n.19 for a reference to 5 million households and 32 million people in the unified North right before 523 CE.

21. Graff (2002: chapter 6–7).

22. Lewis (1999: 625–28); Chang (2007: 177–79).

23. Halsall (2003: chapter 6); Haldon (2003: 101–03).

24. Graff (2002: 93, n. 1); de Crespigny (2004: table 2), and cf. de Crespigny (1990: 7–58).

25. Bielenstein (1987: 194, 199).

26. Graff (2002: 127).

27. Liu (2001, especially 47–48).

28. Tang (1990: 123–24).

29. Bielenstein (1987: 17).

30. Dien (2001), on a manuscript from Turfan.

31. Eberhard (1949: 209–11); Yang (1961: 146–47).

32. Graff (2002: 59).
33. This is a more plausible reconstruction than Goffart's poorly supported thesis that they received a share of tax revenues instead: see Goffart (2006: chapter 6), with Wickham (2005: 84–86).
34. Maier (2005: 62).
35. Wickham (2005: 84).
36. Salaries for Tuoba state officials are attested from the late fifth century CE onward: Eberhard (1949: 93).
37. Huang (1997: 77). The Tuoba state bestowed official titles on defeated fortress chiefs to incorporate them into formal state hierarchies: Graff (2002: 61).
38. Halsall (2003) provides the most recent survey.
39. Klein (1980).
40. Pearce (1987: 519–673); Graff (2002: 108–11).
41. Pearce (1987) and (2001).
42. Elvin (1973: 47) notes the problem that prior to 485 CE, 'until this fiscal system was improved...there was little hope of consolidating imperial authority...conversely, until there was greater imperial authority an improvement of the fiscal position...was hardly possible'. His answer that the government did both at once does not really resolve this conundrum.
43. The contributions to a workshop devoted to this and related issues (Stanford, 2008) conveyed the impression that the pertinent evidence may simply be insufficient to produce clear answers. I am grateful to David Graff, Scott Pearce and Victor Xiong for sharing their expertise with me and my colleagues at Stanford.

12

Tributary Empires: Late Rome and the Arab Caliphate

Chris Wickham

I wish in this chapter to set up a comparison between the late Roman Empire and the early Arab Caliphate, as state structures. Before I do, however, some points about comparison in itself seem to me to be helpful. There are always, before very recent times, three main problems confronting anyone who wishes to compare across historical societies. The first is the nature of our evidence. Different cultures produce different sorts of documentation, and think it important to record – and to preserve the records of – different sorts of things. When one adds to that the hugely different survival rates of our documentation across the vicissitudes of the centuries, the problem of comparing like with like only increases. In the late Roman Empire, outside the tax records of Egypt, the main evidence for state and fiscal structures comes from imperial laws. In the Umayyad and 'Abbāsid Caliphate of the mid-seventh to early tenth centuries, again outside the tax records of Egypt, the evidence for state and fiscal structures comes from the huge political narratives compiled around AD 900 by al-Baladhurī and al-Ṭabarī. You would think that Egypt would therefore be the axis of any comparison between Rome and the Caliphate, and on one level it is, but actually sixth-century (i.e. Roman) and eighth-century (i.e. caliphal) tax and administrative records for Egypt are not that different. The fiscal structures of the two states, or empires, were in reality very different, in many ways, but it is the *other* sources which show this, and we have to use *them* differently and expect different information to be privileged in them.[1]

The second problem of comparison is that historiographical traditions are often hugely different from place to place. By now we perhaps expect the historiography of Poland and that of Britain to be different, as they are undertaken, above all, by Polish and British scholars respectively, and are shot through with assumptions about national identity and the importance of different sorts of historical development which, however hard we try – which is not very hard – remain resolutely distinct. It is more interesting that the historiographies of the Roman Empire and of the early Caliphate are so dissimilar, for they are both dominated by scholars from a handful of European countries and the United States, the same countries in each case. The reasons for this are in part unsurprising – the negative impact of Orientalism on Arabist scholarship, and the greater tension involved in studying early Muslim as opposed to early Christian texts, which is longstanding in the discipline, are two obvious ones. The results can be depressing, though; one is faced in much Islamic historiography with the stark choice between believing every word of a narrative and rejecting every word, and more nuanced analyses of textual strategies and the like, which are commonplace for Rome, have only hit the Caliphate very recently.[2] It is also fair to say that there is far less work on political and fiscal structures in the Arab than in the Roman world. The Caliphate is not one of the core empires of this project, but it seems to me a valuable addition to them at least for comparative purposes (and many of its state structures anyway survived in the Ottoman and Mughal empires). But it needs to be stressed that my presentation here is based on the work of relatively few scholars, and even fewer of any quality (particularly, for me, Patricia Crone, Hugh Kennedy and Daniel Sourdel).[3]

The third problem of comparison is selecting what to compare. The process of selection determines the results. Garry Runciman's marvellous *Treatise on Social Theory* is interested in both the structure or allocation of power and in representations, that is in general in culture; but his focus on the roles of social groups leads him in his comparative volume to consider power more than culture, and, inside 'power', to consider production and coercion more than persuasion.[4] Such a process of selection is inevitable, so this cannot be a criticism, of Runciman or of any other writer. Inside that inevitability, however, one has to be precise in one's choice about what to compare. The wider one's field of comparison, the woollier one can become. It seems to me that in order to avoid woolliness, one needs to take single elements, as tightly characterised as possible, and see how they worked differently in two or three, or more, societies, and use that difference in working to construct a sense of how the societies are different in more general ways. For the state, one could take the structural role of cities in each polity, or army pay, or the political influence of major landowners, that is the incorporation of local élites in the central system, or, as others make clear in this volume, legitimisation, or the nature of frontier society. Each will illuminate different elements in the comparison. But we must avoid mixing them up; there is no point in comparing legitimising symbols in society A with frontier defence in society B. (It may seem implausible that anyone would do this, but I have certainly in the past come across attempts at comparing medieval societies which set forms of military loyalty in society A against peasant labour-services in society B on the grounds that they are both part of a vague concept of 'feudalism'. Historians do do this, even though it is obviously pointless once it is spelled out, and it is important to guard against it.)

To make the comparison as tight as possible, I would also, at a more general level, want to use Weber's image of the ideal type, a sociological concept which is over a century old, but which has by no means outlived its usefulness: that is to say a matrix of elements that have a clear relation to each other, but which are not all necessarily found in every real society under comparison. Looking for the presences and absences of the elements in the matrix in society A and then society B is another way of getting into the issue of difference. But, having said that, I want here to focus on a single element, in order to develop the Rome–Caliphate comparison; in this context, an entire ideal type would take too much space to set up and manipulate. I want to discuss the nature of the control central government had over how tax was taken from the provinces and made available for central government use. I think in fact that this element is a crucial guide to how the political economy of large states (empires) works; but, whether this is true or not, it at least seems to me useful for setting out a framework for comparison.

Under Rome, the procedure of actually exacting taxation was highly decentralised; it was essentially entrusted to local élites, for long the city councillors of the Empire's dense city network, who made a lot of money out of tax-raising but also had to underwrite it, and who therefore, like Lloyds underwriters, complained a lot when things went wrong. This of course meant that local power brokers had a stake in the tax system, and the development of this cellular pattern of collection, although it may have initially been a result of weakness (conquering Romans in each province were far too few to collect tax themselves), led to long-term structural stability. When tax increased substantially in the late empire, the system was long in place.[5]

What happened to that tax was that it went to centrally appointed provincial governors, and then, in the late empire which I know best, to the four praetorian prefectures, whose prefects had determined tax levels in the first place. But the Roman Empire was also situated geopolitically around a sea, which made the movement of bulk goods easier than in land-based states like the Caliphate or the Mughal Empire or China (less so the Ottoman empire). It was therefore possible to structure the *direction* of taxation, which did not have all to come through imperial or prefectural capitals. Egyptian grain went to Constantinople, North African (i.e. Tunisian) grain to Rome, to maintain these two great symbolic cities (Rome rarely being a capital after AD 300 or so, but still being symbolic). The produce of different provinces also went to maintain frontier armies, for the army, the main expense of the empire, was mostly situated on the northern and eastern frontiers. This was presumably organised at the prefectural level, and we know less about it, but it was quite complex; the southern Aegean fed the lower Danube army, for example, whereas northern Italy fed the upper Danube army. Some tax stayed at the level of the province, for local garrisons and administrators, but much went outside it, in the way I have just set out. I have argued elsewhere that most of this tax must have been in kind, even though assessment was generally in money; this would have made the movement of goods more cumbersome, but the sea must have helped. Of all the provinces of the empire, only central Spain and central Anatolia (Turkey) had no obvious destination for their taxed goods, and both were fairly marginal territories.[6] But one crucial point about all this structuring is that it was in the hands of central government. Local élites did the collecting, and then salaried officials took over. It must also be added that it did not involve the army, except the military entourages of tax collectors, and except for some requisitioning, in theory set against tax paying, in frontier areas. The army was paid by the state, but it was not an autonomous part of the state's political economy, and the political élite was basically civilian, except for the emperor and, often, a military strongman at the centre.

The Roman Empire was intensely corrupt, but this system remained stable until its end. Structures at the local level changed in the fifth century and early sixth, because local power relationships shifted; city councils were replaced by more informal élite groups including local senators and bishops, who did not have tax-underwriting obligations, and who shared responsibilities for taxation with central officials sent into the localities.[7] But this was in reality just a reformulation of the same process, for the central officials tended to be local men as well. In Egypt, the best-documented province, cities were after c. AD 500 run by a pagarch, a central government appointee, who had a particular responsibility for taxation; but all the pagarchs we know anything about were local aristocrats. Urban landowners kept responsibility for tax-raising, that is to say, but in a different institutional framework. The rest of the system did not change until the Roman Empire was conquered; in the fifth century in the West, by Germanic tribes, in the seventh in much of the East, by the Arabs.

The state system of the first Arab Caliphate, that of the Umayyads (AD 661–750), had many continuities with that of Rome (above all in the local patterns of tax-raising, as we shall see in a moment), but it was also structurally different; I will discuss three elements of this. For a start, its ruling élite was military. I think this is an important distinction, though it needs nuancing. By and large, conquests create political systems dominated by army men, for it is these who do the conquering. But large tax-based states need skilled official hierarchies to run them, who have considerable political power, and who do not, by and large, have the time or the inclination to run armies. There is therefore a tendency in state development for the initially hegemonic army to become only a part of the élite, with landed aristocracies, old and new, able to choose whether to focus on military or civilian political careers. (The lasting total dominance of military values among the élites of the medieval West was because the tax system inherited from Rome, and thus the civilian hierarchy, soon foundered.) In post Diocletianic Rome and in post-Tang

China, the civilian ruling class was hegemonic in a Gramscian sense, and the army was relatively déclassé; successful army leaders seldom founded lasting aristocratic families, but if they did their heirs were civilian; senatorial forays into army-leadership in Rome certainly occurred, but they tended to be brief.[8] Rome and China were extremes, however. The Byzantines, heirs of the eastern Roman Empire but on the military defensive after the Arab conquests, ended up with a much more military landed aristocracy, who dominated in most places, and a civilian élite restricted to the capital.[9] This was the direction the Arabs went too, with some differences. This is a tendency which has analogues in other empires, too, and is worth exploring.

But the Arab polity was different in a second, more important, way too. The caliphs did not settle their armies on the land. 'Umar I around 640 (so say the later narratives) fixed them, in garrison towns for the most part, as a salaried force, and discouraged them from buying land. They were still, however, unlike the armies of Rome, a political élite, the only one under the Umayyads. The civil administration was until AD 700 still Greek-speaking and Christian, or, in Iraq, Aramaic-speaking and Christian or Zoroastrian, and thus politically marginal in the Islamic state, and even though the administration was Arabised after that, it did not gain political coherence and weight until the end of the Umayyad Caliphate in AD 750. The landed aristocracy was still either Christian or Zoroastrian as well, and thus equally marginalised. The choice to keep the Arabs separate was beyond doubt in order to preserve Arab culture and the Muslim religion, in the unusually huge conquered lands of the mid-seventh century, covering over half the east Roman Empire and all the empire of Sassanian Persia, stretching from Egypt to Iran, and spreading out by AD 720 to Spain, Samarkand and the edge of India, which would have overwhelmed the relatively small population of Arabia – only Alexander and the Mongols ever conquered so far so fast, and their empires broke up very quickly, unlike the Caliphate. But 'Umar also inaugurated, presumably without realising it, the particularity of all successive Muslim regimes in the Near and Middle East: the 'state class' or *khāṣṣa*, paid by taxation and, crucially, separated from the hierarchies of landowning, in what Runciman has called the 'warrior' mode.[10] Landowning thus did not bring rights to wider political power, unlike in the Roman Empire or in the rest of European history. Only in the more traditional parts of Iran did large-scale landowning even – and not until after AD 800, when landowners were more often Muslim – make it easier to get into the 'state class'. Landowning brought local status and power, at the level of the city, but this did not carry across to the level of the state. This did not change for any of the Muslim states of the medieval period, or for the Ottomans after. Members of the *khāṣṣa* did buy land, or get it in gifts from caliphs, particularly in 'Abbāsid Iraq after AD 800, but this merely brought them stable wealth, not greater political influence.

'Umar and his successors put an Arab army into every province, and focused the tax system of each on the supply of salaries for the Arabs of the provincial garrison. In Egypt, this meant that the fiscal structure, at the local level basically unchanged from the Roman period, was simply redirected, away from sending food and money to Alexandria and then across the sea to Constantinople; after AD 650 or so, it went instead to the new garrison-city of Fusṭāṭ, today part of Cairo, and to the Arabs there. The problem of the Umayyad system was that this meant that the provincial army consumed the revenue of the province, and that it did not go to the capital at Damascus, or to anywhere else outside Egypt, at least not on a regular basis; and this was so for every other province of the Caliphate, too, in particular the other two seriously rich areas, Iraq and north-east Iran or Khurāsān.[11] This is the third major difference from the Roman Empire, and the one that I want to develop for the rest of this chapter.

The Romans left the actual process of taxing to local élites; after that, though, tax was in the hands of central government representatives. The Umayyads also used local élites to tax, everywhere in the Caliphate, but the level of surveillance over the tax-collection process was far higher, judging by Egyptian records, and evasion seems to have been considerably harder.[12] Conversely, after that, central government had *less* control over where tax went. The ruling élites of the Caliphate were based in a network of concentrated foci, Fusṭāṭ in Egypt as we have seen, Kairouan in Tunisia, Kufa and Basra in Iraq, Merv in Khurāsān, and so on; they regarded it as their right to keep provincial revenues, precisely because they were an élite. The internal political strategies of the Umayyad caliphs were thus focused on how to seize provincial revenues against the resistance of the local Arab armies. In AD 694, the caliph, 'Abd al-Malik, having just won a civil war, sent a loyal and tough governor to Iraq, al-Ḥajjāj, who ruled there for two decades; Iraq was not only rich but also had a tendency to hostility to the Umayyad heartland of Syria. Al Ḥajjāj cut local Arabs out of the army structure, and put a Syrian garrison there instead; the surplus taxation, this time, went to Damascus. Similar procedures can be tracked elsewhere too; by the end of the Umayyad period, Syrian armies were everywhere except in Khurāsān and in the marginal Berber lands of the Maghreb.[13] But it required constant toughness to achieve this, and the control of the caliphs over tax could always be reversed – centralisation was a political victory in al-Ḥajjāj's Iraq, not a structural change. It is significant, for example, that a caliphal claimant in AD 744, Yazīd III, used as part of his manifesto the promise that taxation would stay in the provinces; the issue remained live.[14] I would propose that this fiscal decentralisation was the logical consequence of putting a new, conquering politico-military élite into separate provinces. It is what happened to Alexander's empire too, after all, which thus broke up very quickly. But what the Umayyads at least achieved was a continued political loyalty to a single Caliphate among the fiscally decentralised armies of each province, however fractious they also were.

In AD 749–50, the Umayyads were overthrown by the army of Khurāsān, which chose a new caliphal dynasty, the 'Abbāsids; the latter based themselves in Iraq, and replaced the Syrian army with a Khurāsānī army, also located in Iraq in the new city of Baghdad. The 'Abbāsids centralised the army structure, and slowly removed the salaries of the decentralised armies of the provinces, though at the cost of a set of tax revolts and eventually a civil war in late eighth- and early ninth-century Egypt. This allowed the steady centralisation of the fiscal system, particularly in the 780s–90s and in the 830s–40s. Baghdad became astonishingly large and rich. And the army remained based in Iraq; the 'Abbāsids did not have much of a stable frontier army, and relied on sending troops out from Iraq when they were needed. This military centralisation was, I think, a necessary element in 'Abbāsid fiscal centralisation. The army did not stay the same, however. The Khurāsānīs of the 'Abbāsid revolution were on the wrong side of a civil war in the 810s, and were replaced first by Persian (rather than Arab) levies from Khurāsān, then, from the 830s, by professional Turkish troops, many of them ex-slaves, the beginning of the *ghilmān* or slave armies that recur off and on across the Muslim states of the next centuries. The Turks were brought in by Caliph Mu'taṣim (AD 833–42), a military-minded ruler who wanted a decent fighting force. To choose a non-Arab group of no particular social status (indeed, as ex-slaves, often of very low social status) was also prob-ably seen as a way of taking the army out of the political élite; this was the period when fiscal centralisation massively extended the civilian bureaucracy of the major Iraqi cities, creating the possibility of making a career, gaining real power, without having to handle a sword, for the first time in Arab history. But the principle of the 'state class' was by now sufficiently established that Turkish generals were simply absorbed into it; Turks became provincial governors or administrative officials very fast, and future centuries of *ghilmān* armies never made for a less military ethos for the élite as a whole.[15] If ever it might have done, conquest by a new army anyway always restored the status quo.

So here, in the 'Abbāsid period, we do have a structural change: with the great bulk of both the bureaucracy and the army now in Iraq, there was a structural logic that focused taxation on Iraq and left less of it in the provinces. Indeed, the 'Abbāsid fiscal system at its high point between the 780s and the 850s was even more centralised than that of the Roman empire, in the sense that so much tax went to the centre; the Roman system was centrally con-trolled, but then directed in large part to the frontiers, where the army was. But the 'Abbāsid system was also more fragile. If there was political trouble in Iraq, as with the civil war of the 810s, and, still more, that of the 860s, when Turkish military leaders killed several caliphs, the provinces had less incentive to continue to send money and goods to Iraq. And, whereas in the Umayyad period it was possible to dispute over tax-paying and stay politically loyal, in the 'Abbāsid period this was not so any more. If a province – most likely a provincial governor and his entourage – wanted to keep its taxation, it would have to break away from the 'Abbāsid state and recruit its own army, thus recreating the Iraqi *khāṣṣa* at the level of the province. This happened in Tunisia in the 810s, and in the 860s it was repeated in Egypt under the Turkish Tulunids, as well as in Iran under a succession of Persian dynasties. After the 920s it happened everywhere, and the 'Abbāsid Caliphate broke up.[16]

The 'Abbāsids may have changed the fiscal structure, then, but they did not change the tendency, already visible in the Umayyad period, to provincial separatism. The Romans were more successful here, because, I would suggest, they gave more power to landowning élites, integrating them more organically into the structures of imperial government, thus making provincial breakaway much more risky and messy. (The Mediterranean also helped; land communication across the Caliphate could never be as easy.) What the separation between the 'state class' and the hierarchies of landowning did do, however, was make it easier to break away from the 'Abbāsid Caliphate but replicate its structures of government at the provincial level. Roman state structures did not survive at all well at the level of the province, as post-Roman régimes found out in western Europe;[17] but 'Abbāsid structures did. It was enough to expand the local bureaucracy and recruit an army – which did not even have to be local; Turkish and Berber and other professionals were easy to find – and you could have your own local state. The 'Abbāsid Caliphate by AD 950 or so had divided into a dozen pieces; nearly every one was the Caliphate in miniature. Only in Spain, and also in a handful of polities in northern Iraq and nearby mountain areas, did the fiscal and political structure risk breakdown when this happened; even in Iran, where traditional aristocracies were strongest, the Umayyad and 'Abbāsid presupposition remained that *real politics* was focused on the capital, wherever that might be in any given period.[18] And on the level of the independent province, it was also much easier for the local ruler to keep tax-raising under his direct control; decentralisation never resulted in Egypt, Iraq or Tunisia being divided up into several pieces. The 'Abbāsid system worked best, most stably, at the level of the province, one could conclude; in this respect unlike the Roman Empire.

I have not used much sociological terminology in this paper, but my aim throughout has been sociological, in that I have aimed to allow comparisons to be drawn, in particular in the arena of province-centre relations: between the Roman Empire and the Caliphate of course, but, I hope, also between both of these and states like those of the Ottomans and Mughals, where some of the caliphal patterns recur, and like China, which is maybe more similar to the Roman case. To enrich that comparison, here developed in the case of one single element, one could then choose others, as other scholars do in this book.

But I think that one can get quite a long way with even one comparative element as a guide to structural differences. These then can, and will, be developed elsewhere.

Notes

1. Contrast for example Jones (1964: 366–469), or Carrié (1993), with any of the authors cited in n. 3. This article is intended to be a think piece, and its bibliography is inevitably summary.
2. An excellent example is El-Hibri (1999).
3. See in general, and for what follows, Kennedy (2001); Sourdel (1999); Crone (1980). For monographic studies on taxation, see further Simonsen (1988); Morimoto (1981); Lokkegaard (1953); Dennett (1950).
4. Runciman (1989) (vol. 2).
5. See for example Jones (1964: 456–59 and 722–66); Lepelley (1983).
6. See for an overview Wickham (2005: 62–80).
7. Liebeschuetz (2001: 104–202); Claude (1969: 107–25 and 155–61).
8. See in general for example Kelly (2004); Whitby (2000: 469–95).
9. Kennedy (2001), especially pp. 59–95; Puin (1970: 80–116) for 'Umar's choice.
10. See in general, Crone (1980); for the 'warrior' mode, Runciman (1989, II, pp. 202–08).
11. Kennedy (2001: 63–65 and 71–76).
12. See for a survey Wickham (2005: 133–44), building on Simonsen and Morimoto, cited in n. 3.
13. Kennedy (2001: 33–47).
14. See for example Crone (1994), at p. 41.
15. For the Turks, see Gordon (2001); see in general Crone (1980: 74–88).
16. Kennedy (1986: 171–99).
17. Wickham (2005: 80–124).
18. Kennedy (1986: 200–308), is easily the best survey.

13

Returning the Household to the Patrimonial-Bureaucratic Empire: Gender, Succession, and Ritual in the Mughal, Safavid and Ottoman Empires

Stephen P. Blake

The patrimonial-bureaucratic empire, a model of premodern state organisation first developed by Max Weber, has inspired much of the recent writing on the structure of the empires of the early modern Middle East. Patrimonial-bureaucratic rulers governed on the basis of a personal kind of traditional authority whose model was the patriarchal family. Patrimonial domination originated in the patriarch's authority over his household: It entailed obedience to a person, not an office; it depended on the loyalty between subject and master; and was limited only by the ruler's discretion. Patrimonial states arose, according to Weber, when lords and princes extended their sway over extra household subjects in areas beyond the patriarchal domain. Expansion, however, did not limit the ruler's ambition. Within the larger realm, conceived as a huge household, the ruler/master exercised military and administrative power of an unrestrained character.[1]

Within the patrimonial model of political organisation two basic variants emerged. The first, the patrimonial kingdom, was the smaller entity and was closer in organisation and government to the ideal represented by the patriarchal family. The second, the patrimonial-bureaucratic empire, was larger and more diffuse. Rulers of such empires developed strategies that allowed personal, household-dominated rule of an attenuated kind within realms of considerable area, population and complexity.

To govern successfully a patrimonial ruler needed a body of loyal, disciplined soldiers. Patrimonial armies were made up of troops whose primary allegiance was to an individual rather than to a dynasty or an office. In patrimonial kingdoms the military forces consisted, for the most part, of the household troops of the ruler. In patrimonial-bureaucratic empires, on the other hand, armies were larger and complex. To conquer and order states of such size required a collection of soldiers too great for the imperial household to manage and maintain. As a result, the armies of patrimonial-bureaucratic emperors split into two groups; one, the private household troops of the emperor and, two, the soldiers of major subordinates, the bulk of the army, men who were bound more to their commanders than to the emperor.

Patrimonial administration followed a similar pattern. In the limited compass of the patrimonial kingdom the private domain of the ruler was virtually coterminous with the realm itself, and there was little or no difference between state and household officials. In patrimonial-bureaucratic empires, on the other hand, these groups were not the same. Extension of control beyond the household domain called for extra-patrimonial officials who administered, for the most part, the collection of taxes and the settlement of a limited number of disputes. Such officials, neither dependants nor bureaucrats, worked in an organisation intermediate between the household apparatus of the patrimonial kingdom and the highly bureaucratised system of the modern state. For example, patrimonial-bureaucratic officials filled positions that were loosely defined and imperfectly ordered – a situation very different from the articulated hierarchy of precisely circumscribed offices in modern bureaucracies. Candidates for posts in patrimonial-bureaucratic administrations had to demonstrate personal qualifications – loyalty, family and position – in addition to technical abilities such as reading and writing. Whereas modern bureaucrats were given fixed salaries in money, members of these administrations were often assigned rights to certain of the fees, taxes or goods due the emperor. In a modern bureaucracy a job was a career, the primary occupation of the jobholder; in patrimonial-bureaucratic administrations, on the other hand, officeholders served at the pleasure of the ruler and often performed tasks unrelated to their appointments. Finally, while modern bureaucrats were subject to an official, impersonal authority, patrimonial-bureaucratic emperors demanded of their officials personal loyalty and allegiance. Such rulers ignored the modern distinction between private and official and tried to make household dependants of their subordinates.

In the smallest and most intimate of patrimonial kingdoms, officials received compensation for their services directly from the ruler's household: They ate at his table, clothed themselves from his wardrobe, and rode horses from his stables. Beyond that, however, they had no claim on the resources of the realm. In the larger, more complex patrimonial-bureaucratic empire, on the other hand, rulers found it impossible to maintain personally all members of their expanded administrations. Thus, they began more and more to give officials land revenue assignments. In time an increasing proportion of state revenues was assigned to soldiers and officials. Since these revenues bypassed the ruler entirely, and since the assigned lands were often at considerable distances from the capital, this arrangement meant a loosening of the emperor's control over his officials. Under such conditions the strength of personal, patrimonial authority began to wane, and officials began to appropriate their lands and declare their independence.

As a result, patrimonial-bureaucratic emperors devised a collection of strategies that replaced, to some extent at least, the traditional sources of control. In order to maintain their hold and prevent appropriation, emperors travelled widely and frequently, renewing in countless face-to-face meetings the personal bond between master and subject on which the state was founded. They demanded of all soldiers and officials regular attendance at court and, on their departure, often required that a son or relative be left behind as hostage. They periodically rotated officials from post to post, allowing no one to keep his job for more than a few years. They maintained a network of intelligence gatherers outside the regular administrative structure who reported directly to them. And, finally, in an effort to check the power of subordinates, rulers of patrimonial-bureaucratic empires created provincial and district offices with overlapping responsibilities.

The patrimonial-bureaucratic empire was a model or an ideal type. It included a variety of elements drawn from existing situations and ordered into a functioning but theoretical system. Just as an economy could be judged 'free market' without displaying all the elements of Adam Smith's model, so an empire could be termed 'patrimonial-bureaucratic' without demonstrating all of the particulars of the type. Understood in this way, the model was more a guide or a point of departure rather than a final explanation of any particular historical entity.

While Max Weber provided the description of the basic model, it cannot be dismissed as merely European and parochial. Two early Islamic philosophers – Nizam al-Mulk and Nasir al-Din Tusi – held up the patrimonial ideal as a guide for Islamic rulers. Nizam al-Mulk (1018–92), who served as prime minister for the Seljuk rulers Alp Arslan (1063–72) and Malik Shah (1072–92), wrote in his famous book on kingship – *Siyasat Namah* or *Book of Kings*:

> A man's magnanimity and generosity must be [judged] according to [the excellence of] his household management. The sultan is the head of the family of the world; all kings are in his power. Therefore it is necessary that his housekeeping, his magnanimity and generosity, his table and his largesse should accord with his state and be greater and better than that of other kings.[2]

The second and more important thinker was Nasir al-Din Tusi (1201–74). A polymath (philosopher, theologian, physician, astronomer, astrologer, geometer and mathematician), Tusi wrote *Akhlaq-i Nasiri (Nasirean Ethics)*, one of the most widely read books on political philosophy in the medieval and early modern Islamic world. Like Nizam al-Mulk, Tusi maintained that the father's government of his household should be the model for the ruler's government of his state.[3]

Most discussions of the patrimonial-bureaucratic empire in the early modern Middle East have contrasted the centrality of the emperor and his extended household, on the one hand, with an increasingly independent array of military, administrative, economic and religious institutions on the other.[4] Despite the dual character of the model, much of the research thus far seems to have been devoted to the bureaucratic side of the equation:

- Military organisation – recruitment, control and payment of infantry and cavalry;
- Administrative organisation – establishing revenue, religious and legal hierarchies; and
- Economic organisation – collection of land revenue, role of merchants, development of commerce and control and integration of the European East India companies.

While these are important issues, there seems to have been a relative neglect of the household side of the equation. A refocusing on imperial households would allow an examination of other topics.[5] Three are considered here: gender, the marriages of imperial daughters; succession, the rules that governed the selection of new rulers; and ritual, the ceremonies chosen to undergird imperial claims to political legitimacy.

These issues, moreover, are not analysed in isolation, rather they are considered from a comparative perspective. What does the examination of gender, succession and ritual in the Mughal, Safavid and Ottoman empires reveal about the character and structure of each state? Only comparison can reveal what is shared and unexceptional, on the one hand, and what is unique and distinctive, on the other. Finally, it is clearly impossible to analyse fully each of these matters. The aim here is not to provide authoritative answers but is rather to pose questions and to venture tentative hypotheses. This essay is more a set of prolegomena for research than a series of finished arguments.

Gender

The Mughal, Safavid and Ottoman empires shared a common Turko-Mongolian conception of political sovereignty. According to this theory, sovereignty resided in the entire ruling family – both male and female. In the three early modern empires, however, the marriages of imperial daughters were arranged with quite different objectives in mind.

In the Ottoman Empire (c. 1289–1923) the marriages of rulers and their children were politically motivated. The Ottoman marriage policy can be divided into two phases. In the first, from the late-thirteenth until the mid-fifteenth centuries, sultans contracted legal marriages with the nearby Christian and

Anatolian rulers while, at the same time, introducing concubines, mostly Christian slaves, into their harems. They married their sons into both ruling dynasties while restricting the marriages of their daughters to the sons of the Muslim rulers – reflecting the Islamic sociolegal principle of *kaf'a*, whereby daughters should not be married to men of lower status.[6]

The second phase of the Ottoman marriage policy began with the death of Mehmed the Conqueror (1451–81). Thereafter, Ottoman rulers, based on their claim to world dominion, judged no other dynasty worthy of a marital alliance. The sultans contracted no more legal marriages, and the imperial harem contained only slave concubines. According to Islamic law and tradition, the sons of concubines were just as eligible for the throne as were the sons of free-born Muslims, and, since it was against Islamic law to enslave Muslims, the concubines were usually Christian, either war booty or purchased from slave traders. With the cessation of legal marriage among the male members of the dynasty, the marriages of imperial daughters became increasingly more important. During the sixteenth and seventeenth centuries the Ottoman sultans began to marry their daughters to the high-ranking slave members of their households, and the *damad* or son-in-law began to assume greater responsibility in the ruling establishment. Under Süleyman the Magnificent (1520–66), for example, the grand vizier, the highest ranking state official, was a son-in-law, and Ahmed I (1603–17) married three of his daughters to men who were eventually promoted to grand vizier. For the Ottomans the virtue of these marriages lay in the bonds of loyalty they created between the sultan and his high-ranking and ambitious subordinates. In addition, since these unions were made within the larger extended family, they did not diminish the prestige of the ruling house.[7]

During the rule of the Safavid dynasty (1501–1722) in Iran the practice of *musahara*, cementing political alliances through marriage, became an important tactic for consolidating imperial power. In the sixteenth century imperial daughters were married to the tribal Qizilbash chieftains, as the rulers tried to strengthen their hand vis-à-vis their rebellious subordinates. With the centralisation of power under Shah Abbas I (1587–1629), however, the tribal chieftains lost their power, and the Safavid rulers began to marry their daughters to the sons of prominent Shiite and Sayyid dignitaries and to the military and administrative elite, reflecting the increasing importance of Shiite legitimacy and official position in the new political order.[8]

For the Mughal rulers of early modern India (1526–1739) marriage was also an important political strategy. Like the early Ottomans, the Mughal emperors and their sons married the daughters of their military rivals – especially those of the Rajput rulers of north India. Imperial daughters, on the other hand, were not ordinarily given in marriage at all. This was so unusual that the early modern European travellers – many of whom had visited the Ottoman and Safavid empires as well – took note. Commenting at some length, they provided a number of fanciful explanations: imperial prestige or incest, among them.[9] While extremely uncommon, however, marriages of imperial princesses were not completely unheard of. In 1585, the emperor Akbar (1556–1605) married his daughter to the Uzbek ruler Shah Rukh, and in the late seventeenth century the emperor Aurangzeb (1658–1707) married two of his five daughters to his nephews, the sons of his brothers Dara Shikoh and Murad Baksh.[10]

The Mughal custom of keeping imperial daughters unwed, however, did not mean that they were rigorously secluded in the harem, unable to act in the larger world. Rather, these royal women seem to have been especially accomplished. Several were learned in the religious sciences, others wrote poetry and memoirs, and still others, from their own household resources, built mosques, shrines, caravanserais and established endowments for the poor and the pious.[11]

The principal factor accounting for the different marital role of imperial daughters was the Indian custom of hypergamy, whereby wife-takers were considered superior to wife-givers. A ruler acknowledged military defeat or a client acknowledged dependency by giving his daughter in marriage to his superior. Part of the Indic obsession with hierarchy, most clearly reflected in the caste system, the hypergamous rule meant that Mughal rulers had very few choices when it came to sons-in-law. The rare marriages that did take place – to foreign princes or cousins – underscored the principal.[12]

In the Ottoman and Safavid empires, on the other hand, different considerations seem to have been at work. The Ottoman rulers claimed a status so exalted that no possible bride or bridegroom could be found for them or for their sons or daughters. The sultans and their sons gave up legal marriage entirely, while their daughters were only given to the high-ranking slave members of their households. In the Safavid Empire, by contrast, the need to build political alliances seems to have trumped the desire for status, and imperial princesses were regularly married to military or religious dignitaries throughout the sixteenth and seventeenth centuries.

Succession

What were the rules governing the transition from one ruler to the next in the Safavid, Mughal and Ottoman empires? The Turko-Mongolian egalitarian tradition of sovereignty found its fullest expression in the Safavid Empire. Even though brothers and sons held provincial posts during the sixteenth century, sisters and daughters also had claims to political power. In the succession struggle following the death of Shah Tahmasp (1524–76), his daughter Pari Khanum took the throne for a period of about four months. Khair al-Nisa Begum, the wife of the eventual ruler Muhammad Khudabanda (1578–87), also played a crucial role in political and military affairs. In the early seventeenth century, moreover, sisters as well as brothers were blinded – since both were seen as threats by the new emperor. With the reforms of Shah Abbas I, however, a new patriarchal theory emerged. Sovereignty was limited to the patrilineal line of the ruler, and princes were no longer given provincial posts. Secluded in the harem, they were unharmed but removed from the struggles of the real world. At an emperor's death, his successor was brought from the inner household and seated on the throne, often completely unprepared for the demands of his new job.[13]

In the Ottoman Empire there seems to have been a similar modification of the Turko-Mongolian egalitarian theory. Under the early Ottomans all male members of the family – sons, uncles, nephews and cousins – were considered equally eligible for the throne, and many were given provincial posts. This led, however, in the fourteenth and early fifteenth centuries to a series of bloody succession struggles. In an attempt to reduce bloodshed and dynastic uncertainty Mehmed the Conqueror enunciated a new principle. In his law code he wrote: 'For the welfare of the state, the one of my sons to whom God grants the sultanate may lawfully put his brothers to death. A majority of the ulema consider this permissible'.[14]

In the second half of the sixteenth century, as rulers became more sedentary and administration more routinised, a new rule based on seniority emerged. Imperial princes were no longer sent to the provinces. The practice of fratricide lapsed, and imperial sons were secluded in the harem. Thereafter, a ruler was succeeded by the oldest living male in his family – brother, nephew or cousin. After his death in 1617, Ahmed I was followed by his brother and in the next 22 generations only three times did a son succeed his father to the throne.[15]

For the Mughals also, sovereignty inhered in the entire patrilineal line. Unlike the other two dynasties, however, the Mughals never developed a strategy for limiting competition, and military challenges by brothers and rebellions of sons marked the dynasty from beginning to end.

Babur (1526–30), the founder of the dynasty, had a short reign. His son Humayun (1530–56), on coming to the throne, distributed provincial offices to each of his four brothers, one of whom declared his independence and precipitated in 1540 Humayun's defeat by the Afghans. Akbar, Humayun's son, was challenged by both his foster brother Adham Khan and his half-brother Mirza Hakim. Jahangir (1605–28), Akbar's successor, also rebelled and, after mounting the throne, was immediately challenged by one son, Khusrau, whom he defeated and blinded, while a second son, Khurram, later revolted and was also defeated. Khurram, however, was allowed to keep both his sight and his life and followed his father as the emperor Shah Jahan (1628–58). After executing a son, two nephews and two cousins, Shah Jahan, nevertheless, gave each of his four remaining sons significant provincial responsibilities. Aurangzeb the most ambitious and talented of the four, imprisoned his father and in the War of Succession that followed killed all three of his brothers. Nonetheless, Aurangzeb gave each of his three sons important military and administrative posts and, on his deathbed, tried to avoid the inevitable struggle by drafting a will that (like Chingis Khan's) divided the empire into three equal parts. This strategy also failed and in the battle that followed Bahadur Shah (1707–12) ascended to the throne, killing his two brothers in the process.[16]

While to the modern eye the Safavid and Ottoman attempts to reduce violence and dynastic uncertainty seem eminently reasonable, from another point of view the Mughal free-for-all has more merit than perhaps first appears. Any theory of sovereignty must have succession rules that accomplish two objectives: they must be specific enough to limit the number of contenders while, at the same time, remaining sufficiently open-ended to allow replacements for obviously unqualified or incompetent candidates. The Safavid and Ottoman strategy of secluding imperial princes, while it avoided succession struggles, often brought weak rulers to the throne and opened the way for powerful ministers to wield sovereign power.[17] The Mughal method, on the other hand, despite its messiness, produced four battle-tested and competent emperors who collectively ruled for nearly 150 years.

Ritual

All three empires celebrated the major rituals of the Islamic year: Id-ul-Fitr, the three day festival celebrating the end of the month-long Ramadan fast; Id-i Qurban, the celebration (with the sacrifice of an animal) during the month of pilgrimage, recalling Abraham's near sacrifice of Ishmael; and Id-i Maulid, the celebration of the prophet Muhammad's birthday. In Iran and, to a lesser extent, in the Mughal and Ottoman empires, the festival of Ashura, commemorating the death of the Imam Husain and held during the first ten days of the month of Muharram, was also widely celebrated. In addition to these religious celebrations, each empire also featured a number of secular, dynastic rituals – rites of political legitimacy. In the Mughal Empire there was the imperial birthday celebration and in the Ottoman Empire the circumcision celebrations of imperial princes.

The imperial birthday celebration in Mughal India was a creation of the emperor Akbar. An elaborate ritual of legitimacy and integration, it was woven together from three separate cultural strands: the Islamic, the Indo-Islamic and the Indic. In its final form the ceremony was held twice a year – on Akbar's lunar birthday (according to Islamic Hijri calendar) and on his solar birthday (according to the Ilahi calendar). The central event was an elaborate weighing. One pan of the large decorated scale held the emperor and the other a variety of articles. The articles from the pan were given to the pious and the poor, and, in the assembly that followed, the emperor distributed horses, cash and increases in rank to his important officeholders who in turn presented him with gold, silver and precious jewels.

This new ritual was part of a larger, more comprehensive programme: Akbar was developing an incorporative, inclusive imperial order that would engage the loyalties and energies of the many ethnic, religious and sectarian groups of early modern India. While the emperor exchanged gifts with the nobility, the wide range of goods against which he was weighed suggests that the ritual was intended to include more than just the elite. The silver, cloth, lead, tin, fruits, sweets, vegetables and sesame oil in the lunar ceremony and the gold, silk, quicksilver, perfumes, copper, pewter, drugs, butter, rice, milk, grains and salt in the solar, along with the alms directed to the poor, and the sheep, goats and fowl given to shepherds and peasants, reveal that the ritual was intended to incorporate the entire socioeconomic hierarchy of Mughal India – from high-ranking officeholders and religious specialists to merchants, artisans, shop-keepers, labourers, shepherds, peasants and beggars.[18]

In the Ottoman Empire the imperial circumcision ceremony was a central ritual of political legitimacy. Although circumcision was a universal practice for Muslim males, it seems to have been more a secular, lifecycle ritual than a religious one. It was not one of the five pillars and was not mentioned in the Quran. There were no rules about the age at which it should be done or the celebrations attending it, and it was barely mentioned in the collections of Islamic law.[19]

While the circumcisions of imperial princes were periodically celebrated elsewhere, they never seem to have been elevated in the Mughal or Safavid states to the high ceremonial position they occupied in the Ottoman Empire. Under the Safavids European travellers reported private domestic celebrations among all classes of the population but did not mention large, dynastic ceremonies.[20] In the Mughal Empire also, Muslim boys were routinely circumcised but the celebrations were, for the most part, private. In 1545 at the age of three, Akbar was circumcised in Kabul. The ceremony, a family affair, lasted for 17 days.[21] Although Akbar later decreed that no Muslim boy should be circumcised before the age of 12,[22] in 1573 he organised an elaborate celebration for his three sons: Salim, the future Jahangir, who was four years old; Murad, who was three; and Daniyal, who was one.[23] The emperor Shah Jahan was circumcised at the age of four years, four months, and four days (the traditional time to begin school),[24] and Muhammad Akbar, Aurangzeb's son, was also circumcised at this same age.[25]

In the Ottoman Empire, on the other hand, the circumcisions of imperial princes were great public events – celebrated not just by the imperial family in Istanbul – but by noble and middling families in the capital and elsewhere, who scheduled their circumcisions to coincide with those of the imperial sons. These elaborate ceremonies seem to have begun as early as 1387, when

Murad I circumcised his three sons – Beyazit, Yakub and Savci.[26] Although the circumcision of every Ottoman prince was ordinarily attended by festivities (some more public and elaborate than others), it was the three spectacular festivals of 1530, 1582 and 1720 that were widely remembered and recorded.

In 1530, Süleyman the Magnificent arranged a 20-odd day commemoration in the At Maidan or Hippodrome for the circumcision of his three sons – Mustafa, Mehmet and Selim. Coming on the heels of the Ottoman failure to take Vienna in 1529, the festivities have been interpreted as an effort to deflect attention from the military setback. The tents of the Akkoyunlu, Mamluk and Safavid rulers, all recently defeated by the Ottomans, were on display, and the hostage Akkoyunlu and Mamluk princes were given prominent seats.[27]

In 1582 Murat III (1574–95) organised for his son Mehmed III the most lavish circumcision festival ever – an event which was arguably the most spectacular dynastic ritual of the entire Ottoman period. It lasted for 52 days and was memorialised in a book (*Surname-i Humayun* or *Imperial Festival Book*) that included poetical descriptions and illustrations. As a ceremony of political legitimacy, the grandeur and majesty of the dynasty was the principal theme. Most days were marked by public receptions, processions or performances, which were presided over by the grand vizier, and witnessed by the sultan and his concubines from an enclosed booth. On the actual day thousands were circumcised – orphans, converts, slaves and the poor. Processions of artisans, ulama, students and merchants, performers from Arabia, Egypt, India and Europe, mock battles depicting famous Ottoman victories, fireworks and music – all were witnessed by the sultan, state officials and European and Islamic ambassadors.[28]

In 1720, Ahmed III commemorated the circumcision of his three sons in an elaborate festival that lasted 15 days and was also memorialised in a book.[29] Historians of the Ottoman Empire have interpreted the circumcision ceremonies in a variety of ways. One argument sees them primarily as public spectacles. Thus, Süleyman's ceremony of 1530 was an effort to redirect public attention from a military defeat,[30] and Murat III's extravagant ritual of 1582 was intended to divert public gaze from the disorder of his time – war with the Safavids, rebellion in Anatolia, and debased coinage.[31] But, the circumcision ceremony in the Ottoman Empire, like the birthday ceremony in the Mughal Empire and the celebration of the prophet's birthday in the early modern Moroccan state,[32] could also be seen as a public rite of political legitimacy, intended to strengthen and glorify the dynasty. The 1582 festival, like the Mughal birthday ceremony, included a cross section of the Istanbul populace – artisan groups, Janissary regiments, archers, horsemen, artillerymen, magicians, musicians, puppeteers, fireworks makers, the ulama, Greek and Armenian patriarchs, and merchants. In addition, during the daily assemblies food and money were distributed to the populace and gifts were exchanged between the sultan and the foreign ambassadors and high-ranking officials.[33] The overall attempt seems to have been to promote the legitimacy of the dynasty and to create a sense of identity among the populace of this multi-ethnic, multi-sectarian state.

Conclusion

Max Weber's model of premodern state organisation, the patrimonial-bureaucratic empire, has been widely employed by historians of the early modern Middle East. Most of the analysis, however, seems to have been devoted to the bureaucratic half of the model, to issues of military, administrative and economic organisation. To look more closely at the household dimension of Weber's construct is to open up new, largely unexplored areas of investigation.[34] While the Mughal, Safavid and Ottoman empires all shared a common Turko-Mongolian theory of political sovereignty, quite different ideas about status and alliance governed the marriage strategies of the three imperial households. For the Ottomans and Safavids the marriages of imperial daughters were undertaken primarily to strengthen political alliances, while for the Mughals the Indic obsession with hierarchy severely limited the marriage pool and, as a result, imperial daughters were often not married at all. Different rules also came to govern the shift of power from one ruler to another. In the Safavid and Ottoman states a desire for order and stability led to the seclusion in the imperial harem of a winnowed list of candidates. When the designated successor turned out to be weak or incompetent, a high-ranking subordinate often assumed the responsibility of rule. The Mughals, on the other hand, maintained the egalitarian tradition of Chingis Khan, and rebellions of sons and fights among brothers marked the dynasty from beginning to end. Such disorder, however, did not throw the state into chaos; rather, these struggles seemed to energise the dynasty, resulting in a series of relatively stable, long-lived and productive reigns. Although all three states celebrated the major rituals of the liturgical Hijri calendar, both the Mughal and Ottoman imperial households created new secular rituals of political legitimacy. The imperial birthday celebration, introduced by the Mughal emperor Akbar, and the circumcision celebrations of imperial princes, begun by the early Ottoman emperors but expanded and elaborated in later years, were both intended to help integrate the large, multi-ethnic populations into one imperial whole. For the Safavids, on the other hand, the ritual innovation was religious. As part of its effort to convert the populace to Imami Shiism and thereby to bolster its political and religious claims to legitimacy, the imperial household promoted the elaboration and expansion of the Ashura commemoration of the martyrdom of the Imam Husain. Finally, while considerations of space have forced these comparisons to be drastically condensed, they have, I hope, conveyed something of the distinctive character of each imperial formation, all three drawing elements from a common Turko-Mongolian, Islamic heritage.

Notes

1. The most complete discussion of the patrimonial state and its variants is found in Weber (1968, 1: 229–57, 263–64; 3: 966–72, 1006–69, 1086–92). Weber's remarks on the patrimonial-bureaucratic empire are scattered and fragmentary, not at all easy to integrate or interpret. His style is to construct pure types – the patrimonial state and the modern bureaucratic state – and contrast them. No historical state, as Weber himself points out, exactly matches either type. All present and past state systems are combinations of elements from several types; the patrimonial-bureaucratic empire is a mixture of the bureaucratic and patrimonial states. Actual historical examples differ as they approach closer to one or the other pure type.

2. *The Book of Kings or Rules for Kings: The Siyasat-Nama or Siyar al-Mulk of Nizam al-Mulk*, trans. Hubert Darke (New York: Yale University Press, 1960), p. 178.

3. *The Nasirean Ethics by Nasir al-Din Tusi*, trans. G. M. Wickens (London: George Allen and Unwin, 1964), pp. 153–56, 163–64, 203.

4. For the tributary empire see Bayly & Bang (2003). For the Ottoman Empire see Kunt (1983); Barkey (1994); and Hathaway (1997). For the Mughal Empire, see Blake (1979 and 1991: 17–25). For the Safavid Empire see Matthee (1999: 61–63); Reid (1978 and 1983: 49–77).

5. As attempted, for example, by Pierce (1993), Ruby Lal (2005) and Walthall (2008).

6. Pierce (1993: 28–30).

7. *The Intimate Life of an Ottoman Statesman, Melek Ahmad Pasha (1588–1662). As Portrayed in Evliya Celebi's Book of Travels (Seyahat-name)*, trans. Robert Dankoff (Albany, New York: State University of New York, 1991), pp. 1–20; Pierce (1993, chapters 2–3).

8. Babayan (1998: 349–81); Szuppe (1994 and 1995).

9. *The Travels of Peter Mundy, in Europe and Asia, 1608–67. Vol. 2. Travels in Asia, 1628–34*, ed. Richard Carnac Temple (London: Hakluyt Society, 1914), 2: 202–03; Francois Bernier, *Travels in the Mogul Empire, 1656–1668*, trans. Irving Brock; rev. ed. Archibald Constable (London: Oxford University Press, 1891; reprint ed., New Delhi: S. Chand and Co., 1972), p. 12.

10. Muhammad Saki Musta'idd Khan, *Maa'sir-i 'Alamgiri in The History of India as Told by Its Own Historians*, ed. Sir John M. Elliot and Professor John Dowson, 8 vols (Allahabad: Kitab Mahal Private Ltd., 1964), 7: 196–97.

11. Blake (1998).

12. See Saberwal (1998: 79–81); Thapar (2003: 62–64).

13. Szuppe (1995: 61–122); Babayan (1998: 349–81).

14. Inalcik (1973: 59); Pierce (1993: 15–21).

15. Alderson (1956: 33); Pierce (1993, chapters 3–4).

16. See Richards (1993).

17. Burling (1974: 47–52; 156–65).

18. See Blake (forthcoming).

19. Bouhdiba (1985: 174–85).

20. Jean Chardin, *Voyages Du Chevalier Chardin en Perse. New Ed. Par L. Langles*, 10 vols (Paris: Le Normant, Imprimeur Libraries, 1811): 9: 191–93; John Fryer, *A New Account of East India and Persia, 1672–81*, ed. William Crooke, 3 vols (London: Hakluyt Society, 1912): 3: 138.

21. Abu al-Fazl, *Akbar Nama*, trans. H. Beveridge, 3 vols (Calcutta: Bibliotheca Indica, 1902; reprint ed., Delhi: Rare Books, 1972), 1: 483–85; Gulbadan Begum (Princess Rose Body), *The History of Humayun (Humayun Nama)*, trans. Annette S. Beveridge (Delhi: Idarah-i Adabiyat-i Dilli, 1972), pp. 179–80).

22. Abu al-Fazl Allami, *The A'in-i Akbari*, trans. H. Blochmann, ed. D. C. Phillot, 3 vols (Calcutta: Bibliotheca Indica, 1927–49; reprint ed., Delhi: Low Price Publishers, 1989), 1: 216.

23. *Akbar Nama*, trans. Beveridge, 3: 103.

24. Banarsi Prasad Saksena, *History of Shahjahan of Dihli* (Allahabad: Central Book Depot, 1968), p. 2.

25. Muhammad Saki Musta'idd Khan, *Maa'sir-i 'Alamgiri* (see note 9 above), p. 23.

26. And (1963–4: 17). Mehmed the Conqueror circumcised his son in 1457, see Babinger (1978: 149).

27. Davis (1986: 9–10); Pierce (1993: 74, 97, 170).

28. Atasoy & Cagman (1974: 31–43); Pierce (1993: 191–93); Terzioglu (1995).

29. Atasoy & Cagman (1974: 73–74).

30. And (1963–4: 17); Pierce (1993: 97).

31. Terzioglu (1995).

32. Combs-Schilling (1989).

33. Atasoy & Cagman (1974: 31–43); Pierce (1993: 192–93); And (1963–64: 18–31, 118–30).

34. Cf. Artan et al. (2011).

14

Comparisons Across Empires: The Critical Social Structures of the Ottomans, Russians and Habsburgs during the Seventeenth Century

Karen Barkey and Rudi Batzell

Introduction

In the veritable industry that has been engendered by studies of empire, the-oretically informed comparisons have remained scarce. Two tendencies dominate the recent studies of empire. First we have erudite typologies of what empire is or is not according to a favourite set of criteria used by the scholar,[1] and the second remains within the domain of eloquent political narratives of particular empires or a parallel telling of the fate of different entities.[2] Another approach focused on the subaltern populations dominated by empire remains interested in comparative work, though from a particular point of view more embedded in cultural studies than social scientific analyses. The domain has largely been abandoned to policy analysts.

As we have become engaged in the study of empire, we have been capti-vated by many historical empires' ability to rule over diverse social systems and peoples, sometimes even with contradictory schemas and approaches patched together in one seemingly comprehensive whole. Though we have all agreed that more research is needed into the mechanisms governing imperial polities, we rarely carry through in a comparative framework. In this chapter we demonstrate the significance of imposing rigorous and interesting com-parative frameworks across empires. We observe a range of social outcomes as responses to the general crisis of the seventeenth century. A conjunction of rural economic dislocation, political unrest and revolutionary changes in the means of organised violence provoked imperial states towards varying degrees of action and intervention. We aspire to understand the divergent responses of three similar and contiguous imperial polities by comparing the nature of their imperial rule.

The rise of widespread banditry in the Ottoman Empire and enserfment of the peasantry in the Russian Empire during the seventeenth century crisis is contrasted to the second serfdom and the religious counter-reformation crisis in the Habsburg Empire. While all three empires experienced an economic and resource-based crisis in the seventeenth century, the Ottoman and Russian states actively intervened in their societies to reshape social relations, to take advantage of the social structural arrangements and their relations to elites. The distinctive and deeply consequential social formations of banditry and serfdom emerged from state strategies to cope with the crisis and meet the demands of mobilising society for warfare based on large infantry armies. The Habsburg dynasty did much less to reshape social relations. Rather, monarchs concentrated their efforts in an attempt to unify the empire under Catholicism, while the nobility independently pursued localised enserfment. How do we explain the puzzle of differing responses as well as different levels of imperial state involvement in the management of crises? In this paper, we sketch an answer that is based on a comparative analysis of the nature of state-society relations and the imperial regime types.

We argue that the prebendal regime of the Ottoman state and the mixed patrimonial-feudal regime of the Russian state made it possible for these polities to interfere and remodel state-society relations and reinforce certain groups to the detriment of others. The Ottomans relied on an established, effective, flexible and highly developed central administration, while in Russia, the challenges of the seventeenth century necessitated the rapid creation of a new bureaucratic order controlled by a literate, differentiated central administration. In the Ottoman Empire, the agrarian crisis led landless and uprooted peasants to join bands of roaming bandits, a process which was promptly instrumentalised by the state as bandits were mobilised into the Ottoman army, centrally or via the provincial officials. In Russia, where the general crisis was compounded by the chaos of the Time of Troubles, political agitation from the declining and impoverished military servitors provided the critical pressure to complete the enserfment of the peasantry. Enserfment helped the state to diffuse political tensions after the rebellion of 1648, and ultimately welded landholders together in support of the emerging autocracy. In both cases, the state was instrumental in shaping and enforcing these sociocultural outcomes. In the Habsburg lands, the much less centralised feudal regime managed the crisis in a different manner. Though less significant, banditry happened in the Habsburg lands as well. However, more noteworthy was the callous enserfment of the peasantry by the nobility. Unable to organise complex social-structural responses to the seventeenth century crisis, the Habsburg monarchy pledged to uproot the effects of the Reformation, imposing Catholicism on the Protestant nobles. They chose cultural unity over issues of class relations.

This explanation points in the direction of the original social structural arrangements that defined the imperial regimes. Various means of empire building through marriage, treaties and conquest led to particular state-society relations and distinctive social structures. We examine how the organisation and practice of landholding, the intensity of patron-client ties in agrarian class relations, the degree of state penetration and mediation of the rural networks of production and exchange, and the methods of revenue extraction and military mobilisation shaped the responses and strategies of these imperial states during the crisis of the seventeenth century. It is then important to further explore such relations and their consequences as they unfolded in the seventeenth century. We will explore briefly the nature of the crisis that befell the Eurasian continent in the seventeenth century. Though we know that the 'seventeenth century crisis' has been discussed at length, we choose to summarise the basic findings that are comparable across cases and underplay the debates. We will then explore the differences in state-society relations in the three empires to follow with an analysis of the different responses to the crisis.

This comparison has several merits. Even though a complete and detailed comparison of the three cases along every aspect of the state-society responses to the crisis of the seventeenth century is practically impossible, this comparison sheds new light that will foster research. First, it will certainly serve as a corrective and an elaboration of the comparative framework once provided by Perry Anderson. On the Ottoman case Anderson reproduced the simple decline thesis of his time to strip the Ottomans from any adaptive capability, therefore condemning them to inaction even before the crisis of the seventeenth century. On the Habsburg and Russian cases, he combined the two empires into the same category: an eastern variant of absolutism where the political system was just the repressive arm of the feudal class, simply a device for the consolidation of serfdom. We not only show differences in the nature of the political systems between the two empires, but we also trace its consequences in the different paths through which serfdom took form in the two lands.[3]

Though some comparisons have been made of the effects of the seventeenth century crisis with western and eastern cases, they have not taken into consideration these three contemporaneous land-based imperial structures that were in continuous relations across borders, and affected by each other.[4] Much comparative work remains resolutely Eurocentric and teleological, although Victor Lieberman has written an interesting essay critiquing the 'Orientalist mode' of historical comparison which assumes western trajectories as normative and compresses non-western societies into static and uniform categories coloured by colonial and imperialist historiography.[5] Especially since the question of variation in the outcomes of crises has been explored for Western Europe, it is now necessary to determine the reasons for the variation across empires. It will also bring to bear the different ways in which social and economic crises brought about different processes of state-society relations and degrees of intervention rather than assuming the non-feudal structures of the east to be typical of despotism, as the Ottoman and the Russian have more often been labelled. Although these empires pursued dramatically different policies, we find that the Ottoman and Russian states were much more involved in actively structuring the social order and controlling outcomes than their more feudal European counterpart.

The crisis of the seventeenth century

The fiscal and economic difficulties and social upheavals of the mid-seventeenth century experienced across the Eurasian continent were for a long time discussed and acknowledged as a 'General Crisis'. [6] The notion of crisis, however, has engendered significant debate around its causes, whether economic or political as well as its consequences, and more recently on whether we can even talk about a crisis. What is clearer now is that most of the regions of the European continent experienced some sort of economic and political adversity that was clearly interdependent, though not the same everywhere[7] and certainly not as short-lived and contained as a 'crisis', but rather as protracted and gradual unfolding of economic (price revolution, stagnating productivity while the population increases rapidly) and political (rebellions and uprisings, or wars as in the Thirty Years War) changes. Simultaneously and related, the seventeenth century witnessed the growth of the state and while many have studied the rise of the absolutist state in Europe as state formation, Niels Steensgaard linked the growth of the state to the symptoms of the economic crisis.[8] In Europe then the rise of the absolutist state has been closely related to the intensification of warfare.[9] Since it was the rural classes that paid for the growth of the state especially in terms of the size and provision of armies, we can surmise that part of the economic and rural predicament on the land can be explained by the needs of the state.[10] Warfare, taxation and state making in the context of population changes dramatically shaped rural relations and upheavals in most countries.[11]

The 'military revolution', which occurred in most of Europe between the mid-sixteenth and mid-seventeenth centuries, was revolutionary not in its rapidity, but in the fundamental transformation it helped to drive in state society relations.[12] For western societies, there has been considerable analysis of how military reform during this period often resulted in constitutional conflict between the centralising state and provincial gentry, the dislocation of traditionally influential military classes, the regimentation of society, and the rise of rationalised bureaucracies.[13] At the heart of the military revolution was the replacement of small cavalry forces composed of military servitors, as in the Ottoman and Russian Empires, or traditional feudal clients, as in the Habsburg Empire, with huge gunpowder infantry armies supported by a centralised state. The military revolution was of great importance to the strategies the state pursued in coping with the disruptions and dislocations of the seventeenth century. When war making was the primary activity of the state, changes in the means of warfare were deeply consequential for state-society relations, particularly when reforms threatened entrenched social and cultural structures. By the time of the Thirty Years War in the first half of the seventeenth century, traditional armies had become fodder for new line-formation, musket-based infantries, and each empire, in order to survive, had to adapt.[14]

The three empires we consider, the Habsburg, Ottoman and Russian, all experienced significant fiscal and economic downturns at the end of the sixteenth and the beginning of the seventeenth centuries. In each case, the fiscal difficulties also affected the rural populations where essential relations of production were transformed. Similarly, despite notions of a despotic and static state imposing solutions on an inert society, the Ottomans and Russians survived the military revolution only by creatively responding to social and political pressure and organising significant rearrangements of the agrarian social order, leading to economic, fiscal and political transformation in these empires.

In the Habsburg lands, the decades after the 1600s experienced a deep crisis of an economic and political nature. The Habsburg lands were hit hard by the wars with the Ottomans (between 1593 and 1606), that brought increased taxes and rural devastation, especially in Hungary. Yet, more generally, the Habsburgs were affected by their awkward intermediate position in the trading order of Europe, leaving the empire more vulnerable and less developed than others. The expansion of other European countries towards the Atlantic sea trade had affected their inland trade with the Habsburgs. American silver and gold hurt the mining industry while the Scandinavian increase in copper mining hurt the copper and iron industry. The three structural effects of these were the ruralisation of the towns, the conflict between landlords and their peasantry and the internal differentiation within the magnate class. In each of these crises, the role of the imperial state had been minimal, with its priority remaining a Catholic consolidation through the realm and the accommodation of the nobility to ensure their loyalty. Thus when the nobility independently pursued localised enserfment, the monarchy mostly allowed such outcomes.

In the Ottoman Empire, the severe fiscal and economic crises felt by the state and society was once thought to be directly the result of the price movements that affected the empire from Europe. While some of the fiscal crisis can be related to the price revolution, its effect seems to have been very short-lived.[15] Much more important was the growing military and therefore fiscal needs of the empire, the geopolitical constraints of increasing the revenue flow to the state treasuries as well as rapid population growth that had started in the sixteenth century. Both the state and the people had a difficult time maintaining the war of 1593–1606 against the Habsburgs and the continued warfare with the Safavids from 1579 to 1590 and more intensely from 1588 to 1610.

For a state engaged in multiple wars, the demands of the military, taxation and resources become deeply significant. The Ottoman state experienced a fiscal crisis and the empire felt that on the land. The scarcity on the land, the strains on state revenue and the ensuing conditions of elite competition led to fragmentation of the rural social order, the flight of the peasantry, and re-nomadisation. These developments were harmful to the local commercial activities and were compounded by the changes in the trade routes from the overland routes to the maritime ones controlled by the British and the Dutch. Vagrancy, poverty, joblessness coexisted in the Anatolian countryside leading to the formation of roving armies of bandits and mercenaries. It is with these units of vagrant peasants turned soldiers that the Ottoman state clashed and negotiated to manage critical wars on both the eastern and western fronts.

Russia entered the seventeenth century in a state of profound economic and political turmoil. In the late sixteenth century, the 'economic progress attained earlier in the century was reversed'.[16] Droughts, famine, epidemics, flight from the countryside and other factors coincided with a dynastic crisis after the death of Ivan IV's son in 1598, leading to civil war between contending factions and pretenders. Even as the political crisis was being resolved, class tensions exploded in massive peasant rebellions.[17] This was Russia's 'Time of Troubles', and it marks the beginning of a dramatic century of crisis.[18] This period of absolute chaos was a legacy in part of the tensions and resentment built up under the despotic and at times arbitrary reign of Ivan IV (1547–84). In Russia political crisis, foreign intervention and rebellion compounded the general economic malaise and agrarian dislocation of the late sixteenth and early seventeenth century. At the turn of the century, a three-year crop failure decimated the peasantry. Perhaps a third of the population starved to death, and cannibalism was rampant in the countryside.[19] After the liberation of Moscow from foreign interference and the establishment of the Romanov dynasty in 1613, the Russian state confronted the social tensions unleashed during this period of transformation and dislocation. In addition, Russia's strategic posture shifted away from military campaigns in the south and east. In the Smolensk war (1632–34) and the Thirteen Years' War (1654–67) Russia confronted the West with new intensity and was forced to rapidly modernise, having fallen behind both the Ottoman and Habsburg Empires in military strength. With the memory of the devastation of the Time of Troubles still fresh, the young Romanov dynasty was acutely sensitive to social unrest. Faced with fugitive peasants and declining social status, the cavalry servitors consolidated as a class and used their political clout to conclusively enserf the Russian peasantry after the rebellion of 1648. In Russia, the general crisis of the seventeenth century was made more acute and more revolutionary because of the general underdevelopment of the state and military, and the severe political and social crisis which erupted during the Time of Troubles.

To sum up, we agree with most of the literature on the crisis of the seventeenth century that a general downturn in economic and political fields upset the state society balance established across these three empires since their inception. From 1550 to 1650 state centralisation, the birth of modern warfare and economic transformation left the three empires in a serious predicament exerting pressures on their populations. While we cannot assess the depth of the crisis in each empire, we can make some comparative arguments. First, the effect was not homogeneous in any one empire. Certain regions fared better than others; some urban areas adapted while others sank into agrarian modes of production. As to the agrarian regions, the nature of state-society relations and practices of landholding, the strength of rural relations and depth of state penetration of rural social networks made a difference in how the state was able to mediate, control, and modernise during the crisis of the seventeenth century.

Second, all three empires faced military transformations since they were affected by the military revolution and engaged in warfare across boundaries where technological developments in one place affected the other. During the Thirty Years War, the Habsburg armies were transformed. A military aristocratic complex emerged, where those who had resources and connections to the court were able to construct regiments from mercenaries for hire and conduct war. During the war Ferdinand II finally found his dependency on entrepreneurs such as Wallenstein to be too demanding, and after the Thirty Years War he established a standing army (1649). The importance of this for the state was the monarch's ability to send his army to the field without the meddling of the provincial diets. Despite that, the Habsburg army was only organised into a coherent whole in the eighteenth century. The Ottoman and Russian Empires, on the other hand, engaged in a much more severe military transformation which altered their previous organisational arrangements. These differences need to be underscored and unpacked further, though we will do this after we describe the varying outcomes for each empire.

Analysis: imperial rule in comparative perspective

Origins of empire

The most widely accepted explanations for the different outcomes in each empire have been made in isolation, where specialists have tried to understand the particular dynamics of the crises together with the patterns of rule. They have neither asked the question of why one type of outcome rather than another or thought about comparative cases that might enlighten social analysis.

The enduring puzzle of different responses of imperial states to similar crises remains important. After all, despite some variation, the Habsburg, Ottoman and Russian Empires were large-scale, diverse, land based, contiguous agrarian political formations where much of the resources were collected through rural agricultural modes of production. They were comparable in their apparent expansion, and though they were at different stages of their expansion, they were imbued with imperial ambitions. Furthermore, each maintained authority over their population through the legitimation of a supranational ideology that included a religious claim to be protectors of Christendom or Islam, and an elaborate ideology of descent and lineage. And politically, each of these states maintained control through divide-and-conquer strategies, keeping elites separate, distinct, and dependent on the central state. Such control also entailed vertical integration into the state, but accompanied by fragmentation at the horizontal level of social arrangements. If these empires were similar along so many dimensions, then why were their responses to the crises of the seventeenth century different? Why were the Ottoman and Russian states so proactive and responsible in reshaping the balance of their society, even though such a solution was detrimental to particular groups, especially the peasantry? And why was the Habsburg state so intent on letting the nobility respond rather then the state itself, encouraging submission on the ground?

The answer we argue lies partly in the early styles of emergence and consolidation of empire and partly in the different systems of rule that became institutionalised overtime. In the next two sections we show that the Habsburg Empire differed substantially in the early patterns of consolidation, where their expansion through marriages tied the hands of the rulers. The Ottoman and Russian Empires, on the other hand, expanded by warfare and conquest, both subjecting populations to their will and making alliances to incorporate and assimilate conquered elites. The differences, we show have important consequences for the autonomy and central power of each state. We then move to discuss the different styles of imperial rule, state-society relations and the nature of agrarian relations to understand the particular outcomes in each society.

The Habsburg Empire emerged not only from the Holy Roman Empire, but more generally from a tradition of medieval Christian Europe where the Catholic religion, its institutions and its values were fully fused with the political order, and as descendants of the Holy Roman Empire, the Habsburgs saw themselves as the guardians of all Christendom. Though the election of the first Habsburg to the German imperial crown occurred in 1273 the effective rise of the monarchy as a contender in European affairs happened when Maximilian I (1493–1519) consolidated the empire through a series of marriages, the most important with Spain and Burgundy, followed by Ferdinand's (1520–64) union of the Austrian lands with Hungary and Bohemia in 1521. Ferdinand in many ways finalised an initial phase of consolidation of the Habsburg Monarchy in East-Central Europe, bringing together the hereditary lands and the eastern crowns. The relationship between these two segments of empire was loose, awkward and divided, constraining any attempt by the monarch at centralising. The limits of such an expansionist policy based on marriages is summarised by Ingrao: '...the subjects of these unions were sometimes incompatible, or at least unwilling to surrender their individual rights and independence to the dominant partner. Indeed, before they could receive the homage of their new subjects, the Habsburgs invariably had to swear to respect their privileges and autonomy – a constitutional nicety that would have been unnecessary had they acquired them by conquest'.[20]

This emerging Eastern European entity, described as 'a mildly centripetal agglutination of bewilderingly heterogeneous elements', by R. J. W. Evans, was culturally, geographically and structurally diverse. Yet it was also a classical example of feudal and indirect rule that grew by incorporating various crown lands. Especially in the historically independent and established kingdoms such as Bohemia and Hungary, regional autonomy and the retention of rights based on the existing diets helped reproduce the feudal social structures that already existed. In Bohemia, an ethnically mixed region made of five principalities, the predominantly Czech nobility initially maintained their rights until they were mostly eliminated during the White Mountain struggle and replaced by Austrian Catholic nobility. Early industry, trade and vitality, moreover, distinguished the Bohemian lands. In many regions where land was not amenable to agricultural production, alternatives had developed making Bohemia a leader in manufacturing and economic wealth. Hungary, the other main segment of the newly formed east-central Habsburg monarchy was fiercely independent, maintaining considerable constitutional liberties with the kingdom's bicameral diet and Chancery maintaining authority over the Hungarian lands. A form of Austrian or Habsburg absolutism did not succeed at this time since the Bohemian and the Hungarian kingdoms were too strong and independent. Even after the suppression of the Czech nobility, the Hungarian estates remained far too powerful for a more consolidated state enterprise.

The varied and diverse nature of the multifarious state-regional elite arrangements provided concessions and granted privileges to the peripheries in return for allegiance, preventing the consolidation of a coherent state structure. Habsburg monarchs relied heavily on various nobilities to ensure the collection of the contribution, to control the peasantry, administer justice and rule their own crown lands to maintain traditional order and traditional feudal values. In return the crown contributed to the maintenance of seigniorial wealth, inheritance, power and prestige, maintaining quasi-serfdom and stifling urban and bourgeois development when necessary to favour the nobility. The Habsburg army – an estate-based military force drawn from contingents permitted by individual landlords and in unreliable numbers for a limited length of service – proved insufficient; by the time he died Ferdinand (1564) had secured an army of only 9000 soldiers.[21]

By contrast to the Habsburgs, the Ottomans' expansion came through warfare, conquest and policies of local brokerage where Turcoman leaders made consequential alliances across frontiers with Christian leaders and warriors. Ensconced between the decaying fringes of the Byzantine empire and the various post-Seldjoukite political formations each vying for regional power and control of territory, the Ottomans emerged because of their syncretic, loose and multifarious traditions of their past. They had come as representatives of Turcoman, Mongol and Islamic traditions, with each of these balancing the weight of the other. Therefore unlike Catholic Habsburgs, Ottomans started in a relatively light Islamic ideological grounding as well as with a warring and conquering army where marriage alliances were only used after war to consolidate bonds that had been forged in the process of subjugation.[22] It is only after Ottomans made major inroads in the Islamic world in the sixteenth century that Islam became more rooted in the identification of the Ottoman state. Thereafter the Ottoman sultans both proclaimed Islam to be the state religion and worked hard to bureaucratise Islam into the administrative apparatus of the state.

The Ottoman expansion was carried out on multiple fronts, advancing towards the west as well as against the fellow post-Seldjouk principalities. Regions were distinguished and administered according to their proximity and adaptability. The first style of rule represented a secure relationship with the region of assimilation, for example, the Balkans and Anatolia, similar in many ways to Russian Ukraine, were regions perceived as open to incorporation. In the Balkans, direct control occurred by the reign of Beyazid I (1389–1402) whereas, by contrast, the more entrenched local Anatolian dynasties were not subdued until the reign of Mehmed II (1451–81) and even the time of his grandson Selim I (1512–20). The second set of regions, further away from the centre, were administered as military and economic outposts. The faraway Arab provinces, Egypt, Yemen, Abyssinia, Lahsa, Southern (Basra) and Northern (Baghdad) Iraq, northern Libya, Tunis and northern Algeria had been assigned governors and governor generals, and revenue collection was locally administered by tax farmers, thereby providing a salary for the officials, a revenue to maintain a local army as well as a surplus to send the central treasury.[23] The similarly more distant Balkan provinces of Moldavia, Wallachia, Transylvania, Dubrovnik were never fully conquered and assimilated, and thus were granted self-government in return for an annual tribute to the treasury of the empire.

In general, vassalage, initiated with the first Balkan conquests, allowed local landowners to remain on land, maintain their religion and become Ottoman vassals and see themselves as privileged Christians. The benefit of vassalage was that it left the local leadership in place, but as vassals who had to participate in the Ottoman campaigns and fight alongside the sultans. This early process fit with the policy of accommodation (*istimalet*), a strategy of encouraging local populations and nobilities to accept the new rule through incentives, and concessions, before they become fully incorporated.[24] At a later stage, having provided proof of loyalty during war, vassals would become fully Ottoman, their land converted to fit the Ottoman land system and their participation guaranteed through the tight oversight of a central administration.

The Ottomans early on had established a central slave-based army (the Janissaries) and used the cavalry (the *sipahis*) as their regional landed units who pushed at the frontiers. Their military as such was much more central-ised and organisationally more sophisticated than the Habsburgs who had to wait until the eighteenth century to consolidate their army. The Ottomans strived at what Max Weber has called a prebendal form of imperial rule, where a patrimonial household was able to establish centralised control over nonhe-reditary landed cavalrymen who performed military service in return for the use of the land. The establishment of a prebendal cavalry army along regional lines (though there was a central cavalry as well) was a way to balance the power of the sultan's patrimonial army, the janissaries. By contrast to the Habsburg antagonism between Austrian imperial elites and the regional aris-tocratic elites, the Ottoman central administration furthered strong vertical integration of the regional land holding and military elites into the state. In the Ottoman system, regional and assimilated elites saw the state as the centre of rewards and advancement, and perceived their participation as beneficial to their own future. As such, a political culture of loyalty to the state was wide-spread among elite members of society. The absence of any rooted Ottoman aristocracy with hereditary rights facilitated the centralised control exercised by the Ottoman state.[25]

The Russian Empire developed patterns of state-society relations that were intermediate between the feudalism of the Habsburgs and the prebendalism of the Ottomans. The origins of the Russian Empire lie in the mid-fifteenth cen-tury. Like the Habsburg and Ottoman Empires, the emerging Russian imperial state was legitimated by a supranational religious ideology as the defender of the Eastern Orthodox Christian faith. Russian religious independence from Byzantium began in 1448 when upheavals made a unified Church politically necessary, and therefore an autocephalous Orthodox metropolitanate was ten-tatively established by Moscow.[26] With time, this autonomy was legitimated and embraced as part of the imperial project, and the Orthodox faith came to serve as 'both the cultural underpinning of the regime and as a principle in terms of which Russia was able to define itself as a nation'.[27] Poor in resources and lacking a sophisticated tradition of classical civilisation, the Grand Princes of Moscow nevertheless managed to organise a dramatically successful and ruthlessly centralised state. By the early sixteenth century, a distinct ideology and imagery of autocracy tempered by networks of kinship and clan solidarity within the Boyar elite had emerged.[28] Similar to the Habsburg Empire, Russia had a group of dominant hereditary elites, the great Boyar clans, whose relation to the central administration was constructive rather than oppositional, a sort of 'oligarchic and bureaucratic' element operating behind the 'screens' of autocracy.[29] The Russian state was powerfully centralised though quite small and lacking the bureaucratic, technical and cultural sophistication of the Ottoman Empire. Still both states administered prebendal service land systems to support their provincial cavalry army, creating distinctive patterns of tenure and state-society relations in both empires.

After a series of dynastic wars during the mid-fifteenth century, the Grand Princes of Moscow decisively established and enforced their dominance over the various principalities of *Rus* in the latter half of the fifteenth century. The rise of Moscow, an unlikely outcome in ways, has been attributed to the 'skilful manipulation of the warrior elite' and a conjunction of social and political factors which eliminated significant challenges to the centre from alternative sources of power.[30] Ending the traditional autonomy of the princes and the decentralisation of the military at a remarkably early moment, Ivan III (1462–1505) consolidated central authority and brought all the major Muscovite princes along with their boyar supporters to the imperial court in Moscow for direct service supervised by the Grand Prince.[31] The devastation of the Black Death and the dynastic struggle depleted the numbers and resources of the petty princes and nobility, allowing the Grand Prince to consolidate central control with relatively little struggle. Elites participated in and supported centralisation, and Russia developed an elite culture of obligatory state service.

Perhaps the most critical aspect to emerge during Ivan III's reign was the subjugation and final annexation of Novgorod, because it placed the Muscovite state in a new and enduring military strategic position and led to innovations in property relations with 'momentous consequences'.[32] No longer threatened from three sides, Russia's expansion was defined by its southeastern frontier with the Kazan, Nogai and Crimean Tatars, and a western frontier facing Sweden, Poland and Lithuania.[33] Marking the end of appanage domination under the 'mongol yoke', the annexation of Novgorod province around 1480 set in motion modes of conquest and patterns of state society relations which would define Russian society until the fundamental transformations of the seventeenth century.[34] Most important was the establishment of the *pomest'e* system of cavalry service lands. After gaining control of Novgorod, thousands of elite landholders were deported to the imperial centre opening up millions of acres of land; this land was distributed to the newly recruited military servitors of the central state.[35] Ivan III, having successfully centralised the state, became 'the father of the *pomest'e* system', a practice of provincial landholding and cavalry military mobilisation remarkably similar to the Ottoman *timar* system.[36]

The annexation of Novgorod established patterns of conquest and consolidation, and under Ivan III (1448–1505) and his son Vasilii III (1505–33), Moscow's territory tripled in size as the Grand Princes gathered the lands of *Rus*. The distribution of pomest'e service lands was used to secure the loyalty of the provinces to the central state, a style of rule that would create intense pressures during the crisis of the seventeenth century and the military revolution. The pomest'e service land system grew in military importance and numerical strength, and by the seventeenth century the pomest'e servitors would play a crucial role in the political and social developments. Expanding through conquest and subjugation, the Russian Empire evolved a hybrid of hereditary and service land tenure systems, creating unique tensions and social relations in the agrarian order. Despite its material and cultural limitations, the Russian Empire emerged into the early-modern world as a centralised autocratic state fused with the 'power elite'[37] of the hereditary Boyar clans.

The patterns of expansion of these three, contiguous, land-based empires powerfully shaped the dynamics of consolidation and centralisation of state power and the contours of the agrarian social and economic order. In the feudal patterns of the Habsburg case, expansion and imperial control was extended through marriages, unions which produced confusing entanglements as central authorities promised and to some extent were forced to respect traditional and local rights of princes and other petty potentates. Due to these limitations, the central state left revenue collection, military mobilisation, and control of rural land and labour in the hands of local lords and princes. The Ottomans, on the other hand, had a highly sophisticated and consolidated centralised state, which controlled both a standing army and a prebendal service land system to support its provincial cavalry. Lacking any significant hereditary nobility, elites in conquered territories were gradually assimilated into the Ottoman land system. Landholding elites participated in this system by seeking patronage and favour, giving the state impressive control over the agrarian social order. Finally, in the Russian Empire, a conjunction of social and political factors led to early centralisation, although the apparatus of the state remained primitive and quite limited. As the empire expanded through conquest and ruthless subjugation, state patronage proved more fruitful than the Russian soil, and landholders, including both elite Boyars at the centre and the state created military service class in the provinces, became tightly fused to the central state. Control of labour, not land, would be the most important aspect of contention. As we will examine next, these different modes of expansion and consolidation unfolded into distinct patterns of state society relations in each empire, which would in turn both constrain and enable state responses to the crisis of the seventeenth century.

Social structure and the state: land, labour, property and power

Emerging from distinct patterns of expansion and consolidation, the organisation of property, production and power in rural relations in the Habsburg, Ottoman and Russian Empires helped determine the manner in which each state chose to respond to the economic/military crisis of the seventeenth century. The Habsburgs relied on a strong feudal nobility and the combination of a relatively weak and less centralised state. Lacking the social penetration and mediation of the Ottomans and Russians, the Habsburgs focused on alternative ways of strengthening their hold. From the beginnings of the reign of Ferdinand II through the middle of the century, they relied on centralisation through religious unification and responded to crisis through the further empowerment of the nobility in their estates. The Ottomans who had managed to construct a more centralised state responded to the crisis by absorbing the different trends on the land, adapting their military policies, making participation in the regional armies more open. The Ottomans possessed a much more fluid rural social structure and their ability to adapt and negotiate their policies to find ways to reign in and incorporate banditry into state centralisation was a remarkable feat. Russia relied upon a combination of a centralised and relatively autonomous state, dominant hereditary elites and a large service class. Faced with hybridity and tension, definitions of property rights and the boundaries of land tenure systems were questioned and remade as the state tried to control and appease various groups. Tensions and trajectories which emerged from sixteenth century practices would shape the state's response to the general crisis, and helped determine the social outcomes of enserfment and a rigidly stratified society dominated by an autocratic state.

The Habsburg Empire, a good example of feudal and indirect rule, grew by incorporating various crown lands through key marriage alliances. They granted autonomy to some, such as the Hungarian estates that preserved their medieval prerogatives, while crushing and replacing other nobility, for instance, substituting the Bohemian nobility with its German counterpart. There was no effective imposition of centralised Austrian or Habsburg rule, but rather limited Habsburg intervention in the Austrian, Bohemian and Hungarian regions. Relations with the Austrian, Hungarian and Bohemian domains were different partly due to the strength of the existing social and political structure in each place and partly due to the larger international relations. Hungary and Bohemia had been established kingdoms with their own entrenched and powerful nobilities. Moreover, their internal and external relations were complicated. Bohemia was made of five principalities, and definite regional mixes were part of this complexity. Bohemia was also more advanced than many regions in terms of its manufacturing and mineral producing capacities. On the other hand, Hungary was divided between

Habsburg, Ottoman and semi-independent Transylvanian sections which made it difficult to fully control and allowed the centre only partial control, and in fact, nominal rule. The Czechs were more incorporated, especially after the Battle of White Mountain, which led to the establishment of a foreign aristocracy. The segmented rule of each region fit the imperial style of dynastic rule. To some extent, the protection of the patrimonial rights of the Habsburgs relied on stressing loyalty to the emperor and his family.[38] Well connected aristocratic families of various origins, Catholics or Protestants converted to Catholicism, eventually emerged and cooperated and coordinated with the dynasty, loosely united through family networks and a Catholic Baroque culture. The state's authority and supremacy was based on its landed support.

When we discuss the nature of Habsburg rule and the state society structures that ensured this rule, we have to at least differentiate between the Austrian, Czech and Hungarian lands. Such distinctions complicate the agrarian picture, and even with such distinction, we inevitably fall short of the full view. The Austrian (hereditary) lands remain the most controversial in historiographical terms since here the contention of how much the Habsburg imperial rule helped shape rural relations is not fully resolved. On the one hand, the traditional arguments see the Habsburg centre as not really involved in local rule. In the Austrian lands, the provincial governments were the units of authority within which the provincial estates were embedded. The estates in the Austrian lands included the clergy, nobility and town, and sometimes a few peasant representatives. However, as R. J. W. Evans argues: 'In practice, since the prelates were largely assimilated, the towns largely ignored, and the peasants a marginal and incohesive force, it was nobles who dominated, either as a single, consolidated estate, or more often as separate estates of lords and knights'.[39] Provincial diets were the centre of bargaining with the crown, 'alternately discussing the princely propositions and advancing their own grievances, haggling over taxes and approving recruits'.[40]

On the other hand, more recent arguments have made a case that in hereditary lands the state extended its power to the level of individual peasant households, dramatically shaping the nature of rural relations and the reaction of the peasantry. Calling this process of state intervention, the bureaucratisation of family and property relations, Hermann Rebel argues that the state altered the peasant family structure, regulated the relationship between peasant tenant and noble landlord and made the peasant into an agent of the state.[41] No doubt the imperial state wanted to control the wealth of the region and the peasantry 'became the football with which princes and nobility played the games of state-building and status maintenance'.[42] Yet, such practices led to rural trajectories of social differentiation that were to become crucial in the increasing ruralisation and impoverishment of the peasantry.

Even though such transformations no doubt took place in some locales, it is difficult to generalise from this region to the rest of the empire. The nature of rural relations and state society interaction in the Bohemian and Hungarian regions of the empire were different. Even in regions where the Habsburgs destroyed the nobility, they did not really alter the existing feudal relations. This was the generalised mode of rule in Eastern and Central Europe, a form of Eastern absolutism that developed partly in relation to Western forms of absolutism and partly from internal pressures to consolidate control over the peasantry.[43]

More common was separate deal making with regional elites, in which the Habsburgs provided concessions and granted privileges in return for allegiance. The Bohemian example is a case in point. The Habsburgs were content to rely on Bohemian wealth, allow the region political autonomy, and give the indigenous nobility the right to put their own official into the government. In fact, Ingrao argues that the Bohemian estates enjoyed greater autonomy, extensive legislative and administrative powers than in the Austrian parts of the empire.[44] What did this estate autonomy mean for rural relations? First, even though they were legally serfs the old Bohemian aristocracy had showed a degree of paternalism and care for their peasants.[45] The partial restriction of peasant mobility in Bohemia dates to the post-Hussite Wars period with the legislation of 1487, the Bohemian nobility's pursuit of profit, the market attractions and the slow but increasing control over the peasantry. By the late sixteenth century, the Bohemian peasants were legally bound to the land and the precedent for the deterioration of their position was set. Hungarian independence from the Habsburg centre was even stronger since it relied on the strength of its diet, its independent Chancery as well as the strength of the aristocratic landowners. The agrarian relations in Hungary had been largely determined after the major peasant revolt in 1514, the Dozsa revolt, which was suppressed, and triggered the enserfment of the Hungarian peasantry. Though the National Diet of 1547 provided serfs with the right to migration, the general trajectory for the Magyar peasants was one of gradual and increasing conditions of enserfment and poverty. The Hungarian aristocrats and the lower gentry both exploited and mistreated the peasants who were by far the worst off in the Habsburg Empire.[46]

In every region, Habsburg monarchs relied heavily on the various nobilities to ensure the collection of the Contribution, to control the peasantry, administer justice, rule their crown lands and maintain traditional order and traditional feudal values. In return, the crown contributed to the maintenance of seigniorial wealth, inheritance, power and prestige, maintaining restrictions on peasant life, and stifling urban and bourgeois development to favour the nobility.[47] This feudal compact between the monarchy and the regional landed elite maintained the resource base of the empire, yet at the same time impacted the towns and especially the peasantry who would soon be forced into a second serfdom. Such a compact was beneficial to maintaining imperial state-elite stability, yet it was in the long run not beneficial to economic development.

The crown strove for a coherent and integrated state structure, but it could never fully achieve this within the powerful feudal constraints of the empire. The Habsburgs moved over time towards an autocratic state centred in Vienna, with an increasingly German centred aristocratic culture, yet without full integration. The main reason for the lack of integration was the strength of the Hungarian nobility, which never lost its privileges. The Hungarian nobility was neither integrated nor easily defeated by a military force. Therefore, even as the House of Habsburg emerged as a strong European force, internal state-elite struggles over centralised control continued. As R. J. W. Evans writes, Habsburg rule in Austria, Bohemia and Hungary 'subsisted on a community of interest between dynasty, aristocracy, and the Catholic church [where] loyalty became a calculation, not a sort of disembodied idealism'.[48]

The Ottoman Empire by contrast to the Habsburg imperial domains, had developed a different landholding system, the *timar*, based on another set of property relations and understandings derived from Islamic law and also Byzantine practice in the Balkans. In the beginning of the sixteenth century about 90 per cent of the land was state-owned (*miri*), the result of a Near Eastern understanding of the conqueror's eminent domain and establishing the use of land for the best interests of the Islamic state. In the core regions of the empire, the Balkans and Anatolia, the timar system became established as the principle form of landholding, based on a land grant issued by the state to a member of the cavalry, a *sipahi*. The allocated land that covered a certain number of villages and was organised along income categories remained in the hands of the sipahi for a limited amount of time. In return, the cavalryman was responsible for administering the domain for the state, collecting taxes and raising a retinue to fight in the provincial army. In that sense, the Ottoman landholders, from the lower level timar holder to the governor and governor-general (who also acquired lands in a similar fashion) were servitors of the state and agents who supervised the use of the land for the state. The Ottoman system left no room for a western feudal class with hereditary rights and privileges.

Although some hereditary practices were present early on in Anatolia and the state had to co-opt this strong hereditary elite, state centralisation allowed the service-based, non-hereditary principle to prevail.[49] Another aspect of the timar was rotation, an administrative device used by the Ottomans to regulate access to office. State agents had a limited tenure in any locality, averaging around three years, a practice which was an effective mechanism of central control, securing the lack of entrenchment on land and preventing local patron-client ties from forming. Since the local timar officials could be dismissed, sent out on rotation and shuffled into different districts with each rotation, this system of landholding promoted dependence and service to the state.[50] As a result, even the fierce competition for the limited numbers of landholdings was understood as meritocratic rather than state manipulation.[51] The competition between timar holders, the divisions among them as well as their inability to remain in one area long enough to build resistance gave the state an inordinate amount of control.

The movement and fluidity of state-regional elite relations in the timar system was buttressed by the stability of tenure at the level of the peasantry. The family farm unit (the *cift hane*) was the basic unit of agricultural production, defined as a plot of land of sufficient size and productivity for the maintenance of the household and the payment of taxes to the state. In this arrangement, individual peasant household conditions, independence and little communal solidarity differentiated the Ottoman land relations, especially compared to the Habsburg, and as we shall see, the Russian Empires. The state's interest in limiting mobility was only related to facilitating taxation and even then the Ottoman countryside was flexible, with peasants abandoning their villages for other regions or becoming nomadic, creating a symbiotic flow between sedentary and nomadic modes of rural production.

Peasant relations with the state were regulated through the parallel and independent institution of the local courts where peasants came for justice and to register their complaints. Even though the local magistrate was also rotated according to an internal schedule, peasants made frequent use of the courts, which functioned to deflect anger away from the local tax-collecting patrons and acted as a safety valve, diffusing and mediating class tensions. This became increasingly necessary as timar holders hired multiple intermediaries to collect taxes and moved towards complete professionalisation as an army rather than an agrarian administrative element. However, emphasising their military role eventually undermined the position of the timar holders because cavalry forces would become outdated with the military revolution. Rotation, peasant transhumance and autonomy, as well as alternative institutions made the Ottoman countryside and Ottoman state society relations adaptable. The result was that remarkably weak patron-client ties characterised Ottoman agrarian relations. As Inalcik observes, the foundation for the Ottoman rural social structure 'appears to have been centralist state control over land possession and family labour. An imperial bureaucracy had systematically to struggle to eliminate encroachments of local lords, while concomitantly striving to prevent its own provincial agents from transforming themselves into a provincial gentry'.[52] These weak ties were the outcome of the state's strategies for the administration of rule in the provinces of the empire. As such they were more the result of unintended consequences of their rule, rather than conscious strategies of rule.

The traditional timar landholding system certainly operated as the main administrative and military tool of the state in the core regions. However, such an administrative system was impossible to establish, regulate and maintain across the vast territorial and transportation barriers of the empire. Instead, revealing their flexibility, the Ottomans negotiated the modes of rule and the agricultural organisation differentially with new subject elites. Significantly, the principle against heredity was maintained over long distance. Regions were assigned governors and governor-generals, and revenue collection was locally farmed out to tax farmers, thereby providing a salary for the officials, a revenue to maintain a local army as well as a surplus to send the central treasury.[53] In the more distant and unassimilated tribute paying principalities of the Balkans like Moldavia, Wallachia, Transylvania, Dubrovnik, the interests of the Ottomans were such that they allowed hereditary princes the freedom to rule as they pleased though in return they demanded political-military obligations expressed by the formula: 'be friend of our friends and enemy of our enemies'.[54] Yet, before long they would interfere in the politics of local rule in both Wallachia and Moldavia. Even though the regions where tax farming and alternative arrangements operated were widespread, the larger timar structure remained the backbone of the Ottoman land system in the core provinces of the empire, shaping their understanding of rural relations and accommodating to the multiple variations assessed at the local level.

During the sixteenth century, we can already hear about the initial tensions in the social structural arrangements of Ottoman rule. In the advice literature of the sixteenth century, Ottoman pamphleteers warn of the problems with just rule, the breakdown of the army and issues of improper training.[55] The pamphleteers interpreted many adjustments in rule as a sign of retreat from traditional institutions and therefore decline. They were displeased that the distinction between the *askeri* (military-ruling class) and the *reaya* (the flock/ the people) did not hold any longer and that all kinds of people could become soldiers. While the rigid divisions between groups might have been more fiction than reality since the early beginnings of Ottoman rule, such fluidity of movement was perceived as one of the potentially explosive trajectories of the empire. Rather one of the important developments of this period would be the empire's response to the military transformations of the late sixteenth and early seventeenth centuries. First, the timar holders were the members of the regional elite most affected by the military transformation. Second, the various layers of regulation, taxation and the significant numbers of intermediaries contributed to the murkiness of the Ottoman agrarian layout, providing for the production of multiple losers and winners preventing patterns of class consolidation in response to change. Third, peasant responses varied considerably from moving, leaving the land, joining religious schools to various internal processes of differentiation where the social stratification of the rural classes became increasingly pronounced.

Russia's rural social structure was characterised by a unique hybridity between the hereditary lands of the Boyar elite and the service lands of the pomest'e cavalrymen. While the Habsburg land system relied on strict adherence to the hereditary rights of the feudal nobility, and landholding in the Ottoman Empire was definitively shaped by the state controlled timar system, in the Russian Empire a dominant hereditary elite coexisted, at times uneasily, with the pomest'e service land system. Whatever tensions may have existed, however, were generally subsumed under the principle of compulsory state service for all landholders, begun under Ivan III and finally codified in the mid-sixteenth century by Ivan IV. In Russia, all landholders were required to serve in a hierarchy subordinated to tsar and god.[56] Even the most powerful elites debased themselves before the Grand Prince or Tsar in rituals of subordination, calling themselves slaves of the sovereign. Although these rituals were shocking to Western observers who depicted Russia as the most abject despotism, the relations between state and society were more complex and negotiated.[57] Despite this dominant cultural and legal regime of obligatory state service, property rights and relations between different forms of tenure reveal complexities and tensions within the structure of rural life in Russia.

The nature of property rights in Russia for hereditary landholders has been much contested. Views have reached either the extreme of contending that Russia had absolutely no system of private property whatsoever, or of claiming that private property was held on a similar basis to the fee simple system of Western Europe.[58] More reasonable is Valerie Kivelson's suggestion that 'landholders worked out an idiosyncratic concept of property holding that did not fit either end of the classical either/or debate'.[59] The indeterminancy of property rights and the coexistence of two distinct modes of tenure would structure the demands made upon the state during the crisis of the seventeenth century, as status conscious and economically pressed service landholders would press the state for conversion of the conditional pomest'e lands into hereditary *votchnina* holdings. The crisis of the seventeenth century would precipitate a decisive rearticulation of property relations in the Russian Empire, whereas property relations remained more stable in both the Habsburg and Ottoman lands.

After the reign of Ivan III (1462–1505), the conditional pomest'e land grant became the most important, if not initially the predominant form of land tenure.[60] Similar to the Ottoman sipahi, the Russian cavalry servitors, called *pomeshchiki,* were responsible for arming themselves and appearing at annual musters and collecting taxes from the peasants on their pomest'e. Like the Ottoman timar holders, the Russian service class 'was not a landed gentry which voluntarily came to the aid of the government when asked', but existed, rather 'at the sufferance of the state'.[61] The rank, status and resources of the cavalrymen were entirely dependent on state service. Unlike the strict military caste privileges of the sipahi, however, the pomest'e holders were originally drawn from diverse social and regional sources. Although rotation was not a practice in the pomest'e system as in the timar system of the Ottoman Empire, the state still exerted considerable control over the middle service class. Far from the feudal gentry of the Habsburg Empire, service lands could not be sold or mortgaged; a cavalrymen who attempted to exit his estate by alienating his lands would be beaten with a knout and his lands returned to him.[62] The middle service class remained the state's 'creature', divided by a 'jungle-like atmosphere' of competition for service lands that weakened group cohesion,[63] until the seventeenth century, when it eventually emerged as a status conscious class able to mobilise and shape state action.[64]

During the sixteenth century, we can notice trajectories which would burst into the open during the crisis of seventeenth century leading to essential restructurings of rural relations. Although the military servitors lacked cohesiveness as a class, they were able to secure impressive privileges and acquired pretensions to status traditionally reserved for the Boyar elite. State consolidation in the sixteenth century allowed officials to act with greater independence, and Ivan IV (1547–84) issued reforms and policies which benefited the servitors and expanded the pomest'e land system. The interests of the servitors and the state coincided in opposition to the Boyars, monasteries and other private landholders. Both the state and its servitors desired to reduce private, hereditary ownership and increase the domain of the pomest'e landholding system.[65] Although Ivan IV's experiment with the *Oprichnina* was disastrous in most respects, many Boyar estates were expropriated in favour of the pomest'e system with the result that 'service land holding became the predominant form of tenure' and it appeared in the 1580s as if hereditary landownership might expire altogether.[66] However, Ivan IV's actions should not be construed as class warfare in favour of the servitors against the magnates; rather, these 'developments were in favour of the state, which required a general levelling of privileges of the upper and middle service classes'.[67] Further, as the state demanded more revenue, the needs of servitors and officials coincided in developing more efficient and precise methods of taxation and control of peasant taxpayers.[68]

Along with these changes in property relations came expanding privileges and autonomy for the service class. Most significantly was the intensification of rural class relations, as peasant producers and service landholders were entwined in ever-tighter nets of exploitation and dependence. Violating established restrictions on relations between state-servitor and peasant, Ivan IV permitted the pomeshchiki to set the level of the rent on their service lands and to extract revenue themselves. This increased exploitation because it placed the landholder and the state in competition in expropriating resources from the peasant. It also made the cavalryman's interest in his holding personal, marking a turn away from prebendalism towards a more western style of patron-client relations.[69] Even more significantly, pomest'e landholdings were consolidated in one locality, instead of being spread across the empire in fragmented pieces, making patron-client relations more intimate and exploitation more intense.[70] A significant result of these changes in the pomest'e system in the late sixteenth century was that cavalrymen became less interested in waging war and more inclined to supervise their estates and extract revenue.

Through the sixteenth century, the Russian peasant was not yet enserfed, although his mobility was considerably more restricted than in the Ottoman Empire. Tendencies towards enserfment were evident as early as the end of the fifteenth century, but paralleling the transformation of pomest'e holdings, it was not until the seventeenth century that the real revolution in rural relations took place.

One of the most central facts of life for peasants in Russia was the system of collective responsibility. Although there were significant regional differences, throughout the Muscovite period records show the centrality of this institution,[71] and its origins have been traced back to Mongol influence in Kievian Rus' in the thirteenth century.[72] Just as Islamic legal notions of property rights and land use were crucial in shaping the structure of Ottoman rural relations, so too the principle collective responsibility would provide a basis on which a particularly vicious and deeply entrenched serfdom could develop in Russia. The state cadastres, which assessed the tax-value of the land a commune encompassed, were updated very infrequently. Based on these assessments, peasants were held collectively responsible for paying a set tax which did not change until a new census updated the cadastres. If a family fled, the remaining peasants would have to assume the tax burden. Thus peasants were systematically driven to form bonds of social solidarity to simply survive the taxation regime based on collective responsibility.[73] Collective responsibility had deep roots in Russia, and became embedded in state strategies for controlling the population. Despite administrative growth, 'the country remained understaffed and undergoverned', and with this recognition, 'Muscovite leaders built on indigenous traditions of collectivism and mutual responsibility to develop complex systems through which to co-opt the population into the process of its own subjugation'.[74]

Long before the crisis of the seventeenth century, the state had demonstrated a willingness to limit peasant mobility and subordinate the cultivators to the landholders. In response to labour dislocations and widespread desertion of agricultural land, the state issued a decree sometime between 1448 and 1470 limiting peasant movement to St George's Day (*Iur'ev Den'*) in the late fall after the harvest when debts would have been repaid and taxes collected.[75] This rule became the general law for all peasants in the law code (*Sudebnik*) of 1497.[76] The condition and position of peasants remained relatively stable through most of the sixteenth century. After 1592, complete immobility was extended to all peasants on a temporary basis in an effort to deal with the growing agrarian crisis, a measure which was significantly weakened by a statute of limitations on the retrieval of runaways and by the chaos that erupted during the time of troubles. By the time Russia entered the critical period of the seventeenth century, the state had made itself comfortable with the notion of regulating and restricting peasant mobility. Peasant mobility and legal personality were reduced during the seventeenth and early eighteenth century to such a degree that Russian serfs became little more than slaves.

Discussion: divergent responses to the crisis of the seventeenth century

We have so far examined the manner in which the nature of imperial rule, state society relations and the agrarian social structure of each empire lay down some of the tracks for diverse trajectories of responses to the deep crisis of political and material circumstances. Before we elaborate on the unfolding of these processes in each case, some comparative points can be highlighted. First, the enserfment of the peasantry as one of the most significant outcomes of the crisis binds together the Habsburg and Russian Empires. However, banditry in the Ottoman and serfdom in the Russian Empires are also equivalent in the sense that they were social outcomes that were obtained through active state intervention in rural class relations. The Habsburg Empire remains more of an anomaly since there the central state had less impact on the remodelling of agrarian relations and the rise of a harsh form of second-serfdom. Second, the Habsburg and Ottoman Empires experienced a steady stratification of the peasantry through the crisis, with a clear pattern of differentiation between winners and losers, while through the same period in the Russian Empire the peasantry experienced a levelling effect with steady movement of all towards loss of freedom. Finally, looking at the overall patterns of transformation within each imperial continuity, we can observe that in different ways, the Habsburg and Russian centres were much more cognisant of the necessity for a cultural project of unification than the Ottomans. The way out of the crisis for the Ottomans reflected their more ambiguous attitude towards large-scale projects of unity and homogeneity. The Russian and the Habsburgs were clearly more similar in this. Such differences become clear in the comparative narratives that we provide in this final segment.

The Ottoman and Russian Empires remain the two cases where the agrarian order was significantly transformed by the economic and the military crisis of the period. Both states were affected by the military revolutions afoot and were faced with the urgent need to reform their manner of fighting. The necessity for men and a new understanding of warfare meant that agrarian class relations would be tampered with to fashion the new army. Not only was this done through state intervention, and in both cases the imperial state was intimately involved in the formulation of change, but in the Russian case, the service class was much more successful at imposing its own preferences on the state, while in the Ottoman case, the service class was slowly dismantled, fragmented and became unable to act on its interests.

The central challenge to the Ottoman state during the crisis of the seventeenth century came in the form not of peasant or elite movements rebelling because of agrarian conditions, but as banditry. Armed gangs, often decommissioned from the state's military campaigns, roamed the countryside, available for hire and engaging in pillage to survive. Ottoman strategies of incorporating the peasantry and rotating elites kept both groups dependent on the state, unable and unwilling to rebel. The bandits were also a product of state-society relations, the agrarian tenure system and the lack of fixity on land. Even when these troops had turned to banditry, they remained focused on gaining resources from the state rather than on rebelling. That the state was willing and able to effectively control and manipulate these bandits through various deals, bargains and patronage, attests not to the weakness of the state, but to its strength and ability to manipulate the rural social order to its own central benefit.

In the Ottoman Empire, the transformations of the timar system in the late sixteenth century and the strategy of allowing banditry to become an alternative source of military energy for the empire was initiated during the time of crisis. While this, as we have said earlier, has been typically regarded as one of the first signs of Ottoman decline, it was in fact an alternative means of development under onerous conditions of fiscal and military requirements. Even though timar holders were the elites most damaged by the transformations of the seventeenth century, the system continued to exist and adapt in ways that made sense for the period. No doubt the timar holders were most affected by the decline of traditional warfare that made the group less essential for the state, increased competition for scarce resources and divided them into layers of winners and losers, and in their vulnerability, they often even turned on each other. This created a consolidation of land in the hands of the largest timar holders whose connections and resources saved them from the fate of the smaller holders who perished.[77] Additionally, the length of land tenure increased as timar holders struggled to hold onto their land. Instead of rotation and engaging in war, timar holders paid the state a yearly fee, transforming state controlled land tenure into a form of tax farming.[78] Cavalrymen not only experienced pressure from above as wealthier holders consolidated and converted to tax farming, but also from below as the state recruited peasants and commoners into its new army.

To Ottoman strategists, the need for musketeers was evident for much of the sixteenth century, and became painfully pressing during the war with the

Habsburgs from 1593 to 1606.[79] The reluctance of the cavalrymen to carry muskets led the state to rapidly expand the janissary corps, whose numbers increased dramatically from less than 8000 men in 1527 to 53,499 in 1669.[80] The Ottoman state increasingly dismissed timar holders who were no longer useful and awarded their land to any soldier, no matter his origin, rank or title for fighting with the Ottoman army. In addition to their military obsolescence, the timar holders were increasingly replaced in their duties as tax collectors. The economic crisis of the seventeenth century led the state to rely on more direct taxes collected by palace agents, effectively bypassing the timar holder. The unity of the service class in the Ottoman Empire disintegrated, as wealthier members benefited and less well connected members declined. Tax-farming became an important means of extracting revenue, and timar lands were granted indiscriminately to whomever served the Ottoman state.

The peasantry was also deeply affected by the social and economic forces of the seventeenth century. The *cift-hane* land-labour unit of family production was the foundation for the entire Ottoman agrarian order.[81] The economic crisis of the seventeenth century posed a serious challenge to this structure, as peasants sought flexibility and the state attempted to maintain stability.[82] Mobility and stratification were two outcomes of the demands for flexibility. Furthering the fragmentation of peasant solidarity, Ottoman peasants were increasingly stratified, as wealthier peasants with larger plots of land hired poorer peasants with less land.[83] Peasants had been paying taxes on a stratified system of high, medium and low resources, but with the rural crisis, any collective responsibility disappeared to promote stratified and more individualistic responses. Nevertheless, the overriding fact of peasant life was its fluidity. Peasants often had the option of moving to other villages, and villagers took the easy way out by exiting when times became difficult, demonstrating no intent to mobilise for collective action. As such, the countryside adapted to the crisis, with exit and movement and the state did not attempt to keep the peasantry tied to the land.

The structure of peasant life made it possible for banditry to develop and spread in this time of crisis. Peasants could easily pay an exit fee (*cift bozan akcesi*) and leave behind their land and tax obligations to join 'pockets of free-floating vagrant individuals in the villages'.[84] While the timar holders were refusing to take up modern weaponry, firearms became common in the countryside as rural life was militarised. Bandits (*celalis*) were drawn from the populations affected by the transformation of rural life in the seventeenth century, including vagrant peasants, unemployed soldiers, members of official retinues and religious students.[85] Banditry became generalised, but at the same time was the outcome of state strategies to cope with the restlessness of rural society and to meet the military demands of musket-based infantry warfare. Bandits then were the result of state construction, a strategy deployed to foil class-based initiatives and efficiently supply a large cadre of military recruits.[86] Hardly the champions of an oppressed peasantry as depicted in romanticised interpretations, peasants were the primary victims of banditry's violence and exploitation, a form of violent, informal taxation implicitly accepted by the state. Furthermore, the Ottoman state, by bargaining with bandit chiefs and incorporating them along with their retinues into the imperial structure, made banditry a source of strength and power.[87] Bandits provided an outlet for rural social pressures, which in most European states erupted in violent peasant rebellion. The Ottoman state's skill as a bargainer and dealmaker, however, manipulated relations so that bandits became a source of strength and flexible stability. Contrary to interpretations, which see the demise of the timar system and the rise of banditry as a crucial first step in the decline of the Ottoman Empire, bargaining produced flexibility and durability, not decline. The Ottoman Empire's strategy was successful in eliminating serious dangers of armed insurrection or rebellion.[88] Obviously such arguments underscore the need for us to reconsider the periodisation of Ottoman decline, to reassess forms of state transformation and adaptation, even if these were temporary.

In Russia, the enserfment of the peasantry was a strategy deployed by the state to mediate and control the pressures unleashed by rural dislocation and the military revolution. The Russian Empire's response to the crisis of the seventeenth century reflected the dynamics produced by its hybrid system of land tenure, the willingness of the state to regulate peasant mobility, and the relative underdevelopment of the Russian bureaucracy and military. In order to understand the activity of state and society in response to the challenges of the seventeenth century, it is crucial to remember the devastating social and political effects of the Time of Troubles in Russia; it deepened agrarian restlessness and dislocation and made the newly established Romanov dynasty particularly sensitive to social unrest. Additionally, Russia was slow to modernise its military because of the unique intensity of 'socio-economic and political upheaval' at the moment when Russia had to modernise in order to survive.[89] In response to the refusal of the middle service class cavalry to register as infantrymen in 1630, Russian officials opened the 'new formation regiments' to irregular social groups, such as the Tatars and Cossacks.[90] This proved insufficient however, as warfare demanded ever-larger infantry forces, and the service class, instead of adapting to military change, secured increasing control over land and labour. Thus, during the Thirteen Years War (1654–67) the state imposed mass conscription, drawn largely from the peasantry, drafting by the end of the war over one hundred thousand men into the new army.[91]

The military service class played a critical role in shaping state action in the seventeenth century. During the Time of Troubles, there was 'a definite qualitative change' in the status and class consciousness of the military servitors.[92] Within the dual system of property relations, the servitors eventually 'acquired perquisites and an accompanying cast of mind' typically reserved for hereditary elites. As their military obsolescence became ever more evident, and service landholders came to rely more on land and labour than on military service for support, they mobilised and placed effective political pressure on the state to establish themselves as a closed caste, transform service lands into hereditary holdings and, most importantly, decisively enserf the peasantry. As Valerie Kivelson has described it, the pomeshchiki emerged as a salient political force during Ivan IV's *Oprichnina* and achieved significant influence 'during the Time of Troubles and the early decades of Romanov rule'.[93] Whereas the timar holders in the Ottoman Empire were divided and peasants and other elements incorporated into the fighting forces, in Russia a 1603 decree prohibited the children of slaves, peasants and clergymen from holding pomest'e lands. The servitors succeeded in gradually eroding the nonhereditary principle of service land tenure by obtaining laws which required the transfer of service lands to family members, and during the intense chaos of the Time of Troubles, pomest'e lands were issued, incoherently, on an explicitly hereditary basis. Reflecting the growing ambiguity between the essentially distinct hereditary and service modes of tenure, decrees in 1634 and 1638 referred to 'familial service lands', as absurd contradiction.[94] Although it would not be until the reign of Peter I that service lands were officially abolished, decrees in 1676–77 essentially recognised the revolution in landholding which had taken place, effectively eliminating the pomest'e and extending the rights of the *votchnina* to the military servitors. This transformation reflected, in Richard Hellie's words, 'a complete reversal' of land tenure policy, 'from the dominance of the pomest'e at the expense of the votchnina in the second half of the sixteenth century to the near extermination of the pomest'e by the votchnina a hundred years later'.[95] The crisis of the seventeenth thus precipitated a revolutionary transformation of land tenure on behalf of the service class.

Even more remarkable was the transformation of rural labour in the decisive enserfment of the Russian peasantry. Although restrictions on mobility were extensive before the seventeenth century, the enserfment of the Russian peasantry reached a critical point during the rebellion of 1648. Under pressure from the mobilised and status conscious cavalry servitors, the law code of 1649 repealed the statute of limitations on the recovery of fugitive peasants who frequently escaped the severe exploitation of the petty landholders to the more lax estates of the magnates. This marked the apex of pomeshchiki political influence, as they were able 'to wring the ultimate concession', of final enserfment 'from a reluctant state and an actively opposed boyar aristocracy'.[96] While fluidity and increased stratification characterised Ottoman peasant life in the seventeenth century, the late sixteenth century 'began [the systematic] homogenisation of the Russian peasantry' and serfdom accelerated this process during the second half of the seventeenth century.[97] Russia's response to the demands of the military revolution and the crisis of the seventeenth led to the imposition of a rigid social order. This 'social regimentation and stratification' was an 'extreme case of rapid, thorough-going social division'.[98] The obsolete cavalry servitors succeeded in securing privileges and property rights similar to the dominant hereditary nobility in controlling land and labour, while for peasants, the possibility of 'moving legally no longer existed'.[99] Already in the seventeenth century, peasants became legally exchangeable labour commodities, marking a process in which human beings came to be treated increasingly as chattel.[100] Enserfment was not a 'natural' by-product of objective economic forces so much as 'a series of conscious acts' by a centralised state under pressure from rebellious and class conscious military servitors.[101] Agrarian dislocation and military backwardness aggravated the challenges of the seventeenth century, and enserfment was a crucial strategy to control rural labour and ease elite tensions. Enserfment 'cement[ed]' the petty service landholders to the state and the hereditary elites; after 1648 the petty landholders would never stir 'to oppositional action again'.[102] In mediating elite tensions and modernising its military, Russia paid 'a tremendous price' in human life and dignity, and 'serfdom was certainly one of the costs of the survival of the Russian state'.[103]

But enserfment was only one facet of a general transformation of Russian society in the seventeenth century. The rebellion of 1648 not only provided the agitation military servitors needed to demand the full enserfment of the peasantry, it also marked transformation of governmentality and emergence of a rigidly stratified bureaucratic order. The organisational and bureaucratic requirements of a large infantry army promoted a 'culture of technicality in state activity' marked by a rapid increase in formal documentation, rationalised procedures and state penetration into society.[104] As Valerie Kivelson writes, 'the rebellion of 1648 erupted at a critical moment in Muscovite history, when traditional and bureaucratising discourses clashed' in defining Russia's political culture.[105] Fundamentally driven by the state's response to the military revolution within the constraints of general crisis of the seventeenth century, 'a new, bureaucratic culture quietly arose in state circles behind a carefully maintained facade of traditionalism'.[106] By 1648 the 'effects of innovation could no longer be hidden, and the fierce conflict pitted an old vision of the social order against the new', as status conscious cavalry servitors attempted to secure their place in the emerging modern state.[107] The new, depersonalised bureaucratic state not only succeeded in mobilising large infantry armies; it also penetrated and regulated everyday life in new ways. Any group who violated the 'newly emerging vision of a static social order' – such as vagrants, wondering minstrels and free Cossacks – were subjected to legislation which attempted to 'register these undisciplined groups, tax them and recast them into one of the officially acknowledged categories of people: peasants, townspeople or soldiers'.[108] The state's response to the crisis of the seventeenth century and the military revolution catalysed 'the destruction of old social and political understandings ... [and the emerging] forms of social organisation became important legacies to the centralised, reformist state of Peter I'.[109]

The Habsburg Empire is comparable to the Russian case through the importance of a state absolutism project. While the Russian state was permeated with elements of governmentality and a central bureaucratic culture that they believed was necessary to survive through the crisis and beyond, the Habsburgs adopted a strategy of 'confessional absolutism' as the solution to the diversity of internal responses to the crises and a cultural approach to the unification of the elites with whom rested the key to the survival of a central Habsburg state. In the process, however, the monarchy's inability to enter the realm of agrarian relations in many regions of the empire, and their eagerness to please the nobility facilitated the rise of a phenomenon called 'second serfdom', in its persistent and supplementary harshness for the concerned peasantry. Furthermore in every region, they also allowed a small class of peasants to become the agents of their brethren's exploitation, dramatically shaping rural relations for the centuries to come.

The Thirty Years War was devastating to the peasantries of each region of the empire. All over the Habsburg Empire, the first half of the seventeenth century was a period of destruction, but also a period during which the nobility made concerted attempts at expanding their trade in agricultural commodities, expand their estates and increase their commercial involvement. Everywhere in the empire, the nobility tried to profit at the expanse of the peasantry, using enserfment, taxation and the dreaded *robota* (compulsory labour services) to further their own interests. For the peasants of Bohemia whose enserfment had started already after the Hussite Wars, this last war was ruinous. The devastation of the war, the destruction and loss of life, the spread of disease and lawlessness happened as the war proceeded. In the devastation that resulted from war, the nobility were able to seize the lands that had been abandoned and force the peasants to settle and therefore reconstructed a labour force. Especially after the White Mountain defeat, when the Bohemian aristocracy was replaced by 'a foreign' Catholic nobility, all the old patron-client compacts, the few restraints that had been observed went away. Since these new landowners had no previous ties to the peasantry, they found it easy to repress them. Such repression was facilitated by the constitutional transformation that provided the new Bohemian elite with complete freedom over the peasantry, which were no longer under the jurisdiction of the state.[110] The second serfdom that ensued was made even more onerous by the numerous and increasing exactions, services and fees as well as the robota, the obligation of peasants to perform services on the landlord's land.

If the enserfment of the Bohemian peasantry was dreadful, by all accounts, it was worse in Hungary. Similar to Bohemia, but earlier, in 1608, a law was passed that essentially altered the fate of the peasantry in Hungary. This law transferred the jurisdiction over the peasantry from the state to the authority of counties in Hungary, so that until the mid-eighteenth century, the central government had no authority in rural relations. When the misery of rural relations was exacerbated by the crises in the seventeenth century, peasants paid for the devastation. They provided labour to repair fortifications, they were tied to the land so they provided steady and fixed labour and they remained poverty stricken. It is only after the Thirty Years War, under the rule of Leopold I (1658–1705) that we see attempts at monitoring the peasant situation in Hungary.[111] By contrast to Bohemia and Hungary where legislation provided the nobility with the ability to alter rural social structure to fit their needs, the Austrian portion of the empire experienced more state intervention. Here the presence of large, market-oriented agriculture and what others have labelled 'feudal capitalism' with a free peasantry provided the conditions for the state to intercede to push for more peasant exploitation. That the state had rearranged the social and familial relations in this region during the prior century had the effect of strong differentiation within the peasantry. Therefore, instead of enserfment, especially in Upper Austria, we see deep cleavages within the peasantry, which then become the basis of the rebellion of 1625. Such stratification was compounded by the religious reaction of a strong Protestant population against the policies of the Counter-Reformation emphasised by the Habsburg monarchy. In fact, the rebellions of this period in the Hereditary lands of the Habsburg Empire can be explained by the deeply unequal rural structure and the religious opposition to the policies of the state.

For the Habsburg monarchy, the nature of its earlier arrangements dictated the choice of their involvement and priorities. First, the continuation of strong and dependable feudal relations was of primary importance. Thus, in every struggle, for example between the towns and the nobility, between the peasants and the nobility the Crown chose to support the latter. While the towns had been strong revenue generators for the Crown, during the seventeenth-century crisis, they were overwhelmed by competition by the nobility and abandoned by the state too weak to counter the nobility. Similarly, the monarchy was adamant about protecting the wealth and the privileges of the noble families over the peasantry since it relied on them for the collection of taxes and administration of the provinces. Second, they believed that Catholic unity and uniformity would create a nobility and population loyal to the Crown. There is no doubt that the cultural unity the Habsburgs strived for was the result of the strong state-church association and the geopolitical position of the monarchy at the time of emergence. As the Habsburg Empire emerged from the Holy Roman Empire, Habsburg Christianity embodied a strong perspective of the unity of church and polity, and was firmly grounded in the belief in the exclusive domination of Christianity. The very establishment and proliferation of these Christian churches outside the Catholic Church, with the acquisition of a variety of lands and diverse populations turned the Habsburg Empire into a veritable confessional mosaic. Added to such confessional differences was the fact that such differences were enshrined further in the structure of state society relations since the dynastic alliances left rather weak ties of vertical integration. We can say then the structural problems of an early dynastic alliance-based expansion and segmentation was to be resolved through imposed cultural unity. The result was that with the reign of Ferdinand II and throughout the Counter-Reformation, persecution became excessive and strident, a policy of the crown intent on consolidation and centralisation with religious unification necessary to ensure loyalty to the crown. In what Bireley calls 'confessional absolutism' centralisation, the princely predominance over estates and the advancement of Catholicism became unified into one coherent policy of statemaking.[112]

Conclusion

The comparison of these three empires as they adapted and transformed themselves in response to the material and political crises of the seventeenth century presents us with at least three sociological conclusions. First, this chapter emphasised the degree to which the particular nature of imperial emergence, the manner in which state society relations congealed at initial moments of incorporation and the structuration of relations of rule and production provided the tracks upon which change could be motivated. That is whether imperial formation was effected by dynastic alliances or warfare and assimilation, the particular strength of the imperial state vis-à-vis societal actors partly determined solutions to the crisis. The path dependency that we observe here and recount for each of the empires was significant, though it should also not be perceived as limiting. Here we have tried to provide a long-term and slow-developing process analysis of institutional change and political outcomes. We have done so by paying attention to the unfolding of processes of change within the existing constraints and opportunities.

We have also emphasised in comparative perspective the ability of imperial states to adapt to crises and react and work with the social structural and institutional understandings in their realm to allow for transformations that maintained them for many more centuries. Such analyses are increasingly important as we try to move away from a decline thesis in imperial studies and study imperial transformations as continual iterations of state society arrangements in response to the challenges (external as well as internal) of rule. The Ottoman Empire seems to have demonstrated the most flexibility, and though this willingness to adapt, negotiate and bargain may have allowed it to pursue a different yet successful route towards state centralisation in the short run, in the long run, it seems the strategies of the Habsburgs and Russian Empires resolved the conflicts of empire more completely, and turned these empires into strong and viable imperial entities for the centuries to come.

Finally, the outcomes of the crisis of the seventeenth century were in no way insignificant or temporary. In each empire, these outcomes shaped the centuries to come and instituted new solutions that were reproduced. The most significant example of this was the Russian Empire. Serfdom acquired an importance in the Russian Empire that it assumed nowhere else in Europe, and its impact on the course of Russian history can barely be overemphasised. The commune outlasted serfdom, and was not entirely destroyed until Stalin imposed collectivisation in the 1930s. The homogenisation and repression of the Russian peasantry during enserfment provided the foundation for the unique ideology and practices of the peasant commune. Collective responsibility, land redistribution and elements of a sort of rough, patriarchal democracy were fundamental and unique practices of the Russian peasant commune.[113] In the Habsburg and Ottoman Empires, similarly, the agrarian structure remained a significant aspect of imperial rule, fought over by different social and national groups as empires began the transition into other forms of political organisation.

Notes

1. The best example of this is Maier (2006).
2. The best example in this category is no doubt Lieven (2001), most recent Burbank & Cooper (2010).
3. Anderson (1974).
4. For instance, Downing (1992) remains focused on the West, with only brief sections on Russia, Japan and China emphasising difference, separation and the failure to develop 'medieval constitutionalism', 26–55.
5. Lieberman (1999: 22).
6. Parker & Smith (1978); Aston (1965).
7. Steensgaard (1974 and 1990).
8. Steensgaard (1978 and 1976).
9. Tilly (1990).
10. Steensgaard (1978).
11. Tilly (1975); Mousnier (1970); Porchnev (1972); Avrich (1972); Brenner (1976); Clark (1985).
12. The original outline of the thesis is in Michael Richards (1967) ('The Military Revolution, 1560–1660'), a reprint of a 1956 lecture. Also in this tradition, see Parker (1988); Downing (1992); Rogers (1995).
13. Poe (1996: 604).
14. Asch (1999).
15. See Pamuk (2001).
16. Hellie (1971: 93).
17. Avrich (1972: 10–17).

18. The classic treatment is Platonov (1970). See further Dunning (1997), a discussion of Jack Goldstone's influential model of early-modern state crisis. Dunning points out that Russia is somewhat unusual, and has been passed over in many works on the crisis of the seventeenth century, but argues that the 'Time of Troubles' is evidence that Goldstone's model does in fact apply to Russia.
19. Hellie (1971: 107).
20. Ingrao (1994: 6).
21. Kann (1974: 132).
22. Inalcik (1980); Kafadar (1995); Lowry (2003).
23. Inalcik (1973: 107); Agoston (1993: 17).
24. Inalcik (1954; 1991). Such tactics were widespread among empires, especially as David Laitin (1991) identifies for the Russian and Soviet empires.
25. Barkey (1996 and 1994).
26. Alef (1961).
27. Raeff (1984: 2–3).
28. Keenan (1986); Kollman (1987).
29. Keenan (1986: 132).
30. Keep (1985: 13); Hellie (1971: 27).
31. Alef (1983); Crummey (1987); Hellie (1971: 26).
32. Crummy (1987: 90).
33. Hellie (1971: 21).
34. Hellie (2005).
35. Hellie (2005: 90; 1971: 27).
36. Hellie (2005).
37. Crummey (1983: 5).
38. Sugar (1963).
39. Evans (1979: 166).
40. Ibid.
41. Rebel (1983).
42. Ibid.: 4.
43. Anderson (1974).
44. Ingrao (1994: 11–12).
45. Wright (1975).
46. Kiraly (1975).
47. Ingrao (1994: 43) provides the following figures for the middle of the seventeenth century: 'just thirteen Hungarian magnates controlled 37 percent of the kingdom's villages, while the eighty-two aristocrats who sat in the Bohemian and Moravian diets controlled 62 percent of their crownlands' peasantry'.
48. Cited in Wank (1997: 102).
49. Inalcik (1994: 104–15).
50. These arguments are made clearly in Barkey (1994 and 1996).
51. Inalcik (1994: 116); Barkey (1994: 37).
52. Inalcik (1994: 145).
53. Inalcik (1973: 107); Kunt (1983); Imber (2002: 107); Agoston (1993: 17).
54. Panaite (2003).
55. Many texts have been discussed in relation to the work of pamphleteers. For the sixteenth century, two are significant: Grand Vizier Lutfi Pasha's *Asafname* and Mustafa Ali's *Nushat-I Selatin*. Both were produced at this time and discussed the situation in the Ottoman Empire, see Howard (1988).

56. Kivelson (1997: 650).
57. Ibid. For an interesting debate on the nature of the Muscovite state, see Poe (2002); Kivelson (2002).
58. Weickhardt (1993: 665); Pipes (1994: 530). Weickhardt contends that 'Russia gradually developed a concept of private property for land' similar to practices in Western Europe, and that limitations on private landownership protected the Boyar clans, not the state. Richard Pipes, on the other hand, argues that the 'patrimonial' regime of the tsars, unlike any state in the West, freely violated human and property rights by appropriating 'the estates of their subjects at will... because they considered all the land of the realm to be ultimately theirs'.
59. Kivelson (2002: 495).
60. Blum (1961: 174–80).
61. Hellie (1971: 33).
62. Ibid.: 33.
63. Ibid.: 37.
64. Ibid.: 33.
65. Ibid.: 40.
66. Ibid.: 41.
67. Ibid.
68. Kivelson (1997: 648).
69. Hellie (1971: 45).
70. Ibid.: 46.
71. Ibid.: 121.
72. Dewey (1988: 249–70).
73. Hellie (1971: 121).
74. Kivelson (1997: 653–55).
75. Hellie (1971: 84).
76. Ibid.
77. Barkey (1994: 63–64).
78. Ibid.: 67–68.
79. Ibid.: 69.
80. Ibid.: 69–70.
81. Inalcik (1994: 143–53).
82. Barkey (1994: 109).
83. Ibid.: 110.
84. Ibid.: 144.
85. Ibid.: 141.
86. Ibid.: 178.
87. Ibid.: 195.
88. Barkey (1991).
89. Paul (2004: 37); Poe (1998: 248).
90. Paul (2004: 23).
91. Ibid.: 23–34.
92. Hellie (1971: 48).
93. Kivelson (1994: 199).
94. Hellie 1971: 56–57.
95. Ibid.: 57.
96. Kivelson (1994: 199–200).
97. Hellie (1971: 102).
98. Poe (1996: 613).

99. Hellie (1971: 144).
100. Ibid.: 120.
101. Ibid.: 145.
102. Kivelson (1994: 200).
103. Hellie (1971: 258).
104. Poe (1996: 616).
105. Kivelson (1993: 733).
106. Ibid.
107. Ibid.: 734.
108. Ibid.: 749–50.
109. Stevens (1995: 5).
110. Wright (1975: 244–46).
111. Kiraly (1975: 269–71).
112. Bireley (1994).
113. Atkinson (1990).

Bibliography

Abou-El-Haj, Rifa'at 'Ali (1995) 'The Expression of Ottoman Political Culture in the Literature of Advice to Princes (*nasihatnameler*), Sixteenth to Twentieth centuries', in R. K. Bhattacharya and Asok K. Ghosh (Eds) *Sociology in the Rubric of Social Science: Professor Ramkrishna Mukherjee Felicitation Volume* (Calcutta), pp. 282–92.

——. (1984) *The 1703 Rebellion and the Structure of Ottoman Politics* (Leiden).

Adams, J. N. (2003) *Bilingualism and the Latin Language* (Cambridge).

Adshead, S. A. M. (2000) *China in World History* (3rd ed., New York).

Agoston, G. (1993) 'A Flexible Empire; Authority and Its Limits on the Ottoman Frontiers', *International Journal of Turkish Studies* 9 (1–2), pp. 15–31.

Ajayi, J. F. Ade (Ed.) (1989) *Africa in the Nineteenth Century Until the 1880s, Unesco General History of Africa*, Vol. 6 (Paris).

Ajayi, J. F. Ade & M. Crowder (1985) *An Atlas of African History* (London).

Aksan, Virginia H. & Daniel Goffman (Eds) (2007) *The Early Modern Ottomans. Remapping the Empire* (Cambridge).

Alam, Muzaffar (2004) *The Languages of Political Islam in India* (Delhi).

——. (1986) *The Crisis of Empire in Mughal North India* (New Delhi).

Alam, M. & S. Subrahmanyam (2007) *Indo-Persian Travels in the Age of Discoveries, 1400–1800* (Cambridge).

Alderson, A. D. (1956) *The Structure of the Ottoman Dynasty* (Oxford).

Alcock, S. E., Terence D'Altroy, Kathleen D. Morrison & Carla M. Sinopoli (Eds) (2001) *Empires. Perspectives From Archaeology and History* (Cambridge).

Alef, Gustave (1983) *Rulers and Nobles in Fifteenth-Century Muscovy* (London).

——. (1961) 'Muscovy and the Council of Florence,' *Slavic Review* 20 (October), pp. 389–401.

Alföldy, A. (1970) *Die monarchische Repräsentation im römischen Kaiserreiche* (Darmstadt).

And, Metin (1963–4) *A History of Theater and Popular Entertainment* (Ankara).

Anderson, Perry (1974) *Lineages of the Absolutist State* (London).

Andreau, J. (2007) 'Registers, Account-Books, and Written Documents in the *de Frumento*', Prag 2007a, pp. 81–92.

Andrews, Walter G. & Mehmet Kalpaklı (2005) *The Age of Beloveds: Love and the Beloved in Early-Modern Ottoman and European Culture and Society* (Durham).

Armitage, David (2000) *The Ideological Origins of the British Empire* (Cambridge).

Arnason, Johann P. & K. A. Raaflaub (Eds) (2011), *The Roman Empire in Context: Historical and Comparative Perspectives* (Chichester).

Arnold, T. W. (1893) *The Preaching of Islam. A History of the Propagation of the Muslim Faith* (London).

Artan, T., J. Duindam and M. Kunt (Eds) (2011) *Royal Courts in Dynastic States and Empires* (Leiden).

Asch, Ronald G. (1999) 'Warfare in the Age of the Thirty Years War: 1598–1648', in Jeremy Black (Ed.), *European Warfare: Problems in Focus, 1453–1815* (New York), pp. 45–68.

Asher, C. (1992) *Architecture of Mughal India* (Cambridge).

Aston, T. S. (Ed.) (1965) *Crisis in Europe 1560–1660: Essays from Past and Present* (London).

Atasoy, Nurhan & Filiz Cagman (1974) *Turkish Miniature Painting* (Istanbul).

Atkinson, Dorothy (1990) 'Egalitarianism and the Commune', in Roger Bartlet (Ed.), *Land Commune and Peasant Community in Russia: Communal Forms in Imperial and Early Soviet Society* (New York), pp. 7–19.

Aurobindo, Shri (1958) *The Foundations of Indian Culture* (Pondicherry, reprinted from the *Arya*, 1918–21).

Ausbüttel, F. M. (1998) *Die Verwaltung des römischen Kaiserreiches* (Darmstadt).

Austen, R. (1987) *African Economic History. Internal Development and External Dependency* (London).

Avrich, Paul (1972) *Russian Rebels, 1600–1800* (New York).

Babayan, Kathryn (1998) 'The "Aqa`id al-Nisa": A Glimpse at Safavid Women in Local Isfahani Culture', in Gavin R. G. Hambly (Ed.), *Women in the Medieval Islamic World: Power, Patronage, and Piety* (New York).

Babinger, Franz (1978) *Mehmed the Conqueror and His Time*, Ralph Mannheim (trans.) (Princeton, NJ).

Bailyn, Bernard & Philip D. Morgan (Eds), *Strangers Within the Realm: Cultural Margins of the First British Empire* (Chapel Hill, NC).

Balabanlilar, L. (2007) 'Lords of the Auspicious Conjunction: Turco-Mongol Imperial Identity on the Subcontinent', *Journal of World History* 18 (1), pp. 1–32.

Balazs, E. (1964) *Chinese Civilization and Bureaucracy* (New Haven and London).

Banerjea, Surendranath (1922) *Collected Works of Babu Surendranath Banerjea* (Calcutta).

Bang, Peter F. (2008) *The Roman Bazaar. A Comparative Study of Trade and Markets in a Tributary Empire* (Cambridge).

Barkey, Karen (1996) 'In Different Times: Scheduling and Social Control in the Ottoman Empire, 1550–1650', *Comparative Studies in Society and History* 38 (3), pp. 460–83.

——. (1994) *Bandits and Bureaucrats: The Ottoman Route to State Centralization* (Ithaca, NY).

——. (1991) 'Rebellious Alliances: The State and Peasant Unrest in Early Seventeenth-Century France and the Ottoman Empire', *American Sociological Review*, 56 (6), pp. 699–715.

Bartnicki, A. & J. Mantel-Niećko (1978) *Geschichte Etiopiens*, Vol. 1–2 (Berlin).

Baruah, Sanjib (2005) *Durable Disorder: Essays on the Politics of Northeast India* (Delhi).

Bayly, C. A. (2008) 'Liberalism at Large. Mazzini and Nineteenth-Century Indian Thought', in Eugenio Biagini and C. A. Bayly (Eds), *Guiseppe Mazzini and the Globalisation of Democratic Nationalism*, Proceedings of the British Academy 152, (Oxford), pp. 355–74.

——. (2004) *The Birth of the Modern World* (Oxford).

——. (2002) 'The Orient: British Historical Writing About Asia Since 1890', in Peter Burke (Ed.) *History and Historians in the Twentieth Century* (Oxford), pp. 88–119.

——. (1996) *Empire and Information. Intelligence Gathering and Social Communication in India, 1780–1870* (Cambridge).

——. (1975) *The Local Roots of Indian Politics. Allahabad 1880–1920* (Oxford).

Bayly, C. A. & P. F. Bang (2003) 'Introduction: Comparing Pre-Modern Empires', *The Medieval History Journal* 6 (2), pp. 169–87.

Bell, H. I. (1924) *Jews and Christians in Egypt: The Jewish Troubles in Alexandria and the Athanasian Controversy* (Oxford).

Bell III, M. (2007a), 'An Archaeologist's Perspective on the *lex Hieronica*', in Dubouloz and Pittia (2007), pp. 187–203.

——. (2007b) 'Apronius in the Agora: Sicilian Civil Architecture and the *lex Hieronica*', in Prag (2007a), pp. 117–34.

Bernal, Martin (1987) *Black Athena: The Afroasiatic Roots of Classical Civilisation*, Vol. 1 (London).

Berve, H. (1959) *König Hieron II* (Munich).

Betts, F. Raymond (1972) 'The Allusion to Rome in British Imperialist Thought of the Late Nineteenth and Early Twentieth Centuries', *Victorian Studies* 15, pp. 149–59.

Biagini, Eugenio (1996) 'Liberalism and Direct Democracy: John Stuart Mill and the Model of Ancient Athens', in Biagini (Ed.) *Citizenship and Community. Liberals, Radicals and Collective Identities in the British Isles, 1865–1931* (Cambridge), pp. 21–45.

Bielenstein, H. (1987) 'Chinese Historical Demography A.D. 2–1982', *Bulletin of the Museum of Far Eastern Antiquities* 59, pp. 1–288.

——. (1980) *The Bureaucracy of Han Times* (Cambridge).

Bireley, Robert (S. J.) (1994) 'Confessional Absolutism in the Habsburg Lands in the Seventeenth Century' in Charles W. Ingrao (Ed.), *State and Society in Early Modern Austria* (West Lafayette, Indiana), pp. 36–53.

Blake, Stephen P. (forthcoming), 'The Imperial Birthday Celebration: Akbar's Ritual of Integration and Legitimacy', in Shireen Moosvi (Ed.), *Reason and Toleration in Indian History* (New Delhi).

——. (1998) 'Contributors to the Urban Landscape: Women Builders in Safavid Isfahan and Mughal Shahjahanabad' in Gavin Hambly (Ed.), *Women in the Medieval Islamic World: Power, Patronage and Piety* (New York), pp. 407–28.

——. (1991) *Shahjahanabad: The Sovereign City in Mughal India, 1639–1739* (Cambridge).

——. (1979) 'The Patrimonial-Bureaucratic Empire of the Mughals', *Journal of Asian Studies* 39 (1), pp. 77–94.

Blaut, J. M. (1993) *The Colonizer's Model of the World: Geographical Diffusionism and Eurocentric History* (New York).

Bleicken, Jochen (1995) *Verfassungs- und Sozialgeschichte des Römischen Kaiserreiches*, 2 Bde. (4th ed., Paderborn).

Blum, Jerome (1961) *Lord and Peasant in Russia From the Ninth to the Nineteenth Century* (Princeton, NJ).

Boatwright, M. T. (2002) *Hadrian and the Cities of the Roman Empire* (Princeton, NJ).

Bodin, Jean (1986) *Les six livres de la république*, 6 vols, texte revu par Christiane Fremont, Marie-Dominique Couzinet & Henri Rochais, *Corpus des œuvres de philosophie en langue française* (Paris).

Bohannan, P. & G. Dalton (Eds) (1962) *Markets in Africa* (Evanston).

Bondanella, Peter (1987) *The Eternal City: Roman Images in the Modern World* (Bloomington).

Bouhdiba, Abdelwahab (1985) *Sexuality in Islam* (London).

Bowersock, G. W. (1969) *Greek Sophists in the Roman Empire* (Oxford).

Boxer, Ch. R. (1969) *The Portuguese Seaborne Empire 1415–1825* (London).

——. (1965) *The Dutch Seaborne Empire 1600–1800* (London).

Braudel, Fernand (1979) *Civilisation matérielle, économie et capitalisme, XV – XVIII siècle*, tome 3: *Le temps du monde* (Paris).

Braund, S. (2009) *Seneca, De Clementia, Edited with Text, Translation and Commentary* (Oxford).

Brelaz, Cédric (2005) *La sécurité publique en Asie Mineure sous le Principat (Ier – IIIème s. ap. J.-C.). Institutions municipales et institutions impériales dans l'Orient romain* (Bâle).

Brennan, T. C. (2000) *The Praetorship in the Roman Republic* (Oxford).

Brenner, Robert (1976) 'Agrarian Class Structure and Economic Development in Pre-industrial Europe', *Past and Present* 70, pp. 30–75.

Brewer, John (1988) *The Sinews of Power* (Cambridge, MA).

Brook, Timothy (2009) 'Tibet and the Chinese World-Empire', in Streeter, Weaver & Coleman (Eds), *Empires and Autonomy. Moments in the History of Globalization* (Vancouver), pp. 24–40.

Brunt, P. A. (1981) rev. of 'L. Neesen, *Untersuchungen zu den direkten Staatsabgaben der romischen Kaiserzeit (27 v. Chr. -284 n. Chr.)*, Bonn 1980', *The Journal of Roman Studies* 71, pp. 161–72.

Bryce, James (1914) *The Ancient Roman Empire and the British Empire in India, The Diffusion of Roman and English Law Throughout the World; Two Historical Studie*s, 1st ed. 1901 (London).

——. (1907) *Imperialismo romano e britannico*, Giovanni Pacchioni (trans.) (Turin).

——. (1904) *The Holy Roman Empire,* 1st ed. 1864 (London).

Bryson, R. A. & D. A. Baerreis (1967) 'Possibilities of Major Climatic Modification and their Implications: Northwest India, a Case for Study', *Bulletin for the American Meteorological Society* 48 (3), pp. 136–42.

Buckle, H. T. (1916) *The History of Civilisation in England*, Vol. 1 (London).

Burbank, Jane & Frederick Cooper (2010) *Empires and the Politics of Difference in World History* (Princeton, NJ).

Burke, E. (2000) *The Writings and Speeches, Vol. VII, India: The Hastings Trial 1789–1794*, ed. by P. J. Marshall (Oxford).

Burke, Peter (2005) *History and Social Theory* (2nd edn., London).

Burling, Robbins (1974) *The Passage to Power* (New York).

Burroughs, Peter (1999) 'Imperial Institutions and the Government of Empire', *The Oxford History of the British Empire III: The Nineteenth Century* (Oxford), pp. 170–97.

Burton, Antoinette (Ed.) (2003) *After the Imperial Turn: Thinking With and Through the Nation* (Durham).

Caccamo Caltabiano, M; L. Campagna, and A. Pinzone (Eds) (2004) *Prospettive della ricerca sulla Sicilia del III sec. a.C. Archeologia, Numismatica, Storia*, Atti dell'incontro di studio, Messina 4–5 luglio 2002 (Messina).

Cagnetta, Mariella (1973) *Antichisti e impero fascista* (Bari).

Cain, P. J. & A. G. Hopkins (2002) *British Imperialism, 1688–2000*, Second Edition (Harlow).

Calkins, Philip B. (1970) 'The Formation of a Regionally Oriented Ruling Group in Bengal, 1700–1740', *Journal of Asian Studies*, 29 (4), pp. 799–806.

Campagna, L. (2004) 'Architettura e ideologia della *basileia* a Siracusa nell'età di Ierone II', Caccamo Caltabiano, Campagna and Pinzone, pp. 151–89.

Campanella, T. (1653) *De Monarchia Hispanica* (Amsterdam, novissima editio).

Canepa, Matthew T. (2009) *The Two Eyes of the Earth. Art and Ritual of Kingship Between Rome and Sasanian Iran* (Berkeley, CA).

Canfora, Luciano (1989) *Le vie del classicismo* (Bari).

——. (1980) *Le ideologie del classicismo* (Turin).

Cannadine, David (2001) *Ornamentalism. How the British Saw their Empire* (London).

Caponi, Livia (2005) *Augustan Egypt. The Creation of a Roman Province* (London).

Carbè, A. (1995) 'Nota sulla monetazione di Tauromenion nel III sec. a.C.', M. Caccamo Caltabiano (Ed.), *La Sicilia tra l'Egitto e Roma: la monetazione siracusana nell'età di Ierone II*, Atti del seminario di studi, Messina 2–4 dicembre 1993, *AAPel* 69 (1993) Suppl. 1, Messina 1995, pp. 303–18.

Carneiro, R. (1981) 'The Chiefdom: Precursor of the State', in G. Jones & R. Kautz (Eds) *The Transition to Statehood in the New World* (Cambridge), pp. 37–79.

Carrié, J. M. (1993) 'L'economia e le finanze', in A. Momigliano and A. Schiavone (Eds), *Storia di Roma*, III.1 (Turin), pp. 751–87.

Caruso, G. B. (1875) *Storia di Sicilia (Memorie istoriche)*, Vol. I (Palermo)

Ceserani, G. (2000) 'The Charm of the Siren: The Place of Classical Sicily in Historiography', in Smith and Serrati (Eds), *Sicily from Aeneas to Augustus. New Approaches in Archaeology and History* (Edinburgh), pp. 174–93.

Chabod, Federico (1996) *Italian Foreign Policy: The Statecraft of the Founders* (Princeton, NJ).

Chakrabarty, Dipesh (2000) *Provincializing Europe: Postcolonial Thought and Historical Difference* (Princeton, NJ).

Chaliand, G. (2004) *Nomadic Empires: From Mongolia to the Danube* (New Brunswick, NJ).

Chandra, Bipan (1979) *Nationalism and Colonialism in Modern India* (New Delhi).

Chandra, Bipan, Mridula Mukherjee & Aditya Mukherjee (2000) *India After Independence, 1947–2000* (New Delhi).

Chang, C. (2007) *The Rise of the Chinese Empire. 1: Nation, State, and Imperialism in Early China, ca. 1600 B.C.–A.D. 8* (Ann Arbor, MI).

Chao, K. (1986) *Man and Land in Chinese History: an Economic Analysis* (Stanford, CA).

Ciccotti, E. (1895) *Il processo di Verre. Un capitolo di Storia Romana* (Milano).

Claessen, H. (2002) 'Was the State Inevitable?', *Social Evolution and History* 1, pp. 101–17.

——. (1987) 'Kings, Chiefs and Officials', *Journal of Legal Pluralism and Unofficial Law*, Nos 25–26: Special issue *Chieftaincy and the State in Africa,* guest editor E. van Rouveroy van Nieuwaal, pp. 203–41.

——. (1981) 'Specific Features of the African Early State', in H. Claessen & P. Skalnik (Eds) *The Study of the State* (The Hague), pp. 59–86.

——. (1978) 'The Early State: A Structural Approach', in H. Claessen, P. Skalnik (Eds), *The Early State* (The Hague), pp. 533–96.

Claessen, H. & J. Oosten (Eds) (1996) *Ideology and the Formation of Early States* (Leiden).

Claessen, H. & P. Skalnik (Eds) (1981) *The Study of the State* (The Hague).

——. (Eds) (1978) *The Early State* (The Hague).

Claessen, H.; P. van de Velde & E. Smith (Eds) (1985) *Development and Decline. The Evolution of Sociopolitical Organization* (South Hadley, MA).

Clark, Grahame (1939) *Archaeology and Society* (London).

Clark, Peter (Ed.) (1985) *The European Crisis of the 1590s: Essays in Comparative History* (Winchester/Mass).

Claude, D. (1969) *Die byzantinische Stadt im 6. Jahrhundert* (Munich).

Clogg, R. (2003) 'The Classics and the Movement of Greek Independence', M. Haagsma, P. de Boer and E. M. Moormann (Eds), *The Impact of Classical Greece on European and National Identities* (Amsterdam), pp. 25–46.

Coarelli, F. (1981) 'La Sicilia tra la fine della guerra annibalica e Cicerone', in Giardina and Schiavone (1981), pp. 1–18.

Cohen, C. A. and Lendon, J. E. (2011) 'Strong and Weak Regimes: Comparing the Roman Principate and the Medieval Crown of Aragon', in J. P. Arnason and K. A. Raaflaub (Eds), *The Roman Empire in Context: Historical and Comparative Perspectives,* pp. 85–109.

Cohen, R. (1981) 'Evolution, Fission and the Early State', in H. Claessen & P. Skalnik (Eds), *The Study of the State*, pp. 87–116.

——. (1978) 'State Origins: a Reappraisal', H. Claessen & P. Skalnik (Eds), *The Early State*, pp. 31–75.

Cohn, Bernard S. (1985) 'The Command of Language and the Language of Command', *Subaltern Studies IV*, Edited by Ranajit Guha (Delhi), pp. 276–329.

Combs-Schilling, M. D. (1989) *Sacred Performances: Islam, Sexuality, and Sacrifice* (New York).

Cometa, M. (1999) *Il romanzo dell'architettura. La Sicilia e il Grand Tour nell'età di Goethe* (Roma and Bari).

Condorelli, M. (1982) *La cultura giuridica in Sicilia dall'Illuminismo all'Unità* (Catania).

Constantine, D. (1984) *Early Greek Travellers and the Hellenic Ideal* (Cambridge).

Conti Rossini, Carlo (1937) *Etiopia e genti d'Etiopia* (Florence).

——. (1935) *Italia e Etiopia. Dal trattato d'Uccialli alla battaglia di Adua* (Rome).

——. (1913) 'Schizzo etnico e storico delle popolazioni eritree', *L'Eritrea economica: Prima serie di conferenze tenute in Firenze sotto gli auspici della Società di studi Geografici e Coloniali*, ed. by Fernando Martini (Novara-Roma), pp. 61–90.

Cooper, Frederick (2005) *Colonialism in Question. Theory, Knowledge, History* (Berkeley, CA).

Corradini, Enrico (1914) *Il nazionalismo italiano* (Milan).

Correia-Afonso, J. (Ed.) (1980) *Letters from the Mughal Court: the First Jesuit Mission to Akbar, 1580–1583* (Bombay).

Corsaro, M. (1999) 'Ripensando Diodoro. Il problema della storia universale nel mondo antico' (ii), *Mediterraneo antico* 2 (1999) pp. 117–69.

——. (1998) 'Ripensando Diodoro. Il problema della storia universale nel mondo antico' (i), *Mediterraneo antico* 1 (1998) pp. 405–36.

Crawford, M. H. (1990) 'Origini e sviluppi del sistema provinciale romano', *Storia di Roma*, ii, 1 (Turin), pp. 91–121.

Crispi, Francesco (1890) *Scritti e discorsi politici, 1849–1890* (Rome).

Cromer, Earl of, Evelyn Baring (1914) *Political and Literary Essays*, 3 vols (London).

——. (1910) *Ancient and Modern Imperialism* (London).

Crone, P. (1994) 'Were the Qays and Yemen of the Umayyad Period Political Parties?', *Der Islam*, LXXI, pp. 1–57.

——. (1989) *Pre-Industrial Societies* (Oxford).

——. (1980) *Slaves on Horses* (Cambridge).

Crowell, W. G. (1990) 'Northern Émigrés and the Problems of Census Registration under the Eastern Jin and Southern Dynasties', in Dien (Ed.), pp. 171–209.

Crummey, Robert O. (1987) *The Formation of Muscovy* (New York).

——. (1983) *Aristocrats and Servitors: The Boyar Elite in Russia, 1613–1689* (Princeton, NJ).

Cutelli, M. (1636) *Codicis legum sicularum libri quattuor* (Messanae).

Dale, Stephen Frederic (2010) *The Muslim Empires of the Ottomans, Safavids, and Mughals* (Cambridge).

Danzig, Richard (1969) 'The Many Layered Cake: A Case Study of Reform of the Indian Empire', *Modern Asian Studies* 3 (1), pp. 57–96.

Davis, Fanny (1986) *The Ottoman Lady: A Social History from 1718–1918* (New York).

Davy, W. (trans.) (1972) *Political and Military Institutes of Tamerlane* (Delhi).

De Almeida, H. & George H. Gilpin (2005) *Indian Renaissance: British Romantic Art and the Prospect of India* (Aldershot).

De Crespigny, R. (2004) 'South China in the Han Period', Internet edition (http://www.anu.edu.au/asianstudies/decrespigny/southchina_han.html).

De Crespingy, R. (1990) *Generals of the South: The Foundation and Early History of the Three Kingdoms State of Wu* (Canberra).

De Donno, Fabrizio (2006) '*La Razza Ario-Romana*: Ideas of Race and Citizenship in Colonial and Fascist Italy, 1885–1941', F. De Donno & Neelam Srivastava (Eds) 'Colonial and Postcolonial Italy', Special Issue, *Interventions: International Journal of Post-colonial Studies*, 8 (3), pp. 394–412.

De Gubernatis, Angelo (1899) *Roma e l'Oriente nella storia, nella leggenda e nella visione* (Rome).

——. (1890) *Usi funebri in Italia e presso gli altri popoli Indo-Europei* (Bologna).

——. (1888) *Mitologia comparata* (Milan).

——. (1886) *Peregrinazioni indiane. India Centrale* (Florence).

——. (1867) *Fonti vediche dell'epopea* (Florence).

De Heusch, L. (1987) *Ecrits sur la royauté sacrée* (Bruxelles).

Deininger, J. (1965) *Die Provinziallandtage der römischen Kaiserzeit* (Berlin).

Dennett, Daniel Clement (1995) *Darwin's Dangerous Idea: Evolution and the Meanings of Life* (London).

Dennett, Daniel Clement (1950) *Conversion and Poll-tax in Early Islam* (Cambridge, MA).

De Sanctis, Gaetano (1962) 'Dopoguerra antico', in Piero Treves, *Lo studio dell'antichità classica nell'Ottocento* (Milan-Naples).

——. (1939) *Storia dei Greci* (Florence).

——. (1907–67), *Storia dei Romani,* 7 vols (Turin).

De Sensi Sestito, G. (1977) *Gerone II. Un monarca ellenistico in Sicilia* (Palermo).

Devji, Faisal (2007) 'Apologetic Modernity', *Modern Intellectual History*, 4 (1), pp. 61–76.

Dewey, Horace W. (1988) 'Words of Authority: Russia's Debt to the Mongols in Suretyship and Collective Responsibility,' *Comparative Studies in Society and History*, 30 (2), pp. 249–70.

Diagne, P. (1981) 'Le pouvoir en Afrique', *Le concept du pouvoir en Afrique* (Paris), pp. 28–55.

——. (1967) *Pouvoir politique traditionnel en Afrique Occidentale. Essai sur les institutions politiques précoloniales* (Paris).

Diaz, F. (1989) *L'incomprensione italiana della Rivoluzione Francese* (Torino).

Di Cosmo, Nicola (2004) 'Did Guns Matter? Firearms and the Qing Formation', in Struve (Ed.), *The Qing Formation in World-Historical Time* (Cambridge, MA), pp. 121–66.

——. (2002) *Ancient China and Its Enemies: The Rise of Nomadic Power in East Asian History* (Cambridge).

Dien, A. (2001) 'Civil Service Examinations: Evidence from the Northwest', in Pearce, Spiro, and Ebrey (Eds), pp. 99–121.

——. (Ed.) (1990) *State and Society in Early Medieval China* (Stanford).

Dirks, Nicholas B. (2006) *The Scandal of Empire: India and the Creation of Imperial Britain* (Cambridge, MA).

——. (2001) *Castes of Mind: Colonialism and the Making of Modern India* (Princeton, NJ).

Doornbos, M. (1994) 'State Formation and Collapse. Reflections on Identity and Power', M. van Bakel, Renée Hagesteijn & Piet van de Velde (Eds), *Pivot Politics. Changing Cultural Identities in Early State Formation Processes* (Amsterdam), pp. 281–95.

Downing, Brian (1992) *The Military Revolution and Political Change: Origins of Democracy and Autocracy in Early Modern Europe* (Princeton, NJ).

Doyle, M. W. (1986) *Empires* (Ithaca, NY and London).

Drijvers, J. W. (2006) 'Ammianus Marcellinus' Image of Sasanian Society', in Huyse & Wiesehöfer (Eds), *Ērān ud Anērān* (Stuttgart), pp. 45–70.

Dubouloz, J. (2007) 'Autorité romaine, fermiers de l'impôt et contribuables en Sicile dans les années 70 av. J.-C.', in Dubouloz and Pittia (2007), pp. 147–68.

Dubouloz, J. and S. Pittia (2007) *La Sicile de Cicéron. Lectures des Verrines, Actes du colloque de Paris, 19–20 mai 2006* (Besançon).

Duncan-Jones, R. (1994) *Money and Government in the Roman Empire* (Cambridge).

Dunning, Chester (1997) 'Does Jack Goldstone's Model of Early Modern State Crisis Apply to Russia?,' *Comparative Studies in Society and History* 39 (3), pp. 572–92.

Eberhard, W. (1949) *Das Toba-Reich Nordchinas: Eine soziologische Untersuchung* (Leiden).

Ebrey, P. (1986) 'The Economic and Social History of Later Han', in Twitchett and Loewe (Eds), pp. 608–48.

Eckstein, A. M. (2008) *Rome Enters the Greek East: From Anarchy to Hierarchy in the Hellenistic Mediterranean, 230–170 BC* (Malden, MA, and Oxford).

——. (2006) *Mediterranean Anarchy, Interstate War, and the Rise of Rome* (Berkeley, CA).

——. (1987) *Senate and General. Individual Decision-making and Roman Foreign Relations, 264–194 BC* (Berkeley, CA).

——. (1980) '*Unicum subsidium populi Romani*: Hiero II and Rome, 263 BC–215 BC', *Chiron* 10, pp. 183–203.

Edwards, Catherine (1999) 'Introduction: Shadows and Fragments', C. Edwards (Ed.), *Roman Presences: Receptions of Rome in European Culture, 1789–1945* (Cambridge), pp. 1–18.

Eich, Peter (2005) *Zur Metamorphose des politischen Systems in der römischen Kaiserzeit: Die Entstehung einer "personalen Bürokratie" im langen dritten Jahrhundert* (Berlin).

Eisenstadt, S. M. (1968) 'Empire' in D. L. Sills (Ed.), *The International Encyclopedia of Social Sciences*, Vol. 5, pp. 41–48.

——. (1963) *The Political Systems of Empires* (New York).

Eisenstadt, S. M., Michel Abitbol & Naomi Chazan (Eds) (1988) *The Early State in African Perspective* (Leiden).

El-Hibri, T. (1999) *Reinterpreting Islamic Historiography* (Cambridge).

Elfasi, M. & I. Hrbek (Eds) (1988) *Africa from the Seventh to the Eleventh Century, Unesco General History of Africa*, Vol. 3 (Paris).

Elias, Norbert (1997) *Über den Prozess der Zivilization*, 2 Vols (Suhrkamp: Baden-Baden).

Elliot, H. M. & J. Dowson (Eds) (1851–55), *The History of India as Told by Its own Historians*, 6 vols, (Calcutta).

Elliott, J. H. (2006) *Empires of the Atlantic World. Britain and Spain in America 1492–1830* (New Haven. CT).

——. (1992) 'A Europe of Composite Monarchies', *Past & Present* 137, pp. 48–71.

Elton, H. (2007) 'Military Forces', in Sabin, van Wees, and Whitby (Eds), pp. 270–309.

Elvin, M. (1973) *The Pattern of the Chinese Past* (Stanford).

Erimtan, Can (2008) *Ottomans Looking West? – The Origins of the Tulip Age and Its Development in Modern Turkey* (London).

Ertman, T. (1997) *Birth of the Leviathan: Building States and Regimes in Medieval and Early Modern Europe* (Cambridge).

Evans, R. J. W. (1979) *The Making of the Habsburg Monarchy 1550–1700* (Oxford).

Farooqi, N. R. (1989) *Mughal-Ottoman Relations: A Study of Political & Diplomatic Relations between Mughal India and the Ottoman Empire, 1556–1748* (Delhi).

Ferguson, Adam (1789) *An Essay on the History of Civil Society* (Edinburgh).

——. (1767) *An Essay on the History of Civil Society* (London).

Ferguson, Niall (2004) *Colossus: the Price of America's Empire* (New York).

——. (2003) *Empire: the Rise and Demise of the British World Order and the Lessons for Global Power* (New York).

Ferrero, Guglielmo (1914) *Ancient Rome and Modern America. A Comparative Study of Morals and Manners*, A. Cecil Curtis (trans.) (London & New York).

——. (1910) *Roma nella cultura moderna* (Milan).

——. (1907–09), *The Greatness and Decline of Rome* (London).

——. (1902–07), *Grandezza e decadenza di Roma* (Milan).

——. (1898) *Il militarismo* (Milan).

Flaig, Egon (1992) *Den Kaiser Herausfordern* (Berlin).

Fletcher, J. (1986) 'The Mongols: Ecological and Social perspectives', *Harvard Journal of Asiatic Studies* 46 (1), pp. 10–50.

Folz, R. (1953) *L' Idée de l' Empire en Occident du Ve au XIVe siècle* (Bruxelles).

Fontanier, Victor (1829) *Voyage en Orient entrepris par l'ordre du government français de l'année 1821 à l'année 1829* (Paris).

Formichi, Carlo (1942) *L'Ora dell'India* (Rome).

Forsén, B. & G. Salmeri (2008) 'Ideology and Practice of Empire', in B. Forsén and G. Salmeri (Eds), *The Province Strikes Back. Imperial dynamics in the Eastern Mediterranean* (Helsinki), pp. 1–13.

Fowden, Garth (1993) *Empire to Commonwealth* (Princeton, NJ).

Fowler, R. & O. Hekster (Eds) (2005) 'Imagining Kings from Persia to Rome', *Imaginary Kings. Royal Images in the Ancient Near East, Greece and Rome* (Stuttgart), pp. 9–39.

Fraschetti, A. (1981) 'Per una prosopografia dello sfruttamento: Romani e Italici in Sicilia (212–44 a.C.)', Giardina and Schiavone, pp. 52–77.

Freeman, Edward Augustus (1877) *The Ottoman Power in Europe. Its Nature, Growth and its Decline* (London).

Gabba, E. (1990) 'La prima guerra punica e gli inizi dell'espansione transmarina', A. Momigliano and A. Schiavone (Eds), *Storia di Roma*, ii, 1 (Turin), 55–67.

——. (1986) 'La Sicilia Romana', in M. Crawford (Ed.), *L'impero romano e le strutture economiche e sociali delle province*, Biblioteca di *Athenaeum* 4 (Como), pp. 71–85.

——. (1959) 'Storici greci dell'impero romano da Augusto ai Severi', *Rivista Storica Italiana* 71, pp. 361–81.

Gaglio, V. (1776) 'Problema storico, critico, politico se la Sicilia fu più felice sotto il governo della repubblica romana o sotto i di lei imperatori?', *Opuscoli di autori siciliani* 17, pp. 1–272.

Gallo, F. F. (2006) 'Tra Greci e Romani. Il recupero dell'antico nel dibattito politico a Siracusa (secoli XVI-XVII)', in N. Bazzano and F. Benigno (Eds), *Uso e reinvenzione dell'antico nella politica di età moderna (secoli XVI-XIX)* (Manduria, Bari and Roma) pp. 49–66.

Garnsey, P. & C. Humfress (2001) *The Evolution of the Late Antique World* (Cambridge).

Garnsey, Peter & Richard Saller (1987) *The Roman Empire: Economy, Society and Culture* (London).

Gebbia, C. (1999) '*Cicerone e l'*utilitas provinciae Siciliae', *Kokalos* 45, pp. 27–40.

Gellner, Ernest (1988) *Plough, Sword and Book* (Chicago).

——. (1981) *Muslim Society* (Cambridge).

Genovese, M. (1999) *Gli interventi edittali di Verre in materia di decime sicule* (Milano).

——. (1993) 'Condizioni delle *civitates* della Sicilia ed assetti amministrativo-contributivi delle altre province nella prospettazione ciceroniana delle *Verrine*', *Iura* 44, pp. 171–243.

Gentile, Giovanni (1996) *The Sacralisation of Politics in Fascist Italy* (Cambridge, MA).

Giardina, A. and A. Schiavone (Eds) (1981) *Società romana e produzione schiavistica*, i, *L'Italia: insediamenti e forme economiche* (Roma and Bari).

Giarrizzo, G. (1989) 'La Sicilia dal Cinquecento all'Unità d'Italia', in V. D'Alessandro and G. Giarrizzo, *La Sicilia dal Vespro all'Unità d'Italia* (Turin), pp. 99–793.

——. (1970) 'Introduzione', in S. Scrofani, *Memorie inedite* (Palermo), pp. 7–36.

Gibb, H. & H. Bowen (1950–57), *Islamic Society and the West: A Study of the Impact of Western Civilization on Moslem Culture in the Near East*, 2 vols (London).

Gintis, Herbert (2000) 'Strong Reciprocity and Human Sociality', *Journal of Theoretical Biology* 206, pp. 169–79.

Gladwin, F. (Ed.) (1800) *Ayeen Akbery or the Institutes of the Emperor Akber*, 2 vols (London).

Glete, J. (2002) *War and the State in Early Modern Europe: Spain, the Dutch Republic and Sweden as Fiscal-Military States, 1500–1660* (London and New York).

Göçek, Fatma Müge (1996) *Rise of the Bourgeoisie, Demise of Empire: Ottoman Westernization and Social Change* (New York).

Goffart, W. (2006) *Barbarian Tides: the Migration Age and the Later Roman Empire* (Philadelphia. PA).

Goffman, Daniel (2002) *The Ottoman Empire and Early Modern Europe* (Cambridge).

Goldman, Michael (2005) *Imperial Nature: The World Bank and Struggles for Social Justice in the Age of Globalization* (New Haven, CT).

Gommans, Jos (1998) 'The Silent Frontier of South Asia, c. AD 1100–1800', *Journal of World History* 9 (1), pp. 1–23.

Goody, Jack (1996) *The East in the West* (Cambridge).

Gordon, M. S. (2001) *The Breaking of a Thousand Swords* (Albany, NY).

Goswami, Manu (2004) *Producing India: From Colonial Economy to National Space* (Chicago).

Graff, D. A. (2002) *Medieval Chinese Warfare, 300–900* (London and New York).

Graus, F., Jan Filip & Antonín Dostál (Eds) (1965) *Das Grossmährische Reich* (Praha).

Grenier, Jean-Claude (1995) 'L'Empereur et le Pharaon', *Aufstieg und Niedergang der römischen Welt*, Vol. II 18.5 (Berlin), pp. 3181–94.

Griffin, M. T. (1984) *Nero. The End of a Dynasty* (New Haven).

Grotius, Hugo (1913) *De jure belli ac pacis libri tres*, J. B. Scott (Ed.), *The Classics of International Law*, reproduction of 1646 Amsterdam edition (Washington, DC).

Grousset, R. (1970) *The Empire of the Steppes: A History of Central Asia* (first published 1939; English translation, New Brunswick, NJ).

Gruen, E. S. (1984) *The Hellenistic World and the Coming of Rome* (Berkeley, CA).

Guha, Ranajit (2002) *History at the Limits of World-history* (New York).

——. (1983) *Elementary Aspects of Peasant Insurgency in Colonial India* (Delhi).

——. (1963) *A Rule of Property for Bengal* (Paris).

Gustafsson, H. (1998) 'The Conglomerate State: A Perspective on State Formation in Early Modern Europe', *Scandinavian Journal of History* 23, pp. 189–213.

Haldon, J. F. (2003) *Warfare, State and Society in the Byzantine World 565–1204* (London and New York).

——. (1997) *Byzantium in the Seventh Century: the Transformation of a Culture*, Rev. ed. (Cambridge).

——. (1993) *The State and the Tributary Mode of Production* (London).

Haldon, J. & J. Goldstone (2009) 'Ancient States, Empires, and Exploitation: Problems and Perspectives', in Ian Morris & Walter Scheidel (Eds), *The Dynamics of Ancient Empires* (Oxford), pp. 3–29.

Hall, E. (1989) *Inventing the Barbarian* (Oxford).

Halsall, G. (2003) *Warfare and Society in the Barbarian West, 450–900* (London and New York).

Hamilakis, Y. (2007) *The Nation and Its Ruins. Antiquity, Archaeology and National Imagination in Greece* (Oxford).

Hammer, M. (1830) 'Memoir on the Diplomatic Relations between the Courts of Delhi and Constantinople in the Sixteenth and Seventeenth Centuries', *Transactions of the Royal Asiatic Society*, 2, pp. 462–86.

Hanioğlu, M. Şükrü (2001) *Preparation for a Revolution: the Young Turks, 1902–1908* (Oxford).

——. (1995) *The Young Turks in Opposition* (Oxford).

Hans, L. M. (1983) *Karthago und Sizilien* (Hildesheim).

Hardt, Michael & Antonio Negri (2001) *Empire* (Cambridge, MA).

Hardy, P. (1972) *The Muslims of British India* (Cambridge).

Harker, A. (2008) *Loyalty and Dissidence in Roman Egypt. The Case of the Acta Alexandrinorum* (Cambridge).

Harrington, James (1656) *Commonwealth of Oceana* (London).

Hartmann, P. C. (2005) *Das Heilige Römische Reich Deutscher Nation in der Neuzeit, 1486–1806* (Ditzingen).

Harvey, David (2003) *The New Imperialism* (New York).

Hasan, Farhat (2004) *State and Locality in Mughal India. Power Relations in Western India, c. 1572–1730* (Cambridge).

Hasan, M. (2005) *A Moral Reckoning. Muslim Intellectuals in Nineteenth Century Delhi* (Delhi).

Hathaway, Jane (1997) *The Politics of Households in Ottoman Egypt: The Rise of the Qazdaglis* (New York).

——. (1996) 'Problems of Periodization in Ottoman History: the Fifteenth Through the Eighteenth Centuries', *The Turkish Studies Association Bulletin* 20 (2), pp. 25–31.

Havell, E. B. (1918) *A History of Aryan Rule in India from the Earliest Times to the Death of Akbar* (London).

Haverfield, F. (1911) 'An Inaugural Address Delivered Before the First Annual General Meeting of the Society', *Journal of Roman Studies* 1, xi–xx.

——. (1912) 'Roman History since Mommsen', *Quarterly Review*, 217 (233), pp. 323–45.

Headley, J. (1997) *Tommaso Campanella and the Transformation of the World* (Princeton, NJ).

Hekster, O. (2005) 'Captured in the Gaze of Power. Visibility, Games and Roman Imperial Representation', in Fowler & Hekster (Eds), *Imaginary Kings. Royal Images in the Ancient Near East, Greece and Rome* (Stuttgart), pp. 157–76.

Hellie, Richard (2005) 'The Structure of Russian Imperial History', *History and Theory* 44, pp. 88–112.

——. (1971) *Enserfment and Military Change in Muscovy* (Chicago).

Herklotz, F. (2007) *Prinzeps und Pharao. Der Kult des Augustus in Ägypten* (Frankfurt am Main).

Heyd, Uriel (1961) 'The Ottoman Ulema and Westernization in the Time of Selim III and Mahmud II', *Scripta Hierosolymitana*, Vol. 9: *Studies in Islamic History and Civilization* (Jerusalem), pp. 63–96.

Hingley, Richard (2000) *Roman Officers and English Gentlemen: The Imperial Origins of Roman Archaeology* (London & New York).

Hintze, Andrea (1997) *The Mughal Empire and Its Decline* (Aldershot).

Hobbes, Th. (1996) *Leviathan*, R. Tuck (Ed.) (Cambridge).

Hobsbawm, Eric (2008) *On Empire: America, War, and Global Supremacy* (New York).

Hodgson, M. G. S. (1974) *The Venture of Islam*, 3 Vols (Chicago).

Hogendorn, Jan & Marion Johnson (1986) *The Shell Money of the Slave Trade* (New York).

Holland, Bernard (1901) *Imperium Et Libertas: A Study in History and Politics* (London).

Holm, A. (1898) *Geschichte Siciliens im Alterthum*, Bd. iii (Leipzig).

Hopkins, A. G. (1973) *An Economic History of West Africa* (London).

Howard, Douglas A. (2007) 'The Ottoman Advice for Kings Literature', in V. H. Aksan & Daniel Goffman (Eds), *The Early Modern Ottomans* (Cambridge), pp. 137–66.

——. (1988) 'Ottoman Historiography and the Literature of "Decline" of the Sixteenth and Seventeenth Centuries', *Journal of Asian History* 22, pp. 52–77.

Hoyos, B. D. (1998) *Unplanned Wars: The Origins of the First and Second Punic Wars* (Berlin and New York).

Huang, R. (1997) *China: a Macro History* (Armonk).

Hui, V. T. (2005) *War and State Formation in Ancient China and Early Modern Europe* (Cambridge).

Hunwick, J. (1969) 'Studies in the Tarikh al-Fattash (I), its Authors and Textual History', *Research Bulletin, Centre of Arabic Documentation – University of Ibadan* 5 (1–2), pp. 57–65.

——. (1966) 'Religion and State in the Songhay Empire 1464– 591', in Lewis (Ed.), *Islam in Tropical Africa* (Oxford), pp. 296–317.

Hurlet, F. (Ed.) (2008) *Les Empires. Antiquité et Moyen Âge. Analyse compare* (Rennes).

Huss, W. (1985) *Geschichte der Karthager* (Munich).

Iggers, Georg G. (1995) 'Historicism: the History and Meaning of a Term', *Journal of the History of Ideas*, 56 (January), pp. 129–52.

Imber, Colin (2002) *The Ottoman Empire 1300–1650: the Structure of Power* (New York).

Inalcik, Halil (1994) *An Economic and Social History of the Ottoman Empire*, Halil Inalcik & Donald Quataert (Eds), vol. 1: *1300–1600* (Cambridge).

——. (1991) 'The Status of the Greek Orthodox Patriarch under the Ottomans', *Turcica* 23, pp. 407–37.

——. (1980) 'The Question of the Emergence of the Ottoman State,' *International Journal of Turkish Studies* 2, pp. 71–79.

——. (1973) *The Ottoman Empire: The Classical Age 1300–1600* (London).

——. (1954) 'Ottoman Methods of Conquest,' *Studia Islamica* 2, pp. 103–29.

Ingrao, Charles (1994) *The Habsburg Monarchy 1618–1815* (Cambridge).

Islamoğlu, Huri & Peter C. Perdue (Eds) (2009) *Shared Histories of Modernity. China, India and the Ottoman Empire* (New Delhi).

Itzkowitz, N. (1962) 'Eighteenth Century Ottoman Realities', *Studia Islamica* 16, pp. 73–94.

Jenkyns, R. (Ed) (1992) *The Legacy of Rome* (Oxford).

Johnson, Chalmers (2004) *The Sorrows of Empire: Militarism, Secrecy, and the End of the Republic* (New York).

Jones, A. H. M. (1964) *The Later Roman Empire*, 3 vols (Oxford).

Jones, C. P. (1978) *The Roman World of Dio Chrysostom* (Cambridge, MA, and London).

Jones, E. (2003) *The European Miracle: Environments, Economies and Geopolitics in the History of Europe and Asia* (3rd ed., Cambridge).

Jones, Gareth Stedman (1983) *Languages of Class: Studies in English Working Class History 1832–82* (Cambridge).

Kafadar, Cemal (2007) 'Janissaries and Other Riffraff of Ottoman Istanbul: Rebels Without a Cause?' in Baki Tezcan and Karl K. Barbir (Eds) *Identity and Identity Formation in the Ottoman World: A Volume of Essays in Honor of Norman Itzkowitz* (Madison), pp. 113–34.

——. (1995) *Between Two Worlds: The Construction of the Ottoman State* (Berkeley, CA).

——. (1994) 'The Ottomans and Europe', in T. Brady Jr, H. A. Oberman & J. D. Tracy (Eds), *Handbook of European History 1400–1600: Late Middle Ages, Renaissance and Reformation – I: Structure and Assertions* (Leiden), pp. 589–636.

Kamen, R. (2003) *Imperio. La forja de Espana como potentia mundial* (Madrid).

Kann, Robert A. (1974) *A History of the Habsburg Empire 1526–1918* (Berkeley, CA).

Kapila, Shruti (2007) 'Race Matters. Orientalism and Religion, India and Beyond c. 1770–1880', *Modern Asian Studies*, 41 (3), pp. 471–513.

Kaplan, Amy & Donald Pease (Eds) (1993) *Cultures of United States Imperialism* (Durham).

Kara, İsmail (2005) 'Turban and Fez: *Ulema* as Opposition', in Elisabeth Özdalga (Ed.) *Late Ottoman Society: The Intellectual Legacy* (London & New York), pp. 162–200.

Karpat, Kemal H. (2001) *The Politicization of Islam: Reconstructing Identity, State, Faith, and Community in the Late Ottoman State* (Oxford).

Katsenstein, Peter (2005) *A World of Regions: Asia and Europe in the American Imperium* (Ithaca, NY).

Kaye, J. W. (1880) *A History of the Sepoy War in India, 1857–58*, Volume III (London).

Keenan, Edward L. (1986) 'Muscovite Political Folkways,' *Russian Review* 45 (April), pp. 115–81.

Keene, H. G. (1891) *Mádhava Ráo Scindia otherwise called Madhoji* (Oxford).

——. (1887) *The Fall of the Moghul Empire of Hindustan* (London).

Keep, John L. H. (1985) *Soldiers of the Tsar: Army and Society in Russia, 1462–1874* (Oxford).

Kelly, Christopher (2004) *Ruling the Later Roman Empire* (Cambridge, MA).

Kennedy, H. (2001) *The Armies of the Caliphs: Military and Society in the Early Islamic State* (London).

——. (1986) *The Prophet and the Age of the Caliphates* (London).

Kennedy, Paul (1987) *The Rise and Fall of the Great Powers. Economic Change and Military Conflict from 1500 to 2000* (New York).

Khazanov, A. M. (1978) 'Some Theoretical Problems of the Study of the Early State', in: H. Claessen & P. Skalnik (Eds), *The Early State*, pp. 77–107.

Khazanov, A. M. & A. Wink (2001) *Nomads in the Sedentary World* (London).

Kieniewicz, J. (1983) 'Europejska ekspansja i Imperium/European Expansion and Empire, *Przegląd Historyczny* 74 (4), pp. 749–57.

Kiraly, Bela K. (1975) 'Neo-Serfdom in Hungary', *Slavic Review* 34 (2), pp. 269–78.

Kivelson, Valerie (2002) 'On Words, Sources, and Historical Method: Which Truth About Muscovy?', *Kritika* 3 (3), pp. 487–99.

——. (1997) 'Merciful Father, Impersonal State: Russian Autocracy in Comparative Perspective' *Modern Asian Studies* 31, pp. 635–63.

——. (1994) 'The Effects of Partible Inheritance: Gentry Families and the State in Muscovy', *Russian Review* 53, pp. 197–212.

——. (1993) 'The Devil Stole His Mind: The Tsar and the 1648 Uprising', *The American Historical Review* 98 (3), pp. 733–56.

Klein, K. D. (1980) 'The Contributions of the Fourth Century Xianbei States to the Reunification of the Chinese Empire', Ph.D. Thesis UCLA.

Koch, E. (1994) 'Diwan-i 'Amm and Chihil Sutun: The Audience Halls of Shah Jahan', *Muqarnas*, Vol. 11, pp. 143–65.

Koçu, Reşad Ekrem (2004) *Yeniçeriler* (2nd ed., Istanbul).

Koenigsberger, H. G. (1971) *The Habsburgs and Europe 1516–1660* (Ithaca, NY).

Kollman, Nancy Shields (1987) *Kinship and Politics: The Making of the Muscovite Political System, 1345–1547* (Stanford).

Kühnen, A. (2008) *Die Imitatio Alexandri in der römischen Politik* (Münster).

Kulke, Herman (Ed.) (1995) *The State in India, 1000–1700* (Delhi).

——. (1993) *Kings and Cults: State Formation and Legitimation in India and Southeast Asia* (Delhi).

——. (1982) 'Fragmentation and Segmentation versus Integration? Reflections on the Concepts of Indian Feudalism and the Segmentary State in Indian History,' *Studies in History* 4 (2), pp. 237–64.

Kunt, I. Metin (1983) *The Sultan's Servants: The Transformation of the Ottoman Provincial Government 1550–1650* (New York).

Kuşmani, Ubeydullah & Ebubekir Efendi (2007) *Asiler ve Gaziler: Kabakçı Mustafa Risalesi.* Aysel Danacı Yıldız (Ed.) (Istanbul).

Laitin, David (1991) 'The National Uprisings in the Soviet Union', *World Politics* 44 (October), pp. 139–177.

Lal, Ruby (2005) *Domesticity and Power in the Early Mughal World* (Cambridge).

Lane, F. C. (1973) *Venice a Maritime Republic* (Baltimore & London).

Lapidus, Ira M. (2002) *A History of Islamic Societies* (2nd ed., Cambridge).

La Rosa, V. (1987) *'Archaiologhia* e storiografia: quale Sicilia?', in M. Aymard and G. Giarrizzo (Eds), *Storia d'Italia. Le regioni dall'Unità a oggi: la Sicilia* (Torino), pp. 701–31.

Layne, Christopher & Bradley A. Thayer (Eds) (2007) *American Empire: a Debate* (New York).

Lazenby, J. F. (1996) *The First Punic War: A Military History* (Palo Alto, CA).

Lehmler, C. (2005) *Syrakus unter Agathokles und Hieron II. Die Verbindung von Kultur und Macht in einer hellenistischen Metropole* (Frankfurt am Main).

Lendon, Jon (1997) *Empire of Honour* (Oxford).

Lepelley, C. (1983) 'Quot curiales, tot tyranni', in E. Frézouls (Ed.), *Crise et redressement dans les provinces européennes de l'Empire (milieu du IIIe – milieu du IVe siècle ap. J.-C.)* (Strasbourg), pp. 143–56.

Lerouge, Charlotte (2007) *L' image des Parthes dans le monde gréco-romain. Du début du Ier siècle av. J.-C. jusqu' à la fin du Haut-Empire romain. Oriens et Occidens, 17* (Stuttgart).

Levtzion, N. (1971) 'A Seventeenth-Century Chronicle by Ibn al-Mukhtar. A Critical Study of Tarikh al-Fattash', *Bulletin SOAS* 34, pp. 571–93.

Lewis, Bernard (2002) *What Went Wrong? The Clash Between Islam and Modernity in the Middle East* (London).

——. (1980) 'Slade on Turkey,' in Osman Okyar and Halil İnalcık (Eds) *Türkiye'nin Sosyal ve Ekonomik Tarihi, 1071–1920: Birinci Uluslararası Türkiye'nin Sosyal ve Ekonomik Tarihi Kongresi Tebliğleri (Hacettepe Üniversitesi, Ankara; 11–13 Temmuz 1977)* (Ankara), pp. 215–26 [reprinted in Bernard Lewis, *Islam in History: Ideas, People, and Events in the Middle East*, new ed. (Chicago: Open Court, 1993), pp. 67–83].

Lewis, Bernard & Benjamin Braude (1982) (Eds), *Christians and Jews in the Ottoman Empire, the Functioning of a Plural Society*, 2 Vols, (New York).

Lewis, J. M. (Ed.) (1966) *Islam in Tropical Africa* (Oxford).

Lewis, Mark Edward (2009) *China between Empires: The Northern and Southern Dynasties* (Cambridge, MA and London).

——. (2009) 'Gift Circulation and Charity in the Han and Roman Empires', in W. Scheidel (Ed.), *Rome and China. Comparative Perspectives on Ancient World Empires* (New York), pp. 121–36.

——. (2007) *The Early Chinese Empires: Qin and Han* (Cambridge MA and London).

Lewis, Mark Edward (1999) 'Warring States Political History', in M. Loewe and E. L. Shaughnessy (Eds) *The Cambridge History of Ancient China from the Origins of Civilization to 221 B.C.* (Cambridge), pp. 587–650.

——. (1990) *Sanctioned Violence in Early China* (Albany).

——. (1988) *Of Rule and Revenue* (Berkeley, Los Angeles, CA and London).

Lewis, Naphtali (1983) *Life in Egypt under Roman Rule* (Oxford).

Lieberman, Victor (1999) 'Transcending East-West Dichotomies: State and Culture Formation in Six Ostensibly Disparate Areas,' Victor Lieberman (Ed.), *Beyond Binary Histories: Re-imagining Eurasia to c. 1830* (Ann Arbor, MI), pp. 19–102.

Liebeschuetz, J. H. W. G. (2001) *The Decline and Fall of the Roman City* (Oxford).

Lieven, Dominic (2001) *Empire: The Russian Empire and its Rivals* (New Haven & London).

Lintott, A. (2008) *Cicero as Evidence. A Historian's Companion* (Oxford).

Liu, S. (2001) 'Jiankang and the Commercial Empire of the Southern Dynasties: Change and Continuity in Medieval Chinese Economic History', in Pearce, Spiro, & Ebrey (Eds), pp. 35–52.

Lo Cascio, Elio (2000) *Il Princeps e il suo impero* (Bari).

Locke, John (1988) *Two Treatises of Government*, Peter Laslett (Ed.) (Cambridge).

Lockhart, P. D. (2007) *Denmark, 1513–1660: the Rise and Decline of a Renaissance Monarchy* (Oxford).

Loewe, M. (2004) *The Men Who Governed Han China: Companion to a Biographical Dictionary of the Qin, Former Han and Xin periods* (Leiden).

Loewe, M. (2006) *The Government of the Qin and Han Empires 221 BCE–220 CE* (Indianapolis, IN and Cambridge).

Løkkegaard, F. (1950) *Islamic Taxation in the Classical Period* (Copenhagen).

Longrigg, Stephen H. (1925) *Four Centuries of Modern Iraq* (London).

Loomba, Ania (1998) *Colonialism/Postcolonialism* (London & New York).

Lowry, Heath W. (2003) *The Nature of the Early Ottoman State* (Albany).

Lubbe, A. (1982) *Imperium europejskie. Ekspansja Europy a powstanie europejskiej gospodarki światowej / European Empire. European Expansion and Formation of the European World Economy* (Warszaw).

Lucas, C. P. (1914) *Greater Rome and Greater Britain* (Oxford).

Ludden, David (2006a), 'A Useable Past for a Post-National Present: Governance and Development in South Asia', in *Journal of the Asiatic Society of Bangladesh*, Golden Jubilee Volume (1956–2006), 50 (1–2), pp. 259–92.

——. (2006b),'History and the Inequality Predicament', Wertheim Lecture, University of Amsterdam, School of Social Science Research, published in full online at http://www.iias.nl/asia/wertheim/ and excerpted in the *International Institute for Asian Studies Newsletter*, 28 (Autumn), pp. 28–29.

——. (2005), 'Development Regimes in South Asia: History and the Development Conundrum,' *Economic and Political Weekly* 40 (37), 10 September, pp. 4042–51.

——. (2003) 'The First Boundary of Bangladesh on Sylhet's Northern Frontiers', *Journal of the Asiatic Society of Bangladesh*, 48 (1), pp. 1–54.

——. (2003b), 'Maps in the Mind and the Mobility of Asia', *Journal of Asian Studies*, 62 (3), pp. 1057–78.

——. (Ed.) (2002) *Reading Subaltern Studies: Critical History, Contested Meaning, and The Globalization of South Asia* (Delhi).

——. (2002b), *India and South Asia: A Short History* (Oxford).

——. (2002c), 'Specters of Agrarian Territory in South India', *Indian Economic and Social History Review*, 39 (2&3), pp. 233–58.

Ludden, David (2002d), 'Modern Inequality and Early Modernity,' *American Historical Review*, 107 (2), pp. 470–80.

——. (1999) *An Agrarian History of India* (Cambridge).

——. (1996) 'Caste Society and Units of Production in Early Modern South India', Burton Stein & Sanjay Subrahmanyam (Eds), *Institutions and Economic Change in South Asia: Historical and Contemporary Perspectives* (New Delhi), pp. 105–33.

——. (1995) 'Urbanism and Early Modernity in the Tirunelveli Region,' *Bengal Past and Present*, 114, Parts 1–2, Nos. 218–219, pp. 9–40.

——. (1993) 'Orientalist Empiricism and Transformations of Colonial Knowledge,' in C. A. Breckenridge & Peter Van der Veer (Eds) *Orientalism and The Post-Colonial Predicament* (Philadelphia), pp. 250–78.

——. (1990) 'Agrarian Commercialism in Eighteenth Century South India: Evidence from the 1823 Tirunelveli Census,' in Sanjay Subrahmanyam (Ed.), *Merchants, Markets and the State in Early Modern India* (Delhi), pp. 215–41.

——. (1985) *Peasant History in South India* (Princeton, NJ). ACLS History E-Book (Available at http://ets.umdl.umich.edu/cgi/t/text/text-idx?c=acls;;idno=heb02438/) Second paperback edition published as *Early Capitalism and Local History in South India* (Delhi, 2005).

Luttwak, Edward (1976) *The Grand Strategy of the Roman Empire* (Baltimore).

Lyttelton, Adrian (1973) *Italian Fascisms: From Pareto to Gentile* (London).

MacFarlane, Charles (1829) *Constantinople in 1828: a Residence of Sixteen Months in the Turkish Capital and Provinces, with an Account of the Present State of the Naval and Military Power and of the Resources of the Ottoman Empire*, 2 vols (London).

MacMullen, Ramsay (1988) *Corruption and The Decline of Rome* (New Haven).

——. (1966) *Enemies of the Roman Order* (Cambridge, MA).

Macůrek, J. (Ed.) (1965) *Magna Moravia: Sbornik k 1100 výroči přichodu byzantské mise na Moravu* (Praha).

Madsen, Jesper Majbom (2009) *Eager to be Roman. Greek Response to Roman Rule in Pontus and Bithynia* (London).

Maier, Charles (2006) *Among Empires: American Ascendancy and its Predecessors* (Cambridge, MA).

Maier, G. (2005) *Amtsträger und Herrscher in der Romania Gothica: Vergleichende Untersuchungen zu den Institutionen der ostgermanischen Völkerwanderungsreiche* (Stuttgart).

Maine, Henry Sumner (1861) *Ancient Law: Its Connection With the Early History of Society and Its Relation to Modern Ideas* (London).

Mair, L. (1977) *African Kingdoms* (Oxford).

Majeed, Javed (1999) 'Comparativism and References to Rome in British Imperial Attitudes to India', in Catherine Edwards (Ed.) *Roman Presences. Receptions of Rome in European Culture 1789–1945* (Cambridge), pp. 88–110.

Majumdar, B. B. (1934) *History of Political Thought from Rammohun to Dayananda*, Vol. I, *Bengal* (Calcutta).

Małowist, L. (1967) 'Märkte und Städte im westlichen Sudan vom 14. bis 16. Jahrhundert', *Jahrbuch für Wirtschaftsgeschichte* 2, pp. 281–305.

——. (1966) 'Le commerce de l'or et d' esclaves au Soudan Occidental', *Africana Bulletin* 4, pp. 49–72.

Mann, Michael (1986) *The Sources of Social Power*, Vol. 1 (Cambridge).

Marchand, S. L. (1996) *Down from Olympus. Archaeology and Philhellenism in Germany, 1750–1970* (Princeton, NJ).

Mardin, Şerif (1988) 'Freedom in an Ottoman Perspective', in Metin Heper & Ahmet Evin (Eds) *State, Democracy, and the Military: Turkey in the 1980s* (Berlin & New York), pp. 23–35.

——. (1962) *The Genesis of Young Ottoman Thought: A Study in the Modernization of Turkish Political Ideas* (Princeton, NJ).

Markus, R. A. (1997) *Gregory The Great and His World* (Cambridge).

Marsigli, Luigi Ferdinando (1732) *Stato militare dell'imperio ottomanno/L'état militaire de l'empire ottoman* (La Haye).

Matthee, Rudi (1999) *The Politics of Trade in Safavid Iran: Silk for Silver, 1600–1730* (Cambridge).

Mauny, R. (1961) *Tableau géographique de l' ouest africain au Moyen Age* (Dakar).

Mazza, M. (1980–1981), 'Economia e società nella Sicilia romana', *Kokalos* Nos 26–27, pp. 292–353.

Mazzini, Giuseppe (1907) *The Duties of Man and Other Essays* (London).

——. (1877) *La questione d'Oriente: Lettere slave, politica internazionale* (Rome: Commissione per la pubblicatione delle opera di Giuseppe Mazzini, 1877 [1857]).

——. (1861a), 'Dal Papa al Concilio', in *Scritti editi ed inediti*, Vol. 7 (Milan), pp. 225–47.

——. (1861b), 'Dell'iniziativa rivoluzionaria in Europa', in *Scritti editi ed inediti*, Vol. 5, (Milan), pp. 55–84.

McNeill, William H. (1982) *The Pursuit of Power. Technology, Armed Force and Society since A.D. 1000* (Chicago).

Meillassoux, Cl. (Ed.) (1971) *The Development of Indigenous Trade and Markets in West Africa* (Oxford).

Memmi, Albert (1965) *The Colonizer and the Colonized* (New York).

Meriç, Cemil (1981) *Bir Facianın Hikâyesi* (Ankara).

Meriç, Ümit (1975) *Cevdet Paşa'nın Cemiyet ve Devlet Görüşü* (Istanbul).

Meyer-Zwiffelhoffer, E. (2002) *Politikōs árchein. Zum Regierungsstil der senatorischen Statthalter in den kaiserzeitlichen griechischen Provinzen* (Stuttgart).

Mignolo, Walter D. (2000) *Local Histories/Global Designs: Coloniality, Subaltern Knowledges, and Border Thinking* (Princeton, NJ).

Millar, Fergus (1977) *The Emperor in the Roman World* (London).

Millward, James A. (2004) 'The Qing Formation, the Mongol Legacy, and the "End of History" in Early Modern Central Asia', in L. A. Struve (Ed.), *The Qing Formation in World Historical Time* (Cambridge, MA), pp. 92–120.

Modesto, Johannes (1989) *Gregor der Grosse. Nachfolger Petri und Universal Primat* (St Ottilien).

Mohamed, Duse (1911) *In the Land of the Pharaohs. A History of Egypt from the Fall of Ismail to the Assassination of Boutros Pasha* (London).

Momigliano, A. (1984) 'La riscoperta della Sicilia antica da T. Fazello a P. Orsi', in A. Momigliano (Ed.), *Settimo contributo alla storia degli studi classici e del mondo antico* (Rome 1984), pp. 115–32.

Mommsen, Th. (1887) *Römische Staatsrecht*, Vol 1–2 (3rd ed., Leipzig).

Monteil, V. (1964) *L' Islam Noir. Une religion à la conquête de l' Afrique* (Paris).

Montesquieu, Charles de Secondat Baron de (1759) *De l'esprit de lois*. Nouvelle édition, revue, corrigée, & considérablement augmentée par l'auteur, 4 vols (Copenhague & Geneve).

Monypenny, W. F. (1905) 'The Principles of Empire: The Imperial Ideal', in C. S. Goldman & R. Kipling (Eds), *The Empire and the Century: A Series of Essays on Imperial Problems and Possibilities* (London), pp. 5–29.

Moreland, W. H. (1929) *The Agrarian System of Moslem India* (London).

Morimoto, K. (1981) *The Fiscal Administration of Egypt in the Early Islamic Period* (Dohosha).

Morris, Ian & W. Scheidel (Eds) (2009) *The Dynamics of Ancient Empires* (New York).

Mousnier, Roland (1970) *Peasants Uprisings in the Seventeenth Century: France, Russia and China*, Brian Pearce (trans.) (New York).

Muldoon, James (1999) *Empire and Order: the Concept of Empire, 800–1800* (Basingstoke).

Murphy, Cullen (2007) *Are We Rome? The Fall of an Empire and the Fate of America* (New York).

Musti, D. (1988) 'La spinta verso il Sud: espansione romana e "rapporti internazionali"', in *Storia di Roma*, i (Torino), pp. 527–42.

Mutlu, Şamil (Ed.) (1994) *Yeniçeri Ocağı'nın Kaldırılışı ve II. Mahmud'un Edirne Seyahati: Mehmed Dâniş Bey ve Eserleri* (İstanbul Üniversitesi Edebiyat Fakültesi Yayınları).

Mutschler F.-H. & Armin Mittag (Eds) (2009) *Conceiving the Empire. Rome and China Compared* (Oxford).

Nandy, Ashis (1983) *The Intimate Enemy: Loss and Recovery of Self Under Colonialism* (Delhi and New York).

Neumann, Christoph K. (1994) *Das indirekte Argument – ein Plädoyer für die Tanzîmât vermittels der Historie: Die geschichtliche Bedeutung von Aḥmed Cevdet Paşas Ta'rîh* (Münster).

Niane, D. T. (Ed.) (1984) *Africa from the Twelfth to the Sixteenth Century, Unesco General History of Africa*, Vol. 4 (Paris).

Nicolet, C. (1988) *L'Inventaire du Monde: Géographie et Politique aux Origines de L'Empire Romain* (Paris).

——. (1980) *The World of the Citizen in Republican Rome* (Berkeley and Los Angeles, CA).

Nishijima, S. (1986) 'The Economic and Social History of Former Han', in Twitchett and Loewe (Eds) (1986), pp. 551–607.

Novick, Peter (1988) *That Noble Dream: The 'Objectivity Question' and the American Historical Profession* (Cambridge).

Oakeshott, Michael (1983) *On History and Other Essays* (Oxford).

Oates, Joan (1979) *Babylon* (London).

Oberg, K. (1955) 'Types of Social Structure among the Lowland Tribes of South and Central America', *American Anthropologist* 57, pp. 472–87.

Ogot, B. A. (Ed.) (1992) *Africa From the Sixteenth to the Eighteenth Century, UNESCO General History of Africa*, Vol. 5 (Paris).

O'Leary, Brendan (1989) *The Asiatic Mode of Production: Oriental Despotism, Historical Materialism, and Indian History* (London).

Ömer Fâ'ik Efendi (1979) *Nizâmü'l-atîk (İstanbul Üniversite Ktb. TY nr. 5836)*, Ahmet Sarıkaya (Ed.), Senior thesis (İstanbul Üniversitesi).

Ortolani, G. E. (1813) *Sulle antiche e moderne tasse della Sicilia* (Palermo).

Owen, Roger (2004) *Lord Cromer: Victorian Imperialist, Edwardian Proconsul* (Oxford).

Pagden, A. (1998) *Spanish Imperialism and the Political Imagination* (New Haven).

——. (1995) *Lords of All the World: Ideologies of Empire in Spain, Britain and France c. 1500–c. 1800* (New Haven).

Pais, Ettore (2007 [1894]), *Il Sud prima di Roma: Storia della Sicilia e della Magna Grecia* (Lecce).

——. (1938) *Roma: Dall'antico al nuovo impero* (Milano).

——. (1922) 'La storia antica negli ultimi cinquant'anni con speciale riguardo all'Italia' in *Italia antica. Ricerche di storia e di geografia storica*, Vol. 1 (Bologna), pp. 1–29.

Pais, Ettore (1920) *Imperialismo romano e politica italiana* (Bologna).

——. (1908) *Ricerche storiche e geografiche sull'Italia antica* (Turin).

——. (1898) *Storia d'Italia: Dai tempi più antichi alla fine delle guerre puniche. Storia di Roma* (Turin).

Palme, B. (1999) 'Die *officia* der Statthalter in der Spätantike: Forschungsstand und Perspektiven', *Antiquité Tardive* 7, pp. 85–133.

Pamuk, Sevket (2001) 'The Price Revolution in the Ottoman Empire Reconsidered', *International Journal of Middle Eastern Studies* 33, pp. 69–89.

Panaite, Viorel (2003) 'The Voivodes of the Danubian Principalities as Haracguzarlar of the Ottoman Sultans,' in Kemal Karpat with Robert W. Zens (Eds) *Ottoman Borderlands: Issues, Personalities and Political Changes* (Madison, WI), pp. 58–78.

Pani, M. (2003) *La Corte dei Cesari* (Roma-Bari).

Parker, Geoffrey (1988) *The Military Revolution: Military Innovation and the Rise of the West, 1500–1800* (Cambridge).

Parker, Geoffrey & Lesley M. Smith (Eds) (1978) *The General Crisis of the Seventeenth Century* (London & Boston, MA).

Paul, Michael C. (2004) 'The Military Revolution in Russia, 1550–1682', *The Journal of Military History* 68 (January), pp. 9–45.

Peachin, Michael (2007) 'Exemplary Government in the Early Roman Empire', in Hekster, de Kleijn & Slootjes (Eds), *Crises and the Roman Empire* (Leiden), pp. 75–96.

Pearce, S. (2001) 'Form and Matter: Archaizing Reform in Sixth-century China', in Pearce et al. (Eds), pp. 149–78.

——. (1987) 'The Yü-Wen Regime in Sixth Century China', Ph.D. thesis Princeton University.

Pearce, S., A. Spiro & P. Ebrey (Eds) (2001) *Culture and Power in the Reconstitution of the Chinese Realm, 200–600* (Cambridge, MA and London).

Pearson, M. N. (1996) *Pilgrimage to Mecca. The Indian Experience, 1500–1800* (Princeton, NJ).

——. (1976) 'Shivaji and the Decline of the Mughal Empire', *Journal of Asian Studies* 35 (2), pp. 221–35.

Perdue, Peter C. (2004) 'The Qing Formation in Eurasian Time and Space: Lessons from the Galdan Campaigns', in L. A. Struve (Ed.), *The Qing Formation in World Historical Time* (Cambridge, MA), pp. 57–91.

Perkins, Ph. (2007) *'Aliud in Sicilia.* Cultural Development in Rome's First Province', in P. van Dommelen and N. Terrenato (Eds), *Articulating local cultures. Power and identity Under the Expanding Roman Republic*, Portsmouth, RI 2007, *JRA* (Suppl. 63), pp. 33–53.

Perlin, Frank (1993) *Monetary, Administrative, and Popular Infrastructures in Asia and Europe, 1500–1900* (Brookfield, VT).

Pesch, O. H. (1994) *Das Zweite Vatikanische Konzil: (1962–1965): Vorgeschichte, Verlauf, Ergebnisse, Nachgeschichte*, 2. Aufl. (Würzburg).

Pierce, Leslie (1993) *The Imperial Harem: Women and Sovereignty in the Ottoman Empire* (New York).

Pinzone, A. (2000) 'La "romanizzazione" della Sicilia occidentale in età repubblicana', in Pisa and Gibellina (Eds), *Terze giornate internazionali di studi sull'area elima*, pp. 849–78.

——. (1999a), *Provincia romana. Ricerche di storia della Sicilia romana da Gaio Flaminio a Gregorio Magno* (Catania).

——. (1999b), *'Civitates sine foedere immunes ac liberae*: a proposito di Cic. *II Verr.* III 6, 13', *Mediterraneo Antico II*, 2, pp. 463–95.

Pipes, Richard (1994) 'Was There Private Property in Muscovite Russia?', *Slavic Review* 53 (2), pp. 524–30.

Piterberg, Gabriel (2003) *An Ottoman Tragedy: History and Historiography at Play* (Berkeley, CA).

Platonov, Sergey (1970) *The Time of Troubles. A Historical Study of the Internal Crisis and Social Struggle in Sixteenth- and Seventeenth-Century Muscovy*, John T. Alexander (trans.) (Lawrence, KS).

Pocock, J. G. A. (2003) *The Machiavellian Moment: Florentine Political Thought and the Atlantic Republican Tradition* (1st ed. 1975, Princeton, NJ).

——. (2002) *Barbarism and Religion, Vol. 1, The Enlightenment of Edward Gibbon, 1737–64* (Cambridge).

Poe, Marshall (2002) 'The Truth About Muscovy,' *Kritika* 3 (3), pp. 473–86.

——. (1998) 'The Military Revolution, Administrative Development, and Cultural Change in Early Modern Russia,' *Journal of Early Modern History* 2 (3), pp. 247–73.

——. (1996) 'The Consequences of the Military Revolution in Muscovy: A Comparative Perspective,' *Comparative Studies in Society and History* 38 (4), pp. 603–18.

Polanyi, Karl et al. (1957) *Trade and Markets in the Early Empires* (Glencoe).

Pomeranz, K. (2000) *The Great Divergence: China, Europe, and the Making of the Modern World* (Princeton, NJ).

Porchnev, Boris (1972) *Les Soulevements Populaires en France au XVIIe Siecle* (Paris).

Portale, E. C. (2004) '*Euergetikotatos ... kai philodoxotatos eis tous Hellenas*. Riflessioni sui rapporti fra Ierone II e il mondo greco', in Caccamo Caltabiano, Campagna & Pinzone, pp. 229–64.

Porter, Sir James (1771) *Observations on the Religion, Law, Government, and Manners of the Turks* (2nd ed., London).

Prag, J. R. W. (Ed.) (2007a), '*Sicilia nutrix plebis Romanae*'. *Rhetoric, law, and taxation in Cicero's* Verrines (*BICS* Suppl. 97) (London).

——. (2007b), '*Auxilia* and *Gymnasia*: A Sicilian Model of Roman Imperialism', *The Journal of Roman Studies* 97, pp. 68–100.

——. (2007c), 'Roman magistrates in Sicily, 227–49 BC', in Dubouloz and Pittia (2007), pp. 287–310.

Prakash, Gyan (Ed.) (1995) *After Colonialism: Imperial Histories and Postcolonial Displacements* (Princeton, NJ).

Prasad, P. (1997) 'Akbar and the Jains', in I. Habib (Ed.), *Akbar and His India* (New Delhi), pp. 97–108.

Price, Simon (1984) *Rituals and Power: The Roman Imperial Cult in Asia Minor* (Cambridge).

Pufendorf, Samuel (1998) *De Jure Naturae et Gentium*, 2 Bde. hrsg. Frank Böhling, *Gesammelte Werke*, hrsg. *Wilhelm Schmidt-Biggermann*, Bd. 4, 1–2 (Berlin).

——. (1910) Severinus De Monzambano (Pufendorf), *De Statu Imperii Germanici*, Fritz Salomon (Ed.) (Weimar).

——. (1675), *Dissertationes Academicae Selectiores* (Lund).

Puin, G. R. (1970), *Der Dīwān von ʿUmar ibn al-Ḫaṭṭāb* (Bonn).

Pullè, Francesco (1898) 'Profilo antropologico d'Italia', in *Archivio per l'antropologia e la etnologia*, Vol. 28, 1 (Florence), pp. 19–168.

Quataert, Donald (1994) 'The Age of Reforms, 1812–1914', in Halil İnalcık with Donald Quataert (Eds) *An Economic and Social History of the Ottoman Empire, 1300–1914* (Cambridge), Vol. 2, pp. 759–943.

——. (1992) 'Janissaries, Artisans, and the Question of Ottoman Decline, 1730–1826', in Eloy Benito Ruano and Manuel Espadas Burgos (Eds) *17 Congreso Internacional de Ciencias Historicas, Madrid – 1990*, Vol. 1 (Madrid), pp. 264–68.

Rabb, T. K. (1976) *The Struggle for Stability in Early Modern Europe* (Oxford).

Raeff, Marc (1984) *Understanding Imperial Russia* (New York).

Ranking, G. S. A. (trans.) (1990) *Muntakhabu-t-Tawarikh by Abdul-Qadir ibn-i-Muluk Shah al Badaoni, 3 Volumes* (New Delhi).

Rankov, B. (2007) 'Military Forces', in Sabin, van Wees & Whitby (Eds) (2007), pp. 30–75.

Rebel, Hermann (1983) *Peasant Classes: The Bureaucratization of Property and Family Relations under Early Habsburg Absolutism, 1511–1636* (Princeton, NJ).

Reed, Howard A. (1951) 'The Destruction of the Janissaries in 1826: How Sultan Mahmud II Abolished the Corps', Ph.D. dissertation (Princeton University).

Reid, James J. (1983) *Tribalism and Society in Islamic Iran: 1500–1629* (Malibu, CA).

——. (1978) 'The Qajar Uymaq in the Safavid Period, 1500–1722', *Iranian Studies* 11, pp. 117–43.

Richards, Jeffrey (1980) *Consul of God. The Life and Times of Gregory the Great* (London).

Richards, John F. (1993) *The Mughal Empire. The New Cambridge History of India: 1.5* (Cambridge).

Richards, Michael (1967) 'The Military Revolution, 1560–1660,' in Michael Roberts (Ed.), *Essays in Swedish History* (Minneapolis, MN), pp. 195–225.

Robertson, William (1769) *History of the Reign of the Emperor Charles V,* 3 vols (London).

Rocco, Alfredo (1973) 'The Formation and Functions of the Corporations', in Adrian Lyttelton (Ed.), *Italian Fascisms: From Pareto to Gentile* (London), pp. 292–97.

Rogers, Clifford J. (Ed.) (1995) 'The Military Revolution in History and Historiography,' *The Military Revolution Debate. Readings on the Military Transformation of Early Modern Europe* (Boulder, CO), pp. 2–10.

Romeo, R. (1973) *Il Risorgimento in Sicilia* (Bari).

Rosenthal, F. (1958) (trans.), *The Muqaddimah of Ibn Khaldun: An Introduction to History,* 3 Vols (New York).

Rostowzew, M. (1910a), *Studien zur Geschichte des römischen Kolonates* (Leipzig and Berlin).

——. (1910b), s. v. *frumentum*, in *Paulys Realencyclopädie der classischen Altertumswissenschaft*, vii, 1, pp. 126–67.

Rothschild, Emma (2001) *Economic Sentiments. Adam Smith, Condorcet, and the Enlightenment* (London).

Roy, Arundhati (2004) *An Ordinary Person's Guide to Empire* (Boston).

Roy, Ram Mohan (1999) 'Brief Remarks Regarding Modern Encroachments on the Ancient Rights of Females', in B. C. Robertson (Ed.), *The Essential Writings of Raja Rammohan Roy* (OUP India, Delhi), pp. 147–55.

Runciman, Steven (1965) *The Fall of Constantinople, 1453* (Cambridge).

Runciman, W. G. (2009) *The Theory of Cultural and Social Selection* (Cambridge).

——. (2001) 'From Nature to Culture, from Culture to Society', *Proceedings of the British Academy* 110, pp. 235–54.

——. (1983, 1989, 1997), *A Treatise on Social Theory*, 3 Vols (Cambridge).

Russell, Ralph & Khurshidul Islam (1969) *Three Mughal Poets: Mir, Sauda, Mir Hasan* (London).

Ryan, Alan (2007) 'Newer Than What? Older Than What?', in Ellen Paul, Fred Miller Jr & Jeffrey Paul (Eds) *Liberalism Old and New* (Cambridge), pp. 1–16.

Saberwal, Satish (1998) 'A Juncture of Traditions,' in Martin Doornbos & Sudipta Kavirag (Eds), *Dynamics of State Formation: Europe and India Compared* (London).

Sabin, P., H. van Wees & M. Whitby (Eds) (2007) *The Cambridge History of Greek and Roman Warfare. Volume II: from the Late Republic to the Late Empire* (Cambridge).

Sahlins, Marshall (1968) *Tribesmen* (Englewood Cliffs, NJ).

Said, E. W. (2006) *On Late Style. Music and Literature Against the Grain* (London).

Salmeri, G. (2005) 'Central Power Intervention and the Economy of the Provinces in the Roman Empire: the Case of Pontus and Bithynia', in S. Mitchell and C. Katsari (Eds), *Patterns in the Economy of Roman Asia Minor* (Swansea), pp. 187–206.

——. (2004) 'I caratteri della grecità di Sicilia e la colonizzazione romana', in G. Salmeri, A. Raggi and A. Baroni (Eds), *Colonie romane nel mondo greco* (Roma), pp. 255–307.

——. (2001) 'La Sicilia nei libri di viaggio del Settecento tra letteratura e riscoperta della grecità' *Analecta Romana Instituti Danici* 28, pp. 65–82.

——. (1998) 'L'arcipelago antiquario', in E. Vaiani (Ed.), *Dell'antiquaria e dei suoi metodi*, Atti delle giornate di studio (*ASNP* Quad. 6), (Pisa 1998 [2001]), pp. 257–80.

——. (1992) *Sicilia Romana. Storia e storiografia* (Catania).

——. (1991a), 'Dalle province a Roma: il rinnovamento del senato', in A. Momigliano and A. Schiavone (Eds), *Storia di Roma*, ii, 2 (Turin), pp. 552–75.

——. (1991b), 'Grecia *vs* Roma nella cultura siciliana dal XVII al XX secolo', in E. Gabba and K. Christ (Eds), *L'impero romano tra storia generale e storia locale*, ii, Biblioteca di *Athenaeum* 16 (Como), pp. 275–97.

——. (1986) 'Sui rapporti tra Sicilia e Africa in età romana repubblicana e imperiale', in A. Mastino (Ed.), *Africa romana*, iii (Sassari), pp. 397–412.

——. (1982) *La politica e il potere. Saggio su Dione di Prusa* (Catania).

Saller, Richard (1982) *Personal Patronage under the Early Empire* (Cambridge).

Sarkar, Jadunath (1935) *The Fall of the Mughal Empire* (Calcutta).

Sarris, P. (2006) Review of Wickham 2005, *Journal of Agrarian Change* 6, pp. 400–13

Sartori, F. (1983) '*Suburbanitas Siciliae*', in *Festschrift für Robert Muth*, Innsbruck (1983), pp. 415–23.

Sarvarkar, V. D. (1972) *Hindu-pad Padshahi. Or a Review of the Hindu Empire of Maharashtra* (1st ed., 1925, Repr. Delhi).

Schäfer, Gerd (1974) *König der Könige -Lied der Lieder. Studien zur Paranomastischen Intensitätsgenitiv* (Heidelberg).

Scheidel, W. (forthcoming), *The Wolf and the Dragon: State Power in Ancient Rome and China.*

——. (forthcoming a), 'The Budgets of the Han and Roman Empires', in W. Scheidel, ed., *State Power and Social Control in Ancient China and Rome.*

——. (forthcoming b), 'The 'First Great Divergence': Post-Ancient State Formation in Eastern and Western Eurasia'.

——. (Ed.) (2009) *Rome and China. Comparative Perspectives on Ancient World Empires* (New York).

——. (2009a), 'From the "Great Convergence" to the "First Great Divergence": Roman and Qin-Han State Formation and its Aftermath', in Scheidel (Ed.) (2009), pp. 11–23.

——. (2009b), 'The Monetary Systems of the Han and Roman Empires', in Scheidel (Ed.) (2009), pp. 137–208.

——. (2006) 'Stratification, Deprivation and Quality of Life', in M. Atkins and R. Osborne (Eds), *Poverty in the Roman World* (Cambridge) pp. 40–59.

Schwartzberg, J. E. (1978) *Historical Atlas of South Asia* (Chicago).

Schwarz, H. (2001) *Soll oder Haben? Die Finanzwirtschaft kleinasiatischer Städte in der Römischen Kaiserzeit am Beispiel von Bithynien, Lykien und Ephesos (29 v.Chr. – 284 n.Chr.)* (Bonn).

Schiavone, Aldo (2000) *The End of the Past. Ancient Rome and the Modern West* (Cambridge, MA).

Schneider, Rolf Michael (2006) 'Orientalism in Late Antiquity. The Oriental in Imperial and Christian Imagery', in J. Wiesehöfer & Ph. Huyse (Eds), *Ērān ud Anērān. Studien zu den Beziehungen zwischen dem Sasanidenreich und der Mittelmeerwelt* (Stuttgart), pp. 241–78.

Scinà, D. (1823) *Discorso intorno ad Archimede* (Palermo).

Sciuti Russi, V. (1994) *Mario Cutelli. Una utopia di governo* (Acireale).

——. (1984) *Il governo della Sicilia in due relazioni del primo Seicento* (Napoli).

Scott, James C. (1976) *The Moral Economy of the Peasant: Rebellion and Subsistence in Southeast Asia* (New Haven, CT).

Scrofani, S. (1988) *Viaggio in Grecia*, R. Ricorda (Ed.) (Venezia).

Seeley, John R. (1909) *The Expansion of England* (London).

Sen, Armatya K. (1981) *Poverty and Famines: An Essay on Entitlement and Deprivation* (New York).

Sergi, Giuseppe (1901) *The Mediterranean Race: A Study of the Origins of European Peoples* (London).

——. (1898) *Arii e Italici. Attorno all'Italia preistorica* (Turin).

Serrati, J. (2000) 'Garrison and Grain: Sicily between the Punic Wars', in Smith and Serrati (Eds) (2000), pp. 115–33.

Service, E. (1975) *Origins of State and Civilisation. The Process of Cultural Evolution* (New York).

Sharar, A. H. (1975) *Lucknow. The Last Phase of an Oriental Culture*, E. S. Harcourt and Fakhir Husain (trans.) (London).

Sherk, R. K. (1988) *The Roman Empire: Augustus to Hadrian* (Cambridge).

Simonsen, J. B. (1988) *Studies in the Genesis and Early Development of the Caliphal Taxation System* (Copenhagen).

Skalnik, P. (2004) 'Chiefdom: a Universal Political Formation?', *Focaal. European Journal of Anthropology* 43, pp. 76–98.

——. (1983) 'Questioning the Concept of the State in Indigenous Africa', *Social Dynamics* 9 (2), pp. 11–28.

——. (1978) 'The Early State as a Process', in H. Claessen & P. Skalnik (Eds) *The Early State*, pp. 597–618.

Skiotis, Dennis N. (1971) 'From Bandit to Pasha: First Steps in the Rise to Power of Ali of Tepelen, 1750–1784', *International Journal of Middle East Studies* 2, pp. 219–44.

Slade, Adolphus (1867) *Turkey and the Crimean War: a Narrative of Historical Events* (London).

——. (1837) *Turkey Greece and Malta*, 2 vols (London).

Smith, Chr. and J. Serrati (eds) (2000) *Sicily from Aeneas to Augustus. New Approaches in Archaeology and History* (Edinburgh).

Smith, J. Masson (1978) 'Turanian Nomadism and Iranian Politics,' *Iranian Studies* 11, pp. 67–68.

——. (1975) 'Mongol Manpower and Persian Population,' *The Journal of the Economic and Social History of the Orient* 18, pp. 282–88.

Smith, Vincent A. (1906) *A History of India* (Oxford).

Sørensen, Villy (1976) *Seneca. Humanisten ved Neros Hof* (Copenhagen).

Solmi, Arrigo (1908) 'Rassegne analitiche: La diffusione della civiltà romana e della civiltà britannica', in *Rivista italiana di sociologia* 12 (2), pp. 254–61.

Sommer, Michael (2005) *Roms Orientalische Steppengrenze* (Stuttgart).

Soraci, C. (2003) '*Sicilia frumentaria*. Contributi allo studio della Sicilia in epoca repubblicana', *Quaderni catanesi di studi antichi e medioevali* n.s. 2, pp. 289–401.

Sourdel, D. (1999) *L'état imperial des califes abbassides* (Paris).

Spawforth, A. J. S. & S. Walker, (1985–86), 'The World of the Panhellenion I + II', *Journal of Roman Studies* Vol. 75 (1985), pp. 78–104 & Vol. 76 (1986) pp. 88–105.

Spencer, Diana (2002) *The Roman Alexander* (Exeter).

Springer, Carolyn (1987) *The Marble Wilderness: Ruins and Representation in Italian Romanticism, 1775–1850* (Cambridge).

Spruyt, H. (1994) *The Sovereign State and its Competitors: an Analysis of Systems Change* (Princeton, NJ).

Stanford (2008) 'The First Great Divergence: Europe and China, 300–800 CE', Workshop Stanford University, April 6–7, 2008.

Steel, C. E. W. (2007) 'The Rhetoric of the *de frumento*', in Prag (2007a), pp. 37–48.

——. (2001) *Cicero, Rhetoric and Empire* (Oxford).

Steensgaard, Niels (1990) 'The Seventeenth-Century Crisis and the Unity of Eurasian History,' *Modern Asian Studies* 24 (4), pp. 683–97.

——. (1978) 'The Seventeenth Century Crisis', in Parker & Smith (Eds), *The General Crisis of the Seventeenth Century*, pp. 32–56.

——. (1974) *The Asian Trade Revolution of the Seventeenth Century: The East India Companies and the Decline of the Caravan Trade* (Chicago).

Stein, Burton (1990) *Peasant State and Society in Medieval South India* (Delhi).

——. (1985) 'State Formation and Economy Reconsidered,' *Modern Asian Studies* 19 (3), pp. 387–413.

Steinhart, E. (1981) *'From Empire to State: The Emergence of the Kingdom of Bunyoro – Kitara c. 1350–1890'*, in Claessen & Skalnik (Eds), *The Study of the State* (The Hague), pp. 353–70.

Stępniewska, B. (1972) *Rozprzestrzenianie się Islamu w Sudanie Zachodnim od XII do XVI wieku/The spread of Islam in West Sudan from 12th to the 16th c.* (Wrocław).

Stevens, Carol Belkin (1995) *Soldiers on the Steppe: Army Reform and Social Change in Early Modern Russia* (DeKalb).

Stone, M. (1999) 'A Flexible Rome: Fascism and the Cult of Romanità', in C. Edwards (Ed.) *Roman Presences* (Cambridge), pp. 205–20.

Struve, Lynn A. (2004) 'Introduction' in L. A. Struve (Ed.) *The Qing Formation in World-Historical Time* (Cambridge, MA).

Subrahmanyam, Sanjay (2006) 'A Tale of Three Empires: Mughals, Ottomans, and Habsburgs in a Comparative Context', *Common Knowledge*, 12 (1), pp. 66–92.

Sugar, Peter F. (1963) 'The Nature of the Non-Germanic Societies under Habsburg Rule', *Slavic Review* 22 (1), pp. 1–30.

Swain, S. (1996) *Hellenism and Empire. Language, Classicism, and Power in the Greek World, AD 50–250* (Oxford).

Syme, Ronald (1939) *The Roman Revolution* (Oxford).

Szuppe, Maria (1995) 'La Participation Des Femmes De La Famille Royale A' L'Exercise du Pouvoir en Iran Safavide au XVI Siècle (Seconde Partie),' *Studia Iranica* 24, pp. 61–122.

——. (1994) 'La Participation Des Femmes De La Famille Royale A' L'Exercise du Pouvoir en Iran Safavide au XVI Siècle (Premiere Partie),' *Studia Iranica* 23, pp. 211–58.

Tall, M. Ly (1972) 'Quelques remarques sur le Tarikh el-Fettach', *Bulletin de l' IFAN*, B, 34 (3), pp. 471–93.

Tang, C. (1990) 'Clients and Bound Retainers in the Six Dynasties Period', in Dien (Ed.) pp. 111–38.

Taylor, Miles (1995) *The Decline of British Radicalism 1847–60* (Oxford).

Tempest, K. (2007) 'Saints and Sinners: Some Thoughts on the Presentation of Character in Attic Oratory and Cicero's *Verrines*', in Prag (2007a), pp. 19–36.

Terray, E. (1984) 'Sociétés segmentaires, chefferies, Etats: acquis et problèmes', in B. Jewsiewicki & J. Létourneau (Eds) *Mode de Production: les défis africain* (St Foy), pp. 106–15.

——. (1974) 'Long Distance Exchange and Formation of the State: The Case of the Abron Kingdom of Gyaman', *Economy and Society* 3, pp. 315–45.

Terzioglu, Derin (1995) 'The Imperial Circumcision Festival of 1582: An Interpretation', *Muqarnas* 12, pp. 84–100.

Tezcan, Baki (2009a) 'Lost in Historiography: An Essay on the Reasons for the Absence of a History of Limited Government in the Early Modern Ottoman Empire', *Middle Eastern Studies* 45, pp. 477–505.

——. (2009b) 'The Second Empire: The Transformation of the Ottoman Polity in the Early Modern Era,' *Comparative Studies of South Asia, Africa and the Middle East* 29, pp. 556–72.

——. (2002) 'The 1622 Military Rebellion in Istanbul: a Historiographical Journey', *International Journal of Turkish Studies* 8, pp. 25–43.

Thapar, Romila (2003) *Early India: From the Origins to AD 1300* (London).

——. (1981) 'The State as Empire', in Claessen & Skalnik (Eds), *The Study of the State* (The Hague), pp. 409–29.

Tillotson, G. (2000) *The Artificial Empire: the Indian Landscapes of William Hodges* (Richmond).

Tilly, Charles (1992) *Coercion, Capital and European States, AD 990–1992* (rev. ed. Oxford).

——. (1990) *Coercion, Capital and European States, A. D. 990–1992* (Oxford).

——. (Ed.) (1975) *The Formation of National States in Western Europe* (Princeton, NJ).

Timur, Taner (1989) *Osmanlı Çalışmaları: İlkel Feodalizmden Yarı Sömürge Ekonomisine* (Ankara).

Treves, Piero (1962) *L'idea di Roma e la cultura italiana del secolo XIX* (Milan-Naples).

——. (1962b) 'Gaetano De Sanctis', in *Lo studio dell'antichità classica nell'Ottocento* (Milan-Naples).

Trimingham, J. (1964) *Islam in East Africa* (Oxford).

——. (1959) *Islam in West Africa* (Oxford).

Troll, Christian W. (1972) 'A Note on the Early Topographical Work of Sayyid Ahmad Khan', *Athar al Sanadid, Journal of the Royal Asiatic Society of Great Britain and Ireland,* 2, pp. 135–46.

——. (1978) *Sayyid Ahmad Khan. A Reinterpretation of Muslim Theology* (Delhi).

Tsigakou, F. M. (1981) *The Rediscovery of Greece: Travellers and Painters of the Romantic Era* (London and New York).

Twitchett, D. and M. Loewe (Eds) (1986) *The Cambridge History of China, Vol. 1: The Ch'in and Han Empires, 221 B.C.–A.D. 220* (Cambridge).

Tymowski, M. (2009) *The Origins and Structures of Political Institutions in Pre-Colonial Black Africa* (Lampeter, NY).

——. (2006) 'Use of the Term "Empire" in Historical Research on Africa: A Comparative Approach', *Afrika Zamani. An Annual Journal of African History, special issue – Comparative African History: Prospects and Challenges,* guest editor Anthony L. Asiwaju, Nos 11–12, 2003–2004 (print 2006), pp. 18–26.

——. (2005) 'Le territoire et les frontières du Songhay à la fin du XVe et au XVIe siècle – le problème du centre et de territoires peripheriques d' un grand Etat de l' Afrique Occidentale', in *Des frontières en Afrique du XIIe au XXe siècle,* UNESCO (Paris), pp. 213–237.

——. (1999) *Państwa Afryki przedkolonialnej / States of Precolonial Africa* (Wrocław).

——. (ed.) (1996) *Historia Afryki do początku XIX wieku / History of Africa to the Beginnings of the 19th c.* (Wrocław).

——. (1990) 'La légitimation du pouvoir de la dynastie Askia au Songhay du XVIe siècle. Islam et culture locale', *Hemispheres. Studies on Cultures and Societies* 7, pp. 189–198.

——. (Ed.) (1979) *Historia Mali* (Wrocław).

Urbańczyk, Th. (2008) *Slave Revolts in Antiquity* (Berkeley, CA).

Üstün, Kadir (2002) 'Rethinking *Vak'a-i Hayriye* (the Auspicious Event): Elimination of the Janissaries on the Path to Modernization', M.A. thesis (Bilkent University).

van Creveld, Martin (1999) *The Rise and Decline of the State* (Cambridge).

Vansina, J. (1962) 'A Comparison of African Kingdoms', *Africa*, 32, pp. 324–35.

——. (1962b), 'Long Distance Trade Routes in Central Africa', *Journal of African History* 3, pp. 375–90.

Vasaly, A. (1993) *Representations: Images of the World in Ciceronian Oratory* (Berkeley, CA).

Veyne, P. (2005) *L'empire gréco-romain* (Paris).

——. (1976) *Le Pain e le cirque* (Paris).

Viswanathan, Gauri (1989) *Masks of Conquest: Literary Study and British Rule in India* (New York).

Vitoria, Francisco de (1991) *Political Writings*, Pagden & Lawrance (Eds) (Cambridge).

——. (1917), *De Indis et de Iure belli relectiones*, E. Nys (Ed.), Classics of International Law (Washington).

Voltaire, François Marie Arouet de (1963) *Essai sur les moeurs e l'esprit des nations*, ed. R. Pomeau, 2 vols (Paris).

Von Premerstein, Anton (1937) *Vom Werden und Wesen des Prinzipats* (München).

Wallerstein, I. (1974) *The Modern World System. Capitalist Agriculture and the Origins of the European World-Economy in the Sixteenth Century* (New York).

Walthall, Anne (Ed.) (2008) *Servants of the Dynasty. Palace Women in World History* (Berkeley and Los Angeles, CA).

Wank, S. (1997) 'The Disintegration of the Habsburg and Ottoman Empires', in Karen Dawisha & Bruce Parrott (Eds), *The End of Empire? The Transformation of the USSR in Comparative Perspective* (Armonk), pp. 94–120.

Wasilewski, T. (1967) 'Morawskie państwo -zwane również Wielkomorawskim/Moravian State – also Called Great Moravian State', article in: *Słownik Starożytności Słowiańskich – Lexicon Antiquitatum Slavicarum*, W. Kowalenko, G. Labuda & Z. Stieber (Eds) (Wrocław), t. 3, pp. 291–94.

Weber, Max (1972) *Wirtschaft und Gesellschaft* (Tübingen).

——. (1968) *Economy and Society*, Guenther Roth & Claus Wittich (Eds), 3 vols (New York).

Weickhardt, George G. (1993) 'The Pre-Petreine Law of Property' *Slavic Review* 52 (4), pp. 663–79.

Whitby, M. (2000) 'Armies and Society in the Later Roman World', in Alan K. Bowman, Peter Garnsey & Averil Cameron (Eds), *The Cambridge Ancient History*, XIV (Cambridge), pp. 469–65.

White, Hayden (1975) *Metahistory: The Historical Imagination in Nineteenth Century Europe* (London).

White III, Lynn T. (1998) *Unstately Power: Volume 1. Local Causes of China's Economic Reforms* (Armonk, NY).

Whitmarsh, Tim (2001) *Greek Literature and the Roman Empire: the Politics of Imitation* (Oxford).

Whittaker, Chr. (1994) *The Frontiers of the Roman Empire* (Baltimore, MD).

Wickham, C. (2005) *Framing the Early Middle Ages: Europe and the Mediterranean, 400–800* (Oxford).

——. (1994) *Land and Power: Studies in Italian and European Social History, 400–1200* (London).

Wicks, R. S. (1992) *Money, Markets and Trade in Early Southeast Asia* (Ithaca, NY).

Wiesehöfer, J. (2006) 'Statt einer Einleitung: 'Randkultur' oder 'Nabel der Welt'?', in Wiesehöfer & Huyse (eds), *Ērān ud Anērān. Studien zu den Beziehungen zwischen dem Sasanidenreich und der Mittelmeerwelt* (Stuttgart), pp. 9–28.

Wilcocks, Charles (1925) *Sixty Years in the East* (London).

Wilde, M. J. (2007) *Vatican II. A Sociological Analysis of Religious Change* (Princeton, NJ).

Wilkinson, S. K. (1995) 'Central Civilisation', in S. K. Sanderson (Ed.), *Civilisations and World Systems. Studying World Historical Change* (Walnut Creek), pp. 46–74.

Willi, A. (2008) Sikelismos. *Sprache, Literatur und Gesellschaft im griechischen Sizilien (8.-5. Jh. v. Chr.)* (Basel).

Wilson, Peter H. (1999) *The Holy Roman Empire* (Basingstoke).

Wilson, R. J. A. (2000) 'Ciceronian Sicily: an Archaeological Perspective', in Smith and Serrati (Eds) (2000), pp. 134–60.

Wink, André (1990) *Al-Hind: The Making of the Indo-Islamic World* (Leiden).

Winterling, Aloys (2003) *Caligula* (München).

Wittfogel, Karl August (1957) *Oriental Despotism. A Comparative Study of Total Power* (New Haven, CT).

Wolters, Reinhard (1999), *Nummi Signati: Untersuchungen zur römischen Münzprägung und Geldwirtschaft* (München).

Woolf, Greg (1994) 'Becoming Roman, Staying Greek: Culture, Identity and the Civilising Process in the Roman East', *Transactions of the Cambridge Philological Society* 40, pp. 116–43.

Wright, William E. (1975) 'Neo-Serfdom in Bohemia,' *Slavic Review* 34 (2), pp. 239–52.

Wyke, Maria (1999) 'Screening Ancient Rome in the New Italy', in C. Edwards (Ed.), *Roman Presences: Receptions of Rome in European Culture, 1789–1945* (Cambridge).

Yang, L. (1961) *Studies in Chinese Institutional History* (Cambridge, MA).

Yıldız, Aysel (2008) 'Vaka-yı Selimiyye or the Selimiyye Incident: A Study of the May 1807 Rebellion', PhD dissertation (Sabancı University, 2008).

Yoffe, N. & G. Cowgill (Eds) (1988) *The Collapse of Ancient States and Civilisations* (Tuccon).

Young, Robert (1995) *Colonial Desire: Hybridity in Theory, Culture and Race* (London & New York).

Zapperi, R. (1962) 'La fortuna di un avventuriero: Saverio Scrofani e i suoi biografi', *Rassegna storica del Risorgimento* 49 (1962) pp. 447–71.

Žemlička, J. (1993) 'Mähren – Grossmährisches Reich', article in *Lexikon des Mittelalters*, 6 (München), pp. 106–11.

Ziegler, N. P. (1978) 'Some Notes on Rajput Loyalties during the Mughal Period', in J. F. Richards (Eds), *Kingship and Authority in South Asia* (Madison, WI), pp. 215–51.

Zürcher, Erik J. (1993) *Turkey: A Modern History* (London & New York).

Index